Walker —
To a g[...]
Thanks [...]
our emp[...] Best,
Jan

Walker,
I know you love and
appreciate this fine part of
the world, all from a
geographer's perspective!
I'm glad we've been able
to tromp around in some
choice places.
Thanks for your efforts to
help keep it green,
Kathryn
21 / [...] / '17

How things have changed!

UNIVERSITY PRESS OF FLORIDA

STATE UNIVERSITY SYSTEM

Florida A&M University, Tallahassee

Florida Atlantic University, Boca Raton

Florida Gulf Coast University, Ft. Myers

Florida International University, Miami

Florida State University, Tallahassee

University of Central Florida, Orlando

University of Florida, Gainesville

University of North Florida, Jacksonville

University of South Florida, Tampa

University of West Florida, Pensacola

Kathryn Ziewitz and June Wiaz

Green

Empire

The St. Joe Company and the Remaking of Florida's Panhandle

University Press of Florida

GAINESVILLE   TALLAHASSEE   TAMPA   BOCA RATON

PENSACOLA   ORLANDO   MIAMI   JACKSONVILLE   FT. MYERS

Copyright 2004 by Kathryn Ziewitz and June Wiaz
Printed in the United States of America on recycled, acid-free paper
All rights reserved

09 08 07 06 05 04   6 5 4 3 2 1

Library of Congress Cataloging-in-Publication Data
Ziewitz, Kathryn, 1957–
Green empire: the St. Joe Company and the remaking of Florida's Panhandle/
Kathryn Ziewitz and June Wiaz.
p. cm.
Includes bibliographical references and index.
ISBN 0–8130–2697–0 (alk.paper)
1. St. Joe Company—History. 2. Real estate development—Florida—Florida
Panhandle—History. 3. Real estate business—Florida—Florida Panhandle—
History. 4. Land use—Environmental aspects—Florida—Florida Panhandle—
History. 5. Conservation of natural resources—Florida—Florida Panhandle—
History. I. Wiaz, June M. II. Title.
HD266.F62Z54   2004
333.33'09759'9—dc22   2003066567

The University Press of Florida is the scholarly publishing agency for the
State University System of Florida, comprising Florida A&M University, Florida
Atlantic University, Florida Gulf Coast University, Florida International
University, Florida State University, University of Central Florida, University
of Florida, University of North Florida, University of South Florida, and
University of West Florida.

University Press of Florida
15 Northwest 15th Street
Gainesville, FL 32611-2079
http://www.upf.com

Contents

Illustrations

Preface

As the year 1999 dawned, it was becoming apparent that the Florida Panhandle was at a crossroads. Several years earlier, the St. Joe Company—the state's largest landowner—had begun its official transition from papermaking conglomerate to real estate developer. The St. Joe Company was setting out to do big things in the place where it owned the most land, things that might change the face of this often-overlooked part of the state.

So what was the background of this company that owned a million Florida acres? How was the "new" St. Joe Company different from the old St. Joe Paper Company, which once kept log trucks rolling and seemed to have an endless sea of pine forests? What were its plans and guiding principles? Who were the people making these momentous decisions? With growth coming a decade and a half after the state passed its landmark Growth Management Act, could the region somehow reap the wisdom from its more noticed, and more exploited, southern region to achieve a more sustainable, ordered pattern of growth? Was there a way to bring better jobs and other social benefits without losing the quiet and open spaces that made the obscure Panhandle so wonderful? The questions went on and on.

Because a book that dealt with such questions did not yet exist, and we both lived in the region, we decided that it was worth writing. Thus began a project lasting more than three years.

The resulting effort is meant for all those in Florida and beyond with an interest in how a place is shaped by forces natural and man-made. We hope to add an ecological, historical, and policy perspective to the actions taking place as the St. Joe Company and its subsidiaries embark on their ambitious new developments. More than anything, we have tried to tell a story—or, more accurately, the intersection of two stories: the overlap between the story of the Panhandle's history and environment and the story of the St. Joe Company. Although news accounts do a good job relaying the latest events in the unfolding saga, a deeper sense of context helps to show common threads and themes underlying the current events.

The Green Empire story is important because the newest wave of change sweeping across the Panhandle will leave a more permanent mark than any land use that has come before, even the wholesale timbering of a century ago. Although the St. Joe Company is not the only agent of change, it is, because of the scope of its plans and its political and fiscal power, the leader. At this time, issues of equity and representation in decision making and public resource allocation are paramount. The remaking of what we call the Green Empire, meant to refer to both the land owned by the St. Joe Company and the corporate empire, is occurring during a time of increasingly fuzzy differentiation between public and private spheres of influence, decision making, and funding.

Green Empire is written for those interested in natural history, planning, and Florida's history, and for those, like us, who simply want to peek ahead to imagine the future Florida Panhandle. Readers with an interest in Florida's wildlife and natural resources will find attention paid to the Panhandle as a center of biodiversity and to implications of developing real estate in such an area. Followers of the stories of Disney and Arvida will find common players and patterns in the St. Joe story, and those interested in neotraditional or "New Urbanist" planning may be interested to see how these principles are faring in Florida's latest real estate frontier. Students of Florida's political history will find the St. Joe story an important part of understanding how the state came to look the way it does demographically and physically.

Green Empire draws on the combined tradition of environmental and corporate histories. Its target audience is Floridians, especially residents of Northwest Florida. But because the state is such a tourist mecca, we hope it will also find a wider than regional audience. To some extent, Florida is a state that belongs to all Americans, and many non-Americans, because her natural heritage and built environment together draw so many and probably always will.

Acknowledgments

A work of this duration and magnitude could not have come together without treading on many trails blazed by others. Following the story took us to many fields, some expected and some not: biology, history, business, planning, with a few twists and tangents, including the American savings and loan debacle of the 1980s and the sugarcane fields of South Florida. As it turned out, the overlapping stories of St. Joe and the Panhandle had more layers than an onion.

To find the trail heads, we relied on previously published books, interviews with residents across the region, newspaper accounts current and past, and the periodical *Florida Trend,* which was consistently helpful as the publication of record for Florida business over the later decades of the St. Joe Company's affairs. We are grateful for the expertise of librarians from Jacksonville to Pensacola, especially those in Panama City and the Florida State Library in Tallahassee. In the course of more than three years of researching, writing, and editing this book, a countless number of people pointed us to information that we otherwise would not have discovered even with computer search engines. Helpful individuals shared considerable expertise, proffered advice, critiqued drafts, and offered aid and encouragement. In particular, we wish to thank Audrey Parker, Patricia Murfee, Carole Timins, Jan Godown, Jerry Ziewitz, and Barry Moline for reviewing chapters, and Brenda Mills and Gloria Pipkin for helping us to slash the manuscript almost in half.

Naturalists, historians, and other active citizens across the Panhandle helped us to better understand the special things about the region, not the least of which includes the graciousness and grit of its residents. In the weary final months of shaping this book, individuals such as Kim Ogren of the Funders' Network for Smart Growth and Livable Communities shared resources that helped to complete our effort. We are also grateful for the patience and encouragement of our editor, Ken Scott, and the cheerful assistance of Bennie Watson, at the University Press of Florida.

We also wish to thank the St. Joe Company itself, which although unwilling to open up its corporate historical files to us, and uneven in its cooperation for the duration of the project, at times granted access to individuals with invaluable perspective—Peter Rummell, Jerry Ray, Clay Smallwood, and Winfred Thornton, most notably. In addition, we are grateful for the insights shared by several board members and investors, especially James Schmitt and James Dahl, who were involved during the years the St. Joe businesses were finding a new direction.

From the start of this project, our guiding principle has been to be bold but factual. We have tried our best to get it all right, as evinced by hundreds of footnotes. But in a book of this length there are bound to be some interpretations of events with which some might disagree, and perhaps a few honest mistakes as well. We hope the errors and conflicting views are few but recognize that writing about development in Florida can be a philosophical minefield.

Foremost, we wish to thank our families and friends who have had to tolerate years of self-imposed tunnel vision on our part as we pursued a final draft: we could not have done it without your support.

Finally, we dedicate this work to the principled residents as well as government workers of the Florida Panhandle and elsewhere who display the courage and endurance to work toward preservation and improvement of their communities. These are people who take to heart the words of Gunter Grass, who said, "The job of a citizen is to keep his mouth open."

Chronology

1971	Antitrust rules force St. Joe Paper Company to divest Florida National Banks; trustees first enter into a series of lawsuits to clarify the intent of Alfred duPont's will with respect to the management of his estate and appointment of trustees.
1972	Labor unions strike at Port St. Joe; pollution control devices installed at paper mill; state sets coastal control setback for coastal building; St. Joe buys Talisman Sugar Cane farm and swaps stock with the Charter Company.
1977	Attorneys general of Florida and Delaware sue the Alfred I. duPont Trust to increase cash flow to Nemours.
1980	Case brought by attorneys general of Florida and Delaware results in larger cash payment to Nemours.
1981	Ed Ball dies; Robert Davis begins Seaside.
1984	Gran Central Corporation established.
1985	St. Joe Paper Company signs contract to sell Topsail Hill.
1986	St. Joe Paper begins to go public, selling off 14 percent of its stock, leaving the A. I. duPont Trust with 86 percent ownership.
1990	The A. I. duPont Trust sells St. Joe Paper stock for $45.75 per share, reducing its ownership to 69 percent.
1992	State of Florida purchases 20,000 acres from St. Joe in Walton County as part of Topsail settlement.
1996	St. Joe Paper Company finalizes sale of its Port St. Joe paper mill and changes its name to St. Joe Corporation.
1997	St. Joe hires Peter Rummell; company name again changed to St. Joe Company and listed on New York Stock Exchange; St. Joe purchases Prudential Realty, creating Arvida Realty Services, and buys controlling interest in Arvida (development) Company.
1998	Jeb Bush elected governor.
1999	St. Joe sells its roughly 50,000–acre sugar plantation as part of Everglades restoration; St. Joe breaks ground at WaterColor and SouthWood; Port St. Joe paper mill closes permanently; FAA approves conceptual plan for relocated airport in Bay County.
2000	St. Joe "spins off" Florida East Coast Industries.
2002	St. Joe sells its Arvida real estate brokerage business. Alfred I. duPont Testamentary Trust reduces its ownership of the St. Joe Company to 49 percent, giving up majority control.
2003	St. Joe has more than twenty commercial and residential projects in north Florida under construction.

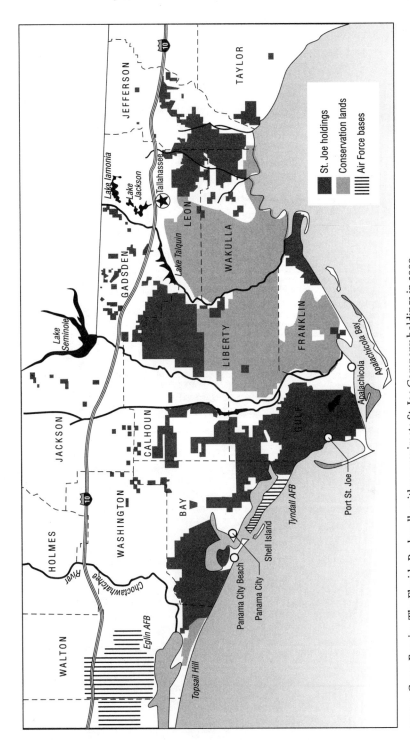

Legend:

- St. Joe holdings
- Conservation lands
- Air Force bases

MAP 1. Green Empire: The Florida Panhandle with approximate St. Joe Company holdings in 2000.

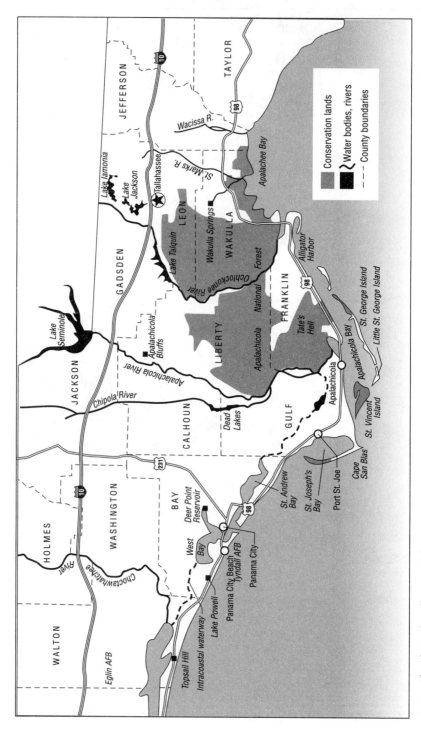

MAP 2. Florida Panhandle natural features.

Abbreviations

CDD	Community Development District
CIA	Central Intelligence Agency
CRA	Community Redevelopment Area
DCA	Department of Community Affairs
DEP	Florida Department of Environmental Protection
DRI	Development of Regional Impact
EDA	Economic Development Alliance of Bay County
EPA	U.S. Environmental Protection Agency
EZ	Enterprise Zone
FAA	Federal Aeronautics Administration
FAMU	Florida Agricultural and Mechanical University
FEC	Florida East Coast (Railroad)
FBI	Federal Bureau of Investigation
FDOT	Florida Department of Transportation (sometimes referred to in text as "DOT")
FGN	Florida's Great Northwest, Inc.
FSU	Florida State University
FWS	U.S. Fish and Wildlife Service
OTTED	Office of Tourism, Trade, and Economic Development
PEER	Public Employees for Environmental Responsibility
RPC	Regional Planning Council
S&L	Savings and loan institution
TNC	The Nature Conservancy
TOP	Transportation Outreach Program
WMD	Water Management District
WWTP	Wastewater Treatment Plant

1

⊙ ⊙ ⊙ ⊙ ⊙ ⊙ ⊙ **A Slice of Paradise**

TO EXPLORE SOUTH Walton County, Florida, is to enter an enchanted realm. The Gulf of Mexico laps the beach with its clearest blues and greens. Sprinkled at intervals are freshwater lakes framed by glittering pines just hundreds of yards from the salty coast. Bonsai-like scrub of wizened oaks, pines, and dwarf magnolias carpets sand dunes, forming intimate thickets where small creatures skitter and birds flit. Hillocks of sand, soft and impossibly white, crest and dip in luscious formations.

It is a landscape of freshness and clarity, with a quality both timeless and brand new. Since about 5,000 years ago, when geologic forces sculpted the present configuration of water and sand, the shore has endured this way, give or take sporadic refinements wrought by hurricanes, forest fires, and the opening and closing of inlets. Sheer isolation, and the firm hold of pine plantations on much of the land, kept south Walton County much as the Choctaw Indians knew it well into the age of computers and satellites. The few villages were clusters of beach cottages and fishing outposts.

The many charms of south Walton County's shores lay undisturbed over the years, as the dunes of Panama City Beach to the east in Bay County were scraped and replaced by condominiums and motels and the harbor at the fishing village of Destin to the west in Okaloosa County was corralled by high-rise, high-priced slabs of steel and concrete. During the 1970s, a large resort, Sandestin, claimed several thousand acres at the west end of Walton County.

East of Sandestin, however, the territory still belonged as much to foxes and gopher tortoises as to fishermen and beachcombers with their modest share of vacation homes. A generous lacing of wetlands in the flatwoods beyond the shore provided an ideal habitat for a host of flora, including carnivorous pitcher plants and an array of wildflowers. Bobcat, bear, and deer roamed the woods, along with more obscure creatures like the endangered flatwoods salamander.

To be sure, the stamp of modern humankind could be detected—mostly in the forest, which changed over time from natural woodlands to pines of one kind planted in straight rows. As the decades passed, the encroachment of modern life was most obvious at night, in the growing orbs of light issuing from Panama City Beach to the east and Destin to the west.

However, even at the turning of the millennium, nature's dark blanket of sky still fell heavily over south Walton County, at Deer Lake, Grayton Beach, Dune Allen, and Topsail Hill—beaches easily counted among the most beautiful in Florida. Moonlight, stars, and microscopic phosphorescent creatures in the sand and surf added glitter to summer nights when loggerhead turtles crawled from the sea to lay their eggs on the beach, as they have since the beach formed at the end of the Ice Age. In the dark of night, tiny native beach mice forayed to gather a meal of sea oats, or, conversely, to become a meal for a hungry coachwhip snake.

But the hold of the darkness is tenuous. South Walton County has been discovered, and its face is changing rapidly. Each month more electric beams pluck a few threads from the blanket of darkness. More cars ply the scenic roadway. More scrub gives way to homes. South Walton County now faces the paradox of all such places so attractive to people—will it be able to keep intact the very elements that make it so appealing? Can the same resources be both exploited and preserved?

The growing pains facing the area are being intensified by the emergence of a new real estate powerhouse—the St. Joe Company. The former St. Joe Paper Company, once known for its sweeping pine plantations, paper mills, railroads, and behind-the-scenes politicking, turned to real estate in a big way in 1997. It launched its first high-profile ventures on the inimitable south Walton shores. This new company now stands to shape the future as keenly as the old company did the past for six decades, not only in south Walton but also across northwest Florida.

FIGURE 1. South Walton County beach and dunes. Photo by Kathryn Ziewitz.

As of the year 2003, the St. Joe Company owned approximately 1 million acres of Florida land, a Green Empire with roughly 900,000 acres concentrated in the Panhandle. The company's Green Empire arcs from southeast of Tallahassee some 150 miles, as the crow flies, to its westernmost holdings in Walton County. St. Joe's major holdings in northwest Florida span eleven counties, with minor holdings in two other northwest counties. St. Joe property crosses into Georgia then dips all the way south to the Gulf of Mexico. The company owns forty miles of coastal frontage, including riverfront, Intracoastal waterway, and Gulf of Mexico shore front, as well as land on bays and lakes.[1] St. Joe (the shorthand name usually applied to the company) is the largest owner of the vast tree farms that wrap much of north and west Florida in what are called "greenbelts."

By sheer scale alone what St. Joe does matters. What it does will matter greatly—to the area's economy, people, and the land. The makeover of the St. Joe Company is bringing a sea-change to the Panhandle, one to which this book seeks to add historical and environmental perspectives.

The Shift toward Real Estate

The company's shift toward real estate was more gradual than it first might appear, dating back to the 1980s. If any place can be pinpointed for the beginning of the change, it would have to be Walton County. The huge Sandestin development that began in Okaloosa County, just across the county line, brought an attention-getting, south Florida–style resort complex to the Panhandle in the 1970s, one that was decidedly upscale. Then, in 1981, a very different resort development began on the beaches of south Walton. That year, Robert Davis broke ground for Seaside between the villages of Seagrove Beach and Grayton Beach.

Davis, a Birmingham native, had the good fortune to inherit eighty acres of prime south Walton waterfront from his grandfather. He also had the talent to develop it with enough imagination to turn a former backwater into an international destination.

At Seaside, Davis shunned the typical construction of condominiums or gated communities in favor of zero lot-line detached homes that offered the best of laid-back southern charm, without the yard cars. And there was more to Seaside than beach homes. It was to be a town, not just a development. Besides the houses with their mandatory white picket fences, there was to be a grassy commons for performances and a hall for public lectures, as well as shops and restaurants, all within walking distance. Furthermore, it was intended to allow all its residents equal access to the shore. The beach was to be more of a commons than a frontage for the most expensive dwellings. Initially, only a few beach walkovers claimed the dunes beachward of the roadway, and the master plan called for only low-density beach-side housing.[2]

Seaside was like the Schwinn of the 1950s but with a gel seat—nostalgic but hip and laid back. Standards were high, embodied in a strict building code.

Davis enlisted help from some leading thinkers in the fields of architecture and urban planning to help bring his vision to the blueprint stage and beyond. Prestigious architects and planners from Berkeley to New York visited Seaside. Davis hired Andres Duany and Elizabeth Plater-Zyberk, an up-and-coming husband-and-wife team of Miami architects, to develop Seaside's building code. Leading British architect Leon Krier helped to tweak the master plan, and Davis gave him a building lot in return.[3]

The beaches of south Walton County were part of what some people derisively called the Redneck Riviera. But Seaside turned that image on its head. The cachet of its remarkable surroundings and its whimsical buildings were eye candy for the *Town and Country* set, with the white powder sands of south Walton County to top it off. Like Disney World, it was truly hard to resist.

Within a few short years, the likes of Prince Charles and Princess Diana were strolling its pleasantly walkable grounds.

The idealism embodied at Seaside was attention-getting, and so was its balance sheet. In 1984, lots sold for $14,000 and cottages could be built for under $50,000. By the start of the new century, those same lots and early cottages carried a half-million-dollar price tag.[4]

Coincidentally, in 1981, the same year Robert Davis was constructing his first cottage, the aging don of the St. Joe Paper Company was spending his final days at a clinic in New Orleans.[5] Ninety-three-year-old Edward Ball had helped create and run the far-flung St. Joe Paper Company empire over six decades. Ball had stepped down as company president in 1968 but kept his position as chairman of the Alfred. I. duPont Testamentary Trust, the entity that owned the lion's share of St. Joe stock and oversaw it and its sister companies.

The A. I. duPont Trust was the repository of wealth that gunpowder magnate Alfred I. duPont brought to Florida in the 1920s and that Ball used to expand the company's holdings after duPont's death in 1935. The perpetual Trust is a curious combination of decision-making body of the St. Joe business conglomerate and benefactor of the health-care charity Alfred duPont specified in his will, the Nemours Foundation. A portion of funds from the St. Joe businesses helps finance the nonprofit foundation. As chairman of the all-important Trust, Ball stayed as involved as possible in company business, given his gradual loss of hearing and vision, until illness finally wrenched away his grip on worldly affairs. He died June 24, 1981.[6] No longer would Edward Ball offer up his famous nightly bourbon toast: "Confusion to the enemy!"

Among his legacies, Ball left behind valuable tracts of Gulf-front land in Walton County, land that abutted Seaside. Ball had crossed the sandy tracks of Walton County an average man's lifetime before and had personally arranged for the purchase of twelve miles of Gulf-front Walton land for eleven dollars an acre.[7] He contracted to purchase it from heirs of the Santa Rosa Plantation in 1925 for his boss and mentor, Alfred I. duPont. At the time, duPont, whose wife, Jessie Ball duPont, was Ed Ball's sister, was collecting real estate in north Florida. Under duPont, and later the St. Joe Paper Company, the Walton County land continued as it had under the Santa Rosa Plantation, as a source of timber and turpentine. Ball would not live to see Davis's new ideas come to fruition. If he had, there is no doubt he would have marveled at the cash flow that was emerging from the plat of scrub and forest next to St. Joe's.

For six decades, the old-guard St. Joe Paper Company had presided over its Panhandle acres in predictable fashion, growing and harvesting pines and turning them into pulp at its mill in Port St. Joe. It ruled a backwoods empire with loggers and mill workers as its foot soldiers. Its principal business was maximizing the gain from the natural resources the land yielded up, in typical industrial-age mode. Above all, it held onto its land. St. Joe spurned most purchase offers while continuing to make acquisitions over the years when bargains appeared.

In the new economy, the land itself has become the commodity. With tourism one of the world's most lucrative industries, and the consumer's appetite for coastal living showing no signs of diminishing, the very appeal of the place can be harnessed and sold, even in the once-remote reaches of Florida's Panhandle. And, as Davis demonstrated, it can be sold at a premium if certain aesthetic dictates are applied. On previously undeveloped Panhandle shores, the new postindustrial economy has dawned. It is heavy on tourism and real estate, and its new foot soldiers are real estate agents.

In 1981, the death of Edward Ball and the birth of Seaside appeared to be events with no relation to each other, save that the semicircle of Davis's eighty acres was surrounded by thousands of acres of St. Joe Paper Company forest. Robert Davis and Edward Ball were certainly a study in contrasts. Davis was a fresh-thinking developer and scholar whose credits included innovative townhouses in Miami's counterculture haven, Coconut Grove.[8] Ball, on the other hand, was a conservative codger whose formal education was limited to eight grades. As a young man, Ball mined for gold and sold law books and furniture. Thanks to the business alliance with Alfred duPont that began after his sister's marriage to the millionaire, he eventually rose to command the St. Joe industrial empire.

Whereas Davis's methods employed cutting-edge thinking, Ball's company was of another era. The St. Joe Paper Company was slow to warm to such modern conveniences as computers. Instead, even into the 1990s, executives kept track of company holdings on an old Esso road map.[9] They made deals the old-fashioned way, over a drink or two of bourbon.

Ball might have guffawed to think the newfangled experiment springing up next to his land was even worthy of his attention. Eighty acres was but a fraction of the land he had controlled. The St. Joe Paper Company owned a neat 3 percent of the state's land, making it Florida's largest private landowner.

His company had run railroads and banks, as well as helped to make some politicians and break others. The company owned the Florida East Coast and Apalachicola Northern Railroads, choice buildings in Miami, Jacksonville, and Panama City Beach, and a sugarcane farm in the Everglades. All this was in addition to the St. Joe Paper Company's namesake industry, the pulp and paper business. St. Joe Paper operated a pulp and container plant in Port St. Joe, Florida, and eventually operated twenty more plants across the United States as well as several in Ireland, producing rolls of sturdy paper and corrugated boxes.

How could a tiny town of quaint pastel vacation cottages possibly rival the accomplishments of a company such as St. Joe? The answer can be understood only by appreciating the enormous appeal of Seaside, whose nostalgic cottages and walkable town would become a focal point for the New Urbanism movement.

Indeed, in 1981, few people could imagine the far-reaching impact Robert Davis's gulf-front town would have. Many locals poo-poohed his premise that people would pay a pretty penny for houses that were not even right on the beach. Davis's town was a marked departure from the condos, golf resorts, and gated communities that had succeeded in attracting affluent consumers to Florida in the past.

Curiously, the passing of two decades has worked a strange convergence of the two enterprises—Seaside and St. Joe. Seaside is almost built out and has lost some of its starry idealism. Simple cottages with whimsical gingerbread have given way to increasingly showy retreats, including mansions with Greek columns that stand shoulder to shoulder on the beachfront side of the village, blocking out the view of the Gulf. Day-trippers jockey for parking spaces and shopkeepers struggle to find help willing to spend the gas money to work service jobs in a place they cannot afford to live.

Meanwhile, the St. Joe Paper Company has ceased to be a paper company and is now one of the largest real estate companies in the Southeast. Its first major resort development, WaterColor, is taking shape smack up against Seaside and will eventually encircle it. The St. Joe forest that many Seaside visitors might have assumed would forever remain a green backdrop to the pastel cottages is itself sprouting vacation retreats with their own color schemes, codes, and covenants.

As it turned out, St. Joe would look to the example of Seaside to catapult it into the future. After fits and starts attempting to break out of a corporate stalemate accentuated by volatility in the paper industry and ambitious but unsuccessful early development ventures, St. Joe took a decisive turn to real estate. The company's new focus was cemented in 1997, when its board of directors brought on Disney executive and former Arvida developer Peter Rummell as chief executive officer. The savvy new leadership of the remade St. Joe Company was mindful of what Robert Davis had discovered two decades earlier: people liked being in this beautiful, out-of-the-way place, and some would pay extra if they could experience the clean beaches in a human-scaled setting without tattoo parlors or featureless condominiums. St. Joe, like other nearby developers who are cashing in on Seaside's cachet, is offering its own slice of paradise to well-heeled consumers. Unlike other developers, St. Joe has the advantage of debt-free ownership of some of the best remaining undeveloped coastal acreage in Florida.

Lifting the Green Curtain

Beginning with its coastal holdings, St. Joe is at last lifting the "green curtain" of pine forests that formed a barrier to development for so long. The state's largest landlord has plans not only to put northwest Florida on the map but also to turn the Florida map upside down, touting a region that has stood apart from the rest of the state since territorial days as Florida's newest real estate hot spot. It has even gone so far as to come up with a name for the area that is variously referred to as the Florida Panhandle, west Florida, or the Redneck Riviera. St. Joe has branded the one-time land of pulpwood and turpentine "Florida's Great Northwest."[10] As the coast of peninsular Florida approaches build-out, the expanses of remote western Florida that seemed locked in stasis for so many years now exist as a portfolio of so-called "raw land" in a developer's dream come true.

Early in the new millennium, St. Joe is opening the tap to what it calls its "pipeline" of building projects on thousands of acres across northwest Florida. So far, these range from resorts and master-planned communities to more typical subdivisions, industrial, commercial, and mixed-used developments, all on land that previously supported pine trees, cattle, and other agricultural pursuits. The reverberations of this change of corporate focus are enormous because of both the company's direct plans and the ripple effects bound to follow.

At local gatherings company officials are often reticent, saying that change will come slowly and in keeping with a community's wishes. The company reassures observers that it holds so many acres that it intends to develop, at most, only 5 percent of its holdings over the current decade.[11] Although the company clearly does not want to alarm locals, its plans are manifold and ambitious. However, even 5 percent of its holdings amounts to over 50,000 acres. Outside of the Panhandle, the new St. Joe Company speaks more aggressively about its plans. It has pitched its properties on Wall Street, in computerized slide-show presentations that extol the virtues of the land and the company's newfound development expertise while pointing to what is says is a deep demand for Florida real estate among wealthy baby boomers.

What would be hyperbole in most other cases may be reality with St. Joe because of its unique status as Florida's largest landlord, its powerful political connections, and the depth of corporate talent it has assembled. The question is not so much whether St. Joe can deliver the New Florida of the Great Northwest as what it will look like, whom it will benefit, and what will be the cost to the environment and to the taxpayer. St. Joe stands to shape the region's future as keenly as it has its past and as much as Disney has shaped central Florida. It is worthy of note that several former Disney executives are in key positions at the new St. Joe Company, further begging comparisons to Disney and its impact on the state.

The St. Joe Company has the resources and management capabilities to write a bright, new chapter for the Panhandle, a region that has taken a back seat to the rest of the state since the days of steamships and King Cotton. By and large, the lightly populated land in the St. Joe domain has reaped neither the rewards nor the damage from the surge of development that has claimed much of peninsular Florida.

With the land and capital at its command, St. Joe can afford to create high-quality habitats and new employment opportunities for people while preserving the natural integrity of local ecosystems. It could even foster restoration of areas that have suffered from past and ongoing forestry practices. St. Joe has an almost unparalleled opportunity to develop for the public good as well as for its own bottom line.

St. Joe's emergence as a real estate developer comes at a time of newfound awareness that the Florida Panhandle's ecosystems possess a biodiversity found few other places on Earth. The question of how the region's abundant natural resources, hitherto only faintly appreciated, can be preserved, has assumed urgent importance. As steward of much of the realm, St. Joe literally holds the future of some species in its corporate hands. In the face of these concerns, St. Joe has repeatedly asserted its intentions to offer up a kinder, gentler mode of development than the sprawling growth that has consumed large portions of coastal Florida.[12]

At the same time, the company is driven by promises to its stockholders that it will increase its before-tax earnings by 20 percent each year.[13] Whether the company can deliver on its profit goals and be an ecological role model at the same time is problematic. As businessman and environmental advocate Paul Hawken writes in *The Ecology of Commerce,* bridging the worlds of ecology and commerce is difficult but not impossible. It requires businesses to "integrate economic, biologic, and human systems to create a sustainable method of commerce."[14] Whether St. Joe places a priority on mustering the restraint and vision necessary to be part of what Hawken labels a "restorative economy" is one crucial question of this book.

The answer to that question depends on the interplay of a combination of forces: natural, political, and economic. Into the crucible of decision making go issues such as property rights, environmental regulation, and growth management. This book hopes to enhance understanding of the issues at stake by recounting two fascinating, overlapping histories—the history of the land of northwest Florida and the history of the St. Joe Company. The St. Joe companies old and new have more in common than is apparent at first blush; most of all, they have the same raw material to work with, the Panhandle land that has passed through several incarnations of its own. After looking to the past, the balance of the book delves into key issues at stake as the new St. Joe Company begins to turn dirt.

We look at the company's emerging developments and some of the growth impacts associated with them. Another area of inquiry is how the St. Joe Company will benefit from publicly subsidized infrastructure, from roads to schools to airports, and the company's role in augmenting a regional economy that is transitioning from past emphasis on the harvest of natural resources and tourism to a more diverse economy. This book also takes stock of St. Joe holdings that have been sold or are likely to be sold for preservation purposes.

One matter was settled early on—the Green Empire, at least its prime coastal areas, is both marketable and lucrative. Indeed, St. Joe's first venture, an exclusive enclave of homes in south Walton County called The Retreat, sold out ahead of schedule, at prices of $15,000 per linear foot for the lots alone. Here, the company made a whopping $29 million profit on ninety homes set on eighty-seven acres with beach access. These homes rest on the eleven-dollars-per-acre land purchased in Ed Ball's 1925 land deal.[15]

The new St. Joe Company markets a high quality of life as a key selling point for its many developments in the Great Northwest. St. Joe touts the assets of both the natural environment that is the setting for its planned communities and the caliber of the built environment it promises to deliver. The Panhandle's green vistas and open spaces offer baby boomers a contrast to populous cities like Atlanta and Birmingham, perhaps even Orlando and Miami. Northwest Florida presents sugar-sand beaches, rivers, and public land for recreation, along with recreational facilities St. Joe will create on its own land. Along with the ubiquitous golf courses, St. Joe is creatively pursuing ideas involving hunting and eco-tourism at several venues.

As for quality in construction, St. Joe's acquisition of the building and community management company Arvida in 1997 gave it a top brand name in Florida development. Arvida has a track record of appealing to St. Joe's initial target market, upper- and middle-income buyers in the New South. Before joining the

St. Joe Company fold, Arvida developed, built, and operated master-planned communities in coastal Florida, the Atlanta area, and North Carolina. St. Joe swallowed the company virtually intact, its management included. St. Joe also purchased leading real estate firms across the state, rapidly building a daunting real estate services operation that also carried the Arvida name, only to sell off the new firm a few years later.

The St. Joe approach to delivering quality of life is apparent at WaterColor and seems to amount to what could be called high-end, place-based aesthetics. The emerging resort is a hybrid of a conventional upscale resort and the traditional neighborhood development, or New Urbanist, style pioneered at Seaside. It offers an assemblage of single- and multifamily dwellings built with Florida touches in a pleasantly walkable setting, with plenty of green space and public areas. It differs from Seaside in making more provision for automobiles, in siting a beach club and sixty-room inn on the beach side, and in having more land to work with, and thus more elbow room between structures.

St. Joe CEO Peter Rummell, before turning the first shovel of sand to break ground for WaterColor in September 1999, paid homage to the extraordinary setting that invites high quality-of-life expectations: "We know we're lucky, and we also have a responsibility to be good stewards of it. That's a responsibility we'll be taking very seriously." Less than a hundred yards away, the surf washed up on the beach and pelicans soared overhead in a vibrant blue fall sky. The company's goal for WaterColor, Rummell said, is best described as "making places"—places like Napa Valley, Santa Fe, Nantucket, and, of course, Seaside. All of these, Rummell pointed out, are special places that evoke a certain feel, based on their natural and man-made attributes.[16]

To emphasize the company's commitment to respecting what is authentic about south Walton, Rummell noted that the first on-site employee at Water-Color was a horticulturist. St. Joe followed in the steps of Seaside by choosing to emphasize the native flora, although showy palms reside in the median of the main road along WaterColor. Almost half of the initial phase of WaterColor was slated for green space, either grassy parks or natural areas. Rather than engage in the wholesale land clearing that is the industry norm, St. Joe work crews painstakingly cleared only around the footprint of buildings to preserve existing vegetation. Landscape plantings included some non-native ornamentals but relied mostly on the rich assortment of native plants, from blueberries to rosemary to varieties of saw palmetto.[17]

Of course, quality of life transcends aesthetics and choice of plantings. Certain facts illustrate St. Joe's challenges in delivering an overall high quality of life. In many areas, northwest Florida's residents as a whole do not enjoy the state's highest quality of life. Median incomes for most counties in St. Joe territory are below the state average. Except for Leon and Wakulla Counties, a greater proportion of children and adults in these northwestern counties live in poverty than the statewide 15 percent.[18] The 1990 census found that the number of residents with college degrees ranked below the state average of 18 percent for every Green Empire county except Leon County, home of Tallahassee, Florida State University, and Florida A&M University.[19] Overall, Panhandle residents have poorer nutrition and exercise habits, smoke more, and get in more motor vehicle crashes, according to a study by the Big Bend Health Council. The same study found that Gulf County was among the top in the state for deaths from cancer—163 per 100,000, compared to the state average of 121, over the period 1994 to 1998.[20]

Some indicators of social well-being matter little to the casual visitor, who can come to enjoy the beach and some golf, then pack up the family and return to a good job and good school elsewhere. Other aspects do matter, even to the casual visitor, who does not want to languish on a long ambulance ride because of sparsely located medical facilities or be inconvenienced because service workers, who are priced out of the community, are in short supply.

Health care and education are high on St. Joe's list of areas to improve to carry out its long-term plans. While beachfront development seems to sell itself, there is a limit to the number of beach and resort homes that St. Joe can build, and after that, the company has said it intends to "build value inland." To fill the thousands of nice, new St. Joe/Arvida homes on its drawing boards, the company needs to attract the new breed of active retirees as well as families. As inland development proceeds, newcomers will require additional schools, medical care, and jobs, as well as transportation and other infrastructure, from sewerage to police to fire protection.

Many of the weak links that the new St. Joe acknowledges about its Panhandle realm are the same ones that faced Alfred duPont and Edward Ball when they began assembling the Green Empire in the 1920s—isolation, limited transportation linkages, and poverty. The very nature of the land, with its major river systems and numerous wetlands, along with its geography—on the way to nowhere else—account in part for the region's socioeconomic shortcomings. These factors made it possible for duPont to accumulate so much land in northwest Florida. There was little competition for it when Edward Ball came calling with Alfred duPont's checkbook.

From the start, the St. Joe Company has worked hard to line up transportation improvements that will directly benefit its projects, and, it says, boost the entire region. The company's role in securing hundreds of millions of public

FIGURE 2. WaterColor groundbreaking with elaborate sand-sculpted model homes. Photo by Kathryn Ziewitz.

dollars raises questions about who pays for improvement, and who benefits. The same questions initially hounded duPont when he formed the Gulf Coast Highway Association to start paving the Panhandle in the 1920s and 1930s.

This time around, a regional airport, interstate connectors, and new and re-routed highways and marinas and ports are the big-ticket items. Making places, and convenient ways to reach them, is an expensive endeavor. For instance, it takes approximately $10 to $12 million per mile to convert an existing two-lane highway to four lanes in an urban area.[21] A new regional airport for the Panama City area, which St. Joe supports, carried a price tag estimated at $218 million.[22]

Meanwhile, St. Joe Company officials assured area decision makers they would pursue a goal of bringing well-paying new jobs to the region to complement their real estate developments. St. Joe even created a new position for an economic development vice president, filling it with the Alabama economic growth expert credited with luring Mercedes-Benz and Boeing factories to that state.

Deals and Ideals

While the St. Joe Company goes about its business of making places in the Great Northwest, some residents only want to hold onto the paradise they already know. They question how much environmental destruction will accompany the company's energetic drive to "make places." How, they ask, will the company preserve one of the brightest spots in the quality-of-life rubric for northwest Florida—its abundant and varied natural resources?

Returning to south Walton County, the environmental issues surrounding the makeover of the Green Empire come into sharp focus. Here the stakes have been high, with thousands of acres of land in dispute and millions of dollars changing hands. St. Joe has had a major part to play in the use, development, and conservation of south Walton lands. It has been involved as land buyer, seller, commercial forest operator, and party to lawsuit with the state over conservation lands acquisition.

Here, as much as anywhere in St. Joe territory, vocal, confident residents have waged a spirited lobby to keep growth in check and protect natural resources. Some activists in south Walton County might be conveniently dismissed as the often-maligned "got miners," people who move to a beautiful place, build a home, then protest the arrival of any neighbors who might spoil their million-dollar views. However, there's a difference: today's activists were yesterday's participants in a bold, state-sponsored planning initiative that strove to map out the future of beautiful south Walton County according to a grass-roots consensus.

The intensive planning effort, which began in 1993, produced a vision that was a progressive planner's dream. South Walton County was to be like a string of pearls, with dense village clusters separated by parks and forests and strung together by a scenic roadway that was paralleled by a bicycle and pedestrian path. The plan contained sprawl by limiting building to defined clusters. Greenway corridors were slated to preserve scenic and ecological values and provide alternative transportation and recreation. Energy efficient design and development, water resources and wetlands protection, and affordable housing were all components of the vision forged. Robert Davis participated in the discussions. He proposed siting a university in the area, restoring planted forests to their natural state, and emphasizing eco-tourism.[23]

The plan was without a doubt the most high-minded one ever proposed in the Panhandle, where the concept of planning at all was relatively new, as the 1994 final vision document duly noted.[24] Yet the vision appeared to be attainable, by virtue of the state's support, and its well-funded land-buying program for conservation and recreation lands. In 1992, the state had purchased approximately 18,000 acres of prize land that had once belonged to St. Joe Paper in Walton County.

The centerpiece of the acreage was the parcel known as Topsail Hill, so named because its towering dunes resembled a ship's sail from offshore. Behind the beach were coastal lakes so clean they were used as the state's standard for water purity. Topsail also had "more varied natural communities than almost any other property of its size in Florida," according to The Nature Conservancy (TNC), the preservation-oriented land-buying organization.[25]

Topsail Hill, and the thousands of acres of former St. Joe pine forests surrounding it, were caught up in controversy for years, starting in the mid-1980s, when developers who had purchased the land from St. Joe went bankrupt, along with two savings and loan institutions that had bankrolled their overly ambitious project. A huge piece of the foreclosed land was sold in a dramatic auction at the Walton County courthouse in DeFuniak Springs. The winning bidder was The Nature Conservancy, which supplied the cash to close the deal, then sold the acreage to the state under the Preservation 2000 Program. The land now exists as Topsail Hill State Preserve and Point Washington State Forest.

For a long time after the startling 1992 purchase, a simmering battle raged over the scope of the purchase. One camp of Walton Countians maintained that the state had taken too much conservation land; they felt some land should be returned to the private sector to beef up tax rolls and encourage free enterprise. The other camp argued that, on balance, more conservation land should be added over time to complete greenways and fulfill other public purposes.

The innovative visioning effort begun in the early 1990s was in fact an attempt to forge a compromise between the two camps through a plan that called for both conservation and development. The state allocated over $1 million and established the South Walton Conservation and Development Trust to manage the multiyear planning effort. Implementation of the visionary plan, however, was another matter. The plan had no legal weight and could only be fulfilled by being translated into the county's comprehensive plan.

The South Walton Trust is still used as a reference document at the Walton County planning office, but fulfillment of the vision has been patchy. The trust vision has been realized in the bicycle paths that have sprouted up along south Walton County's scenic Highway 30-A, but thwarted by homes that have been built outside the bounds of the originally conceived town clusters. Affordable housing, wetlands preservation, completion of greenway corridors, and the establishment of a town center have all been continuing subjects of dispute. Citizens and homeowner groups have squared off against a succession of development plans that have emerged for area beaches. Since 1992, the special place that has been an inspiration to so many passionate advocates of better planning has become mired in traffic jams and studded with expensive second homes.

Now that the St. Joe Company has turned to real estate, it is among the developers who are rapidly changing the once-sleepy south Walton coast into a boom town. The company won permission to develop resort facilities on a stretch of

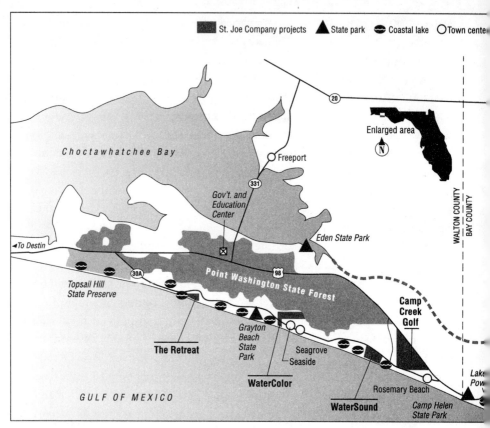

MAP 3. South Walton County: Topsail Hill, Point Washington State Forest, and beaches of south Walton County.

pristine coast that included four and a half acres inhabited by the federally endangered Choctawhatchee beach mouse. In exchange for this encroachment on habitat, St. Joe is subsidizing intensive management for the mouse that constituted the company's greatest obstacle to maximizing its prime beachfront holdings. The Fish and Wildlife Service signed off on the permit in July 2000. "If anyone saves the beach mouse, it will be us," insisted St. Joe vice president for communications, Jerry Ray.[26] It might be apropos that concern for the little mouse be placed in the hands of a former Disney executive, the present CEO of St. Joe, Peter Rummell.

Ray's confidence reflects the company's bold assurance that what is good for the St. Joe Company is good for northwest Florida, hands down. Hiring in-house horticulturalists and biologists before bulldozer operators as St. Joe has done is rare anywhere, and especially in northwest Florida. But, then, few have the hubris to declare they are "making places" out of places that are so inherently well made by nature. The Gulf fritillary butterflies that wander errantly into the tent set up for the WaterColor groundbreaking have been visiting this same, authentic place since time out of mind. The beach mice, sea turtles, and migratory birds that make landfall along this coast put their seal of approval on the place long ago; in fact, they cannot live without it.

Visiting the unfolding developments at the western edge of St. Joe's empire stirs uneasy reflections about appearances, authenticity, and the power of human manipulation. Coincidentally, those were key themes of a 1998 movie, *The Truman Show*, in which Jim Carrey portrayed a man carrying on a cozy but increasingly restless existence in a charming world, which unbeknown to him was an elaborate movie set filled entirely with actors.

The movie was filmed at Seaside. In fact, the clearing on which the Water-Color groundbreaking took place in October 1999 was made for *The Truman Show*. The sand that once supported Jim Carrey's trailer was peopled by well-dressed realtors, business owners, politicians, and St. Joe Big Brass, as well as a few Seasiders and local news reporters. This event was orchestrated carefully enough to please a movie director. A watercolor artist sat perched on a stool at the base of the dunes alongside the tent, adding a few finishing touches to her masterful rendering of the seaward view. A jazz musician played while attendees sampled hors d'oeuvres and iced tea from an upscale local restaurant.

Natural fiber walkways protected the dunes from whatever erosion dozens of curious feet might cause treading the narrow path to the beach. Small signs warned, "Please Do Not Disturb the Vegetation." Never mind that construction was about to start a few short weeks after the groundbreaking, destroying vegetation on hundreds of acres, starting with the construction of the WaterColor sales office across the road.

St. Joe's plans for WaterColor changed in response to concerns from residents at Seaside and other local watchdogs. Density was scaled back, bridges once considered for motor traffic were recast as foot bridges, and shoreline buffers were made even more generous. St. Joe's approach at WaterColor gained the company support and respect from the majority of citizens and officials alike, reflecting the generally positive reception the company enjoys in spite of having more than a handful of critics.

Outside the perfect world that exists only in artificial cocoons like the *Truman Show* set, contradictions, mistakes, and tradeoffs are inevitable. If south Walton County is an example, the squeaky wheel principle—vociferous public involvement—may have some influence to tweak the newly aroused conscience of a company that, apart from its function as an income source for the Nemours Foundation, has not often been noted for a tender heart. However, as some locals are learning, sometimes the vision that prevails has more to do with power than consensus.

The management team of place makers is a talented and interesting mix of former Disney executives, the intact Arvida group, and a shrinking number of old-guard paper company holdovers. Other top executives include a former state legislator, a leading Florida growth management lawyer, and a Texas banker, with the former executive of a leading land conservation organization thrown in for good measure.

Out of this eclectic mix, one hopes that commerce and high ideals can find a happy meeting place in the Florida Panhandle, a place where beach mice can roam on dark starry nights and its human occupants can obtain satisfactory employment. In spite of the chipping away of the south Walton County landscape over recent decades, it remains full of fresh promise, as does the rest of the area.

The St. Joe Company conducts its own state-of-the-art visioning exercises at its Jacksonville headquarters along the St. Johns River. From there issue strategic plans that are wrapped in proprietary secrecy and shared with select movers and shakers across Florida. These visions are likely to stick, barring unforeseen challenges to the company's energetic, creative ambitions. What these plans are is the subject of speculation from Tallahassee to Panama City and beyond. One thing is sure: few visions have the corporate power behind them that this one does—the power to write the newest chapter in the story of the northwest Florida landscape.

The Lay of the Land

*I grew up in the Panhandle of northern Florida and
the adjacent counties of Alabama, in circumstances
that eventually turned me into a field biologist. . . .
The physical surroundings inclined youngsters toward an awe of nature. That part of the country had
been covered, four generations back, by a wilderness
as formidable in some respects as the Amazon.*
E. O. Wilson, *Biophilia*

ST. JOE'S HOLDINGS IN northwest Florida range across a diverse and bountiful, although not necessarily pristine, natural landscape. The region's treasure
trove of flora and fauna suffered greatly from overzealous logging and unrestricted hunting long before the founders of the St. Joe enterprises came to Florida in the 1920s. Since that time, the Panhandle's environment has endured new
assaults on its forests, coasts, and wetlands. In spite of the losses, though, the
region's broad green and sandy expanses still harbor a natural heritage that is
nationally recognized.

As the St. Joe Company mounts a drive to remake the Florida Panhandle, an
acquaintance with the region's environmental history is helpful in understanding the complex land-use issues—ranging from habitat alteration to controlled
burns to land preservation—that are linked to the St. Joe Company's initiatives.
In addition, a look at the Panhandle's environmental history shows that its
economy has historically been tied to its natural resources, a trend that continues in a new way with St. Joe's emphasis on the area's natural assets in its marketing campaigns.

Biodiversity Hotspot

Each of the major ecosystems of the southeastern United States meets in the Panhandle, making it an epicenter of biodiversity. "So many species of plants and animals flourish in the wet, temperate climate of the Panhandle that the region may support the highest species diversity of any similar-size area in the U.S. and Canada," asserts one government report.[1] There are snakes and lizards that come from the West or tropics of long, long ago, rhododendron and beech forests usually found farther north, pitcher plants in common with the Carolinas, as well as the cabbage palms, sawgrass, and fernlike coontie of peninsular Florida. Reptiles, amphibians, and carnivorous plants are among the types of wildlife thriving in great numbers or varieties here.

Some of the flora and fauna is so unusual and limited in its range that it is imperiled. The Nature Conservancy, a nonprofit organization devoted to land preservation and restoration, ranks the Florida Panhandle as one of six biological hot spots in the nation, based on the area's preponderance of rare and narrowly distributed species. "The Panhandle's longleaf pine woodlands, ravine forests, rivers and coastal bays are home to more than 50 imperiled species and hundreds of threatened ones," according to TNC.[2]

The region's natural diversity is reflected in its topography, which has much more relief than the rest of the state. The northern hills, which reach 345 feet at the highest point, grade to a variety of flatlands and wetlands, eventually meeting the Gulf of Mexico. Traversing this varied Panhandle terrain are three out of four of Florida's major rivers: from east to west, the Apalachicola, the Choctawhatchee, and the Escambia, rivers that TNC's Florida director Bob Bendick described as "exceptional" in their biodiversity.[3]

The broad floodplain forest of the Apalachicola is one of the richest habitats on Earth, supporting more than forty kinds of trees. Among them is the Ogeechee tupelo, the blossoms of which honeybees make into renowned, noncrystallizing tupelo honey. The same swamps once sheltered the huge ivory-billed woodpecker and flocks of Carolina parakeets, both doomed to extinction with the fall of the giant cypress forests. This region, now labeled an International Biosphere Reserve by conservationists, supports frogs, salamanders, bugs, beavers, bears, and warblers, along with its diverse plant life. The Apalachicola River harbors rare and ancient Gulf sturgeon, endangered mussels, and a multitude of other aquatic life. At its mouth in Apalachicola Bay, fresh water and nutrients mix with the tang of Gulf waters to produce oysters, fish, crab, and finfish.

FIGURE 3. View of the lush Apalachicola River Valley from Alum Bluffs (on the east bank of the river). Photo by Kathryn Ziewitz.

Nestled on the steep slopes of gullies and ravines along the Apalachicola River near the crossing of Highway 20 is a biodiversity stronghold known locally as the Garden of Eden, a description that seems apt given the variety and antiquity of plant and animal life there. Its steep hillsides are thick with unusual trees, shrubs, and herbs, including rhododendron and the yewlike endangered Torreya tree. Many of the plants were established during the Ice Ages and remained in a sort of living vegetation museum long after glaciers retreated. In the leaf litter that carpets the fragrant bottoms of these ravines live rare creatures including lungless salamanders, frogs, and an as-yet incompletely described set of other bugs and small critters.[4] Similar pockets of herbal Eden exist scattered across the Panhandle highlands.

Other standout features of the Panhandle are its artesian springs. In the opinion of Florida naturalist Archie Carr, the "supernatural beauty of the springs" was the basis for the tales of the Fountain of Youth spread by Spanish conquistadors.[5] In the eastern Panhandle, where limestone from an ancient sea floor reaches the surface, the action of water both above and below the ground creates caves, sinkholes, and springs.

Wakulla Springs is by far the most famous, having served as the filming location for Tarzan movies and the camp horror classic, *The Creature from the Black*

Lagoon. An average of 200 million gallons a day pours out from its subterranean font, which is supplied by the water stored in the Floridan Aquifer.[6] The spring is ringed with cypress draped in Spanish moss that creates a decidedly Gothic appearance. Its compelling scenery continues deep underground in its intricate system of caves and passages, which divers began mapping in 1954 and are still exploring. The spring has yielded up a complete mastodon skeleton, which was reassembled and now towers grandly at the Museum of Florida History in Talla-hassee, along with Indian points of bone and flint.[7] Ed Ball acquired this idyllic treasure for himself in 1934, during his scouting trips for Alfred duPont.

A Landscape Shaped by Fire and Water

The region's most widespread natural habitat, the longleaf pine savanna, was nearly eliminated in a post–Civil War logging frenzy. Early travelers described the longleaf pine landscape as an airy grassland dotted with trees that created a cathedral-like atmosphere. Under the widely spaced pines was a low understory dotted with clumps of gray-green wiregrass and a myriad of wildflowers. Pale-ontologist David Webb places the origins of the longleaf pine savanna during the Ice Ages or the geologic period leading up to them several million years ago.[8]

The ecosystem stretched from the coastal plains of Georgia to Texas, encom-passing more than 75 million acres where creatures from bison to panthers once roamed. "All of the southeastern U.S. was longleaf pine ecosystem before the white man came here," said Angus Gholson, a longtime resident of hilly Chatta-hoochee who maintains an extensive herbarium and is one of the Panhandle's most esteemed botanists.[9]

Before people came, summer lightning ignited fires that would sweep across the land unimpeded until finally meeting a river or the coast. In a region where thunderstorms occur 80 to 130 days a year and lightning strikes are frequent, those species that were suited to fire dominated, with longleaf pines a promi-nent example. These long-lived trees weather their early years in a grasslike stage, pouring most of their energy into growing an oversized taproot. An abundance of expendable, moist needles shields the plant from low-intensity fires. Then, the pine shoots up out of its grass stage with its growing tip safely out of the reach of the typical ground fire. After surviving its early years, the majestic trees can live for 400 to 500 years. Some virgin pines had a girth ap-proaching fifteen feet.

In the absence of fire, longleaf pines in the grass stage are smothered by the accumulation of forest leaves and other litter. In the highlands, pine savanna gives way to other forest types, such as the thickets of turkey oak that today fill whole counties on logged-out longleaf pinelands.

In the lower elevations of the Panhandle, the predominant native landscape was called "pine barrens" by old-timers and is known as flatwoods by today's ecologists. In virgin flatwoods, longleaf, pond, and slash pine were the usual trees, with stands of cabbage palms and picturesque and slow-growing cypress interspersed throughout. Today this habitat supports expansive tree farms of slash and loblolly pines maintained by the St. Joe Company's Timberland division as well as other silviculture companies.

Lack of fire here alters plant communities by allowing dense thickets of shrubby vegetation, islands of evergreen hardwood trees, and the swamp plant called "titi," pronounced "tie-tie," to exert a choking hold on the terrain.[10] Surprisingly, even the wetlands communities in the flatwoods realm require a regular dose of fire to maintain themselves as they have over time. Burning may not be as even as in higher elevations but instead may skip areas, burning in a mosaic fashion.

Wetlands of one kind or another once covered more than half of Florida, and the Panhandle was no exception. Swamps covered vast areas daunting even to early native inhabitants. There were extensive bogs with a rich mix of grasses, flowers, and pitcher plants. Some wet flatwoods areas have standing water for only weeks or months annually. As short-lived as these wetlands are, they are critical to the survival of a host of amphibians such as newts, salamanders, frogs, and turtles. The federally endangered flatwoods salamander breeds in ephemeral ponds and spends the rest of its life cycle in uplands. This unfortunate dependence on both wetlands and undisturbed forests has endangered its existence, as industrial forestry has destroyed wetlands and replaced native forests across the animal's range.

A vast wet region east of the Apalachicola River includes the memorably named Tate's Hell swamp, which offers up a landscape worthy of its daunting name. Among the wonders of this eerie land are dwarf, or hat-rack, cypress. Trees hundreds of years old may be no taller than six feet, while taller ones may be more than a thousand years old.[11] Sprinkled around these curious trees are carnivorous plants and a large quantity of biting flies, mosquitoes, and other insects. As legend has it, in 1875 a farmer from the tiny settlement of Sumatra (about twenty-five miles north of the town of Apalachicola) wandered into the swamp to retrieve lost livestock. After losing his bearings in the boggy, buggy, snaky wilderness, it was several days before he stumbled out, wretched and deranged, into the fishing village of Carrabelle. Raving, "I'm Cebe Tate and I've been through Hell, boys! Been through Hell!" he unwittingly bestowed upon a huge swamp the name of Tate's Hell. Today, foresters are trying to restore a 200,000-acre expanse of Tate's Hell.

Coasts and Bays

The Panhandle's piney flatwoods and river floodplains eventually run into a coast made up of a succession of bay systems. These bays differ in character and make-up according to variables including presence or absence of inflowing rivers and barrier islands and the intensity with which waves slap the shore. The Panhandle's bays are some of the healthiest and most productive bay systems in North America, with large stocks of seagrass and shellfish including oysters, clams, and scallops. St. Joe's holdings influence, to varying degrees, the watersheds from Apalachee Bay at the easternmost crook of the Panhandle to Choctawhatchee Bay at the west, which St. Joe property barely touches at its easternmost arm.

The shallow marshes and bays that mediate between land and sea are productive nurseries for commercial and sport fish and shellfish. St. Andrew Bay alone supports more than 2,500 marine-dependent species, and Apalachicola Bay supports a commercial fishery that contributes $75 to $80 million to the economy annually.[12] Along the Big Bend region south of Tallahassee, where offshore slopes subdue waves before they approach the shore, a massive swath of ecologically productive salt marshes nurtures a variety of life.

Tracking west, stronger surf has sculpted white beaches, dunes, and barrier islands. From Ochlockonee Bay west to Destin, the Gulf Coast supports the uniquely Floridian ecosystem known as scrub, where rosemary, lupines, and salt-pruned oaks, sand pines, and other trees grow in desertlike conditions. The white sand beaches here are 99 percent pure quartz sand formed from the broken-down granite of the ancient Appalachian Mountains, carried to the Gulf of Mexico by ancient rivers and reworked by an energetic Gulf over the ages. Offshore, the clear, blue loop current of the Gulf of Mexico flows unusually close to shore, capping off the beauty of the Emerald Coast.

Humans Shape the Land

Although today's Panhandle landscape is mostly rural and undeveloped, it is far from pristine. By and large, the canvas of the Panhandle landscape was already painted over at least once by the hands of humans long before Alfred duPont and his associates began piecing together the Green Empire in the 1920s.

Even Native Americans tinkered with the land, primarily by using fire to "green up" groundcover for winter pasturage to attract deer and other grazing animals. Most controlled burns are still conducted according to this tradition, during the cool season, a choice of timing that longleaf pine–wiregrass enthusiasts such as Angus Gholson point out is not sufficient to restore the native longleaf pine ecosystem.

Once colonial powers took an interest in Florida, trade profoundly changed the relationship between Native Americans and the land. Instead of simply providing food and skins used in daily living, animal skins were now a commodity that could be traded for guns, knives, and iron pots.[13] The frenzied taking of animals for skins ushered in the first of the wholesale ravages to the Panhandle's land and wildlife. As areas farther north were largely depleted of deer, the hunting shifted, until west Florida became the center of a deerskin trade that some historians compare to the wholesale slaughter of buffalo on the western plains.

During the period of British rule, from 1763 to 1783, the firm Panton, Leslie and Company became the dominant trading concern in the region. After Florida passed from Britain back to Spain in 1783, the company continued its business, and trading posts popped up on the Wakulla and Apalachicola rivers. This first corporate presence in the Panhandle was a powerhouse every bit as important in its time as the St. Joe Company is today. It gained control over 1.4 million acres of Panhandle land, some of which eventually became St. Joe's.

The Arrival of Crackers and Plantation Owners

Once Florida reverted to Spain in 1783, the lure of its land drew the covetous attention of new arrivals to the north. Settlers in Georgia and Alabama frequently crossed south into sparsely populated Florida to raid cattle during the final Spanish years, and the region became a U.S. territory in effect if not in law well before the official handover in 1821. The land of the Panhandle was now in the hands of new settlers who came in two varieties: yeoman farmers who pushed their own ploughs and plantation owners who held slaves. Both groups of settlers left a lasting mark on the Panhandle's land, culture, and economy.

The yeoman farmers were by far more common than plantation dwellers. These were the "Crackers"—the clannish folk originally from the Scottish highlands, Wales, and Ireland who settled heavily in southern states after crossing the Atlantic.[14] Subsistence homesteaders, they had small farm fields and kept free-roaming cattle, hogs, and sheep. Like the Native Americans before them, they used fire to "green up" the woods for pasturage and felled the trees necessary to clear land for crops. They raised, butchered, and cured their own livestock, grew kitchen gardens and grains, patches of cotton for trade wherever the land could produce it, and made rare expeditions to river or coastal ports to obtain the few necessities they could not make. Settlers were scattered and the region remained lightly populated.

Janisse Ray, author of *Ecology of a Cracker Childhood*, contends that the Crackers' hardscrabble origins and existence contributed to a rough-edged view of nature:

> Crackers, although fiercely rooted in the land and willing to defend it to the death, hadn't had the means, the education, or the ease to care particularly about its natural communities. Our relationship with the land wasn't one of give and return. The land itself has been the victim of social dilemmas— racial injustice, lack of education, and dire poverty. It was overtilled; eroded; cut; littered; polluted; treated as a commodity, sometimes the only one, and not a living thing. Most people worried about getting by, and when getting by meant using the land, we used it. When getting by meant ignoring the land, we ignored it.[15]

The Crackers' proprietary land ethic laid the groundwork for the popularity of the doctrine of "property rights" in the region today. The property rights movement emphasizes the freedom of individuals to use their land as they wish over concerns for wider environmental and social consequences.

Other lasting traces remain of the early Cracker way of life. Instead of congregating at a village with its town square, as was the northern pattern, these more widely dispersed settlers met at mills, trading posts along rivers, or roads. Dusty crossroads became ephemeral town squares. Into the present, the pattern of sparse but wide-ranging inhabitation of the countryside exists, harking back to the transitory herding societies of the British highlands. In this region, boundaries between rural and urban land use are often fuzzy. Many present-day rural residents do not farm or ranch, but commute to jobs across a wide area. The result is a settlement pattern that appears haphazard to some eyes, and is the antithesis of the neotraditional or New Urbanist plans of some community developers. In addition, the widespread though lightly populated settlement of rural areas presents challenges to conservationists hoping to preserve wild areas and reintroduce fire to the landscape.

The plantation culture represented a more complex society than the Cracker homestead. After cotton brought a flush of prosperity to Florida's northern tier, the large plantations came to include parties, horse races, and other high-society refinements similar to other southern spreads. North of the geological line known as the Cody Scarp, which divides the hill country from the lowlands, the land was well suited for raising cotton. Plantations appeared in what are today Jackson, Gadsden, Jefferson, Leon, and Madison Counties. Towns that sprang up there included Marianna, Quincy, and, later, Tallahassee. The plantations locked up thousands of acres of land. Remaining intact plantations still form a version of a greenbelt in the Tallahassee area, hemming in the city on its northern and eastern fringes.

The original Southwood Plantation was established in Tallahassee along the Old St. Augustine Road used since Spanish days. A Virginian, George Ward, who worked in the local land office, was the plantation's founder.[16] The stately, columned house that now serves as the St. Joe Company's sales office for its 3,200-acre SouthWood development is not the original plantation home but rather was moved in the late 1930s from downtown Tallahassee to the site. It was there when the St. Joe Paper Company bought the plantation several years later.

As cotton plantations prospered, myriad efforts began to develop a Panhandle transportation network of roads, railroads, and shipping ports, further shaping the land. In 1824, construction of the Pensacola to St. Augustine Highway began along the route of today's U.S. Highway 90. Slaves farmed out from nearby plantations and soldiers from Pensacola did the work, hacking down the forest and laying logs to create a sixteen-foot-wide "corduroy" road over much of the route that the colonial Spanish had used. Early travelers had to contend with bumping along on logs, but their worst problem was enlisting a ride from undependable ferry operators at river crossings.

For more than a century after Florida became a territory, water remained the most common path of transportation. One port that boomed with the water trade was the tiny town of Apalachicola. It was incorporated in 1829 and within a decade rose to prominence for cotton shipping, ranking third behind New Orleans and Mobile. Apalachicola shipped cotton, hides, sugar, cedar, live oak timbers, and other lumber.[17] Starting in 1827, steamships plied the river.[18]

Antebellum Settlements

The town of St. Joseph, forerunner to the St. Joe Company's namesake town of Port St. Joe, was another town that sprang up during the antebellum boom times. The town was formed as a result of a dispute over land once owned by the Panton and Leslie Trading Company. In 1804, Spain had approved the company's request to take ownership of Indian lands, hundreds of thousands of acres of it, to make up for debts racked up by Indians at the company's trading posts. Spain added to the acreage again in 1811, creating a tract of some 1.4 million acres known as the Forbes purchase, after John Forbes, a Tory businessman who took over and renamed the former Panton, Leslie Company. The tract was bounded on the east by the Wakulla River, the west by the Apalachicola River, and the north by a nebulously drawn "swamp interior" that included the yet-to-be named Tate's Hell.[19]

After Florida became a territory, Forbes land titles were challenged in court. When a court sided with the Forbes Company's arguments, settlers who had taken up residence on home sites claimed by the Forbes Company were faced with having to pay for land they claimed to already own. Rather than pay up, a contingent of these settlers from Apalachicola founded the rival shipping hamlet of St. Joseph in 1835. The town was located some twenty-five miles northwest of Apalachicola, on the shore of St. Joseph's Bay, safely outside of the Forbes tract.

The budding town of St. Joseph brimmed over with grand schemes that set a worthy precedent for the ambitions of Alfred duPont and Ed Ball a hundred years later near the same spot of ground. The "Saints," as the town's citizens became known, hoped to capture some of the busy shipping trade from Apalachicola. St. Joseph Bay offered a superior, deeper harbor but lacked the inland connections that the Apalachicola River provided. So ambitious residents had lovely Lake Wimico, a few miles west of the Apalachicola River, dredged and linked to the mighty Apalachicola via a channel so that steamships could traverse the lake. In addition, town promoters built an eight-mile steam-operated railroad, connecting a lake terminal with the town of St. Joseph.[20] Construction of a north-south road connecting St. Joseph to Marianna was a second link to the interior.[21]

With its transportation squared away, town leaders gained confidence as well as business. The new town was ambitious on the political scene, and won itself an indelible role in history as the site of the nascent state of Florida's constitutional convention from December 1838 to January 11, 1839, when the constitution was signed.

Despite energetic efforts of its residents, however, St. Joseph did not capture the amount of trade it had hoped from Apalachicola. Then, in 1841, just as it tried to make itself over as a health resort, an outbreak of yellow fever swept the town. Notables, including the governor's wife, state delegates, and publishers, succumbed along with the common people and slaves. Three years later in 1844 a destructive September hurricane struck. The two calamities combined were too much for the town to overcome. Town buildings were purchased to be dismantled and reused elsewhere. Even the railroad tracks were removed and shipped for reuse in Georgia. Until another railroad came through in 1909, the beautiful coastline of St. Joseph Bay had more cows than people.

By the late 1830s, the earliest of coastal resorts sprang up in the Panhandle, populated with wealthy residents from the interior who built summer homes along breezy shores to escape the hot and "sickly" summers inland. Two locations were Newport, near St. Marks, and St. Andrew Bay, with its attractive sandy bluffs. Along St. Andrew Bay, the location of present-day Panama City, the population in summer swelled to 1,200 by the year 1845. The vacationers enjoyed sailing parties, formal dances for which ladies wore gowns of silk and lace, "always a promenade on the beach in the evening, and music on the water at night."[22]

Aside from these resorts, the St. Andrew Bay area remained a quiet backwater with subsistence farming, hunting, and fishing the main occupations. Wagons transported salted mullet inland to the planters.[23] Behind the shoreline, the Panhandle lowlands, with their extensive wet areas and sandy soils unsuitable for growing cotton or tobacco, remained sparsely populated, although a few ambitious individuals were platting towns.[24]

Timber and Naval Stores

After the Civil War, forest products filled the huge economic vacuum created by the war and the ravages of the boll weevil to the once-prosperous cotton industry. Well into the twentieth century, the Panhandle economy remained rooted in subsistence and harvest enterprises directly dependent on extracting resources from the land and sea, with industrial and manufacturing ventures scarce. This narrowly focused extractive economy took a heavy toll on the region's natural resources.

The Panhandle's forest products industry can be traced back to colonial times, when English, French, and Spanish sailing ships used pines, oaks, and cedars from the Gulf Coast's maritime forests to repair their wooden ships, a usage that defined the production of rosin, turpentine, and related products as "naval stores." Sailors heated pine sap to make pitch for caulking and used rosin to protect the rigging from decay. They felled longleaf pines to use as tall, straight masts for ships as early as 1743.[25]

Live oak became the wood of choice for making sturdy deck beams, planking, and ship's ribs after white oak had been depleted from maritime forests in northern states. It was considered as durable and strong as teak—"the titanium of its day," in the words of St. Joe Company spokesman Jerry Ray, who cited live oak timbering as an example of the longstanding human use of the Panhandle's resources.[26] Territorial officials were even appointed to protect naval live oak preserves from the "live oak pirates" who made off with the valuable timber.[27] Forests owned by the U.S. Navy were the first public lands set aside in Florida.[28]

The USS *Constitution*, a forty-four-gun frigate, earned the nickname of "Old Ironsides" in the War of 1812 because cannonballs bounced off her live oak planking. In the late 1920s, 900 tons of Santa Rosa live oak, cut down from a Pensacola navy preserve and salted away decades earlier, were used to rebuild the tall ship. In 2002, the developer of the golf course at St. Joe's SouthWood development announced that the U.S. Navy would be using a few of the dozens of live oaks felled for the golf course to help in yet another rebuilding of the *Constitution*.

After the Civil War, turpentining grew in importance. There were few other ways to earn a living, especially for freed slaves. All across the region, turpentine stills and their labor camps popped up. Workers used broad axes to chip a thin slab of bark and wood from the base of a living pine to trigger a flow of sap. Successive "chips" on the tree created a "cat faced" scar that can still be found on old turpentining trees today. At the still, collected sap was boiled over wood fires, the remains in the kettle becoming pitch and the steam yielding turpentine. Turpentine was shipped off to become an ingredient in paint, cosmetics, and medicines, among other uses. The industry remained a dominant one in the state's economy until World War II.[29] As logging increased in importance, naval stores operators worked ahead of the loggers, tapping pines that were eventually felled.

Yellow Gold

Sawmills had popped up across north Florida starting in the 1830s, but after 1870, timbering heated up considerably. Once the characteristics of the southern longleaf pine became widely known in the 1890s, the Panhandle finally yielded up the gold that had been sought since the time of the Spanish conquistadors. This "yellow gold" was found in the pillars of the longleaf pine that still stood watch over the vast majority of the Panhandle's many million acres. Longleaf pine (also called heart pine, southern pine, or yellow pine) was strong, dense wood imbued with resin that made it resistant to rot. The attractive honey hue and absence of knots made the wood highly valued for timber. Stout virgin longleaf pines were used for flooring, staircases, beams, and in general construction during the coincidentally named Gilded Age of the late nineteenth century.

Stands of ancient bald cypress fell along with the longleaf pine. In 1871, the Pennsylvania Tie Company descended on the swamps of Tate's Hell in present

Franklin County. Loggers braved the biting flies and snakes to fell and haul out the huge, thousand-year-old cypresses. Old photos show several men linking hands to span one tree. Horses and mules could not skid the logs, so canals were cut to allow "pull boats" to do the job. Later, timber companies built rail tracks on filled-in land and pilings. The cypress became fodder for the nation's railroad-building frenzy, supplying wood for railroad crossties.[30] The magnificent trees were turned into paneling, as well as more lowly products like barrels and shipping crates.

Lumber camps and sawmills appeared across the forested Panhandle amid the subsistence farms. Jacksonville was north Florida's largest port, but Pensacola was the biggest lumber port in the Panhandle. All along the Gulf Coast, ships came to haul off timber. Timber operations became the mainstay of the regional economy, feeding raw materials to an outside world that—unlike itself—was becoming more industrialized, sophisticated, and hungry for building materials.

"Cut out and get out" logging operations that began in the 1870s were the order of the day for the next four decades. Trees were cut and shipped to places such as New York, New Orleans, South America, and Europe. Northern logging companies that had already exhausted the virgin pine forests around the Great Lakes moved south and set up operations in southern forests. After the nation's timbering tapered off elsewhere, timber companies and sawmills still descended on the Panhandle's virgin forests. Cypress, oaks, and grand longleaf pines were the most sought after.

Lumberjacks with crosscut saws felled the trees and stripped their bark on site. They branded the trees with the emblem of the family or timber company. Then, they dragged or "skidded" the logs by two-wheeled carts hitched up to teams of up to eight oxen until reaching a river or railroad depot. Later, this method was replaced by the use of small-gauge railroads that could be easily assembled and dismantled.

Before railroads, the bountiful rivers of the Panhandle became conduits for timber. The once-quiet rivers, which had known occasional passing steamships or smaller crafts of canoes or jon boats, became clogged with fallen timber. At river depots, the logs would be chained into rafts, often ten miles long, and floated to port cities. Logs were transported along most of north Florida's rivers, including the Apalachicola, Chipola, Choctawhatchee, and Blackwater. Sometimes logs would escape the bonds of the raft and the dense, green timbers would sink to the bottom, where some still lie today, perfectly preserved. As much as 10 percent of the lumber was lost in this fashion and is being retrieved today by entrepreneurs of "deadhead logging."

In the early 1880s, a railroad was built from Jacksonville to River Junction, on the east bank of the Apalachicola River, followed by another that linked River Junction to Pensacola. The new Louisville and Nashville (L and N) Railroad made it easier to get wood products to market and firmly placed new towns on the map, including Chipley and DeFuniak Springs. This railroad had a profound influence on the Panhandle's development by connecting the region from east to west and sparking commerce along its route.

The rampant timbering at the turn of the twentieth century fell only slightly short of the clear-cutting that is possible with today's technology. The biggest and best trees were taken, and trees that were unmarketable for one reason or another were left standing. Snags, stumps, and other remnant trees aside, few pockets of unlogged forest remained in the Panhandle after the loggers were done. Across north Florida, loggers would fell one tract of ancient virgin forest, then move on to the next. One eyewitness noted that after one particularly zealous tree-cutting operation in Liberty County, a person could see all the way from the settlement of Telogia to the hamlet of Wilma, eighteen miles away. The swath cut through what had been a diverse virgin forest, now a part of the western side of the Apalachicola National Forest.[31]

The timber-related industries of the time left a negative impression on Georgia poet laureate Sidney Lanier. "To-day they set up their shanties and 'stills,' quickly they cut down or exhaust the trees, to-morrow they are gone, leaving a desolate and lonesome land," he observed after a journey to Florida in 1874.[32]

A Bottom to the Barrel

Over the course of a generation the Panhandle's ancient longleaf pine landscape almost disappeared. The cut-out-and-get-out logging of this era, combined with later fire suppression that followed in the "Smokey the Bear" era of commercial forestry, reduced the longleaf ecosystem to the present figure of about 2 percent of its former range.[33] The longleaf pine natural community is on the list of Critically Endangered Ecosystems of the United States, according to the Department of Interior.[34]

Wildlife too lost ground from the aggressive removal of the forests. Affected animals included the red-cockaded woodpecker, sometimes referred to as "the spotted owl of the South" because of its dependence on old-growth forests and the political conflicts that accompany that status. The birds were once widespread and common inhabitants of the longleaf pine savanna. They rely on aging trees with heart rot in which to excavate nest cavities for their offspring, spending two to five years carving out a nest. Not only woodpeckers but dozens of other animals use these cavities. With the disappearance of appropriate mature nesting trees, populations of red-cockaded woodpeckers—and other dependant animals—plummeted to today's precarious levels.

While these small and industrious woodpeckers are still present, other creatures were not so lucky. Unrestricted hunting of early settlement days in the Panhandle supplied the follow-up punch to habitat destruction to cause the first major extinctions since the late Ice Ages. Hunting and fishing, with their origins stemming back to the earliest residents, remain a cherished part of the rural tradition to this day. Hunting is an accepted, even necessary, part of wildlife management. However, no-holds-barred hunting beyond the capacity of an animal to reproduce eventually leads to extinction.

Creatures that were hunted to extinction included the passenger pigeon and the Carolina parakeet. According to E. W. Carswell, late Panhandle writer and historian, the last stronghold of these charming, social birds was along the Choctawhatchee River in Walton County. "The people would shoot one and the rest would come to help it; they would be shot until all were killed. That kind of characterizes this area. We shot the last duck, the last turkey, the last whatever, so that when I was a boy there was no turkey or deer in this whole area."[35]

Other animals that disappeared from the Panhandle during this period included the Florida panther and the ivory-billed woodpecker, which had once lived and bred in cypress swamps of the Apalachicola floodplain. One of the last ivory-billed woodpeckers in the United States was seen in a wooded floodplain in the area south of Highway 20 and near the Dead Lakes, according to naturalist Larry Ogren. The area would be in between Blountstown and Wewahitchka. The sighting was confirmed with officials from the Audubon Society, says Ogren, who in the 1950s met up with the local resident who had seen the bird. The man would only tell him, "It's been a long time, and I swore not to reveal the location."[36] According to St. Joe Company Conservation Lands vice president George Willson, Ed Ball had a particular fascination with ivory-billed woodpeckers and took pains to protect them when he found out they were present on company lands in that same area.[37]

By the turn of the twentieth century, the excesses of resource exploitation nationwide helped to spark a conservation ethic. Then, as now, efforts to conserve forests, fish, and wildlife had different philosophical undertones. Some voices, most prominent among them John Muir, argued that nature should be preserved for its own sake, not simply for its usefulness to mankind. Nature was "neither a commodity nor a resource nor a playground but something akin to a cathedral."[38] Others viewed the situation through a more pragmatic lens, and from a different spiritual vantage. Nature did indeed provide resources and commodities for people to exploit. Ultimately, God-given resources existed to serve mankind as it saw fit.

Philosophical differences aside, foresighted leaders of the time agreed that they could see a bottom to the barrel of forests, game, and fish that had seemed bottomless before. Manifest destiny or not, the barrel might come up empty. In 1901, plant scientist Charles Mohr voiced his fears that the queen of timber trees, longleaf pine, could no longer propagate itself naturally, even in areas to which it was perfectly adapted. Mohr lamented that primitive turpentining methods were killing these trees needlessly and that herds of domestic animals were consuming seedlings that sprang up in the wake of logging. He also believed fire to be harmful. Although his views on fire were erroneous, his fears about disappearance of the longleafs were well grounded.

Hitherto, forestry had operated strictly as a form of harvesting. Once trees were taken, timber operators moved on to other areas. Deliberate reseeding or any other kind of restoration was unheard of. In the Panhandle, the onetime vast longleaf pine savanna gave way to farm fields and regrowth of whatever took hold.

Scientists and politicians nationwide put forth ideas for ensuring that the growing young nation would not run out of timber. One idea was to buy and set aside new forest reserves similar to the naval reserves of old—an idea championed by President Theodore "Teddy" Roosevelt that resulted in establishment of public forests in both the western and then eastern United States.

A second answer to shoring up the dwindling forests came through the emerging science of silviculture—the growing of trees as glorified row crops. Establishment of a forestry division within the U.S. Department of Agriculture in 1876 squarely defined this new endeavor as a form of agriculture. Pioneers in a new field, scientific forestry, began to research new methods of raising, harvesting, and using forest products. Southern colleges began to start forestry courses. Georgia State was one of the first, in 1914.[39]

Scientific forestry required a scale and capitalization that was out of the reach of the typical Panhandle landowner. However, the development of the science and art of silviculture would make possible the large-scale harvest of crops of trees by those like Alfred duPont who had the wherewithal to take on such a task. The emerging science of forestry was crucial for the development of the forest products business that would fuel the St. Joe Empire. In large part, the founding of St. Joe's Green Empire rested on faith in the resilience of a despoiled land to spring back to productivity, productivity harnessed in the form of silviculture.

3

Good Ol' Florida Sand and Mud

*My friend, you're going to see a lot of wonderful things
come out of those piney woods.*
Ed Ball, c. 1925

A CONSERVATIVE TRIO from the Tidewater states was among the scores of investors who flocked to Florida in the 1920s. These three, Alfred Irénée duPont, his wife Jessie Ball duPont, and his brother-in-law, Edward Ball, were the architects of the Green Empire. They bought land in the 1920s and 1930s that today makes up the majority of acreage held by the St. Joe Company. The vast tracts serve as debt-free "greenfields" for which scores of new uses are underway.

Origins on the Brandywine and Ball's Neck

The duPont-Ball alliance that would have an enduring impact on Florida's development and politics began at Ball's Neck, Virginia, an isolated peninsula along the Chesapeake Bay. Alfred duPont and others associated with the illustrious Delaware duPont family enjoyed hunting excursions to the backwater of Ball's Neck. The hunting outings culminated in a feast and celebration with music and dancing, a highlight for the gentrified but poor leading families of the area, including the Ball family for which the area was named. Following a visit, the Ball's Neck residents would receive an anonymous check to help pay for new shotguns, clothes, and other expenses.[1]

At one such visit in 1900, Alfred and Jessie danced and laughed together. She was a vivacious teenage schoolteacher and he a married man twenty years her senior. Jessie Dew Ball was smitten with the handsome, fun-loving gunpowder maker. Before he left, Jessie implored Alfred to write. She may have been surprised when he actually did, recounting his "most delightful visit" and suggesting they would meet again some day.[2] The two corresponded on and off over the next two decades before marrying in 1921—a third marriage for Alfred and Jessie's first and last.

The Balls were bluebloods, descended from early English settlers. George Washington's mother was a Ball. But Jessie and Ed's father earned only a modest living as a lawyer, and the family scraped by. In contrast, Alfred duPont was part of a family dynasty that grew in wealth and power from the time its founder, Alfred's great-great grandfather, Pierre Samuel duPont de Nemours, emigrated from France on the heels of the French Revolution and settled along the Brandywine River in Delaware. There, one of his sons began the gunpowder-making business that would eventually build the vast American duPont fortunes. The chemical empire that began with gunpowder today manufactures well-known products, including nylon, Teflon, and Tyvek, a building material being incorporated into new St. Joe/Arvida homes. (The duPont name has been spelled a variety of ways. This book uses "duPont" to refer to family members, while using the capitalized DuPont to refer to the old powder and extant diversified chemical company.)

Alfred hailed from the branch of the family that lived on the same side of the Brandywine as the powder works and took enormous pride and interest in the manufacture of powder. Alfred labored shoulder to shoulder with workmen, putting in an especially arduous stint during the Spanish American War. He became the nation's foremost black-powder maker.

Alfred joined his first cousins Thomas Coleman duPont and Pierre Samuel duPont in taking over the company in 1902, the 100th anniversary of the original company's founding. The E. I. DuPont de Nemours Company was a gold mine with a declared value of $24 million.[3] The business had grown by buying up many of the nation's competing gunpowder and explosives companies. Besides supplying ammunition for every major conflict from the War of 1812 on, E. I. DuPont de Nemours products carved railroad tunnels through mountains and blasted rocks from quarries to supply material for building the nation's roads and buildings. The cousins had gained the company on easy terms from the old guard duPonts who were poised to sell to outside interests.

Alfred's personal life was complicated. In 1907, soon after his first marriage ended in a bitter divorce, he married a sophisticated distant cousin, dashing any hopes that Jessie, by then twenty-two years old, might have had for a closer relationship with Alfred. Jessie left the Chesapeake area for California, where she joined other family members and continued her teaching career.

Alfred built an opulent mansion for himself and his new wife, and christened their private kingdom Nemours. The Nemours name originated with his famous ancestor Pierre Samuel duPont, who appended "de Nemours" to his name after purchasing a country home in the French village of Nemours, as was the habit of the noble class to which duPont aspired. The Nemours name has since been fondly bestowed on duPont landmarks, including an inn built by Jessie duPont in Port St. Joe. It also remains the name of the main St. Joe–related duPont charitable institution, the Nemours Foundation, to which profits from the St. Joe Company's duPont-founded enterprises were designed to flow in accordance with Alfred duPont's will.

Power struggles between Alfred and his duPont cousins over the company and family resentment over Alfred's marriages engendered a bitter family feud that was never resolved. By 1920, Alfred's relations with his second wife had deteriorated. Also, Alfred was losing his end of the power struggle for the E. I. DuPont Company. To make matters worse, the Internal Revenue Service was dunning him for profits from World War I. Alfred apparently found solace during these difficult times in his correspondence with Jessie Ball. A year after his second wife's death, he married Jessie in California on January 22, 1921, with her brother Edward serving as best man.[4] He was fifty-six, she thirty-six.

Alfred duPont and Ed Ball Join Forces

Alfred began searching for new ways in which to apply his wealth and talents outside of the Brandywine and the E. I. DuPont Company. His new brother-in-law was instrumental in shaping these plans. Edward Ball had been making quite a comfortable living as a furniture salesman in California when his sister persuaded Alfred to hire him as an advisor. From the start, his hard-nosed business skills helped Alfred, who had been cheated before in several business dealings.

Although a newcomer to Wall Street, Ed Ball boldly renegotiated loan rates to pare his new brother-in-law's debts. Over time, the two became close friends as well as business partners. Ball's grasp over Alfred duPont's interests grew with each of his successes at improving the bottom line.

Alfred wrote his older brother Thomas about his new right-hand man, "Ed is surely a nice boy, the most lovable human being, next to the Brid [meaning his bride, Jessie], that I know. Being a Ball he is naturally a gentleman, and excuse me from living with anybody less. He is a little pig-headed—another Ball feature (also a duPont feature, I being the exception)—so it is necessary to bat him over the head with a club once in a while; but he has a well-balanced cabeza and is a fine, loyal, hard worker, as tenacious as a bull dog on a tramp's pants—all qualities appealing most strongly to me."[5]

Unlike the other Ball children, young Ed Ball had ended his days of formal schooling at age thirteen. He turned to a variety of enterprises, including felling and selling black walnut trees, gathering nuts and berries for sale, and protecting the family's oyster beds from poachers. He roamed the woods "as a sort of Virginia version of Tom Sawyer or Huck Finn," according to his later associates and biographers, Jacob "Jake" Belin and Braden Ball (no relation to Ed and Jessie.)[6] Unlike Tom and Huck, his adventures usually had a money-making angle. The family's noble poverty was nothing he wanted to imitate. Although his family did not have the ability to shower their children with material things, they did encourage their children's talents and especially indulged Ed, the youngest. According to author Richard Greening Hewlett, "Eddie, the younger son, was a round-faced little fellow who had been badly spoiled by his parents and his older sisters."[7]

By the time his sister married the famous millionaire, Ed had long left the Virginia woods behind. He had grown into a man of modest stature, about five feet six inches tall and weighing under 150 pounds. In later years, when his dark black hair had diminished to a white fringe, he was described as gnome-like.[8] Over the years he had gained experience in a variety of jobs—selling hardware and groceries, law books, and furniture. He had also served a stint as an infantryman in the army in Washington State and had prospected for gold in Alaska.[9] At one point, he toyed with getting a law degree like his father and his brother, Tom, but he decided against it. Although he held no diploma, he was not an uneducated man. He could recite the works of Omar Khayyam and Shakespeare and obviously had a keen grasp of the workings of business mathematics.

Alfred, with the considerable fortune in E. I. duPont de Nemours stock that remained in spite of business failures and back taxes he owed the U.S. Treasury, had enough capital to make a mark in any well-planned enterprise. Ball had a genius for finance that required no sheepskin. As his involvement in duPont-sponsored ventures deepened, Ball acquired personal wealth and power beyond that which any furniture or law book salesman could ever acquire.

To Florida

In 1926, after his cousin Pierre S. duPont became tax commissioner in Delaware and began to scrutinize his finances, Alfred transferred almost all his business interests to Florida and made the Sunshine State his official residence. The duPonts had visited Florida soon after their marriage and had lodged at the late Henry Flagler's Royal Palm Hotel in Miami. Jessie had even taken part in the red-hot south Florida real estate market, investing her own money in 1923 on two Miami Beach lots that she resold two years later for a profit of $127,000.[10] At the time, a crowded field of players was floating extravagant plans for south Florida projects. Although duPont money would later purchase several key downtown Miami properties, for the most part the sensible trio sidestepped the fanfare of the south Florida boom.

The duPonts instead planted themselves far north of the whirl of speculation, in the sedate city of Jacksonville. The leading city of north Florida and, indeed, of the state, by the early 1920s, Jacksonville's population exceeded 100,000. Alfred and Jessie found the city, with its skyscrapers and streetcars, congenial to their needs and sensibilities. From Jacksonville, duPont could handle his banking affairs and have access to the Atlantic Ocean and intracoastal waterway for cruising.

Ed Ball's early Florida duties included supervising the construction of the duPonts' winter home along the banks of the St. Johns River just outside Jacksonville. Alfred christened the Spanish-style mansion Epping Forest in honor of the Ball family into which he had married. Epping Forest had been the name of the manor of Mary Ball, George Washington's mother, in Virginia, a home place that in turn was named after the Ball's ancestral home in England. Once the 25,000-square-foot home was completed in 1927, the couple divided their time between Nemours and Epping Forest, traveling up and down the East Coast in their large houseboat cruiser, which was docked, literally, at their door. Alfred brought to the St. Johns a vestige of his early days as a maker of explosive powder—he installed a small cannon on the lawn that he fired regularly over the St. Johns.

From Jacksonville west across the Panhandle, colder winters and poor transportation dampened the real estate market relative to south Florida. Author Mark Derr contends that the blighting of the state's northern landscape wreaked by the cut-out-and-get-out logging of the late nineteenth and early twentieth centuries was a factor in discouraging the interest of the earliest big-name developers, including Henry Flagler.

FIGURE 4. The mansion at Epping Forest Yacht Club. Photo by Kathryn Ziewitz.

The population of the Panhandle had grown only slowly after the Civil War. Most residents eked out a living from homesteads, the sea, or timber-related businesses. Early Panhandle developers pinned their hopes on new railroads, roads, and ports that often did not materialize. Entrepreneurs made plans on paper that were never realized, as was the case when circus magnate John Ringling proposed a planned community near Crestview, north of present-day Fort Walton Beach,[11] and when preacher and bad poet–turned–businessman William Lee Popham floated plans to build a thousand-room hotel on St. George Island.[12]

Several Panhandle cities grew modestly, among them Panama City, where ambitious residents hoped to develop an important port to serve the new Panama Canal that was under construction when the town was incorporated in 1909. Tourism, however, turned out to bring more business than the shipping trade. By the first decade of the twentieth century, Bay County reclaimed its status as a regional vacation destination, reviving the tourist trade that had lain dormant since the original town of St. Andrews had been destroyed in the Civil War. Whereas Florida's east coast drew the leading scions of the North, the Gulf Coast catered to the wealthy set from the former plantation belt and emerging industrial cities, including Birmingham.

For more than a century this pattern of tourism has repeated itself, with the only variation being the mode and speed of overland transportation. The Panhandle beaches, with their proximity to the Deep South and central United

States, still draw more vacationers by car than any other Florida destination except the Orlando area, an important statistic to developers like the St. Joe Company.

The Panhandle even attracted a few Yankees. In 1913, magazine publisher W. H. Lynn founded the town of Lynn Haven on cut-over land five miles north of Panama City as a retirement area for Civil War veterans—northern ones. A statue of a Yankee soldier stands facing north in this town, one of the few of its kind south of the Mason-Dixon line. In the Tallahassee area, northern industrialists purchased plantations that had declined after the boll weevil and the Civil War.

In the Panhandle, as elsewhere, real estate development was inextricably linked with transportation improvements. The revival of a town along the shores of St. Joseph Bay where the old town of St. Joseph had briefly flowered was directly tied to the arrival in 1909 of a new railroad, the Apalachicola Northern Railroad (ANR). The railroad went ninety-nine miles from River Junction, just south of present-day Chattahoochee (where it connected with the east-west line to Pensacola) to St. Joseph Bay, by way of Apalachicola. Its cars carried lumber from the Panhandle's rapidly falling longleaf pine forests to markets on the East Coast and abroad. Building the line was an engineering challenge, as it traversed steep hills in its northern reaches and spanned the Apalachicola and its vast swamps on its lower portions. The state granted the railroad's builders 495,000 acres of land, many of which were later acquired by duPont companies in the 1930s.[13]

The ANR was essential to both developing and serving deep-water docks that revived the shipping trade at St. Joseph Bay. For starters, the railroad hauled in the pile driver needed to construct the deep-water docks.[14] With the addition of the docks, St. Joseph Bay presented a nearly perfect shipping harbor: protected by the long curving finger of the St. Joseph Peninsula from severe weather in all directions except due north and lacking inflowing rivers that would deposit silt that interfered with navigation.

By July 1, 1913, when the settlement was incorporated with the new name of Port St. Joe, local trade products included sawn lumber, tobacco, sugar cane and fish oil, in addition to the standard rosin, pitch, and turpentine. The town had a large sawmill, an ice plant, and an oyster packing house. Port St. Joe became known as a "Fun Town" because of its popularity with tourists who came by train. Sunday was the prime day, when the train would bring hundreds of day-trippers to picnic and enjoy the shore. "There was swimming and fishing and boating (including picnic trips across the bay to the peninsula on the other side), crabbing, and scalloping, hiking, and bicycle riding."[15] Large slides and a merry-go-round set up in the water provided early water-park amusement for children and adults. A hotel in the center of town near the waterfront, the Port Inn, was a favorite meeting place. People gathered at the park in front of the hotel to hear music from a band stand or they strolled to a pier that led far out to the bay.

The group of St. Louis, Missouri, investors who financed the railroad formed other companies as well to capitalize on their assets. They chartered the St. Joe Dock and Terminal Company, the St. Joseph Land Development Company, the St. Joseph Telephone and Telegraph Company, and the Port St. Joe Company— all companies that were later acquired by Alfred duPont's representatives. As long as the valuable timber lasted, the small town prospered.

Once the longleaf pines, slash pines, and cypress played out, however, Port St. Joe declined, as did the Panhandle economy in general. The riches of the woods were diminishing fast, although some sawmill operations still found enough pines to make a go of business. Turpentining remained a leading industry, with moonshining another important means of putting cash in the pockets of many rural residents. Like other parts of the rural South, the region struggled with the poverty, disease, and limited educational opportunities that went hand-in-hand with geographical isolation and a slow economy.

Assembling the Empire

Consequently, land in Florida's great northwest was a bargain when Alfred du-Pont dispatched Edward Ball and another representative, William T. "Will" Edwards, the husband of one of Jessie's Virginia childhood friends, to the west Florida hinterlands in 1925. In their biography of Ball, the late Jacob Belin and Braden Ball note that "duPont felt, and Edward Ball soon came to agree with him, that the state's northwestern area would attract future visitors once it became possible to travel there with a reasonable degree of ease and comfort."[16] Although some early settlers viewed the beaches as useless because they were unfit for growing potatoes, the duPonts had a more cosmopolitan perspective and saw the white, sandy beaches as holding great potential.

Thirty-seven-year-old Ed Ball took to the sand roads in a dependable six-cylinder Chevrolet to begin his legendary prospecting trips across the Panhandle. He forged his way across the sand-covered corduroy highway from Jacksonville to Pensacola, the only east-west route at the time. This was the Old Spanish Trail, which had not been much improved since its construction by slaves and soldiers in the antebellum years.

Ball found himself a prospector of what he fondly called "good ol' Florida sand and mud"—cut-over land that had lost its value after timbering. Ed Ball would traverse the region, staying in hotels and boarding houses and meeting with prospective sellers in his sparsely furnished room or around the stove at the general store. He dealt with turpentine barons and operators of the movable sawmills that were still harvesting the last of the best. Eventually, sellers would seek him out instead of vice versa. Large tracts often came from land that the state had generously granted to railroads that were later leased and finally sold to timber concerns.

Until scientists developed new uses for the second-growth pines that had begun to regenerate the land, there was not much demand for it. At first, even the duPonts and Ball did not have a clear idea of how they would use the Panhandle land they were buying, but they proceeded with purchases anyway.

Ball signed a contract on May 11, 1925, that optioned 34,000 acres in Bay and Walton Counties with the purpose of obtaining "not less than twelve lineal miles of frontage upon the Gulf of Mexico." The sellers, the Santa Rosa Plantation Company, agreed to provide land "between United States Military Reservation on the tip end of Santa Rosa peninsula on the West and Phillip's Inlet on the East." The owners and their agent also agreed to act as go-betweens with landowners of other tracts in the desired area "for the benefit of the Purchaser," one Edward Ball of Wilmington, Delaware. The agent was authorized to pay up to fifteen dollars per acre. All but two and a half sections (1,600 acres) of the land under consideration was in Walton County, the rest in Bay County.[17] The deal was sealed in 1927.

The land covered the choice tracts that today comprise the St. Joe Company's WaterColor and Camp Creek developments, as well as land now out of the company's possession, including Topsail Hill State Preserve and Point Washington State Forest. Ed Ball may not have obtained all the land he sought, but what he bought for duPont then still makes up the majority of the white sand beaches held by the St. Joe Company. In the year 2000, the company owned five miles of Gulf of Mexico beachfront, most of it in Walton County.[18]

Also in 1925, Ball contracted to buy 12,539 acres in Bay County; two years later, this parcel and seven others were transferred from the possession of Edward Ball (now listed as a resident of Duval County, Florida, instead of Wilmington, Delaware) to the Panama Beach Development Company. This was one of the land-buying companies Alfred duPont established. The other company duPont formed to buy Panhandle land was Gulf Coast Properties. The transfer took place on August 13, 1927, with Panama Beach Development Company picking up the first tract for the $161,226 owed in principal—a price that came to less than thirteen dollars per acre.[19]

Successive deals went down in price. One of the next finds was a collection of more than 66,000 acres in Franklin, Bay, and Walton Counties, along with residential lots in the town of Carrabelle, east of Apalachicola. The price tag was $800,000, just over twelve dollars per acre.[20] DuPont okayed that transaction in 1926. Even adjusting for inflation, the per-acre cost was reasonable—roughly equivalent to $121 in 2002 dollars.

DuPont was among the few still buying real estate at this point, for that spring, the bottom had finally fallen out of the Florida real estate market. A devastating September hurricane further sealed the end of the boom. Together, these events ushered in the Depression years for Florida ahead of the rest of the nation. The duPonts and Ball had anticipated the bust and by this time had sold off the more speculative of their investments.

The duPonts' continuing stake in Florida at this nadir contrasted with the exodus of other deep-pocket investors. Will Edwards saw duPont in almost heroic terms, as someone with "the vision, the will and the courage, to make large investments and Herculean efforts to assist the people back to the path of prosperity."[21] Perhaps so, but duPont's great wealth also gave him the wherewithal to make purchases at fire sale prices, prices that boggle the minds of today's St. Joe Company executives for their low initial cost (or "basis" in finance parlance).

While Ball and Edwards were investigating prospects, duPont was sizing up Florida banks. He began quietly buying stock in the Florida National Bank, eventually taking over the board. Florida National opened branches across the state and weathered the Depression through a combination of conservative lending and shifting cash from bank to bank to forestall runs. The chain of Florida National banks not only weathered the worst of the Depression but acquired new failing banks because of it. The chain that would grow to thirty strong already had eight banks by 1935, with more than $45 million in deposits.[22] The banks stayed a part of the duPont-Ball empire until a federal antitrust action forced Ed Ball to choose between the banks and the Florida East Coast Railroad (FEC) in the 1960s.

Like Henry Flagler before them, the duPonts and Ball knew that transportation was vital to making their land worthwhile. Bumping along across the sand roads must have driven home to Ball the importance of improving transportation. The only paved road in the Panhandle was a nine-mile stretch near Milton, east of Pensacola. Arterial roads were lacking, and into the 1930s, the steamer *Tarpon* still provided the only expedient connection between coastal towns from Pensacola to Port St. Joe.

Alfred duPont founded and became the first president of the Gulf Coast Highway Association, the "Highwaymen," in 1927.[23] He set up quarters in a spacious building near the state capitol that came to be known as the "High-waymen's Hideout" or the "House of Lords."[24] The association lobbied for funding from the state and federal governments, and worked to boost county bond sales. Later, the group evolved into a lobbying block that served the interests of north Florida and acquired the nickname "Porkchop Gang."

When the state legislature met in the spring of 1927, Ed Ball lobbied hard in favor of bills to construct a highway along the Gulf Coast—present-day U.S. Highway 98—and a series of bridges. Most of the projects were approved. DuPont, Ball, and other political and business interests in the Panhandle now expended years of effort to push for additional highways, hash out the routes, and accomplish bond sales at the county level through the worst of the Depression. Starting in the 1920s, highway construction became "the primary function of state government and the medium through which Ed Ball was introduced to Florida politics," according to author Tracy Danese.[25]

Over the next decade, the Highwaymen's efforts secured three new U.S. highways: U.S. Highway 90, which followed the Old Spanish Trail from Pensacola to Lake City, and later, to Jacksonville; U.S. Highway 19, connecting Tallahassee to Tampa in the region that had remained roadless since the days of the early Spanish conquistadors; and finally, U.S. Highway 98, the new scenic route popularly called the Gulf Coast Highway because it hugged the coast for much of its length from Pensacola to Perry. At last, the settlements of the Panhandle connected to each other and to the outside world. As politicians expected, towns that fell along the new roadways prospered over those that were passed by.

Highway 98 was routed from Panama City to the sleepy town of Port St. Joe, where in the twenty-first century, the St. Joe Company proposed to reroute a section of this road. Benefits to the emerging duPont empire raised eyebrows when the highway was first laid down, as does the plan for rerouting. Alfred duPont and his subordinates warded off criticism by pointing to the advantages to the general public of improved transportation, while at the same time, they scouted out parcels of land that would rise in value because of the new roads.

In addition to the highways, bridges were built, including the first bridge to span the mighty Apalachicola. Some of the Highwaymen are immortalized in the naming of bridges—Hathaway Bridge connecting Panama City with Panama City Beach is named after the state road board chairman of the duPont days, Fons Hathaway. Another span across the eastern arm of St. Andrew Bay, which connects to Tyndall Air Force Base, is the duPont Bridge. These bridges spanning far-flung St. Andrew Bay were completed in 1929.[26] The graceful curving bridge across the Apalachicola on coastal U.S. 98 was finished in 1935 with some funding assistance from the Public Works Administration (PWA), and was named for Apalachicola inventor and doctor John Gorrie.

Meanwhile, water transportation was improved by the dredging of an Intracoastal Waterway that offered an inland, sheltered alternative to the open Gulf of Mexico for boats traveling along the coast between Destin and Apalachicola. St. Joe's extensive holdings along this sheltered water transportation route are among the areas ripe for development, either for commercial or tourist and residential uses.

While the road and bridge building was proceeding, the duPont interests continued buying land. Once the Depression set in, prices dropped well below the fifteen dollars per acre duPont had originally set as a ceiling. In 1932, Ball acquired another 145,000 acres in Bay and Gulf Counties, bringing the total duPont acreage to almost half a million acres of Florida sand and mud south and west of Tallahassee alone.[27]

In 1933, Ed Ball and Will Edwards accomplished a couple of momentous transactions. That year, the duPont interests closed on related deals that established the nucleus of the future St. Joe Paper Company holdings and began the Apalachicola National Forest. As duPont biographer Joseph Frazier Wall relates the story, W. T. Edwards had secured options to purchase land and businesses in Port St. Joe in 1932, but at Alfred's advice, held off on closing the deal until new president Franklin Roosevelt was inaugurated. Then, Edwards sold the Forest Service 186,400 acres of timberland duPont had already acquired, raising $450,000 in cash from the U.S. government that duPont used to help purchase the multifaceted Port St. Joe holdings, including most of the town itself.[28]

Jake Belin offers a different version of the story, one conveyed to him by Ed Ball. This tale features Ed Ball's creative problem solving. In this version, one elderly Col. Albert Perkins, representing a bankrupt St. Louis timber company, which had extracted lumber from the Port St. Joe area, was willing to sell a vast acreage—240,000 acres—to the duPont interests. Ball and the colonel, who had fortified himself with strong drink, boarded a launch to look over some of the property in question. But the colonel was hot and uncomfortable and hastened the negotiations along. He readily agreed to a price of $300,000 and questioned why anyone would want the land anyway. Belin was careful to point out the deal was not consummated until Colonel Perkins had a chance to cool off in the shade.[29]

Belin's story continues with the St. Louis Lumber Company's not having clear title to 192,747 acres. This land was part of the bygone Indian territory conveyed to the Forbes brothers by Spain, and since then fraught with the title problems that had caused such trouble a century earlier in Apalachicola. Anticipating trouble, Ball seized on an idea proposed by a friend to try to sell the land to the government. In 1935, he wrote Secretary of the Interior Harold Ickes and offered the land at "a pretty good price, just in case they were interested," according to Belin.[30] In this version, the government paid $670,000.

Whatever the real story, the transaction resulted in the cornerstone purchase of one of the most biodiverse forests in North America. Quite likely the forest sale to the government did wash away Forbes title problems, whether the sale took place before or after acquisition of the other St. Louis interests. And either way, the duPont interests turned a healthy profit on sale of the forest, as Alfred duPont had been buying land at about two dollars per acre at the time, according to Wall.

While purchasing properties for his boss, Ball also made a few purchases of his own. One was the natural wonder Wakulla Springs. In a series of purchases starting in 1934, Ball acquired the springs and two miles of frontage on the Wakulla River.[31] In 1937, Ball constructed a Spanish-style lodge there in honor of Ponce de León, who according to legend, but not fact, was rumored to have visited there. The structure was built for posterity, with a gracious open lobby and adjoining dining room paved in Tennessee marble and flanked in arching windows that overlook the approach to the spring. Ball employed craftsmen to make ornate ironwork and set tiles, as well as add decorative painting to the cypress beams of the lobby's high ceiling. The elegant result has landed the building on the National Register of Historic Places. Among the building's curiosities are a vault for liquor equipped with a heavy-duty metal door, which Ball had constructed and which still stores liquor for today's patrons, and iron grilles on the windows of Ed Ball's former suite, which also was fortified with a sturdy metal door.

Early Plans for Port St. Joe

By the early 1930s, all the ingredients were in place for the making of a new duPont empire far from the Brandywine, and Alfred duPont eagerly set to work to plan his new dominion. Thanks to Ed Ball and Will Edwards, Alfred duPont had secured a vast domain of vacant Panhandle property. Most of the new Panhandle highways and bridges were completed, and the relationships forged during the efforts of the Highwaymen were in place as a political power base to serve into the future.

Port St. Joe won out over the fishing village of Carrabelle as the choice of headquarters for the duPont enterprises because of its deep harbor and the amenities that came in toto with the purchase from St. Louis Lumber.[32] Essentially, the duPont interests obtained almost the whole town with its docks and deep port for oceangoing ships, as well as the Apalachicola Northern Railroad and hundreds of thousands of acres of land.

DuPont studied the options for a local industry that would make use of his hundreds of thousands of acres of newly acquired forest land. The cellulose in pines could be used for a variety of products, from rayon to sponges. At first, duPont considered products that could be finished at a DuPont chemical complex out of state. However, transporting the wood pulp would be difficult; also, the industry would not provide as much employment if the product was not manufactured on site, an important consideration for duPont.

Recent breakthroughs in wood chemistry made paper production another option. Scientists had found that the chemical sodium sulfate could dissolve the high lignin content of southern pines. The chemical separated wood fibers enabling even the resinous soft pines to be converted into usable pulp. Although the end product did not rival the fine papers made from hardwoods and low-resin softwoods like spruce and hemlock, it was well suited for products including the sturdy brown paper known as kraft—a trade name derived from the word "strength" in German. Kraft could be made into wrapping paper and later was used for shopping bags and corrugated boxes.

Florida's first large-scale pulp mill made use of this technology. Opened in Panama City in 1931, just thirty-five miles from Port St. Joe, the huge new Southern Kraft mill's success in converting the region's remaining forest resources to marketable products provided a beacon of hope for north Florida's worn-out forest products industry. It was an example that the yet-to-be-formed St. Joe Paper Company would imitate closely.

Principal considerations for a pulp mill were the availability of pines within reach of the mill, an abundance of fresh water mainly for pulping and washing, plus a handy means of shipping. On all counts, both Panama City and Port St. Joe came out well. The pines were available, either from natural forests or re-seeding that was taking place on logged-out lands, or, later, from planting. Even on Florida's generally sandy soils the typically generous rainfall and long growing season could produce new trees in about twenty years. Unlike wood destined for milling, wood for pulp could be made from a scraggly pine instead of a majestic, 500-year-old longleaf. As for shipping, both cities offered sufficiently deep harbors. The Panhandle's ample above- and below-ground water resources supplied the many millions of gallons used daily.

For a time, duPont consulted with Charles H. Herty, a former president of the American Chemical Society, who was working with a new technique to use pine pulp for another product, newsprint. Even though Will Edwards had gained much interest from regional newspaper publishers in Florida-produced paper, Ed Ball was more interested in kraft paper because of its higher profit margin. Despite the Great Depression the Panama City plant was turning a profit.[33] According to duPont biographer Wall, Ed Ball propagated a false story that newsprint produced from southern pines on an experimental press run absorbed too much ink and yellowed rapidly.[34] Even though Alfred duPont had originally been enthusiastic about producing newsprint, he changed his mind and eventually endorsed Ed Ball's plan to produce kraft paper instead.

Alfred's intentions for Port St. Joe involved more than just making money. From all indications, bettering the standard of living for Panhandle residents was Alfred duPont's sincere desire from the outset. DuPont envisioned rehabilitating the run-down fishing village of Port St. Joe into a working-class showplace with parks, tree-lined streets, and good schools, while also turning a profit on his new paper mill. According to Jake Belin and Braden Ball, duPont believed the mill would have a large beneficial effect: "With the mill and new village, present residents could be relocated and better employed. People outside the area might be attracted to mill work and become better educated in quality schools. Those who remained on their farms might improve living standard over time by raising pine trees or by working as tree harvesters and transporters."[35]

Firsthand reports from Ed Ball after his prospecting trips only strengthened the duPonts' resolve to improve northwest Florida. Ed Ball, even with his background of genteel poverty, was appalled at the dirt-poor existence he encountered among the people inhabiting the sandy, muddy byways of the Panhandle. "At first, I couldn't believe what I was seeing out there in the woods. . . . What I was finding was almost like that fellow wrote about in *Tobacco Road*, he said. "Most people out there lived on a little plot of ground, usually in a house that had no amenities, and had likely never seen a coat of paint. Most of their living came off the land, maybe with a scrawny cow or two, a garden with beans and greens, and usually they'd fish and hunt a lot."[36]

Any dreams Alfred harbored of helping to usher in a socioeconomic transformation of the Panhandle in his own lifetime ended when he became ill in the winter of 1935. He died at Epping Forest in April of that year at age seventy-one. Jessie, Ed Ball, and Will Edwards now had duPont's fortunes and his stated intentions for them, under their care.

DuPont had rebounded financially since his ousting from the Delaware duPont enterprises. He left a fortune of some $56 million, a stunning sum for the time. The state of Florida reaped almost $3 million from his estate; the federal government also took a cut.[37] DuPont's will instructed that Jessie be given a generous annuity. Other family members and beneficiaries received annuities or gifts. To each of his four children and to Edward Ball, Alfred bequeathed 5,000 shares of stock in Almours Securities, the umbrella company formed in 1926 that consisted of Alfred's Florida duPont holdings. This amount of stock was valued at $750,000.

Alfred's will specified that the remainder of his estate was to be left to operate the Florida businesses to generate income for charitable purposes, specifically for children and the elderly. The charity would be administered through the yet-to-be-formed Nemours Foundation, an organization that Alfred instructed in his will was to be a memorial "to my great, great grandfather, Pierre Samuel duPont de Nemours, and to my father, Eleuthère Irénée duPont de Nemours." Alfred and Jessie had discussed at length Alfred's desire to establish the Nemours Foundation in Delaware on the grounds of their mansion there. Alfred's will instructed the trustees of Nemours to "pay over . . . to the said corporation . . . the net income of my said estate, subject to the annuities and legacies herein above mentioned, for the purposes of maintaining the said Estate of Nemours as a charitable institution for the care and treatment of crippled children, but not of incurables, or the care of old men or old women, and particularly old couples, first consideration, in each instance, being given to beneficiaries who are residents of Delaware."[38]

As the vast estate was gradually settled over the next several years, Jessie aggressively laid plans to bring the Nemours Foundation into being by constructing a children's hospital and staffing it with the best medical equipment and personnel available.

Although Jessie was undisputedly in charge of directing the Nemours Foundation, when it came to the vast holdings of Almours Securities, decision making was necessarily more complicated. Jessie served as president from 1935 to 1938, but her brother Ed took over the reins of day-to-day management. As planning for Port St. Joe and its mill went forward, it became clear that Ed Ball did not agree with his benefactor's twofold purpose in developing Port St. Joe. His emphasis would be on further building the corporate empire now at his command. As much as he understood the Tobacco Road conditions that faced many people of the region, he did not share his mentor's vision for rehabilitation of the village—at least not out of the company's wallet.

The Era of the St. Joe Paper Company

Who do we fight today?
Edward Ball's customary morning invocation

Confusion to the enemy!
Edward Ball's customary evening toast

WHILE ALFRED DUPONT had only one decade in which to leave his mark
on Florida, Ed Ball guided the duPont-spawned enterprises over the better part
of six decades, from the 1920s to the 1970s. Ball's firm and pugnacious personal
stamp molded the duPont-founded enterprises into a Green Empire constitut-
ing one of Florida's most powerful economic and political forces. At the same
time, the St. Joe Paper Company reshaped hundreds of thousands of acres of
cut-over land into orderly, profitable, commercial forests.

After Alfred's death, the focus remained on bringing into existence the
planned industrial fountainhead, the paper mill at Port St. Joe. Rather than start
up a mill independently, Ed Ball and his associates at Almours Securities sought
a partner experienced in the paper business to share the cost and provide expertise. Almours settled on the Mead Company, an Ohio firm that had been in the
paper business for a hundred years. Mead agreed to design and operate the mill,
with Almours providing the mill site and trees. Each firm was to put up $1 mil-
lion of the estimated $6 million to build the plant.[1]

In 1936, the two companies formed the St. Joe Paper Company as a joint venture. On the Almours side, the company's officers were Ed Ball, Will Edwards, a
lawyer from a leading Jacksonville firm named Henry Adair, and state represen-

tative and pulpwood dealer G. Pierce Wood of Sumatra, Florida. George Mead and several other officers of his company represented Mead.[2]

The new company set to work dredging a thirty-foot-deep channel from the deep portion of the bay to the mill site. Where steamships had once docked to load virgin timber, new concrete docks were built that extended almost 3,000 feet to accommodate five large ships at a time. The company built the mill on dredge spoils, shored up with a bulkhead that later corroded. These circumstances made it easier for any soil contaminants to eventually make their way into the bay waters. Draglines also went to work digging a canal to link the mill site to the existing Intracoastal Waterway a few miles outside of town. The canal served as a shipping shortcut and decades later became the location where industrial wastewater was discharged from combined municipal and industrial sources in Port St. Joe.

A press release at the time announced a remarkable difference that distinguished this mill from the others like it being built across the Southeast.[3] The St. Joe Paper Company, with financing from the Almours side, stated its intentions to pour more millions of dollars into improvements for the town of Port St. Joe, whose years as the up-and-coming "Fun Town" had ended with the demise of the virgin forests. By 1936, the biggest industry was a "pogy" plant, which extracted oil from menhaden fish and transported it north in tanker cars on the Apalachicola Northern Railroad.

DuPont's notion of a planned model town was similar to the current ventures of St. Joe/Arvida, including homes, parks, and other amenities. However, his vision was directed at a lower- to middle-class population instead of the middle- to upper-class population targeted by today's St. Joe/Arvida. But as dredging, mill construction, and other steps on the business end proceeded, the town improvements, most noticeably housing, failed to materialize. Will Edwards, who continued on with St. Joe Paper throughout his career, was eager to fulfill Alfred duPont's plans, but he faced opposition from Ed Ball.

"The economics of such building were just not there, Mr. Ball felt," former St. Joe Paper executive Jake Belin recalled.[4] The bottom-line oriented Ed Ball felt the millions of dollars that would have gone into Port St. Joe's rehabilitation was money that would be better invested elsewhere, especially as competition in the paper industry heightened.

In 1937, when Mead began construction and there were still no signs of housing, Mead officials pressed Ed Ball for answers. They were concerned the new skilled workers relocating to the town would find no place to live. Indeed, the influx of newcomers hired to build and operate the mill caused the population of Port St. Joe to increase more than fivefold from 1935 to 1938.[5]

But Ball stood firm. It became clear that duPont's protégé would run the company his way, even as far as setting aside the high-minded intentions of his benefactor. As the issue simmered, Ball "reminded his associates that he himself had since made it clear on several occasions that Almours was not going into the housing business,"[6] an ironic assertion in context of the community-development emphasis displayed by the St. Joe Company after 2000.

In spite of Jessie's title as president, first of Almours then of the St. Joe Paper Company, it was clear that her brother was now calling the shots when it came to the company checkbook. She considered building some homes at her own expense. Eventually, Almours offered to sell its town lots at a discount to buyers who agreed to build within a year, a provision put into place to thwart land speculators. Later, the Federal Housing Administration provided a mortgage insurance plan that helped workers finance their homes.[7] For seventeen years the St. Joe Paper Company sponsored a housing program; nevertheless, a shortage of decent, affordable housing would become a perennial problem for the company town.[8]

Ball's failure to deliver on the town improvements was the first of actions that raised questions about whether the duPont fortunes were being applied as Alfred duPont had intended. Over the years, the town would struggle to get schools, centralized water and sewer, and other basic needs. Decades later, when the mill closed, the city suffered a tax shortfall that jeopardized basic city services.

In 1938, no one could protest too hard. Like the Panama City mill before it, the St. Joe Paper Company mill brought well-paying jobs in a desperate time. While skilled paper workers were hired on from mills in other states, unskilled labor came from the local people who had been mostly engaged in fishing and naval stores. They got jobs in the wood yard, with the most back-breaking and dangerous jobs going to the "bull gang," largely composed of African Americans.

Among the new white-collar hires was a young Jake Belin, son of a turpentine operator whose family settled in Port St. Joe when he was ten. Belin eventually rose to the top of the company, taking over as president from Edward Ball in 1968 and eventually becoming CEO. Belin was a descendent of the South Carolina duPonts, a separate branch from the Delaware duPonts, according to another former St. Joe Paper Company executive, Robert Nedley, who delivered Belin's newspapers as a youth.[9] He started work after attending George Washington University and working for a time in a government job in Washington, D.C.

Pulp Production Begins

On March 17, 1938, St. Patrick's Day, the mill sent its first puffs of sulfurous smoke into the skies of Gulf County. Shortly afterward, the Port St. Joe newspaper, the *Star,* published a "Progress Edition" commemorating the opening of the pulp mill. The front and back covers of the special edition were printed on heavy brown kraft paper from the mill. The front-page story on the oversized newspaper heralded the South's "newest and finest paper mill."[10] Illustrations depicted the Sturm und Drang of progress—cranes, steam shovels, the scaffolding around rising mill structures, a cement mixer, a surveyor, a scientist looking through a microscope—symbols similar to those that adorned duPont headquarters in Delaware a thousand miles away.

A full-page ad trumpeted Port St. Joe as "Florida's Coming Metropolis" that "INVITES THE WORLD!" (The Gulf County planning staff, besieged by newcomers at the turn of a new millennium, may feel that message only recently reached its audience.) A column proclaimed the mill a "Dream Come True," noting that the 1935 census reported a population of only 798, leaving plenty of room for growth, since that count even included "colored people and stray cows," the humor attempt at the expense of the local African American population.[11]

The same year the mill opened, the town celebrated the hundredth anniversary of the framing of Florida's Constitution. Along with parades, concerts, speakers, luncheons, and trap and skeet shooting, tours of the new mill were another special event.[12] Tour takers could see the impressive equipment and many steps that it took to turn pines to pulp.

First, workers stripped the bark from logs. Next, wood was chipped and screened to the desired size before being "digested" into cellulose fiber pulp by being cooked in vats and boilers filled with caustic solutions. The pulp was then processed further to align the cellulose fibers, then fed into paper machines that produced the finished product on large rolls.

All this involved a multitude of facilities, from a wood-handling yard to huge storage tanks for black liquor, green liquor, and white liquor—the liquid solutions that were ingredients and byproducts in the paper-making chemistry. One huge building housed the paper-making machines. Warehouses, fuel oil and chemical tanks, a lime kiln, and a vast lumber and railroad yard rounded out the structures on the 124-acre site.

The mill initially burned heavy oil, with two bark furnaces also producing steam for cooking wood chips and running turbines. A recovery boiler burned off turpentine and other byproducts. Photographs of the mill at work in the

1950s show the unfettered billowing of smokestacks in the days predating environmental controls.

Making kraft paper took an enormous amount of water, as much as 35 million gallons of it daily by the time the mill tripled its operations in the early 1950s.[13] Wells pumping groundwater supplied the mill until the 1950s, when a canal that siphoned water from the Chipola River began delivering surface water to the mill. Besides water and wood, the other primary ingredients for turning cellulose into pulp were sodium sulfate, sodium hydroxide (caustic soda), and lime rock. The sodium sulfate supplied the signature aroma of paper mills—various sulfur gases, which the human nose detects even at concentrations of as little as one part per billion. Literally thousands of other chemicals are used or created as byproducts in each of the main processes.[14]

It took several years of fine-tuning before the operation was running to Ed Ball's satisfaction. The plant did not turn a profit its first year and made only a small one the second. While the Great Depression was certainly a factor, Ed Ball thought maximizing production would help bring the business into the black. He wanted the capacity of the mill expanded in spite of Mead's insistence that it was operating at full throttle. When Mead resisted, Ball responded by buying out the company. By 1940, St. Joe Paper Company became a solely duPont enterprise. Production rose from 340 tons per day to 400 tons. That same year, the mill turned its first sizable profit.

1940 Reorganization Puts Ed Ball in Control

Taking full control of the paper mill was only one change Ed Ball made in the company in 1940. In fact, Ed Ball orchestrated a sweeping reorganization that took effect after Alfred duPont's estate was settled. After the reorganization, Ed Ball emerged with the title of president for fourteen out of twenty-four Alfred duPont–funded companies.[15]

Almours Securities was liquidated in December 1938. DuPont relatives who were beneficiaries in Alfred duPont's will received their share of the Almours assets in cash, an arrangement that removed these relatives from business decisions. Alfred's considerable remaining assets went to establish the Alfred I. duPont Testamentary Trust (also called the Estate), the overarching entity that encompasses the duPont Florida investments and charities into the present.

Monies from the liquidation capitalized the St. Joe Paper Company. Alfred duPont's real estate companies that had made the original purchases in the Panhandle—Gulf Coast Properties and the Panama Beach Development Company—became part of the St. Joe Paper Company. Other interests under the Trust umbrella were the chain of Florida National Banks, the Apalachicola Northern Railroad, and the Port St. Joe–based telephone company. At the same time the paper company was getting off the ground, Almours upgraded the rattly ANR, which had been running on tree stumps, to diesel power. It also modernized the phone company, which had begun with twelve phones located at intervals along the railroad line.

Besides his new Florida businesses, Alfred duPont had also left behind considerable stock in his rival cousin Pierre duPont's General Motors Company, and in the family chemical business, E. I. DuPont de Nemours Company, as well as the Nemours mansion and grounds and Alfred's childhood home in Delaware. (The animosity between Alfred and his relatives did not sever all corporate entanglements to the E. I. DuPont de Nemours Company and family. Indeed, financial ties to the DuPont Company remained a substantial part of the St. Joe portfolio, at least into the 1990s, when St. Joe Paper sold much of its GM and DuPont chemical company stock. Even in year 2000, one of the St. Joe Company directors was a retired executive of E. I. DuPont de Nemours.)

As the initial source of capital for St. Joe Paper Company and the other Florida duPont enterprises, the Alfred I. duPont Testamentary Trust became the businesses' major shareholder. To this day, the Trust remains the St. Joe Company's largest shareholder, although over time, the Trust's stake in the company has diminished. In 1981, the Trust controlled 75 percent of the shares in the St. Joe Paper Company. In 2000, the Trust still owned a majority, 58 percent, of St. Joe Company shares. Then, in 2002, the Trust interest in the company took a historic dip to 49 percent, reducing its share to just below majority ownership as part of a stock offering that pumped new capital into the company.

The profit from the Trust's businesses was earmarked to fund the Nemours Foundation, the charity established for medical treatment of children and care of the elderly. According to a 1963 publication produced by the Trust, Alfred believed that "the possessors of great wealth" should pass on "the bulk of it" for humanitarian purposes.[16]

The businesses that were under the aegis of the Alfred duPont Testamentary Trust were charged with funding the charities. While other trusts satisfied the need for an ongoing revenue stream in a more traditional manner, by making various financial investments, the A. I. duPont Trust differed by actively running its own businesses to generate revenues. Over the years, however, critics charged that the Green Empire businesses prospered without fully honoring the charitable obligations set out in Alfred duPont's will.

In the view of Jessie duPont's biographer, Richard Greening Hewlett, Alfred's widow faithfully carried out her husband's wishes through the Nemours Foundation and under it, the Alfred I. duPont Foundation that operated a hospital in Delaware. Eventually, Nemours established a hospital and several more clinics in Florida as well. Also, Jessie duPont established several charities of her own, the Jessie Ball duPont Fund and a couple of small Jacksonville-based trusts.[17] In her lifetime, Jessie Ball duPont gave more than $100 million to colleges, churches, and other charities.[18] Nevertheless, critics from the 1940s on charged that the Estate sent only a trickle of the Trust's wealth to the charities while redirecting most capital it generated into empire building.

During the years of Ball's management, the Trust's assets grew into an increasingly complex web. Its highest profile company in the Panhandle was St. Joe Paper. The 1940 amendments to St. Joe Paper's original articles of incorporation show a company that already entertained a future beyond forestry, pulp, and paper. The company charter empowered it to "engage generally in the real estate business in all of its branches; to hold, buy, own, hire, control, work, develop, sell, convey, lease, mortgage . . . and otherwise deal in or dispose of real estate and property." The company by its charter could even "lay out and plan city, town and village sites."[19]

The St. Joe Paper Company also reserved the right to build and or operate roads, wharves, bridges, railroads, and to prospect for metals and minerals, including oil and gas, as well as engage in banking, securities, and publishing businesses. In the early 1960s, Ed Ball did start up a newspaper to rival the *Tallahassee Democrat,* but he shut it down after only five weeks due to poor revenue.[20] In light of the early amendments to St. Joe Paper's articles of incorporation, the seeming conversion of the "new" St. Joe to real estate powerhouse in the latter part of the 1990s appears less radical.

Ed Ball's Battle for the FEC

Once the paper mill was up and running, Ed Ball turned his sights to Henry Flagler's old rail line, the Florida East Coast Railroad. It had operated profitably until the triple blows of the 1926 Florida real estate crash, the Depression, and the deadly Labor Day hurricane of 1935, which washed out painstakingly laid railroad tracks in the Florida Keys. The FEC went into receivership and formally declared bankruptcy in 1941. Ball began investing some St. Joe Paper Company capital into buying FEC mortgage bonds at bargain rates. In some cases, he purchased bonds at prices as low as six cents on the dollar from bondholders who wanted to salvage their investment as the railroad's troubles dragged on with the Interstate Commerce Commission.[21] In March 1941, the St. Joe Paper Company filed its plan to take over and reorganize the railroad.

But St. Joe Paper was not the only business interested in owning the FEC. A group of bondholders and another party had submitted reorganization plans as well. In spite of its slump, the FEC was of value not only for transportation, but also for valuable tracts of land it owned in the developing Florida east coast, including tracts in Miami. A complex set of negotiations among parties with interests in the FEC ensued, involving Interstate Commerce Commission (ICC) rulings, reversals, and court opinions. Through it all, Ball doggedly kept pursuing his goal. Not until 1959, eighteen years after his initial bid, did he win control of the FEC.

As the long struggle for the FEC unfolded, it pitted Ed Ball against one of Florida's U.S. senators, Claude Pepper. Pepper and Ball started out as friends with a mutual interest in bringing roads to the Panhandle.[22] After a decisive moment in February 1944, however, they became enemies. Senator Pepper was the only senator to vote to uphold President Roosevelt's veto of a revenue bill that included tax exemptions for holders of speculative bonds—the very class of FEC bonds Ball had purchased. Congress overrode the veto, but Ball reacted to Pepper's stance by working in the background against Pepper in the senatorial races of 1944 and 1950, when Pepper lost his seat to George Smathers.

The conflict between the two men was intensely personal, as chronicled by historian Tracy Danese in *Claude Pepper and Ed Ball: Politics, Purpose and Power.*[23] Pepper dove into the ongoing battle for the FEC, arguing before the ICC that allowing the duPont Estate to gain control of the rail line would hurt the public interest by expanding the duPont Estate's economic grip on the state. That estate, he noted, was "operated principally by one man, Mr. Edward Ball."[24] For his part, Ed Ball resented Pepper's intrusion into his business affairs. "In Ball's view, Pepper's verbal tactics deliberately distorted the facts for the singular purpose of wrongfully depriving him of his property rights," Danese wrote.[25]

In 1945, Pepper, joined by Nevada Senator Pat McCarran, investigated the St. Joe Paper Company and whether its intentions on the FEC were monopolistic. McCarran's investigation gathered a large body of evidence that in the eyes of the senator showed that Ed Ball had become an enormously powerful individual in Florida. McCarran contended that "the economic life of the State and well-being of its people may be affected more by [his] . . . power than by the power of the government of the state itself."[26] McCarran's report was not endorsed by his colleagues and the criticisms he leveled remained dormant until other lawmakers brought up the same issue during congressional hearings in the 1960s.

After handsome Miami lawyer and former congressman George Smathers took Pepper's place on Capitol Hill in 1950, he sponsored an amendment to the Bank Holding Act that exempted personal trusts from the act's prohibitions on engaging in other commercial businesses along with banking. Without the exemption, the Green Empire could not have continued to operate both its Florida National Bank Chain and the Florida East Coast Railroad as businesses associated with a perpetual trust. For another decade, the duPont-Ball Green Empire did both.

The Empire in the Courts

Under Ed Ball's management, lawsuits became an everyday matter. These included lawsuits over property tax bills with counties, disputes over property ownership, and in the case of Ed Ball personally, divorce litigation that went as far as the Florida Supreme Court. According to a friend of longtime company president Jake Belin, St. Joe Paper would keep tax lawsuits in the courts for years until it appeared that a "favorable" judge had been assigned to the case. The state and local governments simply could not afford to fight all of the legal gauntlets that Ed Ball and St. Joe threw them as cases progressed through the state's court system.

The St. Joe Paper Company and its sister businesses usually came out the winner, but not always. In Port St. Joe, the pioneer Maddox family went to court to maintain possession of the only waterfront land parcel that was not a part of the land that conveyed to the duPont interests from St. Louis Lumber. After the St. Joe Company claimed the property as theirs, the Maddox family enlisted two attorneys to do battle with Ed Ball's battery of lawyers. "Mr. Ball made a remark that he could take the land and it would not cost him a cent because he had seven attorneys on retainer," recalled Dave Maddox about his parents' legal battle.[27] A Marianna court agreed that, thanks to proof from the Maddox family's scrupulous recordkeeping of receipts and correspondence, the family owned the land by virtue of having made faithful interest payments even through the lean years of the Depression.

Not inclined to rest his case, Ball then tried to put building restrictions on the Maddox parcel, and again they went to court, this time to the Florida Supreme Court in Tallahassee. Ball lost in this venue as well and was made to hand over a deed with no restrictions to the Maddox family, which he did in November 1939.[28] Today that parcel is a park owned by the state of Florida that affords access to the St. Joseph Bay shoreline.

In 1943, Ball faced another legal action, this time from his wife of ten years, Ruth Latham Price Ball. It was a wonder that Ruth Price ever married Ed Ball. Before they wed, the inveterate deal maker drew up a prenuptial agreement that set forth nineteen rules governing physical appearance, allowable relationships and activities, especially with respect to the opposite sex, and how they should impart constructive criticism to each other (never in front of third parties). Florida entrepreneur Raymond Mason, who partnered with Ed Ball on various business ventures during the 1960s and 1970s and wrote a book about Ball, called the prenuptial contract "a marvelous attempt to avoid the well-publicized problems of any marriage."[29] But the intricate contract failed to produce a good marriage. In her divorce complaint, Ruth said she was emotionally neglected by workaholic Ball. Ball, in turn, charged that his betrothed was unable to bear him an heir, and knew of that condition even before they wed. Ball's effort to acquire an annulment instead of a divorce failed. With Florida Supreme Court Judge and close friend of Ed Ball's, B. K. Roberts, taking on the case, the Ball divorce was finalized. Ruth received $250,000 and custody of their joint property at the time of the initiation of the divorce.[30] The couple had kept a house in the comfortable Riverside section of Jacksonville, near Epping Forest. Ed Ball reverted to bachelorhood, remaining single until his death.

Although others questioned how Ball could keep track of his many lawsuits, he maintained that having a few lawsuits going at all times kept him "sharp and on target."[31]

Wartime

During World War II, the paper and pulp industry became an integral part of the national defense effort. The St. Joe Paper Company seized the opportunity to aid and benefit from the war effort. The armed services used an astounding amount of products made of pulp and paperboard, and using American trees helped to avoid disruption in supply. Uses for pulp and paperboard ranged from an ingredient in gunpowder and supply parachutes to surgical dressings, waterproof maps, blood plasma boxes, and casing for ammunition shells. The sturdy kraft paperboard was particularly important for packaging foods such as C-rations, arms, and medical supplies.[32]

Workers stayed busy trying to meet production goals that reached 11,500 tons monthly by 1945. As the war dragged on, women filled positions vacated by men who had joined the services—some whose deaths were reported in the employee newsletter. Jessie Ball duPont contributed to the "Bundles for Britain" relief effort by arranging for byproducts of kraft board manufacture to be made into felt blankets for Britons who had been bombed out of their homes.[33]

Meanwhile, Ed Ball supported the war effort by offering his property at Wakulla Springs to the military. Servicemen from nearby Camp Gordon Johnson in Franklin County dined and danced at the Mediterranean Revival–style lodge, and officers' families were housed there. In April 1943, the Amphibious Training Center of Camp Gordon Johnson staged a "mock combat." Soldiers demonstrated techniques of amphibious warfare using a variety of weaponry and swimming through burning gasoline spills. Soldiers detonated a dummy Japanese boat in the river and planes from a nearby airfield strafed the spring. The army filmed the exercise and used it for training through the 1960s.[34]

Ball, a seasoned bond buyer and seller from his days of promoting state transportation bonds, was happy to purchase war bonds. One particular war bond issue he supported provided bourbon along with each purchase.[35] Ball purchased enough bonds to warrant an entire rail car full of bourbon, perhaps explaining the many bottles of 1940s vintage Kentucky Tavern, not Ball's usual brand, found sitting in a second-floor closet of the old home at Southwood when Rummell became CEO.[36]

The heightened demand for paper products during the war helped the new paper company prosper by adding a new product line, corrugated board containers. More and more shippers were changing from wooden crates to these containers. Charles Herty, the same scientist who had been in the forefront of southern forestry research for so long, was instrumental in finding a way to use kraft in making the reinforced containers. St. Joe Paper produced its first corrugated board in 1943 from a new plant built alongside the pulp mill at Port St. Joe.[37] In 1945, the company followed up on its new business line by adding another corrugator to its box plant.

Into the Modern Era

After World War II, the St. Joe Paper Company continued to expand its forestry and container plant operations. St. Joe Paper Company engineers designed from scratch a box plant for Houston. By the end of the 1950s, the company had full or partial interest in box plants in nine U.S. locations from Texas to Pennsylvania.[38] Then, in 1957, St. Joe Paper crossed the Atlantic to take over operation and management of a paper mill and box plant in Waterford, Ireland. The emerging consumer age maintained the strong demand for shipping containers that had begun during wartime, and the St. Joe Paper Company continued to add plants to satisfy and expand its share of the market. Eventually, St. Joe came to own partially, if not fully, more than twenty container plants in the United States and Ireland. The company sold all its container plants in its makeover of 1995–96.

In the company town of Port St. Joe, the postwar boom was apparent in the new enterprises that sprang up both on St. Joe property and adjacent to it. In 1950, St. Joe Paper built a new, modern building to house the expanded box plant.

Starting in the late 1950s, when he began overseeing the paper mill in Waterford, Ireland, Ed Ball became a frequent visitor to western Ireland. In one of his more flamboyant moves, Ed Ball and a consortium of other investors sprang for their own castle in Ireland, Ballynahinch.

In the Green Empire, too, Ball kept expanding the St. Joe Paper Company's reach. In December 1947, the Henderson family of Tallahassee agreed to sell its Southwood Farm to St. Joe Paper. A letter on file with the Tallahassee Historic Trust mentions a price of $90,000,[39] although by April 1948, the *Daily Democrat* announced the farm had sold to St. Joe for $81,000.[40] St. Joe bought the Southwood Farm intact, including the 1,760 acres of farmland and a courtly columned home that was moved onto the site from a previous location in downtown Tallahassee in 1939.

In the 1940s, Ball claimed the rolling hills of Southwood as his official residence even though he spent only weeks out of most years there. His chief agricultural interest at Southwood was raising purebred cattle, more as an expensive hobby than anything else, as its cash flow was negative. Still, he liked to refer to himself as "farmer" on forms that required an occupational peg, such as his passport. He also identified himself as a farmer in his testimony before Congress in the 1960s, when his companies faced antitrust scrutiny. (His license plate, however, read "taxpayer.") From time to time, Ball would entertain notable public figures at the farm. In 1960, Ball hosted a visit by the British envoy to the United States, Sir Harold Caccia, and his wife, Lady Caccia.[41]

The stately house had a reputation of being haunted. Pensacola publisher and former St. Joe Paper Company director Braden Ball, in his book, *Around West Florida in 80 Years*, recounts the story of he and his wife, Theda, twice being visited by an apparition with "clammy fingers."[42] Another story tells of a guest having a radio cord wrapped around his neck while sleeping. When St. Joe/Arvida executive Tim Edmond first came to Tallahassee to develop South-Wood, he planned to stay there for the night. A full moon illuminated Ed Ball's old four-poster bed as Edmond settled in for the night. But he did not stay long. "I realized that if there were ghosts in this world, they were going to find me in

Mr. Ball's bedroom," Edmond told Bill Varian of the *Tallahassee Democrat.* "I slipped on my pants and checked into the Governor's Inn."[43]

St. Joe already owned the woodland to the immediate south of the Southwood Farm and got busy collecting more. By the mid-1950s, St. Joe owned well over 50,000 acres of Leon County land. Southwood and another 150,000 acres stretching southward remain among the most valuable of the company's inland holdings because of proximity to both the state capital and the coast.[44]

St. Joe conducted its affairs very quietly, leading some people to suspect that St. Joe had some "ulterior intentions" for Southwood, involving the exploitation of resources, namely oil. Other oil prospectors drilled one well in the area more than 6,500 feet down before declaring the effort a bust in 1944.[45] Although the land failed to produce a gusher, it was prime agricultural land and thus a fine location to establish a new centralized tree nursery for the company. By 1952, the Woodlands division of the company tended to five million slash pines growing at a nursery at Southwood.[46]

St. Joe's Forestry Operations

The large-scale tree nursery at Southwood was another step by the St. Joe Paper Company toward assuring a future supply of trees. A paper mill was a huge and permanently rooted investment, requiring a stable supply of nearby wood. From the outset, the company worked to make its own forest land as productive as possible, and to foster modern silviculture on nearby private lands that had been stripped bare by early logging. The company sought uniformly aged trees that could be harvested together and favored faster growing slash pines over longleaf pines.

St. Joe Paper was single-minded in its attempts to maximize pulp production from its lands. Whereas other paper companies sought integrated use of their land—with a portfolio of products from turpentine, saw timber, pilings, poles, and more—St. Joe was interested primarily in wood for pulp.

The supply of trees from noncompany lands was crucial. Even with its vast holdings, in 1963, the company's Woodlands division still depended on outside sources for 60 percent of the wood it used. Years before the mill opened, Alfred duPont and Ed Ball had arranged for demonstrations to introduce the concept of silviculture to local landowners. Landowners were lukewarm to the idea. They would have to buy the seedlings, prepare the ground, and plant each seedling by hand. All this was a lot of work for a crop that would not mature or pay for itself for two decades. Some landowners eventually warmed up to the idea, however, especially when they heard a mill would be constructed nearby. After all, duPont money had brought roads to the area for the first time—it was logical to count on the same money to buy pines many years hence.

St. Joe had resources for commercial forestry that a struggling farmer with his woodlot did not. Early on the company started growing a stock of young pines and hiring professional foresters to supervise operations. The Florida Forestry Division helped as well. When the seedlings were ready, state crews began planting on duPont-owned land. Some cut-over lands in the region, including in the Apalachicola National Forest, were replanted by New Deal work programs such as the Civilian Conservation Corps, the Works Progress Administration, and the Public Works Administration. Trees from the forest were bid for by private concerns, which logged and then sold them. St. Joe Paper, as the nearest mill, was the main customer.

With sometimes shocking rapidity, the new kind of forestry advanced by St. Joe and the other paper companies began to change the face of the land once more. Where abandoned cotton fields or logged-out forests once stood now appeared legions of pine trees, resembling soldiers on a drill field at attention, row upon row. A single species—the hardy, efficient slash pine—supplanted the previously dominant longleaf pine ecosystem and the wide variety of other trees and vegetation associated with it. The St. Joe Paper Company reinvented hundreds of thousands of acres of cut-over forest land in this fashion.

By necessity, a form of salvage forestry called "stumping" preceded silviculture. Forest operators used explosives and heavy machinery to remove the massive stumps of virgin trees that still studded the land. Because early loggers had worked without the benefit of machine saws, they often cut the trees at a convenient height above ground, so stumping yielded plenty of wood for the effort. The stumps, along with the heartwood at the center of the tree, contained resin and burned magnificently. These parts of the trees were prized as "fatwood" or "lighterwood" used for starting fires or for torches.

During the Depression, stumpers hired fast and daring boys to do the dangerous work of setting off explosives to blast the stumps out of the soil. The boys set the caps under the stumps, lit the fuses, and sprinted off. Sometimes the boys suffered burns and other injuries; at least one lost his life when a box of caps ignited.[47]

After stump removal, the next step in preparing the ground for silviculture was dragging huge anchor chains to remove any standing trees. Two bulldozers would suspend the thick chains between them and raze the forest, a practice that continues today especially in tropical rainforests. In the process, forests that had naturally regenerated into a mix of hardwoods and softwoods, usually turkey oak and pine, were obliterated. One place this occurred in the 1950s was in northern Bay County, where St. Joe Paper, Hunt Oil, and International Paper began silviculture operations. Over a period of several years, the landscape there was changed so completely that an outdoorsman who thought he knew the woods could find no more familiar landmarks.

Jim Barkuloo, a retired fisheries and wildlife biologist, was one of those outdoorsmen. Barkuloo recalled that by the 1950s, there were already plenty of planted pines in the southern portions of Bay, Walton, and Gulf Counties, but that farther north, the naturally regenerating forest contained plenty of open areas with oaks. "All of a sudden, there was a lot more demand for pine, so they took chains and pulled them behind bulldozers, then burned and planted thousands of acres and square miles in pine trees," he said.[48] Barkuloo attributes the large-scale clearing and planting in large part to the "greenbelt" tax, which requires a certain density of planting to allow land to qualify as a managed forest deserving of a generous agricultural tax discount. The discounted ad valorem taxes did not apply to forest land that was allowed to reseed naturally or to land kept for conservation purposes. This distinction, combined with market demand for pulp, helped spur much of the land clearing that so drastically reshaped the Panhandle during the 1950s and 1960s.

One result of the massive clearing was loss of habitat for deer and turkey. Whereas the regenerating forest predominated by turkey oak trees was not the original habitat, it contained acorns and a variety of vegetation to feed and shelter turkey and deer, making "excellent" conditions for turkey and deer, according to Barkuloo.[49] Once the oaks were cut and pines planted, turkeys retreated to creek floodplains where heavy machinery could not clear the mixed forests. Deer did well in early years of planted pines' growth, but ran out of food once trees grew tall, shading out food sources. The deer would then have to migrate to younger pine forests.

Fire was a threat to the St. Joe Paper Company's investment in its carefully planted forests, and the company installed hundreds of miles of fire lanes to limit the spread of conflagrations. The company sent out its firefighters to help put out woods fires whether they were on St. Joe land or not; International Paper followed the same policy. By the mid-1970s, the company had 1,000 miles of graded fire lanes and 3,000 miles of plowed firebreaks.[50] The cleared lanes prevented fires from jumping and allowed fire-fighting equipment to reach the blazes.

"It was unlikely that if these same lands were owned in smaller parcels by numerous individuals there would be anything like these extensive firebreaks," noted Bay County historian Marlene Womack.[51] The fire lanes also provided access for Panhandle residents to get to favorite swimming and fishing holes or hunting spots. The fire lanes became a source of controversy in the late 1990s, when the reorganized St. Joe Company closed off many of them from public access.

One of St. Joe's early foresters was Chattahoochee-born botanist Angus Gholson, whose first job after obtaining his forestry degree from University of Florida was supervising St. Joe forests in western Bay County, near the area where the company hopes today to plant a regional airport. When he began in 1948, the area today known as Moore's Pasture was still unfenced. Hunters roamed the second-growth woods, sometimes running dogs to chase bobcats and deer. Farmers let their cows forage the woods and set fires to enhance growth of new vegetation in keeping with land-use patterns that had continued for generations.[52]

The new doctrines of scientific forestry brought an end to those ways. "We clear-cut all the longleaf pine, planted slash, and immediately adopted the Smokey the Bear program with no burning," Gholson recalled. He credited the St. Joe Paper Company with bringing jobs to people who, he said, "didn't have anything." The company foresters worked hard to ensure there was an adequate supply of wood for the pulp mill at all times, he said.[53]

While silviculture brought much-needed jobs, the combination of intensive land clearing and fire suppression had huge ecological impacts that were not understood for decades. In fact, the word "ecology" was just entering the lexicon during these years. While the logging of the virgin forests was a devastating ecological event, the side effects of silviculture that followed may have been even more damaging. "When you clear-cut a place that contains longleaf pine and you plant another species there, you're changing what nature has done for millions of years," Gholson said.[54] He has since become a critic of industrial forestry practices, including burn suppression and mechanical cultivation, advocating fiercely for longleaf pine/wiregrass restoration and the adjustments in commercial forestry that it requires, including warm-season burning.

Clay Smallwood, president of St. Joe Timberland, holds a different outlook on the importance of restoring longleaf pine habitat. In a February 2001 interview, Smallwood maintained that longleaf pine dominated only after the arrival of white settlers who set fires to increase forage for cattle. "It's interesting to me when people say our native communities were longleaf and wiregrass. It depends where you draw your zero line at. If you look in the late 1800s, yes. If you go back to the Indian days here, there was a lot of hardwood here all over Florida, very little longleaf pine," Smallwood said.[55] Smallwood's view of the natural history of longleaf defies a body of scholarship that asserts the dominance of longleaf in the pre-Columbian era.

Its natural history aside, one undisputed fact is that longleaf does not produce the same speedy returns that faster growing pine species do. "Instead of 25- to 28-year rotations, you may have to look at 35- to 40-year rotations. Now you're looking at carrying the cost of your stand establishment 10 or 15 more years. What does that do to your cost of monies, your rates of returns to your investors?" Smallwood asks. "If my company is publicly owned, I have a fiduciary responsibility to my shareholders to generate a certain rate of return based on what my bosses tell me that needs to be," Smallwood said.[56]

Gradually, foresters nationally recognized the value of controlled burns, both to prevent catastrophic fires and to improve the forest's value to wildlife. Public forests, including the Apalachicola National Forest, and some private timber companies began controlled-burn programs. St. Joe eventually embraced cool-season controlled burns, which it routinely uses to clear understory vegetation.

The use of heavy machinery by St. Joe Paper Company and others to clear sites before planting changed not only the type of forest, but the variety of plants that made up the forest floor. The hundreds of species found in the native grassland-longleaf matrix were replaced by a much lower diversity of grasses and shrubs. One plant that does not return is wiregrass.

"If the land is cultivated, it's over for wiregrass," Gholson says. "During the days of logging by mule or by oxen, there was very little damage done to the vegetation that was left. . . . But now with big [trucklike] tires, you can log in any weather, and on any terrain."[57] Other innovations in forestry that have disturbed the natural ground cover are "bedding"—the creation of raised beds for planting pine seedlings—and roller-chopping, which damages ground cover by uprooting, crushing and macerating the earth and the plants in it.

Over the years, St. Joe Paper logged in several areas that were particularly important for rare native plant life. One area was along the hilly sand ridges of Calhoun and Gadsden Counties that flank the eastern side of the Apalachicola Valley in the reputed "Garden of Eden" area. According to Gholson, in the 1950s, St. Joe clear-cut "all the timber they could use" from the relatively unproductive upland sand ridges. The company pushed topsoil into windrows, then planted slash pines. Thirty years later, the company began clear-cutting its harvest of rather scrawny trees that had grown. Gholson noticed that the heavy machinery was working all the way up to the edge of the botanically rich steephead ravines, and alarmed, contacted Jake Belin at St. Joe Paper.

Gholson recounted the conversation: "Mr. Belin, this is Angus Gholson up in Chattahoochee. . . . I played baseball against your brother, if you remember." Belin said yes, he remembered him, and he asked Gholson what was on his mind. Gholson told him he was interested in the company's activities along the Apalachicola. "They're getting awful close to those steep slopes and I wanted to ask you if you could do something to prevent the erosion," he said. At the time of Gholson's phone call, The Nature Conservancy and the state were getting interested in conserving these botanic hotbeds, and Gholson was supportive of these parties' interest in the areas.

According to Gholson, Belin's reply was, "I want you to know one damn thing. I don't need The Nature Conservancy or the state of Florida."[58] (By 2001, 13.5 percent of St. Joe's revenues came from conservation land sales, many of them brokered by The Nature Conservancy, marking just one financially driven turnabout in company attitudes.)

Ecologist Bruce Means is another champion of the remaining fraction of the longleaf pine landscape who had run-ins with St. Joe over timbering in botanically unique areas. In the mid-1980s, Means was studying an impressive old-growth forest of beeches and magnolias on St. Joe Company land in Wakulla County. It was the Panhandle's finest, and only, remnant of a beech-maple forest that had attained its full stature in the absence of fire, with thirty-inch-diameter Florida maples, spruce pines, and other rarities. Shortly after Means's visit, St. Joe Paper clear-cut the tract. Means says he does not know if the clearing was prompted by his findings or already scheduled, but "we lost the ONLY tract I have ever seen that was dominated by really large, old-growth *Acer barbatum* [Florida maple]."[59]

Shortly after this incident, Means escorted a group from the Florida Natural Areas Inventory, a hybrid state of Florida and Nature Conservancy organization that flags high-value natural areas, onto a botanically promising site in a steephead east of the Apalachicola River, also on St. Joe property near old Aspalaga Landing. The creek had etched its bed down into hardrock limestone and its sidewalls were covered with plants bathed in seepage. Means believes the site may have been where Tallahassee plantation owner and amateur naturalist Hardy Bryan Croom originally found the now-endangered Torreya tree back in the nineteenth century.

Means learned that The Nature Conservancy had approached St. Joe about purchasing the lush natural grotto. Shortly afterward, Means said, "St. Joe went in and clear-cut the steep slopes very nearly down to the creek edge." The clear-cutting muddied the creek and opened up the forest canopy, drying out the valley and its sensitive shaded vegetation. Means summed it up as "a real disaster."[60]

Angus Gholson believes the actions of the St. Joe Paper Company contributed to the endangerment of the Torreya tree. "I think that St. Joe was responsible for the demise of the Torreya. When they cleared all that land, they interrupted the moisture regime." The stressed trees were weakened in their defenses against the pathogens that are interfering with reproduction, he contended. "If things continue the next five to ten years as they have the last five to ten years, I suspect the demise will be a fact."[61]

Other timber practices that were damaging to wildlife and habitats included draining and ditching wetlands to prepare the way for planted forests. St. Joe Paper's Woodlands division oversaw the drainage of so-called "useless wet or marshy areas" to provide additional planting space. One area the company carried out these practices was in its Tate's Hell holdings in Franklin County, land that is now being painstakingly reworked to restore its natural patterns of water flow.[62] Forestry in these wet places typically involves bedding, where alternating mounds and ditches disturb natural water flow.

In its forestry practices, the St. Joe Paper Company of old was no different from its industry peers. In the 1950s, draining wetlands still was the norm and was even encouraged by the U.S. Department of Agriculture and the state. In an interview around this time, St. Joe Paper Company spokesman Robert C. Brent spoke of the company's original intention of "rehabilitating" north Florida. One of his key tasks was to drain the abundant wetlands. Brent went on to become head of the Woodlands division and a director of the St. Joe Paper Company.[63]

Patterns of land-use change in northwest Florida mirrored those in the South as a whole. In the post–World War II years, farmers and private landowners sold increasing acreage to corporations. Other nationwide forest products companies surpassed the land holdings of the St. Joe Paper Company, as they too expanded their silviculture acreage. By 1980, the biggest three companies operating in the South were International Paper, with 4.9 million acres in southern states, Georgia-Pacific, with 4.8 million acres, and Weyerhaeuser, with 3.1 million acres. Other contenders were Kimberly-Clark, Scott, and Proctor and Gamble.[64] However, none had more acres in Florida than St. Joe. As early as 1952, St. Joe Paper already had 750,000 acres in planted pines, only 50,000 acres below the year 2000 acreage kept in planted pine.[65] Even in the year 2003, the St. Joe Company was still very much in the tree business.

5

Pork Chop Emperor

*Ed Ball was the most important man who could be summoned
to any political meeting in Florida, and probably still is.*
Robert Sherrill, *Gothic Politics in the Deep South*, 1968

IN THE POLITICAL SPHERE, Ball's influence took up where duPont's Highway-men left off. During the 1920s and 1930s, special-interest lobbyists like the High-waymen so dominated the statehouse that they were referred to as "the third house" and often shared the podium with elected officials. The influence of such lobbyists continued unabated after Alfred duPont's death. Ball exerted power in Florida and beyond and formed an extensive network of contacts that reached as far as Iran and as high as the FBI and the White House.

In the post–World War II years, politicians and their backers from rural areas who dominated the Florida legislature came to be known collectively as the Pork Chop Gang. The name came from the observation that deep southerners such as those in rural north Florida preferred pork, whereas the residents of south Florida, who hailed predominantly from the northern United States, fa-vored lamb. Until 1968, Pork Choppers enjoyed a distinct political advantage in that legislative districts were mapped out by area, not population.[1] The Pork Chop Gang directed a disproportionate share of state tax dollars to public works projects in their lightly populated districts. These included the roads and bridges that were so important in making the St. Joe properties more accessible and valuable.

State money from gasoline taxes helped to pay for the highway projects. The gas tax was one fee that Ed Ball did not mind paying—or asking others to pay. Ball and his Highwayman predecessor, Alfred duPont, also supported passenger tolls on bridges. According to Jake Belin, the last conversation the two had before duPont died was in regard to a toll over a bridge in Jacksonville. DuPont urged Ball to convince the Florida legislature to keep the toll. "Don't let them take the tax away. We need it to build more bridges. People who use a facility should pay the cost," Alfred reportedly told Ball.[2] Nevertheless, Ball remained reluctant to open his own pocketbook for taxes.

Ed Ball usually remained in the shadows while pulling political strings. As author Leon Odell Griffith wrote, "Ball works his magic by telephone. . . . He can call a bank president who, in turn, may contact a particular legislator. Then, over the years, Ball has given land for public roads and performed other benevolent acts that guarantee a receptive attitude from legislators for him or his emissaries."[3] In that regard, the new St. Joe Company maintains a long company tradition.

Critics complained that state dollars went to build some Panhandle roads that seemingly went nowhere. In her book *The Other Florida,* author Gloria Jahoda marveled at the splendid roads in Wakulla County that traversed Wakulla's "most challenging places: swamps, live oak hammocks, and the dark recesses full only of Ball's timber, wild bears and hogs, songbirds, snakes, bobcats, and a few bald eagles. . . . Let there be asphalt in the backwoods, and never mind Miami."[4] But Ball was unapologetic. He knew that roads that benefited the company's interests also benefited others in the rural counties through which these byways, particularly Route 98, would pass. Moreover, as Ball reminded critics, he gave away "every inch" rather than sold the state the rights of way for roads that bordered St. Joe lands.[5]

Transportation funding again became a major push for the Florida Panhandle beginning in the late 1990s. St. Joe openly supported many of the changes and made a number of Ed Ball–like strategic right-of-way donations for new roads.

Halcyon Days

By and large, the 1940s and 1950s were halcyon days for Ed Ball and the St. Joe companies he controlled. The diminutive, round-faced Virginian had grown into his role as emperor. Some even referred to him as that, although to his person all but relatives called him "Mr. Ball." The greenbelt was expanding and maturing, and the company's stake in the growing container industry was likewise increasing. Although there were always enemies to whom Ball could toast "confusion," he usually triumphed over them in the end. Besides Pepper, these enemies came to include Miami mayor Robert King High, who was at odds with Ball over issues ranging from what he saw as the FEC's neglect of its downtown Miami terminal to the fate of other duPont properties in downtown Miami. High made a bid for governor in 1966, but Claude Kirk, Ball's favored candidate, defeated him. Another of Ball's outspoken opponents in the heart of the Green Empire was Apalachicola newspaper publisher Joseph A. Maloney, who lamented what he saw as an economic thralldom imposed by the St. Joe "pine curtain" similar to the iron curtain of the Eastern Bloc.[6]

Ball continued to expand his little black book of influential and knowledgeable associates. These included newspaper publisher John Holliday Perry, who operated a chain of Florida newspapers. Perry marshaled editorial support for Ball's public works projects and served as a director on one of Ball's banks. One of Perry's employees, the younger Braden Ball, went on to take over as publisher for the *Panama City News Herald* and *Pensacola News Journal* papers. He also served as a director of the St. Joe Paper Company and co-wrote a biography of Ed Ball with Jake Belin. Another Ball ally in Florida was Tallahassee lawyer B. K. Roberts, a Sopchoppy native who began working for Ball while still a law student at the University of Florida. Roberts's boyhood friend, Governor Fuller Warren, appointed him as a Florida Supreme Court justice in 1949, and he served until 1976.

Ball also spent time in Jacksonville and abroad with Gilbert Smith, whom Jake Belin described as "a man whose career had a sort of James Bond appearance."[7] Smith worked for the CIA in Europe during the early 1950s and later went to work on Wall Street as a broker and businessman. Smith helped Ball find his fantasy Irish castle. The two also investigated undisclosed business opportunities overseas on extended trips during the 1950s, including forays to the north African city of Tangiers.[8] Another acquaintance and business partner with an espionage background was William Pawley, who is credited with first alerting the United States to the presence of Russian missiles in Cuba. Pawley later sold a sugarcane farm to the St. Joe Paper Company.

Yet another of Ball's acquaintances in high political places was Spessard Holland, a Bartow native and World War I pilot who was elected Florida governor in 1940, then served as U.S. senator. Holland was a strong property rights advocate and was in accord with Ball on other issues that affected the Green Empire. Congressman Robert "Bob" Sikes, who represented northwestern Florida for thirty-eight years in Washington, D.C., was another close associate who advocated for Ball on many occasions. Then there was George Smathers, who served three terms as a Florida senator before going on to become a lobbyist after his retirement from the U.S. Senate in 1969. These were conservative Democrats whose ideology jibed with Ball's. Smathers and President John F. Kennedy were close friends. According to the former receptionist at the paper mill, Kennedy himself telephoned Ed Ball on more than one occasion, as did other prominent politicians.[9]

Ball maintained hotel suites in Washington, D.C., and New York to facilitate company business. These rooms were undoubtedly more luxurious than the modest rooms he kept for many years in Jacksonville at the Robert Meyer Hotel.

One of Ball's affiliations in D.C. was with the FBI and the inimitable J. Edgar Hoover. According to information obtained from the FBI under a Freedom of Information Act request, Ball had been a fan since the 1930s of the FBI and Director Hoover. An April 17, 1935, memo to J. Edgar Hoover from the special agent in charge in Jacksonville introduced Ball as the brother-in-law of Alfred I. duPont and mentioned anticrime ads that duPont's bank had run in Jacksonville. The advertisements in Jacksonville's *Florida Times-Union* asked, "Does Crime Pay?" and alleged corruption among Jacksonville police due to a botched investigation of embezzlers at Florida National Bank.

"Mr. Ball is an especial friend of the Bureau and the Jacksonville Office. He is vindictive to say the least," the agent wrote to Hoover.[10] Hoover, in turn, appeared to use the anticrime ads that were adulatory of the bureau to promote himself by forwarding the ads to the U.S. attorney general.[11]

Within two years of these ads, Ball made attempts to directly meet with J. Edgar Hoover and have him be a "guest at his home and on one of the DuPont yachts."[12] Hoover and Ball also frequently were in Miami and may have met there on occasion. FBI internal correspondence in the 1930s shows that the agency viewed FNB and Ball as valuable in their own right and because of the deep affiliations to the duPonts.

By 1964, J. Edgar Hoover's FBI and Ed Ball formalized their mutualism. A memorandum from the agent in charge in Jacksonville to "The Director" recommended that Ball could serve as some sort of informant or facilitator for the bureau. The agent reported that Ball had high-level business interests and was frequently referred to as "the most powerful single individual in the State of Florida."

"Through his control of the aforementioned companies [A. I. duPont Trust interests] he can provide unlimited services so far as access to leading political figures and leading financial personages is concerned," the memo said. Ball had offered his Southwood home as a meeting place for "important business officials" the agent wrote. The memo called Ball "an outstanding contact of this Division."[13] In 1969, the Jacksonville FBI agent forwarded to Ed Ball the book *J. Edgar Hoover on Communism,* the last available official record on the relationship between Ball and the FBI.

Expansion of the Company Town

In the company town of Port St. Joe, the 1950s and 1960s brought a major expansion of the town's main industry and the arrival of several others. In 1950, the St. Joe Paper Company undertook to triple the mill's output. By 1954, the mill produced an average of 1,200 tons of product daily, up from its early maximum of 400 tons daily,[14] making it one of the largest pulp mills in the world at the time.

The only hitch was that the massive water withdrawals needed to cook and wash the pulp were straining the local groundwater supply. Eight wells 150 feet deep and another eight wells 600 feet deep pumping day after day were causing water levels to drop.

Another water source would have to be found. Company engineer Robert Brent set to work devising a solution that made use of the Panhandle's abundant supplies of river water. He oversaw construction of an eighteen-and-a-half-mile canal that diverted water from the Chipola River, a spring-fed tributary of the Apalachicola. It pumped water from the Chipola into a ditch, then channeled it under creeks and the Intracoastal Waterway before delivering it to the mill in a huge pipeline. The canal was an engineering challenge that ultimately succeeded in supplying the 35 million gallons of water the newly expanded plant needed daily and extra for other town industries or municipal needs.

By the early 1960s, the St. Joe Paper Company's combined operations reached a production level of several hundred million square feet of corrugated board in the form of boxes and packaging components annually.[15] The company installed a new 500-ton-per-day bleached pulp plant. Now St. Joe produced mottled white paper along with the brown kraft paper used in grocery bags and a multitude of other uses. Eventually St. Joe became one of the biggest producers of bleached "top board" that was placed over brown boxes to make them more attractive to consumers. Later, the product became even more in demand as bulk superstores such as Sam's and Price Club used them for displays.[16] One byproduct of the bleaching process was the chemical dioxin, which made its way into the local environment at very low levels. Scientists suspect

FIGURE 5. Rolls of kraft paper being shipped from Port St. Joe mill, c. 1960s. Photo courtesy of Billy Howell, Port St. Joe, Florida.

that dioxin in amounts as small as parts per trillion or less may cause a variety of health problems.

Industries in Port St. Joe in the 1960s comprised one of the state's largest complexes of chemical companies. Glidden company opened a plant near St. Joe Paper. The plant used "tall oil," a byproduct from pulp and paper making, to produce rosins and other derivatives. It underwent several changes in ownership and was eventually purchased by Arizona Chemical. Other industries included an alum manufacturing plant and a facility that produced magnesium oxide from oyster shells and nearby dolomite deposits.

During these postwar years, the city of Port St. Joe grew along with its industries. Residents of the town and the surrounding countryside turned to St. Joe's Green Empire for jobs. Some former employees, like retired Electrical Department head Billy Howell, remember the days of St. Joe Paper fondly: "St. Joe was a good company to work for: all who wanted to work could work."[17] The pay was good, and so were the benefits.

Jessie Ball duPont instituted a program for scholarships for the children of employees in 1951, the same year she accepted the position overseeing the state's higher education system as a member of the Florida Board of Control (later called the Board of Regents). Many mill workers and their children gained a college education through this program. Longtime paper mill superintendent Ferrel Allen recalled how the company paid for his education while he continued to work part time at the mill.[18]

By the early 1940s, the town also had its own hospital. The mayor was careful to make sure that Jessie duPont approved the plans before going ahead with building. The Nemours Foundation did not spend any of its considerable resources on a new health facility for Port St. Joe; mostly, this was because Nemours specialists would not have a sufficiently large pool of patients for its specialized care.[19] (More than half a century later the hospital that operated from the same aging building was finally refurbished.)

Even though these were prosperous times, Ed Ball and the St. Joe Paper Company held back on making civic improvements. During the war, Port St. Joe mayor J. L. Sharit, who had worked with Jessie duPont on war relief efforts, appealed to her to ask the company to help finance the cost of a water and sewer system when her brother balked at the prospect. Finally, Jessie had the mayor and company executive Will Edwards scrounge up water treatment equipment from closed military bases. She purchased them for the city with her own, not St. Joe Paper Company, funds.[20] The company did donate land for schools.

Port St. Joe was decidedly a company town, and the direction favored by the St. Joe Paper Company was usually supported by the actions of local political boards and the local newspaper. Rising St. Joe Paper Company executive Jake Belin even served several terms as mayor in the 1950s.[21] The overlap between local government and the company seemed at the forefront when the St. Joe Paper Company sold a parcel of land in 1968, this time to relocate the county seat to Port St. Joe from Wewahitchka. The county paid the St. Joe Paper Company $84,000 for the parcel of 43.8 acres. The price worked out to $1,900 per acre for land assessed at $10 an acre at the time, as congressional testimony later revealed.[22] The new courthouse, conveniently located less than two miles from the St. Joe paper mill, was dedicated by a crowd including Governor Claude Kirk and Congressman Bob Sikes.[23]

As powerful as Ed Ball and the St. Joe Paper Company were, there is only a grain of truth in the story that credits Ball with placing Port St. Joe in the same time zone as the corporate office in Jacksonville. The change finally came in 1972, although it began back when the St. Louis investors were building the Apalachicola Northern Railroad. The Apalachicola River was the dividing line between the Eastern and Central time zones in Florida. Each time the train crossed the river, the operators would have to reset their watches until they decided to simplify things and use Eastern time the entire way.

In 1918, the city of Apalachicola requested to use Eastern Time—even though it was on the western bank of the Apalachicola—and was given permission by federal authorities. Port St. Joe, by then an official city roughly fifteen miles farther east, did not make the same request but nonetheless continued to use Eastern time unofficially. The situation caused great confusion when ships, especially foreign vessels, would dock at the port. When they gave an estimated arrival time, they often would assume that Port St. Joe was on Central time, which seemed logical looking at the Apalachicola as the demarcation line. Because of the confusion, dozens of longshoremen, the harbor pilot, and customs officials often would have to wait, sometimes in rough weather, not knowing whether the arrival time was meant to be Central or Eastern standard time.[24]

In 1972, after being lobbied by officials including Port St. Joe Harbor pilot Capt. Dave Maddox, state and U.S. lawmakers, and Florida governor Reubin Askew, officials at the national Coast and Geodetic Survey in Rockville, Maryland, finally acquiesced. Since then the time line has veered from the lower Apalachicola along the Intracoastal Waterway then down the Gulf-Bay County line to the Gulf of Mexico. Gulf County is the only county in Florida, if not the country, that is split into two time zones.

Even though Ball was not the force behind the redrawn time zone, had such a change been inimical to him and St. Joe, the alteration arguably might not have taken place. It so happened that the official time-zone adoption conveniently put Port St. Joe on the same schedule as the St. Joe corporate office in Jacksonville.

Greenbelts and Greenbacks

Although Ball may not have exercised the power to change time, his ability to keep the Green Empire's dollars from the bite of taxes was prodigious. Over the years, the blessing of minimal property taxes on pine plantations saved St. Joe millions of dollars. In 1948, when Governor Fuller Warren reluctantly conceded that a sales tax was a necessary antidote to the state's budget deficit, Ed Ball sided with him. He considered the sales tax the lesser of tax evils, relative to the other tariffs he abhorred—inheritance tax, state income tax, higher property taxes, severance taxes and corporate taxes in general. Others considered the sales tax regressive, imposing a relatively higher burden on those at lower income levels.

Meanwhile, low tax rates on land kept in commercial forestry—nicknamed the "greenbelt tax"—limited the amounts St. Joe paid into the coffers of poor, rural Panhandle counties. The greenbelt designation applied to anyone who could satisfy claims that their land was devoted to some form of commercial agriculture. The category came about to protect farmers from being forced to sell out because they could not afford to pay the high property taxes associated with developed land. While state, federal, and university programs assisted with the technical aspects of the developing science of forestry, state governments, including Florida's, assisted the spread of tree farms by extending to commercial foresters the same favorable tax structure that applied to traditional agriculture.

As Florida's largest forestry outfit, the St. Joe Paper Company stood to gain the most from the tax breaks that accompanied its dominant land use of the time, a use that is still paramount even as St. Joe diversifies into real estate. Greenbelt taxes had a profound effect on land use that remains a factor today. The deep tax discount discouraged land use for either development or conservation. Biologist Jim Barkuloo, who attributed much of the 1950s and 1960s land clearing to the tax, noted, "On the one hand, the tax encouraged silviculture to the loss of forest diversity and wildlife habitat. On the other, it kept big chunks of land from other kinds of development that would be taxed at a higher rate. Wild land has to either be planted into a certain density of marketable trees, or put into an environmental easement, which is loaded with restrictions. Or, the owner must pay higher taxes."[25]

The St. Joe Paper Company legal team stayed busy challenging the application of property taxes, even at the reduced greenbelt rates. In 1968, St. Joe Paper sued Leon County officials, claiming that the valuations placed on its forestry lands were "illegally excessive."[26] Ignoring the value of its standing timber, St. Joe Paper argued that income derived from the land should be the sole standard of value. In fact, there were other criteria, including present use, and highest and best use in the immediate future. A district court upheld Leon County with only a minor adjustment to some of the Southwood Farm property.

Even with that decision, St. Joe Paper did not dutifully pay all of its taxes. In 1988, when the company was getting ready for the first time to develop its Southwood properties, St. Joe agreed to pay $393,000 in back property taxes to settle with the Leon County Property Appraiser's Office. Nevertheless, St. Joe continued to challenge assessments of its Leon County land, saying that 44,000 acres of timberland had been overvalued, according to Leon County Property Appraiser, Bert Hartsfield. A court upheld Hartsfield's appraisals for 1989–91.[27]

Finally, in 1998, the "new St. Joe" ceased to argue with the valuations made by Leon County. Hartsfield attributed the 1998 settlement to the changing of the guard at the company. "This is a direct result of the new management at St. Joe. They're trying to present themselves as good corporate citizens," Hartsfield told the *Tallahassee Democrat*.[28]

Over the years, St. Joe challenged assessments of its lands in Bay and Walton Counties as well. In 1976, St. Joe appealed a Bay County Circuit Court decision to uphold the tax assessor's valuation of 87,000 acres of St. Joe Paper Company land. The county had assessed the land anywhere from five dollars per acre for swamp and bottom land to sixty-five dollars for the highest quality timber stands. The county's expert witnesses and the St. Joe representative offered very different figures as to the taxable value of the land. The average of the county's three experts was approximately $7.2 million; St. Joe's two witnesses estimated the value of the 87,000 acres to be more than $4.2 million. However, the Court of Appeals ruled that the Bay County tax assessor had failed to meet the burden of proof required of him by statute and reversed the decision of the Circuit Court. As a result, St. Joe's greenbelt tax bill was lowered even further, mainly because the assessor had been a bit haphazard in his valuations.[29]

St. Joe's appeal in Walton County one month before Ed Ball's death in 1981 was less straightforward. St. Joe disagreed with a decision of the Circuit Court that its beachfront and lakefront properties should be taxed at a higher, non-agricultural rate. At the time, St. Joe was not actually using the lands in question for silviculture. The company argued that the appraisal methods were too "speculative" since the Walton County property appraiser was considering possible alternative use of the land in the future, such as for residential subdividing. St. Joe argued that it would not develop the beachfront or allow public access because to do so would expose its timber stands to traffic, the possibility of fire, garbage and other negatives. In essence, the contested coastal strip and another lakefront plot were serving agricultural purposes by acting as protective buffers, St. Joe said. The court disagreed with the buffer rationale, noting that argument could be made for any large agricultural tract that fronts a publicly used area.[30]

Within five years, St. Joe sold a huge parcel of south Walton beachfront for a development that ended in foreclosure as part of the Topsail Hill debacle. Fifteen years after that, St. Joe used additional portions of the land subject to the tax dispute for several of its coastal developments in Walton County.[31]

The lawsuits did not stop after Ball's death. St. Joe was in court in Bay County in 1995. This time the state and county property appraiser were on the offensive, trying to reverse a decision by the Bay County Circuit Court. The court had ruled that the property appraiser, Richard Davis, erred when he denied agricultural classification for 238 acres of land fronting the Gulf of Mexico. The land, although zoned for silviculture, was not being used for that or any other agricultural purpose. In fact, St. Joe previously sold this land, known as Harbor Point or St. Michael's Landing, for development in the 1980s in a deal that later collapsed. The circuit court judge, N. Russell Bower, ruled that the property appraiser had somehow abused his discretion. The appeals court did not buy that contention and reversed his decision.[32] St. Joe's tax bill for the acreage, which lay between Tyndall Air Force Base and Mexico Beach, jumped from $480 to $74,554 without the greenbelt discount.[33]

Yet the court noted a troubling aspect of the decision. Although it was clear that the 238 acres were not being used for forestry, the valuation needed to reflect the classification of the land in accordance with the comprehensive plan. The zoning restrictions under the plan as it existed at the time of the appeal would not have allowed nonagricultural use of the property. Courts have consistently ruled that property appraisers cannot be speculative in their assessments. But when a company owns considerable acreage zoned for agriculture but does not use this acreage for that purpose, they themselves appear to be speculative. Could St. Joe's property in Bay County be rezoned from silviculture to a more intensive use? Yes, according to the appraiser, but not "without a struggle" (that is, an amendment to the comprehensive plan).[34] There have been plenty of those in Florida's counties. Indeed, five years after this appeal, the St. Joe Company proposed to develop a portion of this 238-acre gulf-front property.

In practical terms, the fact that forestry concerns pay lower taxes means that others must pay more taxes to foot county bills for education, fire and police protection, and other public services. "Anytime somebody doesn't pay, then somebody picks up the slack," points out deputy property assessor Mack Webb of Bay County, where St. Joe has extensive holdings.[35] That group would include lower income Panhandle residents who might reside in modest single- or double- wide trailers mere yards from tree farm land that is taxed at a fraction of their own.

Troubled Times

As the 1960s unfolded, Ball faced new social forces that presented a stiffer challenge than any of Ball's previous individual enemies. And he faced a battle that threatened to break apart the Green Empire itself. Emperor Ball rallied his Pork Chop allies to face off against these threats, starting with two in particular—unions and the civil rights movement. Ball predicted that if the Pork Chop Gang lost its influence, "the NAACP [National Association for the Advancement of Colored People] and the Unions would take over." In fact, he felt these organizations already had done so in the cities.[36]

After Ball finally gained control of the FEC in 1959, he wasted no time in taking on the railroad unions. He pared the railroad's operating expenses by trimming the staffing levels on trains and making other adjustments that infuriated the unions. In 1960, Ball hired a young railroad executive from Southern Railway named Winfred Thornton—as of 2002 still head of the A. I. duPont Trust—to be in charge of the FEC to carry out the changes. Workers called for a strike, and for the next nine years the FEC was the object of the longest running railroad strike in U.S. history. During the strike's early years, diesel engines and railroad cars were dynamited dozens of times. Unionized workers never did get their jobs back. In the nasty, protracted strike, Thornton gained a reputation as "the biggest hatchet man in the history of American railroading."[37]

"It was difficult for a number of years," recalled Winfred Thornton. "But it [not dealing with the unions] allowed FEC to maintain independence. We got rid of antiquated work rules and incorporated a more modern arrangement."[38] For example, there was a rule that 100 miles of travel equaled a day's work. If an engineer got on the train in Jacksonville and got to New Smyrna Beach in three hours, that was a work day. Thornton maintained that the union was also too generous with overtime and the number of workers necessary to operate the trains.

The labor dispute had such a negative impact on both railway workers and the economy of Florida's east coast that in 1963 President Kennedy appointed a board to attempt to mediate. However, Ball rejected the group's recommendations.[39] Thornton's assessment was that Kennedy was using his weight to try to get Ball to deal with the unions, but apparently even the president could not persuade Emperor Ball. At one point, the strike became a national security concern because the shutdown impaired military operations at Cape Canaveral in the wake of the Cuban missile crisis and the Soviets' launch of the first manned space probe. The FEC spur line supplied the Cape. Ball suggested to President Kennedy that he send in troops to put down the strike, a suggestion he did not take. Instead, the next year, President Johnson allowed the trains to operate with strikebreakers, with FBI agents present to keep order.[40] At the time, Ball was still active as an FBI adjunct, a connection he may have exploited. However, files obtained from the FBI make no mention of these events.

The strike finally ended with the unions vanquished. However, Ball's intransigence during the strike helped prompt a House investigation of the duPont-Ball empire in Florida that opened up the Green Empire's affairs to nationwide scrutiny. Union representatives had taken their grievances to sympathetic ears in the nation's capitol. Before long, the duPont Estate's 1956 exemption from the federal Bank Holding Act was common knowledge. Oregon senator Wayne Morse charged that the duPont Estate had committed "grave abuses of power."[41] Texas Representative Wright Patman, a populist who took a special interest in the workings of private trusts established by the wealthy, researched the Alfred I. duPont Estate. He issued a massive report filled with income and tax tables to illustrate his argument that the Estate was ducking taxes under the guise of charity.

In 1964, Patman opened hearings on a bill that would remove the A. I. duPont Estate's exemption from the 1956 Bank Holding Act. Witnesses took turns defending or attacking the duPont Green Empire. Defenders included Thornton, Florida senator Spessard Holland and Congressman Bob Sikes, William Pawley, several bank executives, the editor of the Port St. Joe *Star,* and Ed Ball himself.

Ball was seventy-seven years old and crafty as ever when he took his seat behind a microphone at the polished table to defend his empire's business practices. When Wisconsin senator William Proxmire questioned him about the Estate's finances, he responded that as "an old farmer," he was hard pressed to come up with precise figures. Proxmire fired back: "Not many farmers in Wisconsin have this kind of control of more than a million shares of General Motors and 764,000 shares of duPont stock."[42] Ball did volunteer some figures, which he said showed that companies controlled by the Estate did indeed pay taxes. Ball firmly sought the moral high ground, invoking the words and charitable purposes set down in Alfred duPont's will and arguing that the proposed legislation was punitive and un-American.

Witnesses who testified against the Estate included Miami mayor Robert King High, George Meany of the AFL-CIO, the head of the Railway Labor Executives Association, and *Apalachicola Times* publisher Joseph Maloney. Maloney charged that "Mr. Ball's pine curtain" stifled economic development in the Panhandle. The company, he said, was "a sleeping giant, anesthetized by the power of the duPont estate."[43]

In the end, Ball failed to convince Congress that the Trust should maintain its privileged status quo. Following the hearings, Congress passed a bill ending the A. I. duPont Estate's exemption from the 1956 Bank Holding Act. As a charitable trust, the Alfred I. duPont Estate could no longer operate both banks—by then, the largest bank chain south of Philadelphia and east of the Mississippi— and the array of other Green Empire businesses. One economist had determined that in 1962 the worth of these combined holdings was $2 billion.[44] By the federal law President Johnson signed on July 10, 1966, the Green Empire had to divest either its banks or other holdings within five years.

6

⑥ ⑥ ⑥ ⑥ ⑥ ⑥ ⑥ **Challenges to the Empire**

> *Quite frankly, the company is worth more dead than alive.*
> Alfred duPont Dent, grandson of Alfred I. duPont

THE 1966 LAW ENDING the Alfred I. duPont Trust's exemption from the Bank Holding Act spelled the end of an era for the Green Empire, or at least it seemed to. Ed Ball disappointed the railroad unions when he failed to promptly surrender the railroads and other duPont nonbanking assets. Instead, Ball set to work seeking ways to fulfill the letter of the law while keeping as much of the empire as possible intact and under his control. It took almost the whole five years before the Estate reorganized and until 1977 before the Ball-duPont interests lost effective control of the banks. Even then, some would question whether Ball had given up behind-the-scenes control.

During this period, Jessie Ball duPont's influence over the Green Empire went from minimal to nonexistent. Throughout the 1960s, her attempts to take a more active role in the company businesses were frustrated by her brother's unresponsiveness to her requests, even though she remained chair of the board of directors of the St. Joe Paper Company until her death. She died at the Nemours mansion in Delaware in September 1970.

The Stalled Divestiture

Nearly five years rolled by after the congressional hearings without any sign of the duPont Estate divesting the banks, railroad, or other corporate holdings. The railroad strike, too, continued. Ball had no intention of giving up the Florida East Coast Railroad and fought equally hard to keep control of the banks. Ball's first gambit was to push for a branch banking law in Florida. Branch banking would allow the Estate to keep one bank, which could then govern subsidiaries under it. Florida's new governor was Claude Kirk, the first Republican governor in a century and a man who supported Ball's branch banking plan. But Ball had to let go of this plan when the Florida legislature sank the initiative. Next, Ball floated a plan to link his banks with two other Florida bank chains, including Charter Bankshares, which was owned by Jacksonville businessman and Ball associate Raymond Mason.[1] Federal regulators nixed this plan.

Then, shortly before the July 1, 1971 deadline, the Estate made its next move. Ball and the other trustees sold 3,213,103 shares of Florida National Bank holdings valued at $60.6 million. Ball enlisted the help of his globetrotting James Bond–like friend Gilbert Smith, then on Wall Street, and yet another duPont firm, the securities business F. I. duPont and Company, to sell the new shares created in the restructuring.[2]

The A. I. duPont Estate ended up with 24.9 percent of the Florida National Bank shares, just below the legal limit of 25 percent. When Ed Ball's 6.4 percent interest and Jessie Ball duPont's 4.5 percent interest were included, however, it was clear that the Ball-duPont empire still ruled the banks. "Ed Ball may have lost control of the bank on paper, but his influence was surely sustained," wrote Braden Ball.[3]

In 1973, the Federal Reserve Board ruled that the Estate had not truly divested. A new "Fed" policy stated that ownership of only 5 percent could constitute control, meaning the Estate would have to give up control of more FNB shares.

One need not have told FNB's directors that Ball and the duPont Trust were still in charge. In 1977, Ed Ball and St. Joe Paper set its sights on 17,000 acres of Florida Panhandle land. The land was owned by businessman Jimmy Hatcher and his business associate Cary Everett, who was a director of the Florida First National Bank in Chipley, one of the chain of Florida National Banks supposedly by then divested from duPont and Ball. Hatcher and Everett were partners in the Chipola Land Company.

When Hatcher and Everett suffered financial reversals in the mid-1970s, Ball pressured the two partners to sell the 17,000 acres at $140 an acre—far less than the going rate. He required a $350,000 loan previously obtained by the Chipola Land Company through the Florida National Bank at Chipley be paid from the sale proceeds even though it was not due until the following year.[4]

According to Everett, at the closing in Panama City, Ball, accompanied by Jake Belin, made clear the extent of his reach. Ball noted that he not only owned 24.9 percent of Florida National, but that he personally was the largest single stockholder in the banks, and he wanted that loan paid. Ball then added insult to injury, according to a later letter of resignation by the banker. He slammed down his eyeglasses and singled out Everett, demanding that he pay back a personal loan to Florida National at Madison, a loan Ball and Belin could not have known about unless given access to confidential bank files. Ball then advised that all would fare better "if we kept the details of our transaction to ourselves."[5]

An FBI file reveals that once St. Joe acquired the land, a company headed by the son-in-law of Ball's business associate Raymond Mason, the Louisiana and Life Insurance Company, intended to show it to some visitors from the Middle East.[6]

It appeared that Jake Belin and Ed Ball had improperly obtained confidential information from inside Florida National Banks since neither was an officer or director. "How many times over the years," Everett wondered, "had Florida National Banks been in 'cahoots' with Mr. Ball and St. Joe Paper to coerce people and maneuver people and companies into financial disaster?"[7]

Everett resigned, expressing his dismay that Jacksonville was running the FNB at Chipola with the bank directors serving only as "rubber stamps." "Whether the 'DuPont Trust' under the domination of Mr. Ball has illegally used the protection of a charitable trust to accumulate capital without taxation and put together this vast monopoly when these earnings were very probably intended to be used for the welfare of the crippled people of America is not for me to say," he wrote.[8] Everett looked to the court system to consider breaking up the St. Joe monopoly. But the wily Ball had another idea.

Under the gun from the Feds to again divest FNB shares, Ball arranged to sell nearly a quarter of the bank shares owned by the duPont Estate to the Florida National Associates, Inc., an investor group composed of Florida National Bank directors, employees, and customers. The group was pretty much a reconstituted version of the prior administration, minus some duPont Estate–connected employees whose departure the federal regulators required.

Federal regulators required too that the Florida National Bank give up its seat on the Estate's group of trustees. In 1977, the sale became final. Later, the Florida National Banks were taken over by the First Union Bank, now Wachovia. This bank is still tied to the affairs of the St. Joe Company; it serves as the company's transfer agent and registrar and counts the proxies for its annual meetings.

Not everyone in the ranks of the duPont Estate approved of the sale to Florida National Associates. William Mills, a trustee of the A. I. duPont Estate who also served as an executor of the Jessie Ball duPont Estate, filed several lawsuits objecting to Ball's plans. Mills was a tax lawyer who had worked for Ball since 1949 and had served as a go-between for Jessie and Ed. Mills and Alfred's grandson, Alfred duPont Dent, went on in the 1970s to question whether the A. I. duPont Estate would not be better served by selling of the Green Empire businesses and switching to more traditional stock and bond investments.

Mills, Dent, and others questioned the management of the Trust funds. By 1974, the attorneys general of the states of Florida and Delaware had launched a suit against Ed Ball and the A. I. du Pont trustees to remove Ball and the trustees and foster a greater contribution to sick children and the elderly. After all, the charitable objectives of the Trust were the reason it received favorable tax status. The standard requirement for a charitable organization's payout was 5 percent, but the Trust was averaging only a woeful 1 percent. After legal hijinks from Ball's end that frustrated the office of the Delaware state solicitor, the parties agreed to a compromise, a 3 percent contribution.

Another suit brought by Mills sought to remove Ball as an A. I . duPont trustee, alleging he was senile and a "scoundrel."[9] Years later, at the age of ninety-two, Ball retaliated against Mills by filing a suit charging that the Jessie Ball duPont fund he oversaw had improperly disbursed monies, a charge an appeals court found to be unjustified.[10] Mills's ideological partner Alfred duPont Dent even had alleged that Ed Ball had murdered Alfred duPont before a redraft of his will became legally binding. The redraft would have taken considerable power from Ball. Dent's accusation was never proven, and may simply have been the result of a rumor propagated by Ball's detractors.

St. Joe's New Businesses

Although Ball still had close ties to the Florida National Banks, he no longer controlled them outright. On its face, the Green Empire appeared to have shrunk. However, the empire compensated for its loss of the banks by venturing into several new fields. In 1971, the same year the initial divestment took place, the St. Joe Paper Company swapped stock with the Charter Company, owned by business tycoon and Ball companion Raymond Mason. St. Joe Paper acquired just over 20 percent interest in Charter, making it Charter's largest single stockholder. In return, Charter received 8 percent of St. Joe Paper common stock.

Mason built the Charter Company from a virtually bankrupt lumberyard and mortgage company into an international corporation that ranked number 173 on the Fortune 500 in 1975.[11] Charter had interests in oil, land, and finance both in the United States and abroad. After Jessie duPont's death, the corporate overlap was made complete by Raymond Mason's purchase of the Epping Forest mansion.

In 1972, the St. Joe Paper Company made another major capital acquisition. It bought the south Florida Talisman sugarcane operation from an acquaintance of Ed Ball, William Pawley. The purchase included the roughly 50,000-acre farm and sugar mill on the southeastern shore of Lake Okeechobee near Belle Glade.

Pawley was a former U.S. ambassador to Brazil and Peru and a CIA operative who helped found the Flying Tigers airline company that became the CIA's Civil Air Transport, most famous for its evacuation of the U.S. Embassy in Hanoi during the Vietnam War. Pawley was seen as a hero for providing intelligence about Cuba during the tense times of the Bay of Pigs and Cuban missile crisis. In fact, Pawley's Cuban associates provided the first, "remarkably accurate," information that Russians were at work in Cuba building missile sites, according to writings of *Washington Star* journalist and staunch anti-Communist Clare Boothe Luce, a friend of Pawley's.[12] His *New York Times* obituary in 1977 noted that "he had a flair for supersalesmanship and high adventure" and could fill "several old-time dime novels."[13]

During the Cuban Revolution, Ball aided displaced anti-Castro Cubans, putting up some exiles, including Mrs. Batista, at a hotel he owned in Mississippi, the Edgewater. The Talisman farm, which Pawley purchased in 1964, offered employment for exiled Cubans.[14] Pawley initially retained a 40 percent interest in Talisman after selling to St. Joe in 1972 but ultimately sold his shares to Gulf and Western, shares which St. Joe later bought to gain full possession of the farm and sugar mill.[15]

Turbulence with Unions and Civil Rights

When St. Joe bought Talisman, Pawley was having financial problems and his sugar business was operating in the red. To top off Pawley's troubles, the United Farm Workers were striking Talisman in protest over working conditions, which included twelve-hour shifts with no days off and no meal breaks. Picketers included Talisman workers, then mostly Cubans from Miami's Little Havana, truck drivers, and others sympathetic to the workers' cause.

One of those on the picket line outside Talisman's gates on a foggy night in

January 1972 was a college student named Nan Freeman. Eyewitnesses saw Freeman accidentally flung onto the road and killed by a truck, an explanation at odds with William Pawley's statement to the press that Freeman had died elsewhere along the dangerous Highway 27 and her body later placed at Talisman's gates. An autopsy confirmed the eyewitnesses' account, and Freeman's parents sued Talisman over what appeared to be a cover-up. The suit was settled out of court.[16]

Around the same time, a civil rights attorney with the Department of Justice asked the FBI to investigate a complaint. The United Farm Workers, headed by Cesar Chavez, charged that Talisman Sugar Corporation was holding workers as virtual prisoners. But the FBI dropped its investigation, apparently without visiting Talisman, after a Miami judge ruled against the United Farm Workers.[17]

After the St. Joe Paper Company took over, it made swift changes at Talisman. Winfred Thornton assumed the role of Talisman president and director.[18] Company officials posted armed guards at the gates. As it had done when the duPont Estate took over the FEC, the company dealt with its labor problems forcefully, by thinning labor's ranks. St. Joe was one of the first to switch over to harvesting machines, Winfred Thornton was proud to say. The machinery reduced the need for seasonal cane cutters, even though mechanical harvesting was not well suited to Talisman's mostly mucky soils. Although the heavy machines degraded the soil much more rapidly, they cost half as much and took a quarter the time as did harvesting done by hand labor.[19] Plus, machines did not protest for better working conditions.

Under the St. Joe Paper Company, Talisman became a profitable operation. A branch line from the FEC railroad helped deliver its sweet product to market. St. Joe sold its sugar lands to the state of Florida in the late 1990s to use as water storage as part of the massive Everglades restoration project.

Also in 1971, another strike plagued the Green Empire, this time at the paper mill in Port St. Joe. Three unions at the mill struck, the International Brotherhood of Pulp, Sulfite and Paper Mill Workers (now the United Paperworkers International Union), the International Brotherhood of Electrical Workers, and the International Association of Machinists. The strike paralyzed operations at the mill and brought port commerce to a standstill.[20]

Workers at the paper mill had a much better livelihood than sugarcane cutters. They earned good salaries for their level of education and relative to other wages in the area. Nevertheless, they contended with many hazards on the job. Retired electrical department supervisor Billy Howell recalled just one of the plant's danger spots, the electrostatic precipitators that removed salt from mill emissions. Precipitators discharged high-voltage electricity that caused salt, in the form of dust, to adhere to charged plates and drop to the ground where it could be collected and reused. The precipitator was very high voltage and sent electric arcs flying around the equipment. "Working in a paper mill was about as dangerous as being in Vietnam," according to Howell, who worked at the mill for forty-two years until his retirement in 1989.[21]

Even careful workers suffered accidents because of their own or others' mistakes. Accidents claimed worker's limbs, and even their lives in some cases from accidents in the lumber yard, or around the chlorine gas and elsewhere.[22]

Workers stubbornly persisted in a protracted strike for better fringe benefits. The strike ended March 20, 1972.[23] The dispute came at a bad time for both the unions and management. President Nixon had just imposed wage and price freezes, making the unions' demands more of an uphill battle; in addition, the mill was in the start of a major renovation. Senator George McGovern, then running for president, sent a telegram to Ball urging him to put an end to the strike. Ball's response berated McGovern for misreading what was happening at the mill, which Ball called a "tragic situation for the innocent people who have been misled into striking." He ended the tart epistle by saying that a greater tragedy would be McGovern's election as president.[24]

The strike at Port St. Joe was less explosive than the FEC strike. There were no incidents of violence, nor was there vandalism. If he had any doubts about his own personal safety, Ed Ball could always retreat to his suite at Wakulla Lodge, where he had installed iron bars on his windows and a steel-plated door decades earlier.

After this strike, the paper makers' union never returned to its former power. When layoffs began in the years after Ed Ball's death, the unions did little. "Hoffa would have bombed the plant or closed it down," reflected historian Philip Adkins. "There was a real symbiotic relationship, with a no strike clause."[25] Even as the mill was closing permanently in the late 1990s, the union was largely ineffectual in seeking a severance package for its members.

Another labor issue that surfaced in the 1970s was the matter of racial discrimination. As Ball feared, the NAACP did prove to be a thorn for the St. Joe Paper Company. The issues raised would not be resolved for three decades.

In 1965, Congress had passed Title VII of the Civil Rights Act, the act that prohibited discrimination in employment and allowed minority workers to bring lawsuits aimed at stopping discriminatory practices. The southern paper industry was among the slowest to make the required civil rights adjustments, and among those, the St. Joe Paper Company dragged its feet more slowly than most, according to historian Timothy Minchin.[26]

Jobs for blacks at the mill continued to be the lowest paid, most physically demanding tasks as part of the "bull gang," the paper industry's slang for miscellaneous yard duties—cleaning, unloading chemicals, hauling, and the like. Often blacks had to train whites for jobs that they themselves would not be given. They had different time clocks and racially coded time cards, separate eating areas and bathrooms. These segregated facilities were maintained until the late 1970s. The local unions were themselves segregated until 1968, and the minority local unions found themselves subservient to their all-white counterparts.[27]

African American workers at the mill filed complaints with the Equal Employment Opportunity Commission (EEOC) in 1968, but the company denied that discrimination took place. The EEOC complaint and subsequent grievances at the mill changed little. In 1976, the EEOC attempted to negotiate a settlement in the ongoing dispute. St. Joe Paper was prepared to give the workers cash payments. The workers, on the advice of an international union representative, held out, pressing instead for reforms in the company's labor practices.

Four St. Joe workers went to Tallahassee to meet an attorney for the NAACP. They filed suit, calling for the company to stop discriminating and to preferentially hire black applicants to fill certain job vacancies.[28] Once again, however, St. Joe's response was to do almost nothing. The case came to be known as *Winfield v. St. Joe Paper Company.*

In 1981, the U.S. District Court rendered a summary judgment on the basis of "overwhelming statistical proof" that the company had practiced racial discrimination in the selection of salaried employees at the mill.[29] Yet as late as 1984, the pattern of segregation and discrimination, especially the near absence of promotions to black workers, continued and was documented in court proceedings.

In 1988, the U.S. District Court for the Northern District of Florida handed down a consent decree to settle past EEOC charges and Title VII claims. The decree included a total of $3.8 million for cash awards to workers and lawyers' fees.[30]

The decision also granted black workers the rights for promotion into formerly "white" jobs, but plant officials let workers struggle in these positions by not affording them adequate training or stopping harassment when it took place. *Winfield* continued into the 1990s and carried over even after the paper mill was sold in 1996. Finally, the case was settled in 1997, when the U.S. Court of Appeals rejected the plaintiffs' appeal for further relief. Some black workers felt vindicated; others felt that the company and judicial system had, given the many years of lost wages, handed them the shaft.

The town of Port St. Joe remained largely segregated with the poorer black neighborhood north of the proverbial railroad tracks. A north-south road that stopped abruptly at the tracks could easily have continued on with an inexpensive crossing that would connect with the white neighborhood immediately to the south. Decades ago, the St. Joe Paper Company told the mayor, Frank Pate, that the absence of a crossing was a "safety feature." Pate was elected in 1966 on a platform that included opening up the black neighborhood so there would be two ways in and out.[31] Within several years, Pate lived up to his promise and a new road fed into the neighborhood, connecting it to Highway 71 to the northeast, but not directly to the white side of town.

Passing the Baton

Ed Ball's unflagging stamina confounded his detractors. His feisty performance at the congressional hearings in 1966, at age seventy-seven, confirmed that he was still a powerful man. The rules for the St. Joe companies called for mandatory retirement at age sixty-five, but Ball the emperor took exception for himself. Still, he had suffered several heart attacks, starting with a serious one in 1957 on a train, during which he sedated himself with bourbon until he received medical care.

Over the years, Ball resisted change and rebuffed his sister's suggestions that he bring on young staff with new ideas. In fact, for his whole career with the Green Empire, Ed Ball had stuck with the eccentric but competent secretary he had inherited from Alfred duPont, Irene Walsh. At last, when he turned eighty in 1968, Ball declared himself ready to step down as St. Joe's president and CEO.

Thereafter, Ball was freer to pursue his intriguing international business ventures while still warding off St. Joe's enemies. Until his death, Ball maintained an active role in the Green Empire through his key role as chairman of the A. I. duPont Testamentary Trust.

Ball handed over his title as president of the St. Joe Paper Company to longtime employee Jake Belin, who had already been appointed to the board of trustees of the Alfred I. duPont Estate the year before. Belin inherited a number of challenges from Ball, starting with the A. I. duPont Estate's 1971 deadline to divest. Belin, too, was at the helm of day-to-day operations for the strikes at both the paper mill and Talisman. Another problem was that the paper mill, last updated in the 1950s, had begun to fade into obsolescence.

Despite all these challenges, Belin assumed his new role handily and carried on in a management style similar to Ball's. According to one observer, Ball had sought a replacement who was "as near like himself as possible, and Jake was hard as nails in business dealings."[32] Belin remained in the position of company president until 1984 and as a director for the A. I. duPont Trust until his death in May 2000.

Like Ball, Belin knew how to work the telephone to take care of troublesome situations, and also like Ball, he knew how to get to the top. He had a working relationship with every Florida governor from 1940 on. Unlike Ball, Belin lived in Port St. Joe, although he also maintained a Jacksonville residence. He was a staunch member of community organizations including the Long Avenue Baptist Church. In 1968, the year Belin took over, the town's population had climbed to 4,400. The St. Joe Paper Company employed 1,200 people, a quarter of them from Port St. Joe, according to Raymond Mason.[33]

Belin was fascinated with Confederate history, especially Stonewall Jackson and Robert E. Lee, of whom he spoke "as though they were friends."[34] His principal residence in Port St. Joe was modest—no larger than the dwellings of the neighboring mill workers' on the flat, sandy lots in the port town of St. Joe. As Belin rose to head the company, he, like Ball, appeared more interested in power itself than in its trappings. He did not own a flashy car; he would pick one from the company motor pool for his treks between Port St. Joe and Jacksonville, a distance of about 260 miles.

As the 1970s began, Belin oversaw the third major wave of construction at the paper mill plant that had occurred over its lifetime—the first being the initial construction in the late 1930s, and the second the major expansion that tripled production in the 1950s. Along with taxes, unions, and civil rights, the St. Joe Paper Company added new environmental regulations to its list of burdens.

In response to the burning rivers and choking smog that gave birth to the environmental movement in the 1960s and early 1970s, the federal government passed environmental laws—the Clean Air Act in 1963, the National Environmental Policy Act in 1969, and the Clean Water Act in 1972, among them. These groundbreaking laws had a profound impact on all industries that directly polluted air or water, as paper mills did on a daily basis. The Endangered Species Act, passed in 1973, also affected the company's management of its timberlands. Red-cockaded woodpeckers and bald eagles were among the animals inhabiting St. Joe lands that received new federal protection.

The St. Joe Paper Company spent $40 million modernizing its facilities, including installing air and water pollution controls in the early 1970s.[35] Air emissions included the mix of gases from the pulp processing and bleaching and partially combusted fuel chemicals. Through much of the mill's life, it burned heavy No. 6 fuel oil, belching out acrid smoke.

Among the other charges he hurled at Ed Ball, 1972 presidential contender George McGovern accused Ball of being one of Florida's worst polluters.[36] Industries in this era of burgeoning environmental awareness could no longer ignore the fate of their waste streams.

Around this time, the company also backed the building of a new $9 million combination industrial-municipal sewage plant, the construction of which the Environmental Protection Agency also supported. This was more a prudent business move than an act of corporate responsibility because the company, not the municipality, was by far the major user of the system. The liability for wastes entering the environment rested with the city, not the town's industries, of which St. Joe Paper contributed roughly 96 percent of the volume.

The Edward Ball School of Conservation

On several issues that cropped up in the early days of Florida's environmental movement, the St. Joe Paper Company took a stance that raised the ire of environmentalists. For one, Ed Ball favored the construction of a controversial airport, the Everglades Jetport, which had it been built, would have proved convenient for his trips to the Talisman sugarcane farm but damaging to birds, panthers, and other wildlife in the vast wetlands complex.[37]

Also, for four decades Ball supported the construction of a canal across north-central Florida. Originally, the Cross-Florida Canal was intended to cut a shipping canal across the state from Yankeetown on the Gulf Coast to Jacksonville on the Atlantic. In between, the route was to follow the Withlacoochee, Oklawaha, and St. Johns Rivers, after channelizing the rivers' natural twists and turns and connecting them with dredged canals. The route would provide a shortcut for shipping products—such as pulp from the mill at Port St. Joe—to the port at Jacksonville, supposedly helping boost business at both ends.

The Cross-Florida Canal had been proposed as early as the 1920s, and during the 1930s, Ed Ball purchased bonds to support the project's construction as yet another improvement to the Green Empire's transportation infrastructure. However, Congress stopped funding for the project in 1936. A study by the U.S. Geological Survey pointed out that blasting a channel deep enough for ship traffic would damage the Floridan Aquifer, leading to saltwater intrusion and disrupting the flow of fresh water at several springs.[38]

Even so, the idea was revived after World War II. The U.S. Army Corps of Engineers had kept the project on its list, but it lacked funding. In 1960, John F. Kennedy pledged his support for the canal if elected. Ball, in turn, threw his support behind Kennedy, and thereafter committed funds to study the feasibility of the project in a slightly pared back version, as the shallower Cross-Florida Barge Canal. Construction began, including channelizing miles of the pristine Oklawaha and impounding that river with the Rodman Dam. Mullet and catfish that once migrated freely into Silver Springs could no longer get through. Seventy million dollars of taxpayer money was spent before the Nixon administration halted construction.

In his later years, Ball acquired a reputation as a conservationist, in large part because of two special wildlife havens with which he was associated—Southwood and Wakulla Springs. These were two of the seven refuges Ball established starting in 1966. The Edward Ball Wildlife Foundation, according to associate Raymond Mason, was to be "a perpetual trust with sanctuaries in seven Florida locations."[39] Besides Southwood and Wakulla Springs, these included several ranches in the Panhandle and Big Bend areas, the Bona Allen Ranch in Calhoun County, the 7,500-acre Box-R Ranch northwest of Apalachicola in Franklin County, and the M-K Ranch in Gulf County.

The foundation also set aside company land for another nature preserve in Marion and Sumter Counties in north-central Florida called the Seven Springs Wildlife Sanctuary and dedicated a sanctuary and nature walk at the University of West Florida in Pensacola. At its height, the foundation also sponsored some research as well as classroom programs. After environmentalists quarreled with Ball over management at Wakulla Springs, however, Ball lost his enthusiasm for the foundation and cut off its funding.

The so-called "perpetual" trust for wildlife endured a brief fifteen years. Its greatest conservation legacy is the preservation of Wakulla Springs and its surrounding woods as a natural area. After Ball's death, trustees of the Nemours Foundation sold Wakulla Springs to the state; the state turned it into Edward Ball Wakulla Springs State Park and Lodge. Meanwhile, the trustees gave most of the Wildlife Foundation's monetary assets to Florida State University rather than to conservation endeavors, establishing the Ed Ball chair of international law.[40] Ball made another gift to FSU in the 1960s, when he deeded seventy acres to the university for an oceanographic research lab at Turkey Point on the Gulf Coast forty-five miles southeast of Tallahassee. In 2000, St. Joe unsuccessfully attempted to reacquire the marine lab acreage from FSU for a recreational marina, creating local controversy.

Under the reorganized St. Joe Company, the remaining former sanctuaries were being used in a variety of ways, from housing and commercial development at Southwood to a duck hunting operation at the M-K Ranch, which previously had been leased to a Japanese company to grow rice and later converted to silviculture.

Wakulla Springs

It was at Wakulla Springs, a property owned personally by Ed Ball rather than by the paper company or any of its offshoots, that Edward Ball was most scrutinized for his conservation decisions. Ball visited the lodge regularly over the years, using it in a similar fashion to the paper company's Southwood farm, as both a retreat and a place to meet with influential people. The lodge also remained in service as a hotel. Since the 1870s, the spring had served as a place for political rallies, and area residents boasted that all successful candidates for governor kicked off their campaigns at Wakulla. Ed Ball kept this tradition alive, hosting several functions where politicians he supported launched their races for governor.[41] Ball's other guests included businessmen, ambassadors, and members of royalty, according to historian Tracy Revels, who wrote an extensive history of Wakulla Springs called *Watery Eden*.[42]

Guests enjoyed tours on glass-bottomed boats around the huge spring and down a stretch of the wildlife-packed Wakulla River. The tours were, and still are, narrated by local guides with a reputation for charming patter and a sharp eye for the many creatures present. Alligators, turtles, limpkins, and anhingas, nicknamed "water turkeys" or "snake birds," were the most abundant animals.

In the 1950s, some boosters in the Wakulla area and Tallahassee began suggesting that more could be made of Wakulla as a tourist attraction to help the economically depressed area. "Why can't Ed Ball and his bunch get on the ball and do something big with Wakulla Springs?" one editorial writer in nearby Crawfordville asked.[43] Then, in 1959, a story ran in several area papers raising the possibility that Wakulla Springs might be the location of a Florida Disney attraction. As company lore has it, Ball rebuffed an overture from Walt Disney, saying, "I don't do business with carnival people." There was great historical irony in former Disney executive Peter Rummell taking over at St. Joe.

While shunning Disney, Ball did form a short-lived alliance with the Audubon Society. In 1963, his Wakulla Edgewater company (Edgewater was the name he used for his other resorts in Mississippi and Panama City Beach) entered into an arrangement with the National Audubon Society whereby Ball's company would operate the resort and the Audubon Society would lease and manage the 4,000 acres around the spring.

Audubon hired a game warden, who added feed corn to the wild food available at Wakulla. The result was "wall to wall" bald pate or American widgeon ducks, recalls one Bay County bird watching aficionado, Audrey Parker. The warden also operated feeding stations for deer and wild turkeys. Ball's more controversial animals at Wakulla though were a succession of pet caged bears,

FIGURE 6. The Edward Ball Wildlife Management Area in Gulf County, one of the diminishing number of forested areas owned by the St. Joe Company and leased to the state for public hunting. Photo by Kathryn Ziewitz.

beginning with an injured and rehabilitated black bear named Algae. But Ball was not equally protective of all animals that teemed in the area. He once advised the manager of the springs to invest in a good shot gun to shoot those "damn cormorants" that were eating the fish.[44]

The arrangement with Audubon held until 1969, when Ball's Wakulla Edgewater company undertook major projects at the spring. Ball's Edgewater outfit dynamited the fringes of the spring and river run to give new, larger glass-bottomed tour boats a greater turning radius.[45] The blasting stirred up sediment that took years to settle. At the same time, the concrete dock that still exists was put in. The National Audubon Society considered these and other "improvements" a travesty, and withdrew its sponsorship of the sanctuary.[46]

The controversy over management at the spring was a prelude to years of legal disputes well described by Tracy Revels. The first case began in 1970, when Wakulla's manager blocked off a stretch of a dirt road that ran through Ball's property. Locals claimed the little-used road had been in public use for over sixty years, but Ball's lawyers argued that closing it had been necessary to prevent pollution, poaching and vandalism. The situation paralleled ongoing arguments in modern-day Gulf County, where a legal dispute flared over closing off local forest roads the St. Joe Company insisted were private. Ball lost the Wakulla case, and the road remained open to the public.

The most famous battle began after Ball strung a fence downstream from the sparkling spring run, limiting public access and triggering controversy over property rights and submerged lands. The fence blocked access to the spring from south of the fence. Ball's supporters, including *Tallahassee Democrat* editor Malcolm Johnson, argued that the fence was vital to protect the springs from trash and ruin by careless visitors. Audubon and the Chamber of Commerce agreed, but fisherman eager for access to the resource, as well as boaters and some environmentalists, were more concerned about Ball's mismanagement of the springs and river than potential for damage from public access.[47]

Despite a series of challenges, most notably by Jack Rudloe, an aquatic specimens collector from nearby Panacea, and Thomas A. Morrill, a writer and former science teacher from Tallahassee, the fence remained.

Ball denied that he planned to further commercialize Wakulla Springs, saying he had no intention of turning Wakulla Springs into a "honky-tonk." However, Ball had at one time considered piping the spring's water to south Florida, according to Braden Ball. The idea withered because "at that time, the economics were against such an effort."[48]

The next dispute over Wakulla Springs related to the cage of Ball's "pet" bear. In 1975, Ball applied to the Army Corps of Engineers for a permit to extend his bear cage thirty-five feet into the Wakulla River for the benefit of the bear.[49] Morrill objected, as did Florida Audubon field representative Charles Lee. Lee wrote to the Corps, arguing that Ball had not developed a comprehensive plan for the future development of Wakulla Springs. (In 2002, Charles Lee was still with the Audubon Society as its lead lobbyist and had assumed a leading role in Florida's environmental politics.) Ball got his permit, but the Edward Ball Wildlife Foundation had to sign a document acknowledging that the placement of the bear cage did not override state ownership of the river and bottomlands.[50]

For the remaining six or seven years of his life, Ball continued to visit Wakulla, counting alligators and feeding his caged bear by hand. After Ball's death, Wakulla and Ball's other holdings were passed along to the Nemours Foundation. After several years, the trustees of the Nemours Foundation, including Jake Belin, realized that Wakulla would continue to operate in the red. Governor Bob Graham proposed that the state buy the nearly 3,000 acres of Wakulla Springs and Nemours was receptive, selling it for $7.15 million in 1985. The sale closed in May 1986, marking the first of the state's purchases of Green Empire land for conservation purposes.

In the fall of 2000, Ed Ball was honored as a "Great Floridian" in a reception at Wakulla Springs. After the ceremony, St. Joe CEO Peter Rummell joked with park manager Sandy Cook, "Too bad this isn't ours anymore."[51] He pondered the whether public-private partnerships might be possible. Perhaps the idea was not impossible, responded Cook, politely but cautiously, noting the state's recent successful acquisition of additional land to expand the buffer between the springs and the rest of Wakulla County, Florida's fastest growing county on a per capita basis. Perhaps in the future, he said. "We're working our way up" toward Wakulla Springs, he said in this good-natured banter.

Ball's High-Flying Finale

Well into his eighties, Ed Ball actively pursued business deals in the United States and abroad, particularly the Middle East. One particularly busy year, 1973, Ball clocked 300,000 miles by air.[52] Ball often traveled with Charter president Raymond Mason aboard the private Gulf Stream jet owned by Charter, the oil and insurance company with which St. Joe had made a corporate meld in 1971.

During these high-flying days of the early 1970s, Ball met with notable and notorious persons, including oil tycoon J. Paul Getty and U.S. financier-later-turned-fugitive Robert Vesco. Ball's associate Gilbert Smith, the jaunty ex-CIA man turned banker, was involved in arranging a meeting between Ball and the court of Iran to discuss business plans, including ideas for real estate development in southern Iran. One meeting in Teheran concerned a joint venture to form an international bank.[53] The ambassador to Iran, former CIA director Richard Helms, also was involved in the discussions.[54]

Also in the 1970s, Charter Oil engaged white-collar criminal Robert Vesco and Billy Carter, the brother of President Jimmy Carter, to negotiate trade deals with Libyan dictator Muammer al-Qaddafi, causing a scandal that came to be known as "Billygate." The scandal occurred during the period when St. Joe and Charter owned substantial shares of each other's stock.

The Iranian Revolution of 1979 dashed Ball's plans for Iranian business developments. By then, Ball had been forced to give up his driver's license, which meant retiring his license plate that read "taxpayer." He could no longer speed along the lightly trafficked Panhandle roads, as he had for decades. He moved to a plush condominium in Jacksonville overlooking the wide St. Johns River. After years of travel by trains, cars, and planes, Ball was finally grounded.

As his health declined, it no longer was a question of if Ball would die, but when. In 1981, he checked into the Ochsner Clinic in New Orleans seeking treatment for an abdominal aneurysm. Besides taxes, the things that most troubled Ball were Communists and death. Although there was not much he could do about the latter, even to the end Ball surrounded himself with anti-Communist allies. The founder of the clinic in New Orleans, Dr. Alton Ochsner, was an expert on tropical medicine but also prominent in right-wing politics. According to Thomas Karnes, author of the book *Tropical Enterprise,* Ochsner was a consultant to the U.S. Air Force on the "medical side of subversive matters"[55] and ran his own foundation to aid Cuban exiles. Ochsner was president of the Information Council of the Americas, a New Orleans propaganda operation that likely did work for the CIA.[56]

Edward Ball died on June 24, 1981, at age ninety-three. After a funeral service in Jacksonville, Ball's body arrived in Wilmington, Delaware, via a four-jet escort. His remains were interred in a multistoried crypt at Nemours alongside those of Alfred and Jessie.

Ed Ball died childless. But he left many legacies—the most obvious of which was the multi-billion-dollar business conglomerate that he had parlayed from Alfred duPont's initial investment of around $40 million in the 1920s. Along the way, Ball had also amassed a personal fortune. He died a millionaire 200 times over. For an old, self-described "farmer," he had managed well, even without a large salary. Most of his $200 million estate went to the Nemours Foundation, as had the estates of Alfred and Jessie. Ball earmarked his fortune for the care of medically needy children in Florida.

To his successor, Jake Belin, Ball bequeathed what might have been his most personal possession—a gold whiskey jigger. Belin handled Ball's elaborate funeral arrangements. He and the other Ball successors were left to decide whether and then how to keep alive the rare bird that the Green Empire was—a business complex with one foot in the mercenary world of Wall Street and another in the world of philanthropy.

⑥ ⑥ ⑥ ⑥ ⑥ ⑥ ⑥ ## A Company in Transition

The status quo is changing, and it will be very hard to turn back.

James Schmitt, financial analyst

AFTER ED BALL'S DEATH in 1981, speculation was rampant that the new guard at St. Joe could not hold together the Green Empire. For more than a decade, the board of directors continued to bicker, and sue, over the A. I. duPont Trust's obligations to charity. They disagreed about whether the Trust should break apart and sell off St. Joe Paper and some, or all, of the other assets under its wide umbrella to raise the cash to fulfill its charitable mission. Meanwhile, analysts and potential buyers pondered the value of the conglomerate's holdings and how to get a piece of the action.

Even within the company, determinations of its value had fluctuated wildly. Ball and the trustees went from valuing the Trust at $1.1 billion in 1979 to $640 million the following year. The business magazine *Florida Trend* conducted independent research and conservatively put the worth of the duPont Trust's holdings at closer to $1.5 billion or more if all the Trust's assets were liquidated—more than twice the value assigned by the trustees.[1]

Especially valuable were the Florida East Coast (FEC) holdings, the treasure that Ed Ball had fought so hard to win and keep. The railway had more than 785 miles of track on its main line from Jacksonville to Miami and its branch line from Ft. Pierce to Lake Harbor.[2] It had minimal debt and highly desirable real estate—roughly 30,000 acres, much of it developable, including half a dozen blocks in downtown Miami. Plus, it served the ports of Miami, Palm Beach, and Port Everglades. FEC's stock price climbed to new highs as speculation mounted that Flagler's old rail line might go up for sale.[3]

The paper mill, at the time in the midst of a $100 million expansion and modernization project that included computerizing its container plants, also drew the attention of rival paper companies. St. Joe Paper ranked fortieth in revenue in the industry, making it a small operation relative to giants like International Paper or Georgia Pacific. But its extensive greenbelt strengthened its standing in the world of forest products; St. Joe ranked as the fourteenth largest owner of timberland.[4]

As the company struggled to generate the cash to pay out to Nemours, phone calls poured in to St. Joe Paper, tendering offers for this or that piece of its holdings. While minority trustees Alfred duPont Dent and William Mills continued to argue for selling off entire business entities to augment the shortfall, Belin, Thornton, and board member Thomas Coldewey stood their ground.

Lawsuits dragged on for several years. Finally, in 1983 the trio of Ed Ball–groomed trustees triumphed. The minority trustees and the states of Florida and Delaware were defeated. The Florida Supreme Court ruled in agreement with Jake Belin that "the company was a better vehicle for long-term investment than a series of paper investments such as stocks and bonds."[5] The surprise ruling allowed the majority trustees to keep the Green Empire together. "The court found that we did [meet our obligations]," Winfred Thornton said in an interview in December 2000. "We had obligated to fund Nemours to perpetuity. You have to make the contributions in a responsible way. The courts accepted our pay-out basis."[6]

The spotlight was now on longtime St. Joe Paper Company president Jake Belin, who was elected to the post of Chairman of the Board of the A. I. duPont Trust after Ball's death. Belin had spent more than four decades watching Ball's long-term plans for asset appreciation unfold. Although he was not yet willing to sell off the prize completely, he was willing to realize profits that would accrue from developing some of the company's most precious land holdings. He began a shift in focus toward real estate that has come to full blossom under the reorganized St. Joe Company.

At one time, company watchers had viewed the Charter Company's Raymond Mason, with whom Ball had jetted around the world in the 1970s, as a successor to Ball. But the acquisitive Jacksonville businessman did not view himself in that role. "I've never been trained to be a trustee of anybody else's assets," he said in September 1981, firmly ruling out a future for himself at the head of St. Joe Paper or the A. I. duPont Trust.[7]

The Charter Company, with which St. Joe had swapped stocks back in the early 1970s, went from being a Fortune 500 company with $5.6 billion in sales in 1983 to Chapter 11 bankruptcy the following year. In 1983, before Charter's finances bottomed out, St. Joe exchanged its Charter stock for treasury stock, gaining $7.7 million in the transaction.[8] By the early 1980s, Charter was dealing with another headache. One of Charter's subsidiaries had earlier contracted with a waste hauler to dispose of spent oil that turned out to contain the hazardous chemical dioxin, creating one of the earliest Superfund sites in the nation at Times Beach, Missouri. Cleanup costs amounted to roughly $200 million.[9]

The corporate overlap between the St. Joe and Charter companies ended just in time to prevent a drag on St. Joe Paper's finances. Cincinnati financier Carl Lindner scooped up the remnants of Charter by buying a controlling interest in the debt-ridden conglomerate.[10] Lindner, an eccentric and powerful deal maker, showed up at the fringes of the St. Joe story at various times, as owner of a Florida Keys resort, the Ocean Reef Club, at least five years after Peter Rummell worked there in the mid-1970s and, during the 1980s, as chairman of Penn Central, the conglomerate that controlled Arvida for decades.

Belin's firm helmsmanship of St. Joe brought continuity to the Green Empire during these bumpy times. Minor differences aside, Belin was as close as you could get to another Ed Ball. Belin had served as a St. Joe director since 1952 and as president of the St. Joe Paper Company from 1968 to 1984. He held the top jobs of CEO and chairman of the board of directors of St. Joe Paper from 1982 to 1991.

Having worked for St. Joe since 1938 at age twenty-four, Belin carried more St. Joe institutional memory than anyone after Ball's death. The lanky Belin was something of a chameleon, at ease in the local cafes of Port St. Joe, speaking on the phone with Florida politicians, or meeting with investment bankers on Wall Street. Belin's passport, too, put on mileage from his visits to Europe and across the globe. "He knew people around the world," said Clay Smallwood, president of St. Joe Timberland.[11]

The number two man at St. Joe after Ball's death was Winfred Thornton, whom Ed Ball hired to run the FEC in 1961 as one of the youngest railroad executives anywhere. Thornton shared Ed Ball's almost total focus on his work, shunning outside diversions. At one time or another, Thorton served as director of almost every company division. He became a director of the St. Joe Paper Company board in 1968. In 1984, he assumed the role of St. Joe Paper Company president, taking over from Belin. Both Thornton and Belin also served as trustees of the A. I. duPont Estate. Sharing the power did not come easy and the two split their oversight. Thornton informally oversaw everything east of the Suwannee, including the FEC interests, and Belin looked over the holdings west of the famed river.

In the late 1980s, Belin briefly looked outside the company for new leadership. He approached Wayne Mixon, then finishing a term as lieutenant governor to Bob Graham, floating the idea that Mixon head up the company under its new real estate development thrust. Mixon, an Ivy League–educated farmer and rancher originally from Alabama, had reservations about taking control of St. Joe as it sought "the highest and best use" for its lands. "I knew full well that I wasn't capable of seeing that job all the way through," he said.[12]

After Ball's death, Belin began to retool the company with a mind to raising cash for Nemours without dipping into principal. In the mid-1980s, St. Joe Paper took two initiatives that were a bold departure from past management. First, St. Joe Paper Company went public, selling 14 percent of its common stock shares in 1986. The Trust retained the other 86 percent. The stock offering meant the company had to disclose more to the public, filing reports with the Securities and Exchange Commission (SEC). Second, the company launched its first forays into real estate development.

The measures made financial sense for St. Joe. For St. Joe Paper Company's early stockholders, though, owning a piece of the company had few obvious advantages. The stock was hard to get (or track, as no one on Wall Street bothered to follow it), expensive (ranging from $8,000 to $15,000 per share from 1985 to 1989) and paid low dividends (for example, $10 per share on profits of $1,152 per share in 1986). For many Floridians, owning a share was better for conversation at cocktail parties than it was for generating returns, at least in the near term. In 1986, there were only 602 stockholders.

St. Joe's Early Real Estate Ventures

Getting into real estate made good sense too. In the 1980s, many developers were struggling with debt and high interest rates. In contrast, St. Joe had a large land inventory and lack of debt. The company reorganized in both 1985 and 1986. In 1985, it created St. Joe Industries as the parent operating company, under which it organized its four main operating industries: forest products, under the newly created St. Joe Forest Products Company; transportation, under Florida East Coast (already reorganized in 1984); the sugar cane farm and refinery under Talisman Sugar; and St. Joe Communications, for its telephone interests.

In 1986, it officially created a real estate division, following action the previous year that identified 81,000 acres as suitable "investment real estate."[13] Two years later, the company raised expectations about performance of this new business division. "The real estate operations are now considered a significant business segment," the company informed stockholders in its 1987 annual report.[14]

St. Joe Paper consolidated its real estate ventures under Southwood Properties, with Jake Belin in charge. Meanwhile, real estate owned by St. Joe's wholly owned subsidiary, Florida East Coast Industries, was placed under the Gran Central Corporation, managed by Winfred Thornton. Consolidation would allow St. Joe to more efficiently plan for "future development, sales and/or leasing of various parcels of property," the company said.[15]

Reflecting on the St. Joe Paper Company's original articles of incorporation filed in Tallahassee in 1936 and amended in 1940, it appears the shift from pines to penthouses, putting greens, and high-end commercial spaces is something long ago anticipated. A decade before Peter Rummell came aboard, the "old" St. Joe was already making inroads into the real estate market. It flexed its corporate muscle to attract buyers to its land, sell conservation land to the state for top dollar, and quash unwelcome growth management provisions. In terms of actually developing real estate, the company then was not as successful as today's St. Joe. Still, its early efforts helped lay the groundwork for today's lucrative projects. And the new St. Joe has benefited from lessons learned by beefing up its managerial skills in precisely the areas that sunk the "old" St. Joe's plans—growth management, marketing, and public relations.

In the 1980s, the real estate ventures of Southwood Properties and Gran Central took on distinctly different characters in keeping with their different bosses. Under Thornton, the pace was restrained and conservative. Gran Central would not start a new commercial building project until the current one was at least 50 percent occupied. By 1989, Gran Central had projects underway in Miami, West Palm Beach, Riviera Beach, and Jacksonville.[16] In time, Thornton seemed to embrace real estate more wholeheartedly, recognizing that building commercial properties is risky mainly when the development requires taking on debt. Jake Belin pursued real estate with a grander approach on the expanses under his command in the Green Empire. Detractors who viewed Belin as a plodder were not well acquainted with his real estate ventures.

In Tallahassee, Southwood Properties turned to real estate with a vengeance. St. Joe proposed a huge residential development to be set on Ed Ball's old

Southwood Farm and environs as the flagship Southwood Properties development. This sidelined project was the progenitor of the SouthWood that is well
under way in the early twenty-first century under Peter Rummell and St. Joe/
Arvida.

The first attempt at Southwood from 1985 to 1989 failed mainly due to excess
and poor public relations. The initial project was nearly three times larger than
the current model, which itself will make up the largest planned development in
northwest Florida to date. The originally proposed Southwood (without the
capitalized "W") was a golf-course community with mainly high-end homes.
Other parcels were also slated for later dense construction. St. Joe Paper tried to
get development approval for the whole project at the outset, so as to avoid restrictions that loomed as a result of new statewide growth management plans
about to go into effect.

Members of the neighboring Grass Roots community challenged Belin and
St. Joe, arguing, among other things, that the project would overwhelm the capacity of the existing roads.[17] When the city of Tallahassee was adamant, too,
that St. Joe provide more low-end housing stock, the company "like spoiled
children, walked away from the table," according to Dorothy Inman-Johnson,
who served as a city commissioner from 1986 to 1994. "We were talking about
$75,000 to $100,000 homes, not housing projects," she explained.[18] That was the
end of the first Southwood project.

"I think you would see at that time, everybody's heels were dug in, and there
was this big divide," St. Joe/Arvida Capital Region president Tim Edmond
reflected from the airy Tallahassee corporate office of St. Joe/Arvida in an interview in 2000. Other contentious issues, besides the project's sheer size, were
storm-water management and protection of the adjacent canopy roads, issues
that were also germane in the new SouthWood.

St. Joe's abrupt departure from the negotiating table was not the company's
final word. Shortly after the breakdown in negotiations, St. Joe clear-cut 200
acres of old-growth longleaf pine on its property there. Longleaf pine forests,
with their propensity to provide habitat for federally endangered red-cockaded
woodpeckers, posed a regulatory complication, whether on forest land or on
land slated for future development. According to several sources, St. Joe took
preemptive measures on its lands during the 1980s to avoid working with endangered species by aggressively harvesting stands of mature longleaf. "The
firm foresaw the threat of protecting old-growth (40–80y [year-old]) forests,
thus doesn't allow its trees to age," one outside analyst wrote in 1995.[19]

Timberland chief Smallwood defended the company's past and present timber practices with regard to red-cockaded woodpeckers. He said in the 1980s,

the company followed the recommended practices of endangered species rules at the time, leaving five-acre blocks around cavity trees where woodpecker colonies were discovered.[20] Scientists have since determined it takes a much larger area of longleaf pines to provide both food and shelter for the birds.

A further postscript to Southwood's first incarnation occurred in 1989 when St. Joe donated 273 acres adjoining Capital Circle, about five miles east of downtown Tallahassee, to the state's Internal Improvement Trust Fund.[21] The land was to be used for the Satellite Office Complex, now called the Capital City Office Complex (CCOC) with room to grow to a projected 2 million square feet by 2112. Belin wrote Republican governor Bob Martinez the very same day that he withdrew plans for the first Southwood in 1989. At the time, state government was outgrowing its office space elsewhere in Tallahassee. The state could have built skyward and closer to the center of Tallahassee, which would have helped enliven the downtown. Or, it could sprawl out and take advantage of St. Joe's offer of free land in what was then cow pasture. Two other large landowners also were offering parcels for the new state office complex. St. Joe's Southwood land was not considered the favorite at the time, yet it prevailed.

"It was quite a battle," recalled Tallahassee City Commissioner Debbie Lightsey. "We almost had enough votes to kill the Capital City Office Complex. But the legislature gets you. We have so many 800-pound gorillas here in Tallahassee. Members of the legislature wanted the Office Complex."[22] Local government feared reprisals from the legislature if they nixed the new government offices at Southwood. So cow pasture beat out downtown and other possible sites with local government having little say-so in the matter. The state committed to invest $5 million in infrastructure at the site within five years and allowed the St. Joe Company to use any excess capacity in storm-water storage facilities constructed by the state.[23]

The land donation was a foresighted act on the part of St. Joe, under the guidance of Jake Belin. The relocation of government offices made St. Joe's surrounding land, now home to the new and improved SouthWood, that much more valuable for future development. In the interim between the Southwood proposals, the state also sunk $11 million into improving roads[24] to accommodate the new government office buildings. Those improvements now benefit the SouthWood development, although remaining traffic woes into 2002 still pointed to the likelihood of more major road projects in the future.

Some saw the land donation as only one part of a well-thought-out strategy that allowed the state and St. Joe to mutually benefit. At the same time St. Joe made its land donation, Tallahassee annexed the new state property and much of Southwood. The city also adopted changes to its comprehensive plan in accordance with a new "Southeast Sector Study," which according to one analysis, "merged St. Joe's development ambitions for Southwood into the city and county's comprehensive plan, directly melding private business strategy with public policy."[25] The Southeast Sector Study indirectly helped St. Joe by suggesting major city spending in that quadrant of the city.

In June 1998, St. Joe decided it wanted some of its donated Tallahassee land back, and the Florida Cabinet tentatively approved a two-for-one land swap that gave St. Joe back seventy-seven acres just north of the new state office complex (still undeveloped) in exchange for 153 other acres of other St. Joe land nearby on two separate parcels.[26] However, before signing the warranty deed six months later, St. Joe added a further stipulation: if the state did not begin construction on an 80,000-square-foot office building or spend at least $2 million on development activities by 2003 on the first parcel (and the other by 2008), the land would revert to St. Joe. The company would instead give the state land at another unspecified location.[27] Governor Chiles and his cabinet approved the modified agreement drawn up by St. Joe's top counsel Robert Rhodes, in December 1998, a month before Jeb Bush assumed office.

By 2003, with SouthWood a reality, the swapped land near the community's commercial town center had increased in value considerably. As the clock had ticked toward the deadline for the reversion clause to take effect, the state sought intensified development rights for the tract, but without a clear rationale for new state construction. The push for "upzoning" seemed contrary to the state government downsizing initiatives in effect at the time.

As the deadline approached, the legal status of the tract remained an enigma, at least to the public. At a Tallahassee planning commission meeting in November 2002 less than two months before the deadline, a consultant stated that he thought St. Joe actually had waived its right to the reversion clause. The consultant, Rick Harcrow, was advising the state Department of Management Services (DMS), the agency that supervised state office buildings under DMS secretary Cynthia Henderson. (Harcrow was an engineering consultant with the same Tampa law firm where Cynthia Henderson had been a partner before she took a job with the Jeb Bush administration.) Neither Henderson nor other officials at DMS responded to repeated questions in 2001 about the status of these parcels, or why the state agreed to the additional stipulation that put a time line on the state's use of the land, a limiting clause not originally present.

In early 2003, St. Joe was pressuring the state to develop the site and granted the state an extension until midyear before it would exercise its right to reclaim the land. Regardless of the ownership issues, St. Joe was anxious to have the parcel developed to help support its fledgling retail center at SouthWood.

Unlocking the Beachfront

As early as 1981, Jake Belin revealed a desire to develop the Topsail Hill area in south Walton County into "the playground of America," with condos, shopping centers, and recreation areas.[28] However, the need to produce cash for Nemours prompted him to put the land up for sale instead. Well-known developers including Arvida/Disney (where Peter Rummell worked at the time) took a look at the gorgeous land about twelve miles east of Destin but balked at the price and remoteness. Instead, a development group from Texas emerged seemingly from nowhere in 1985 and offered to pay $200 million for 20,850 acres of St. Joe's beach and forest, with Topsail Hill its focal point. At nearly $10,000 per acre, it was the priciest deal for raw land to that date in Florida.[29] The project's backers announced plans even more grandiose than Belin's concept, including a regional airport, theme park, and industrial park along with housing and golf courses.

But the joint venture backing the deal failed to make payment on its loans, and the colossal deal fell apart. The buyers had arranged a bizarre series of transactions to secure loans from two savings and loan institutions (S&Ls) that subsequently failed in part or whole because of Topsail. The S&Ls' poorly secured loans for Topsail ended up costing taxpayers over $100 million in the form of a federal bail-out.

The transaction that later cost U.S. taxpayers so dearly had a healthy effect on St. Joe's flagging balance sheet. Thanks to $67.5 million that had been handed over at closing in June of 1986, plus many millions more in interest payments, St. Joe took in an estimated $86 million, according to one analysis.[30] In fact, St. Joe's net income in 1986 increased 129 percent over the previous year, in spite of losses in the forest products business.[31]

After the foreclosure, St. Joe also regained possession of portions of prime beachfront land included in the deal, which it had itself financed separately for the would-be buyers. St. Joe formally repurchased about 600 acres of the 1,700-acre Topsail tract, as well as other large and valuable tracts farther east that it has since developed as The Retreat, WaterColor, and WaterSound.

After the collapse of the deal, a onetime spread of undeveloped land that had spanned six miles of pristine beachfront became a patchwork quilt–like array of more than twenty-five parcels. Besides St. Joe, land owners now included investor groups, S&Ls in Texas and Pennsylvania that had financed the sale and others that began investing later, and eventually the federal government, in the form of the Resolution Trust Corporation (RTC), the organization set up to bail out failed S&Ls. Speculative intentions on the part of investors seemed evident in the fact that parcels had been subdivided and resold even before the 1986 closing between St. Joe and the joint venture. In foreclosure suits over these parcels, the FBI documented a scheme by which investors subdivided land while keeping options to repurchase, with an intent "to rejoin parcels in one ownership for sale to the state of Florida."[32]

Indeed, the state of Florida was keenly interested in obtaining as much ecologically valuable south Walton land as possible for preservation. In 1990, the state arranged a purchase of more than 600 acres of St. Joe's reclaimed Topsail land, but the purchase failed after a state official questioned appraisal prices. Two years later, the state finally gained a toehold on Topsail land, purchasing a twenty-three-acre tract under threat of development.

Then, on May 19, 1992, the state and The Nature Conservancy bid $20 million to purchase 305 acres of foreclosed Topsail Hill land—with 18,000 acres of forest (present-day Point Washington Forest) thrown in as well. The RTC had lumped the foreclosed properties together in preparation for an auction at the Walton County courthouse. Mere hours before the auction began, the governor and cabinet approved the purchase, waiving the requirement for a survey and appraisal in order to get in its bid.[33]

At the heart of the delicate deal was The Nature Conservancy's ace negotiator, George Willson, who had worked furiously to pull it off. (Eight years later, Willson would join the St. Joe Company to broker sales of St. Joe land for conservation purposes.) Conservationists were ecstatic, but others were upset, not so much about the Topsail land, but about the large Point Washington tract that went with it. Governor Chiles, while supporting the purchase, expressed some reservations. "Even if we buy this, I'm not sure we ought not to sell some of it," he said.[34] This sense that the state had overstepped its conservation mandate set the stage for the state-sponsored visioning effort described in chapter 1.

For several years after its winning bid for the foreclosed Topsail and Point Washington land, and in fact into the present, the state continued trying to piece together additional parcels. All the while, the state failed to reach an agreement with St. Joe for its remaining 600 acres at Topsail Hill. In July of 1994, the state took drastic action, condemning 596 acres of the land as crucial to the state's preservation effort at Topsail Hill. St. Joe's Winfred Thornton vowed to challenge the state's action.

St. Joe lawyers from Miami to Jacksonville tackled the problem. They ended up having a major role to play in setting the terms of St. Joe's further development in south Walton County. In December 1995, the state and St. Joe settled their case out of court. The state agreed to pay $84 million for the disputed 600 acres, a sum that was $39 million above the price that state officials had nixed five years earlier. In addition, a consent agreement accompanying the settlement gave St. Joe special treatment in meeting Walton County's comprehensive plan requirements for wetlands impacts and other environmental and recreation considerations. Soon afterward, the state paid St. Joe another $14 million for another south Walton tract, Deer Lake.

Counting unknown profits from sales of smaller parcels after the collapse of the Topsail deal, the company most likely attained or exceeded the $200 million sales price it set back in 1985.

As for the actions of the buyers in the 1986 sale, a Pensacola jury in 1992 convicted nine defendants on various fraud and conspiracy charges related to the Topsail Hill transactions. Among them was William Michael Adkinson, a Panhandle native turned Texas developer who had spearheaded the initial development. In 1998, however, the 11th U.S. Circuit Court of Appeals in Atlanta overturned all convictions, citing technical mistakes that denied defendants a fair trial. The court said prosecutors did not succeed in proving that a conspiracy existed.[35] Adkinson went on to form an array of companies in Florida, including several prominent in Walton County.[36]

Revelations from the trial and in the press showed connections between certain figures in the doomed Topsail purchase and the CIA, Middle East, and offshore banks associated with drug-money laundering. Exhaustive investigations by a federal regulator traced $7 million from a real estate commission paid at closing to a company based on the Isle of Jersey (the same offshore banking haven where Ed Ball and Raymond Mason once owned a hotel), and from there to various points, including a Swiss bank and back to private accounts in the United States.[37] A Houston real estate agent who sent a large sum overseas after the closing told the *Tallahassee Democrat* that the money was earmarked for payment of a debt to a Middle Eastern investor but did not divulge any specifics.[38] In addition, the Miami attorney who incorporated the investment group that signed the original option on Topsail was convicted of laundering cocaine money in 1989.[39] These and other unusual circumstances prompted former *Houston Post* reporter and author Pete Brewton to draw parallels between Topsail Hill and another failed real estate deal in Texas that pumped money from failed S&Ls into covert CIA operations.[40] However, Brewton's investigation into Topsail failed to turn up hard evidence that bank loans were diverted for illicit purposes.

Neither company officials nor the company was ever implicated in investigations. St. Joe officials said they had been given false representations from their buyers.

The long and twisted Topsail Hill saga generated controversies that continue to this day. Meanwhile, a much smaller deal in Bay County followed a similar course. The property involved was another beachfront beauty, with rolling sand dunes and interior pine forests interspersed with wet areas containing marsh grass and sloughs, smack up against the 17,000 acres of conservation land buffering Tyndall Air Force Base.

In early 1986, St. Joe signed over a special deed to 1,000 acres of land near Mexico Beach to a Bay County man who had other businesses related to fishing and development. The sales price was $20 million or an average of $20,000 per acre, with $15 million of that being financed by a promissory note to the buyer, G. M. "Mike" Hobbs. The agreement called for Hobbs to pay back the $15 million in five annual installments, at which time St. Joe would release to him gulf-front footage.[41] After Hobbs was unable to meet the payment schedule for a 700-acre portion of the land, St. Joe foreclosed on the land. Attorneys handling the foreclosure for St. Joe were from the law firm of high-powered Florida senator Dempsey Barron, still in office at the time, a firm that into the twenty-first century continued to do legal work for St. Joe.

The property St. Joe regained included the area disputed in a St. Joe–Bay County greenbelt lawsuit, which the company lost at the Florida Supreme Court in 1995 after winning an initially favorable ruling from the same judge who had presided over the foreclosure case. St. Joe had sought the greenbelt designation even after it had sold the land to Hobbs for development. Then, in 1996 and 1997, the company again sought the greenbelt designation. To further its claims, the company logged and "roller-chopped" the area except for a strip along the well-traveled U.S. 98, and then attempted to plant seedlings that never quite took hold. Photographs in the Bay County property appraiser's office document the destruction that the forestry operations wreaked on the environmentally sensitive area, which had only a few years earlier been under consideration for purchase under the state's land conservation program. By early 2002, St. Joe was floating development plans for the tract.

Other, more modest St. Joe projects begun under Southwood Properties, projects that did come to fruition, included sale of lots at The Retreat and other beachfront locations in south Walton; Summerwood, in Panama City Beach; and The Woods subdivision in Panama City. Among all the Panhandle counties, Bay County was singled out as the one with the most acreage for future development.

Wringing More From the Assets

In the spring of 1990, St. Joe offered more stock for sale. This time, St. Joe Paper sold more than five million shares at $45.72 a share, thereby raising $225 million.[42] If the initial stock offering in 1986 had cracked the door, this one set St. Joe on an irreversible course of change. This stock sale reduced the Trust's share of St. Joe from 86 to 70 percent.

Investors who purchased large chunks of the stock as a play for the company's assets were unwilling to sit idly by and settle for paltry dividends of .3 percent of the share price, which itself grew at only one-fourth the rate of its industry peers. Winfred Thornton, in his role as president of St. Joe Paper, was increasingly finding himself besieged by disgruntled stockholders.

Thornton bore the brunt of their criticism, being viewed as a tortoise to the up-and-coming hares. "Our goal is to build assets," Thornton told the *Wall Street Journal* in a 1994 front-page story, echoing the familiar dictum of the Ed Ball school of long-term investing. "We have a commitment in perpetuity. Those who say the job of St. Joe is to generate a lot of cash are misled."[43]

By the early 1990s, St. Joe Paper was limping along like a giant with shin splints. A downward spiral in liner-board prices contributed to a loss in 1993 of nearly $20 million. As dividends remained minuscule, St. Joe's leadership went to court again. This time, Belin shocked industry onlookers by suing his coworker Thornton. Belin charged that Florida East Coast and St. Joe Paper were unable to generate enough income for the Trust to meet the 3 percent requirement for contributions to Nemours. He advocated revising the trust structure as laid out in Alfred duPont's will to add three more members who would give new perspective and managerial help.

Under pressure from the state to mediate, Belin and Thornton settled in October 1994, each being allowed to pick a new A. I. duPont trustee, with the third trustee coming from a list drawn up by the state attorney's office. The settlement hiked the trustees' pay from $5,000 to $54,000 annually.[44] Also in 1994, St. Joe Paper expanded its board of directors to gain fresh management perspective from outside the company.

One of the new A. I. duPont trustees was Herbert Peyton, owner of Gate Petroleum and one of Jacksonville's top real estate developers. Peyton counted among his prizes the exclusive Ponte Vedra Club, along with the former duPont estate, Epping Forest, which he purchased from a financially ailing Raymond Mason. Peyton's financially aggressive ways were shared by another colorful money whiz, James "Jim" Dahl, who bought a large amount of St. Joe stock after locating in Jacksonville in 1991.

Dahl acquired national notoriety for his involvement with junk bond king Michael Milken. Dahl was one of Milken's top salesmen at the Beverly Hills, California company Drexel Burnham Lambert, which in the 1980s specialized in junk bonds—securities that pay high interest rates because they are issued on companies with low bond ratings. Drexel Burnham was involved with brokering numerous hostile takeovers and had involvement with failed savings and loan establishments that cost American taxpayers billions.[45] Milken was convicted of securities fraud. Dahl, however, received immunity from prosecution in exchange for his testimony.

Dahl retained his securities license and a hedge fund estimated to be worth $50 million.[46] He returned to his native state of Florida, settling in Jacksonville. There, he cofounded an investment firm in 1992, Rock Creek Capital.

According to Dahl, several factors piqued his interest in the St. Joe Paper Company. For one, Dahl appreciated the Green Empire's land, which he had admired since attending Florida State University, where he earned an MBA. The south Florida native bought a plantation in the rolling hills north of Tallahassee in 1988 and began looking for more land. In the year 2000, he owned around 10,000 acres in the Panhandle, including a 2,900-acre former plantation in northern Leon County and another 2,000-acre spread in Madison County. Dahl also owned property in Escambia County on which he and a business partner made plans to locate a hazardous waste facility.[47] Those plans never reached fruition.

"I really got interested in forestry and wildlife management and started adding to my holdings," Dahl said. "Every time that I looked at a tract I saw it was owned by St. Joe." Thus, Dahl familiarized himself with St. Joe's vast and valuable holdings. The Panhandle beaches especially impressed him. "I visited Topsail Hill, [and] became convinced that it was the last frontier," he recalled.[48]

The frontier he saw was financial as well as literal, the animated Dahl explained in a telephone interview. "If you go back to [Ron] Perelman or other venture capitalists . . . they realized they could buy raw material directly, or invest in a company that already owned the material. In the case of St. Joe, an acre of pine forest that cost $1,000 could be indirectly purchased for about $300 of St. Joe stock."[49]

By the mid-1990s, Dahl owned enough stock in St. Joe Paper and FECI— Florida East Coast Industries consisting of the railroad, as well as trucking and real estate divisions—to begin pressuring St. Joe and FECI executives and directors to wring more from their assets. After seventeen years in New York and Beverly Hills cutting highly leveraged deals, Dahl could not believe the ultra-conservative management style of Winfred Thornton, whom he said ran the Trust and the subsidiaries as if Ball and Alfred duPont were still alive.

Some company officials feared that Dahl was attempting a hostile takeover using his extensive financial connections. Dahl responded that he was not interested in engineering a buyout of St. Joe—that he was merely demonstrating his rights as a shareholder.[50] But the takeover jitters were understandable. After all, Dahl's old employer Drexel Burnham had brokered deals for the likes of T. Boone Pickens, Saul Steinberg (who attempted to buy Disney), the notorious Charles Keating, and Ronald Perelman. Drexel Burnham also worked with several high-profile businessmen who at some point had business dealings with either St. Joe or Arvida. These clients were Carl Lindner Jr., with his past ties to both Charter and Arvida; Ted Turner, who paid St. Joe $11 million for a north Florida property in 1999; and Roger Stone, CEO of Stone Container and a partner in the now-bankrupt Florida Coast Paper limited liability corporation that ended up buying St. Joe's pulp mill.

Dahl and others wanted higher dividends, but the Trust's obligations to charity were an issue too. In Dahl's view, St. Joe's management was shirking its fiduciary responsibility by earning only 5 percent return on equity rather than the 15 percent common to similar businesses. The consequences to Nemours hit close to home after Dahl observed his wife, Georgia, working doggedly to raise funds for Nemours. She and other volunteers toiled in the Dahls' garage to get ready for an antique sale to benefit Nemours. "Here were these women working their butts off until 2 a.m. in my garage . . . and here was this Trust not earning enough to maintain its tax-free status," Dahl said.[51] He told St. Joe president Thornton, "If the doctors at Nemours knew how much money you were stealing from them, they would cry."[52]

Dahl, who calls himself an "in-your-face" kind of guy, informed Thornton that he was not going away. But Thornton was essentially reporting to himself by serving in top positions at both the A. I. duPont Trust and St. Joe Paper. It took outsiders such as Dahl and newly appointed board members to shake the tree of what Dahl called its "low hanging fruit" to generate profits.[53]

In the mid-1990s, several investor groups assessed the company's holdings and opportunities. In the summer of 1994, an investment advisor from the old and politically well-connected Wall Street investment firm of Dillon Read and Company presented a study to St. Joe's board of directors during a train ride on the Florida East Coast railroad. The study recommended the immediate sale of the paper mill and leasing of St. Joe's roughly one million acres of timberland. "We were kind of shocked," one company director recalled.[54]

In 1995, another study gave similar recommendations to St. Joe about decoupling itself from its industrial past. James Schmitt, one of Dahl's contemporaries in California and himself a St. Joe stockholder, headed up a painstaking two-year study that analyzed the holdings of Florida East Coast Industries and St. Joe Paper. Schmitt's company, WestCountry Financial, determined that the conglomerate should move toward "an investment rather than operating structure." Among the first steps suggested were selling the paper mill, as well as putting up for sale cutting rights on a quarter-million acres.[55] WestCountry also urged "market separation" between St. Joe Paper and its subsidiary FECI—advice that St. Joe ultimately followed with its "spin-off" of FECI in year 2000 after first attempting to acquire it.

The WestCountry study divided St. Joe's history into four stages: the Formative Era under Alfred duPont; the Wealth Building Era of the Ed Ball years, followed by what WestCountry called the Supervisory Era after Ball's death. The final era was titled Enlightenment, during which the duPont-created empire would become an investment holding company.[56] The report writers believed Jake Belin was already moving the company toward "Enlightenment."

Pausing after the May 2000 St. Joe annual meeting to grant a brief interview, a gaunt but dignified Jake Belin just several weeks before his death displayed a keen business sense that fully embraced the latest stage in the company's mode of business. The company's new emphasis should be "to get income and reinvest it, and become a reinvestment trust, spread the risk over diverse investment markets—stock market, technology, fixed income securities," he said.[57]

Stoked by the urging of new outside directors and the insights of investment analysts, the board at St. Joe Paper began taking decisive steps to cash in. In 1995, the directors unanimously agreed to put the Port St. Joe paper mill up for sale. Even Winfred Thornton, who as recently as six months before its sale had talked of pumping $200 million into further improvements to the mill, voted with the others after arm twisting by Dahl and others.[58]

The Sell-Off to a Limited Liability Corporation

The decision to sell the mill business was a managerial watershed, stripping away the very heart and soul of the old St. Joe Paper Company. Stockholders approved the deal in the spring of 1996, following the endorsement of the sale by the directors of the A. I. duPont Trust, which as holder of 70 percent of the common stock carried the real weight in the decision.

When St. Joe began the process of finding a buyer for its mill and box plants, several candidates had hovered in the background. Workers were surprised when a newborn partnership of Florida Coast Paper (FCP) emerged victorious late in 1995. FCP was a joint limited-liability partnership of the Stone Container Corporation of Chicago and the Four M Corporation of Valhalla, New York, the parent of Box USA. Millionaire Dennis Mehiel, CEO and president of Four M and Box USA, as well as the more well-known Sweetheart Cup brand, had formed a business alliance with Roger W. Stone.

St. Joe and FCP closed the deal on May 30, 1996, agreeing on a purchase price of approximately $334 million for the mill and container plants.[59] Through their FCP partnership, Stone and Four M formally acquired the mill for its strategic location and to meet some of the linerboard requirements of their respective corrugated container facilities, many of which are located in the Southeast. Mehiel coveted St. Joe Container Corporation's sixteen box plants, whereas Stone was interested mainly in the pulp mill. Mehiel's final acquisition of St. Joe's container businesses more than doubled the size of his company.

Many considered the purchase price to be fire-sale level, with the mill and box plants selling close to $200 million less than analysts expected in the last quarter of 1995. Note holders backing the complex and highly leveraged sale put up $165 million in high-interest bonds issued by an eclectic group of financiers. The group included foreign and domestic investors, among them a Swiss investment firm, the United Bank of Kuwait, and Lehman Brothers.[60] Michael Ainslie, who joined St. Joe's board of directors in 2000, at the time of the sale and into 2002 served on the Lehman Brothers board of directors, although he did not consistently include mention of his Lehman directorship in information he provided to St. Joe for its annual proxy filings with the SEC.[61]

The FCP partners had business connections that predated their purchase of the St. Joe mill. Historically, Stone Container was one of Box USA's principal suppliers of raw materials. Stone also had past dealings with California broker Michael Milken, Jim Dahl's former boss. In the 1980s, Roger Stone and his chief financial officer, Arnold Brookstone, had entered the world of leveraged buyouts to expand the company with the help of banks and Michael Milken. In so doing, they ran up considerable debt.[62]

In 1993, when Milken's former business associate, Jim Dahl, and Alfred I. duPont trustee Herbert Peyton were pushing for the sale of the paper and box plants, Stone Container began what the Federal Trade Commission (FTC) would later characterize as an attempt to "orchestrate an industry-wide price increase, in violation of federal antitrust laws."[63] Stone contacted competing companies to determine which had excessive inventory, then purchased some of that supply from his competitors.

Documents from the FTC reveal that Stone made known its desire for taking mill downtime and reducing industry-wide inventories in the belief that so doing would bring about a rise in linerboard prices. The FTC argued that Stone thereby invited its competitors to participate in an orchestrated price increase.

Roger Stone contested the FTC's conclusions, and pointed out how the company's strategy had helped revive the box industry in the fall of 1993. Four of the five FTC commissioners concluded that Stone manipulated supply conditions to create a coordinated price hike. The one dissenting commissioner found no "sinister" aspects of Stone's actions, many of which he called legitimate business decisions. The four-to-one vote resulted in Stone entering into an agreement in February 1998 to settle the charges, neither admitting nor denying guilt.[64]

St. Joe was not named in the SEC action. But Stone and St. Joe had gotten together to discuss pricing of their products before, as a 1978 grand jury determined after investigating possible collusion in the corrugated container industry over the period 1960 to 1974. The grand jury returned price-fixing indictments against fourteen of the defendants, including St. Joe Paper Company and Stone Container.[65]

At the time of the Port St. Joe mill purchase, there was a hopeful upward blip in the global market for corrugated paper, an industry that generated revenue of almost $20 billion in 1995.[66] But the FCP partners agreed to purchase linerboard from their FCP mill in Port St. Joe for $25 less per ton than market rates published in *Pulp and Paper Week*,[67] making it more difficult for the mill to show a profit.

Florida Coast stated in its SEC filing that it thought it could increase both quality and productivity and therefore profitability at the plant. Its strategy included increasing linerboard production through technology upgrades and reducing the frequency of changeovers from one grade to another and thereby decreasing machine downtime.

The workers who survived the transition from St. Joe to FCP, however, recalled that the management seemed more intent on experimenting than on streamlining. Mill workers spoke proudly of their award-winning product— glossy white paper that lined cardboard boxes—and were dismayed at the direction of the FCP management in making frequent process changes that workers interpreted as experimentation. "It went beyond careless," said laid-off millworker Duke Jones. "They were trying hard to produce an inferior product. . . . Moves were made to ensure there wouldn't be a profit."[68]

A former operator at the bleach plant also said that when new management came in they did "a lot of strange things" like changing paper stock in the middle of a shift and virtually ruining 60 to 100 tons of bleached stock at once.[69] Longtime mill superintendent Ferrel Allen, who survived the transition from St. Joe Paper to Florida Coast also made a curious observation: "Stone, for whatever reason, decided to reduce our mottled white [linerboard] production making us less competitive on the open market."[70] FCP partner Four M Corporation/Box USA itself discussed in a 1996 SEC filing the increased demand for bleached linerboard, noting that mottled white containers generally sold "at a premium" over unbleached kraft.[71]

When FCP bought the mill at Port St. Joe, one former worker observed that it was as though they had bought the stomach of a beast and little else.[72] They did not acquire the land to supply it with raw material; rather, the fledgling limited liability corporation arranged wood fiber supply agreements with St. Joe's forestry division.

St. Joe gained nearly $50 million on the sale of the linerboard mill and box plants, plus several million dollars more from the sale of St. Joe Communications.[73] Rather than pay tax on the earnings, St. Joe took advantage of a generous loophole in the U.S. tax code, the so-called partial liquidation provision. That clause allowed companies to distribute proceeds to shareholders from sales of discrete parts or subsidiaries in the form of a special dividend. Shareholders then paid capital gains tax of 28 percent versus the normal income or dividend rate of nearly 40 percent.[74] At the time of the sale, the Alfred I. duPont Trust owned 70 percent of the shares in the St. Joe Company. The Trust, though not technically tax-exempt, was grandfathered to qualify for an exemption since "100 percent of its earnings" supported a tax-exempt 501(C)(3) nonprofit organization in the form of the Nemours Foundation.[75] So it is possible the Trust did not pay even the reduced capital gains tax.

Almost immediately after the sale of the mill, the bottom dropped out of the global paper market, owing mainly to the Asian financial crisis. In the first quarter of 1996, the mill experienced a continued decline in the prices for its products as a result of drops in demand. FCP shut down the mill for several weeks in January, April, and May 1996 for maintenance and to decrease excess inventory. Global paper prices continued to stay low. In 1997, the mill remained closed from April through September and suffered losses and downtime until declaring bankruptcy in 1999.

Ownership of the Florida Coast joint venture changed in 1998, when the Irish-based forest products company Smurfit purchased Stone Container, creating Smurfit-Stone. Roger Stone resigned from his multinational company in March 1999 and four months later bought out Four M subsidiary Box USA with a group of investors. Box USA had purchased St. Joe's container division and had a small interest in the mill.

"It was stupid," Jim Dahl said of Stone's takeover of St. Joe's pulp business. "People do that all the time. . . . It's what happens in the paper industry because of the cyclicality of the business. Potentially he could have made it work by owning that mill and limiting production and [addressing] oversupply and pricing. . . . Stone always has been a highly leveraged company. In this case he [Roger Stone] made a bad buy."[76]

Raid on Rummell

With its drive to unload unprofitable business segments underway, the next step was finding new leadership at the top to keep the ball rolling. At the request of Jim Dahl, St. Joe's board of directors interviewed executive Albert J. Dunlap, "a turnaround specialist." St. Joe and "Chainsaw Al," as he has widely been called, apparently were not a good fit, and in June of 1996, Dunlap left to head the ailing Sunbeam Corporation. According to St. Joe spokesman Jerry Ray, St. Joe came very close to hiring him. Dunlap and other officers of Sunbeam later allegedly engaged in a fraudulent scheme to create the illusion of a successful restructuring and Sunbeam filed for bankruptcy.[77]

Meanwhile, the quest to remedy what Dahl called a "very sleepy" management team ended when the St. Joe directors hired Peter Rummell (at the time president of the Disney Development Company) in early 1997.[78]

Dahl, who said in 2001 that he had since reduced his stake in St. Joe, was satisfied with the changes taking place at the company in the late 1990s. "They've always had the assets but not the management," he told business reporter John Finotti from the *Florida Times-Union* in 1997. "Now they have the assets and the management. The best is yet to come."[79] The Green Empire was well on its way to becoming a financial as well as a geographical empire.

The Making of a Real Estate Powerhouse

Activity breeds activity.
Peter Rummell, May 2000

THE ARRIVAL OF former top Disney "imagineer" Peter Rummell as CEO cemented St. Joe's commitment to a total makeover. After taking the job in January 1997, Rummell began to appease restless stockholders by leading the company through a series of fast-paced changes. The formerly stodgy company acquired controlling interests of other companies and formed new partnerships en route to becoming the premier real estate conglomerate in the state. Keeping track of the acquisitions and developments was like trying to train binoculars on a hummingbird.

Under Rummell, the corporate behemoth began acquiring a new personality—sophisticated, forward-looking, capable of dreaming in color. First and foremost, it was now a company focused on real estate instead of smokestacks. Given its new focus, St. Joe displayed a newfound consciousness of consumers and image.

One of Rummell's first steps was to change the company name from the short-lived "St. Joe Corporation," the name that existed briefly before Rummell's arrival, to "St. Joe Company," "a friendlier, less industrial name," in his opinion.[1] At one point, company leadership considered the symbolic benefits of breaking completely from the "St. Joe" name. Rather than altogether ditch the history embodied in "St. Joe," they settled for minor adjustments and sleek new graphics. Along with the new name came a symbol on the New York Stock Exchange ("joe") and a stylized bluebird logo.

Rummell aggressively sought the talent needed to help him retool St. Joe. He reported to stockholders that recruitment was much easier than he had expected. High-caliber professionals apparently shared Rummell's view that St. Joe offered a wide vista of personal and corporate opportunity. Rummell himself spoke of "endless" opportunities ahead.[2] Rummell added in-house talent from organizations as diverse as the Disney Company, Harrah's, and The Nature Conservancy, although the pool of executives lacked much racial, ethnic, and gender diversity.

Besides the lure of personal and corporate opportunity for growth, new executives had additional incentives in the form of good salaries and stock options. Rummell's own wages reflected the new willingness to reward top management. Whereas Winfred Thornton had made $160,000 a year as St. Joe president as recently as 1994,[3] Rummell's base wages in 1999 were $659,486, plus a bonus of $775,000. In 1997, Rummell received options on more than four million St. Joe shares estimated to be worth $123 million when they expire in 2007.[4]

No sooner were bluebirds flying than St. Joe began acquiring talent in another way—by acquiring partial or controlling interest in several of Florida's leading real estate firms, notably Boca Raton–based Arvida in November 1997, Miami's Codina the next month (with Jeb Bush still on board as consultant to Codina), and Orlando's Commercial Net Realty (CNL) around the same time. The acquisitions made St. Joe an instant Florida real estate powerhouse.

Rummell demonstrated that in the new St. Joe management was as important as assets and that the sixty-year-old company could move with agility. By 1999, a fold-out "pipeline" in the company's annual report listed dozens of residential and commercial real estate projects.

Rummell identified his two overarching goals: "to create great places and to make extraordinary returns for the shareholders."[5] He played to a demanding audience. Stockholders and directors who had agitated for change wanted results in the form of improved earnings and a higher stock price. Rummell and other top employees had extra incentives to grow company wealth—at least in the near term—by virtue of their own generous stock options.

The company set a goal of 20 percent annual growth in earnings.[6] The stock market smiled on Rummell's early moves at St. Joe; the stock price marched up to $36 before tapering off to hover in the low 30s by the summer of 2003. In December 1997, St. Joe declared a three-for-one stock split that benefited existing shareholders. The company also added to the available "joe" stock by putting up a public offering of 4 million common shares held by the A. I. duPont Trust.[7]

Earnings would lag somewhat as St. Joe launched profitable new ventures and continued to shed less profitable lines of business. In the restless Wall Street world of instant stock quotes and quarterly earnings reports, Rummell faced pressure to produce early results. He cautioned stockholders that eagerness for results must be balanced with patience. "I think speed is very important. . . . At the same time, we also have some fabulous assets that will take several years to grow," he wrote stockholders in 1997's annual report.[8]

The view from the top—in Rummell's case, an executive suite in Jacksonville overlooking the St. Johns River—was exhilarating. Even after years of lackluster performance, the company was flush with $500 million in cash and a market capitalization of more than $2 billion, with no debt. Then there were the million acres of the Green Empire, an unfathomable expanse for most real estate developers. Still, some analysts doubted St. Joe's ability to sell the backwoodsy Florida Panhandle to high-end buyers. One business analyst pointed out that more than a third of the company's value was in its land, an asset not easily liquified.

An immediate challenge was that of modernizing the company. When Rummell first came aboard, company headquarters was barely into the computer age, quite a warp back in time from the cutting-edge Disney Company. In fact, Rummell's first glance at the company's holdings were by way of an aging Esso map.[9] Corporate headquarters soon sprouted computers and a state-of-the-art studio where brainstorming sessions took place. Speaking in an interview from his spacious office in September 2000, Rummell said things had changed drastically: "I can take you to a computer screen that can bring up every acre of our million acres. Every acre is now mapped, logged, digitized; we can manipulate it."[10]

Florida's Number One Place Maker

When St. Joe approached Rummell in the mid-1990s, the company and the executive may have been the answer to each other's prayers. At Disney, Rummell was chairman of the division overseeing creative design, research and development, and real estate. While wearing his hat as president of Disney Design and Development, Rummell oversaw development of the new town of Celebration on Disney land. In a 1998 interview, Rummell indicated that he was a "real estate man" who may have not felt completely in his element with the amusement park aspect of his Disney position, even though he had a strong relationship with Disney head Michael Eisner.[11] St. Joe offered real estate opportunities that exceeded even Disney's, and almost carte blanche to do with it as he saw fit—provided it made money.

"The fact is, I came with a mandate," Rummell recalled:

The company went through its catharsis in the early 1990s, trying to decide what they wanted to be, and it was clear that paper wasn't the future, that sugar wasn't the future. They didn't think the railroad was the future. Everybody . . . thought that the million acres was where the future would be as opposed to these old kind of old smokestack industries.

So they went looking for somebody who understood the real estate industry. That's how they found me. So we got rid of the people who understand sugar and railroads and paper and brought in a group of people who understand development. It was a metamorphosis, not better or worse, we just changed stripes, and I think brought some sophisticated management practices along the way.[12]

Rummell was clearly in his element at the helm of St. Joe, where he could apply more than a quarter century of experience from some of the country's leading real estate developers to a vast new canvas of raw land.

The trim, mid-fifties CEO was born in St. Louis to what he described as "kind of an Ozzie and Harriet couple." His father was a midlevel human resources manager at a steel company and his mother a teacher. His family moved from Missouri to upstate New York when Rummell was six, to the small town of Deansboro, where a farm-implement dealer and milk processing plant were the main industries. His surroundings impressed upon Rummell a strong sense of place, an echo of which might be borne out in the human-scale attributes of Disney's Celebration and emerging St. Joe communities. "I grew up on a bicycle. . . . My world was really that little town."[13]

People in Tallahassee who speculate about what St. Joe's SouthWood project will look like may rejoice that Rummell grew up riding his bicycle among rolling hills and cows rather than among fifty-story buildings. SouthWood reprised a surprising number of Deansboro influences—hills, places for biking, a town center. There were even cows nearby.

After earning a master's degree in business administration from the Wharton School of the University of Pennsylvania, Rummell landed a job with one of the most interesting and successful resort community developers in the country, Charles Fraser, at Hilton Head Island in South Carolina. With a phalanx of young enthusiastic MBAs, including Peter Rummell, Fraser created Sea Pines, a low-slung, almost camouflaged resort that was a marked contrast to places like Atlantic City and Myrtle Beach.

At Hilton Head, Rummell was baptized into the contradictions inherent in developing pristine landscapes. To developers, nature is an attraction, but one that needs to be controlled and shaped to suit the needs of their customers, the home buyers. Charles Fraser believed that development was inevitable for a place such as Hilton Head but felt strongly about preserving the place and set about to "create something beautiful."[14]

Rummell learned from Fraser the importance of architectural controls. Although covenants and restrictions are now commonplace at many upscale planned communities, including St. Joe's, at the time, Fraser's use of covenants was daring. Fraser's specifications were unbending and detailed, with forty pages of restrictions accompanying every deed.[15] Fraser recognized that without this extent of control, a coherent vision was difficult to achieve. The need for absolute decision-making authority about external appearances of homes and grounds is a page that Peter Rummell clearly borrowed for his projects, especially Celebration and WaterColor.

Another lesson from Hilton Head was about how to maximize returns on land that was a step down from beachfront in terms of desirability. "Fraser started subdividing land and sold the ocean property because nobody would buy anything interior," Rummell said. "He started running out of beach land and began trying to figure out how you could add value to the back lands. He realized if you put a golf course there, then he's created another whole environment there that has views, and open space and light and air, and so on."[16] Rummell put to use the lesson about "developing value inland" in a big way in northwest Florida with its vast interior acreage.

From Fraser's mistakes, Rummell learned about financial pacing. Fraser went out of business because, in Rummell's words, "his appetite for land was far greater than his bank account." In its early projects, St. Joe was careful to market its developments in stages. Rummell said he had "learned some very basic lessons about finance, about leverage and the lack [of leverage], and how you use it, and the whole issue of pace, not getting too far ahead of yourself, which he [Fraser] never learned."[17]

After Sea Pines at Hilton Head, Rummell went to Florida to work on another Fraser project, the low-scaled Amelia Island Plantation, north of Jacksonville. Whereas high-rise buildings and schlock shops stand out on the north end of the island, the southern part of Amelia Island, where the Plantation is situated, has ample shade trees and native vegetation abutting a wide beach. After four years there, Rummell left Fraser's organization.

After a stint at Ocean Reef, an exclusive resort in the upper Florida Keys, Rummell went to the Arvida Corporation in 1977. He became general manager of the upscale Sawgrass Development in Ponte Vedra Beach, twenty miles southeast of Jacksonville. After six years of managing Sawgrass, Rummell departed a rocky Arvida to spend a couple of years in New York as vice chairman of the Rockefeller Management Corporation. In 1985, Rummell returned to Florida to work once again for Arvida, by then under Disney management. In 1987, when Disney sold Arvida, Rummell stayed with Disney.[18]

During more than a decade at Disney, Rummell was in charge of research and development as well as management of Disney lands next to its theme parks in Anaheim, Tokyo, Paris, and Orlando, where Disney still owned thousands of undeveloped acres. Rummell's notable projects included development of Euro Disney outside of Paris and the New Urbanist/neotraditional town of Celebration, not far from Walt Disney World. Rummell and Disney head Michael Eisner got along well, and Rummell said he learned from Eisner how to channel the efforts of a creative staff. There were, he noted, "huge positives, along with working with Eisner and the people who worked for me. The negative side is that Disney is a huge, bureaucratic, political machine."

Rummell said that at St. Joe he has tried to avoid the paralysis and expense of too many decision-making layers: "We've tried to make responsibilities clear, and to provide clear autonomy to people and to eliminate . . . as a friend used to say, 'the number of layers between me and the hammer.'" At Disney, some good ideas "ended up being five-humped camels that were unaffordable. . . . The virgin idea was a good idea but it got changed and screwed up and compromised and edited."[19] Rummell said he learned from Michael Eisner that in many ways, "the enemy of creativity is flexibility"; creative groups do better with boundaries.[20]

Something to Celebrate

In 1991, Disney announced plans it said would fulfill the late Walt Disney's dream of planting full-time residents in a Disney setting. Disney would carry out Walt's dream, and venture into the field of residential real estate, by building the planned community of Celebration on former ranch land south of Orlando held by Disney since the 1960s. Peter Rummell was the man charged with bringing the town to life. He worked closely with young Disney executive Chris Corr, a former state legislator, now a St. Joe vice president.

At Celebration, Rummell harnessed the wave of interest in New Urbanism or "neotraditional" planning. Celebration, a town with an initial 8,000 homes and planned for a population of more than 20,000, embodied the basics of New Urbanism. Celebration featured a traditional town center, southern architecture, and plenty of room for pedestrians and bicyclists. Disney developed a list of "cornerstones" that expressed the elements that Rummell hoped the town would emphasize: state-of-the-art education, sense of place, wellness, a community feel, and technology.[21] The quaint town center on a small lake features a fountain, several restaurants, a hair salon, and several other retail stores and offices. The press and would-be residents loved Celebration in spite of its lack of diversity. The nascent town quickly lived up to its name, joining Seaside as one of the most celebrated New Urbanist creations.

From the start, Celebration generated so much interest that the company used a lottery system to allow people the privilege of purchasing the mostly up-scale homes. Disney's global reputation and use of big-name architects virtually guaranteed success of the attractive community with the small-town feel. But Rummell also faced tremendous challenges because of tight time lines. In its hurry to meet construction deadlines to satisfy demand, the rapid pace imposed upon the two out-of-state home-building companies was too great to assure quality. A labor shortage and time pressures forced the builders to hire unfamiliar subcontractors, leading to quality control problems.

The first dwellers at Celebration suffered tremendous inconveniences and frustration as the flaws in the new town made themselves known. Some of the original pioneers departed, the disappointments too great. Retired contractor Ron Dixon left Celebration after just one year. "I found that two of the builders did an absolutely terrible job of building townhouses and free-standing houses," he said. He was "also greatly disappointed that over 70 families pulled their children out of the Celebration school and sent them elsewhere. Many families felt the kids weren't learning anything, or even going backwards, forgetting what they'd learned before coming to Celebration. . . . I documented the construction problems and took them to the city manager. Celebration stonewalled and refused to address the problems."[22]

In Rummell's effort to provide cutting-edge education, Celebration incorporated what turned out to be too many novel concepts: self-paced learning relying on computer technology, multi-age grouping, open classrooms, and, at first, no letter grades. Journalists Douglas Frantz and Catherine Collins moved their family to Celebration to experience firsthand the ups and downs of Disney living. In their book *Celebration U.S.A.: Living in Disney's Brave New Town*, they noted that many of the first residents had unrealistic expectations of a perfect Disney world.

Celebration continues to grow and change and many of the people who have ridden out the rocky start now enjoy the living environment that Rummell's vision has afforded. Celebration has been deemed a commercial success.[23] As for authenticity, the town still displays a tendency to improve on reality Disney-style. When fall comes to Celebration, town managers embellish the Florida autumn with artificial leaves strewn around the town center. In winter, the lamp posts produce snow (soap bubbles) at scheduled intervals.

Disney's America

While awaiting final approval for Celebration, Rummell led Disney's attempt to install a national history theme park and commercial and residential housing project called "Disney's America" on 3,000 acres of rolling farmland in northern Virginia. The land was similar to the rolling hills of SouthWood of Tallahassee, although SouthWood's plans did not include a theme park. Disney's foray near historic Haymarket, Virginia fizzled after serious public opposition.

The Disney development would have radically altered the surrounding farmland and pastures, while costing state and local governments hundreds of millions of dollars for ancillary infrastructure: roads, schools, police, fire protection, sewerage, and so on. Disney requested that the state build the highways needed to get people into and out of Disney's America, and Republican governor George Allen, now a U.S. senator, agreed to sell $137.3 million in tax-exempt government bonds for Disney's roads, and spend $13 million to promote the park.[24]

One *Washington Post* editorial referred to the project as "Disney's Trojan Mouse: A Corporate Colony Paid for by Gullible Locals."[25] Another showed a squad of broad-shouldered, well-dressed grinning Disney executives (complete with Mickey ears) shaking a taxpayer's hand, causing much pain to the tiny taxpayer.

The most prominent opponent to Disney's America was a group called the Piedmont Environmental Council (PEC). The grass-roots-sounding group was a formidable foe whose members included millionaire Paul Mellon, candy czar Forrest Mars, and heiress Alice duPont Mills,[26] whose involvement was ironic given that Rummell would soon go on to head up the erstwhile duPont Florida empire. PEC obtained 5,000 documents under Virginia's open records law grudgingly yielded after an official from the state's Department of Economic Development initially refused to release them.

Disney hired the public relations firm of Jody Powell, former press secretary to President Jimmy Carter.[27] Jerry Ray, St. Joe's senior vice president for corporate communications, was one of the founding members of Powell's firm, Powell Tate, and worked on the Disney's America project.

Analysts the PEC hired found a pattern of overestimating benefits and underestimating the costs associated with the project and peripheral growth. In the view of Richard Foglesong, author of the Disney history *Married to the Mouse*, Virginia became "a virtual arm of Disney." Foglesong noted that high-ranking officials overrode staff-level concerns and that state workers were put to work helping Disney while hiding damaging information from the public.[28] The situation was reminiscent of how Florida's legislature blithely welcomed Disney into the state in the 1960s.

Rummell is extraordinarily candid about his experiences with Disney's America:

> The number one lesson out of northern Virginia is never try to get land rezoned ten miles away from [now-deceased former *Washington Post* publisher] Katherine Graham's farm, which we didn't realize at the time. . . . It was a mistake; I mean, it was my project. We did enormous research going in about the political [environment]. . . . And we'd done the research on all the surrounding environments and decided that Virginia was clearly a safer bet than Maryland, because Maryland clearly was no growth.
>
> I mean, we spent hundreds of thousands of dollars doing our preliminary work before we went public. We tied the land up in all kinds of secret names because . . . we didn't want [our] name to come out. And as soon as we went public, they came out of the woodwork, and it was just pure, raw political muscle. . . . We had some secret meetings with the county commission. They clearly were excited about it. [There were] thousands of jobs involved, and [they] were going to do their best to help us.[29]

Rummell added that somehow Disney also missed the Piedmont Environmental Council. "It wasn't infrastructure," he said. "It was all politics. The infrastructure problems were easily solvable. . . . The governor had it lined up to build [highway] interchanges; I mean, it was a huge economic development story for Virginia, huge."

Rummell's candor about his experiences in northern Virginia may hint at how St. Joe and its former Disney executives go about business in northern Florida. The "Disneyfication" of St. Joe—to paraphrase novelist and *Miami Herald* columnist Carl Hiaasen—was disturbing to some, not least of whom was Hiaasen. In his book *Team Rodent,* the outspoken author worried, "St. Joe happens to be the biggest private landowner in Florida. . . . The potential for an environmental holocaust is enormous, and there's no comfort to be taken in the knowledge that a Disney spawn sits in command."[30] Hiaasen's assessment of St. Joe's potential imprint on the state may be seen as alarmist, but the fact remained that while St. Joe itself might develop under 100,000 acres in a lifetime, there would be massive ancillary infrastructure and development.

Pulling the Team Together

Rummell brought together a management team that possessed an impressive depth of experience in finance, real estate development, marketing, and navigating bureaucracy. In his 1999 letter to stockholders, Rummell said his new team was "pound for pound, the strongest group I have had the good fortune to assemble" over his twenty-eight-year career.[31]

The Disney influence was a noticeable part of the new St. Joe corporate culture. In addition to Rummell, former Disney executives joining St. Joe included widely respected attorney Robert Rhodes; the affable Chris Corr, hired to head up public affairs; Robert Shinn, former president of the Celebration Company and head of a short-lived division at St. Joe; and Michael Reininger, head of St. Joe's Creative Services department.

At corporate headquarters in downtown Jacksonville, the Disney legacy is apparent in a set of rooms on the first floor. Here is the headquarters of St. Joe's "Creative Services," complete with backward *e*'s, a place that emits a sense of playfulness and seriousness all at once. It is part sophisticated architectural office, part preschool. The people who work there are "creative managers," explained Jerry Ray, St. Joe's senior vice president of corporate communications.

"This is a place that marries creativity and discipline," Ray said, as he guided the authors past airy work stations to the studio where brainstorming sessions take place with artists who sketch out ideas on huge pieces of paper using colored markers.[32] Although consultants execute many of St. Joe's plans, the ideas start here with a so-called charrette process that many planners use to generate community design ideas. In the fall of 2000, the wall map proclaimed "Florida Wild," an idea for turning one of the Panhandle's least-traveled bits of coast into a marketable product.

But the corporate influence that overshadowed even Disney's was that of Arvida, named for its founder, aluminum magnate Arthur Vining Davis, who like his industrialist peer Alfred duPont, acquired extensive amounts of Florida land—100,000 acres in Dade, Broward, and Palm Beach Counties. Davis organized Arvida as a public company in 1958, four years before his death at age ninety-five.[33]

In its early years, Arvida focused mostly on its Boca Raton Hotel and Resort, but later had a wider impact on its hometown of "Boca" where Davis had plenty of land, and on the west coast of Florida as well. In the early 1960s, Arvida, in the company's own words, "pioneered passage of Florida's condominium law," and built the state's first luxury condominium towers on Lake Boca Raton and then on Longboat Key, near Sarasota.[34] Arvida's legislative tinkering forever changed the face of Florida's coastline.

Residents of the once-remote fishing enclave of Longboat Key watched as Arvida workers built sea walls and planted Australian pines where mangroves had once thrived. Condos rose on the subtropical island once owned by the Ringlings of circus fame. Arvida executives moved in and further shaped the community with their votes. Longboat Key is one of the ritziest of Arvida's creations and few natives remain in this costly paradise. "We've accepted this as Florida's fate," wistfully said one young man who grew up there.[35]

After Davis's death in 1962, his heirs sold the majority interest in Arvida to Penn Central, the holding company whose biggest concern was its railroad. Penn Central owned Arvida for the next twenty-one years. In 1972, with Penn Central under court-ordered reorganization, the company embarked on a whole new direction under the leadership of Californians Charles Cobb and John Temple, both Stanford graduates.[36]

The duo began developing "integrated" communities that combined homes, golf courses, offices, industries, and shopping centers—an old idea in California, but a new one to Florida. After reshaping Boca Raton in the integrated community style, Arvida moved on to land around Atlanta, Sarasota, and Jacksonville, where Rummell managed Sawgrass. Arvida's golden age under Cobb and Temple came to an end after Penn Central in the early 1980s bought a larger share of Arvida and began to micromanage the profitable company.[37]

As morale sank during Penn Central's stewardship, Rummell and many others left Arvida. Starting in 1983, the company went through a succession of owners, prompting one former company chairman to dub the company "little orphan Arvida."[38] That year, senior managers, joined by Texas venture capitalists, the Bass Brothers, arranged a leveraged buyout of Arvida from Penn Central.[39] After only five months, the Arvida-Bass bunch sold to Disney for $200 million in Disney stock. Chuck Cobb stayed with Arvida under Disney, going on to head Disney Development Company and serve on Disney's board of directors. For Disney, the deal helped bring real estate expertise as the company began pondering what to do with its 25,000 undeveloped acres.

Under Disney's management, Arvida continued development of its most ambitious project to date, the 10,000-acre town of Weston in Broward County. Arvida initiated Weston in the early 1970s under the name Indian Trace. It proposed to blast artificial lakes out of limestone, drain wetlands, and insert as many as sixteen residential units per acre. At the time, that area edging into the Everglades was sparsely populated and home to eagles, snail kites, wood storks, and Florida panthers.[40]

The plans pitted developers against citizens, many of whom previously had not considered themselves environmentalists. The controversy became one of the most heated environmental battles of the 1970s. In the end, Arvida got to build, but had to cut the number of homes from 40,000 to 20,000.[41]

Not long after Weston greeted its first residents in 1986, Arvida again changed hands. This time, Disney sold Arvida for $400 million to a successful Chicago conglomerate named JMB. Earlier in 1987, the same year JMB acquired Arvida, many top managers left the company as the result of a court battle with Disney over stock options. By 1994, JMB owned or operated a whopping $20 billion in assets.[42]

After purchasing Arvida, JMB formed Arvida/JMB Partners I, a limited partnership. Apart from the housing recession of the early 1990s, this venture did well, generating a profit of $47 million in 1997. A second partnership operating in California, however, lost money.[43]

After some Arvida/JMB investors attempted to buy out other partnership shareholders, JMB sold Arvida to St. Joe in 1997. St. Joe paid $12.2 million for a 74 percent ownership in the limited partnership.[44] St. Joe acquired Arvida's management personnel and its information systems. The teaming of St. Joe with Arvida positioned St. Joe/Arvida to dominate Florida's residential building scene, especially in northwest Florida.

One vice president of the Arvida/JMB partnership projected a brighter future for Arvida owing to St. Joe's considerable land and capital.[45] In addition to St. Joe's stake in the St. Joe/Arvida limited partnership, the newly reorganized St. Joe also connected to JMB through 26 percent interest in another limited partnership, Arvida/JMB Partners, L.P. that was developing new residential communities in Florida, Georgia, and North Carolina and owned the signature community of Weston, then nearing completion.[46]

Following the formation of the St. Joe/Arvida development partnership, St. Joe proceeded to get into the brokerage business as well. It purchased several of

Florida's leading brokerage houses, starting with Prudential Florida Realty, purchased in 1998 for $90 million.[47] St. Joe went on to acquire many more real estate firms, combining them into the new Arvida Realty Services, a brokerage firm that opened St. Joe's way for doing business in buying and selling existing homes, whether or not they were Arvida-built.

This portfolio of services Arvida Realty provided was unparalleled in the state, and Arvida Realty Services quickly became Florida's largest full-service brokerage outfit, with roughly 100 offices and more than 3,000 agents. Arvida Realty generated roughly $150 million in revenues in 1998,[48] but little of that was profit to the company. Arvida's brokerage business was making only modest gains in profitability. In April 2002, St. Joe again shocked observers by selling its newly formed brokerage business to NRT, Inc. for more than $160 million in cash.

But there still remained some 150 companies bearing the Arvida name, of which real estate services were just one part. Arvida was better known than St. Joe, and most noted for its planned communities marketed to middle- and upper-income buyers in California, Florida, Georgia, North Carolina, and Texas. By the year 2000, Arvida had developed more than fifty communities. Like Sawgrass, which Rummell managed, these usually featured tennis, golf, swimming, and other recreational activities amid tasteful grounds.

Some considered Arvida past its prime when it entered into its marriage with St. Joe, as a result of its loss of seasoned personnel after Disney sold Arvida to JMB. Rummell disagreed, citing the "instant expertise" that Arvida brought into the fold. Arvida's president was Jim Motta, who already had almost two decades of experience with Arvida in several states before the formation of the joint venture with St. Joe.

Through the years, Arvida had a reputation of building high-end communities, "planned down to the doorknobs."[49] Arvida's own surveys showed the majority of its buyers enjoyed living in its lush developments. Arvida was a commercial success, ranking nationally among numbers of homes sold.

However, Arvida did have a contingent of disgruntled customers after Hurricane Andrew blasted the roofs and gables off a large number of Miami-area Arvida-built homes in 1992. Andrew's powerful winds revealed that beauty is only roof deep, damaging many homes, including those at two upscale Arvida communities: Country Walk south of Miami in Homestead and Lakes of the Meadows in Miami. Both communities were built in the 1980s, mostly by Disney/Arvida before Disney sold its share of Arvida in 1987.

As a result of the damage at Country Walk, the Florida Department of Business and Professional Regulation (DBPR) issued an administrative complaint against Arvida's certified general contractor. A review by an engineering firm showed a pattern of code violations and shoddy workmanship: inadequate bracing and fastening, inferior materials, and other problems with installation of materials.[50]

For Arvida, the affiliation with St. Joe gave one of Florida's most storied developers fresh momentum. The new synergistic relationship carried the Arvida name into the Green Empire, a place until then untouched by the Arvida trademark. The combination of Arvida's community building experience and St. Joe's storehouse of land primed the St. Joe/Arvida team to dominate the Green Empire.

Commercial Development with Codina and Others

In commercial building, too, St. Joe had high ambitions. St. Joe hoped to capture a strong share of the commercial real estate business in a broad triangle from Miami to Washington, D.C., to Dallas. At breakneck speed St. Joe formed alliances with market leaders in its target area. By 2000, St. Joe commercial had more than twenty projects in the works, mostly in Florida, but with a half dozen in Texas and more in the Virginia–Washington, D.C., area.

St. Joe Commercial began by assimilating the management and operations of Gran Central, FECI's longtime real estate subsidiary. When St. Joe "spun off" FECI in 2000, St. Joe lost its ownership in the old Gran Central, by then renamed the Flagler Development Company. However, it and its commercial partners retained agreements to finish ongoing projects and develop and manage other properties within FECI's extensive portfolio.[51]

St. Joe forged its commercial real estate services unit Advantis from prominent commercial and real estate firms in Georgia and Florida. Advantis hungrily eyed St. Joe's vast holdings in the Panhandle with a focus on economic opportunities. "Our economic development program is your economic development program," an Advantis executive said.[52]

In December 1997, only a month after linking with Arvida, St. Joe bought a one-third interest (which soon grew to 50 percent) in the Codina Group, then the twelfth largest privately held company in the state. St. Joe's acquisition of Codina raised questions about whether newly elected governor Jeb Bush's past involvement with the Codina Group would allow him to sufficiently distance himself from many decisions about matters affecting both the state and the St. Joe Company, now officially tied to Codina.

A great many such decisions faced Florida's chief executive, involving transportation projects, disbursement of economic development dollars, and growth management policies. During his bid for governor, some political observers expressed concerns about the governor's role in decisions that would affect St. Joe's bottom line. A Sierra Club official called for careful monitoring of St. Joe's actions. Audubon's Charles Lee, however, called the Codina Bush company "noncontroversial" compared to other development companies and stated that the new St. Joe and old St. Joe are "different animals" in terms of environmental responsibility.[53]

Codina is a well-known Miami firm that has constructed many commercial projects, including several in conjunction with the former St. Joe subsidiary, Florida East Coast Industries through its Gran Central division. One of the largest was a huge industrial park, Beacon Station, near Miami's airport. Codina also built Deering Bay, a Miami area complex with luxury condos, villas, a marina, and a golf course that lost millions before Codina and Bush sold it to Florida developer and major Republican fundraiser, Al Hoffman.[54]

Jeb Bush went to work for the Codina firm in the early 1980s. Cuban-American Armando Codina, a friend and supporter of his father, George H. W. Bush, offered Bush 40 percent of the profits of the company plus an opportunity to invest in other ventures. In return, Codina got the marketing power that came from association with a well-known public figure—at that time, the vice president's son. The firm's name changed to Codina Bush Group.[55]

Twice in the past Bush has left and returned to Codina: first when Governor Bob Martinez appointed him commerce secretary in 1987, and again 1993, when he ran against Lawton Chiles for the governorship and lost in a tight race. Jeb Bush returned to Codina in 1995 and stayed on as a part-time consultant until June 1998,[56] around the time that the press was starting to raise questions about the relationship of the would-be governor to St. Joe, the latter having recently purchased a major share of his old company. Although he worked only part time for half the year, in 1998 Bush grossed $755,136 in salary from the Codina Group.[57]

While with Codina, Bush had several financial coups. Codina had invested in Museum Tower, a downtown Miami office building on West Flagler Street, a run-down part of the city, but one about to be revitalized. After Codina invited Bush to invest in it, he received a 20 percent stake for a contribution of $1,000. By 1990, Bush sold out his share in Museum Tower for $346,000.[58] In a controversial deal in the 1980s, Bush and Codina managed to retain possession of a building in the financial district of Miami even after one of the loans they used to purchase the building defaulted.[59] The two businessmen insisted that they had been "victims of circumstances," in the weakening real estate market.[60]

When asked in an August 2000 interview about the perception that St. Joe's alliance with the Codina Group gives the company special access to governor, Peter Rummell responded:

> We made the deal with Armando because we had huge holdings in south Florida and he's the best commercial developer in south Florida, and so it was a make or buy decision. We could spend three years to cobble together our own commercial organization in south Florida, or we could make a deal with Armando and end up better than something we could make in three years.... Jeb was already gone when we made the deal, [or] he was on his way out.
>
> We were going for Armando, not Jeb. The fact that they're friends is just coincidence. Armando is a man of just enormous integrity. You just have to know him to understand the kind of person he is. To him that question would be mildly offensive.[61]

Yet Rummell acknowledged that ties to high-ranking officials do not hurt.

Former commercial developer Governor Bush, when asked via e-mail about his view of St. Joe and his plans after leaving office, responded, "I think St. Joe's plans with proper coordination with local and state governments offers great potential for NW Florida. I have no idea what my life will be like post service as Governor of our wonderful state."[62] His response did not rule out a return to Codina.

Governor Bush appeared at the side of St. Joe executives at groundbreakings and other occasions that celebrated St. Joe's new "place-making" endeavors. He also found a large number of St. Joe/Arvida–affiliated citizens worthy of appointments to various commissions and boards, and met frequently with St. Joe officials. The company's activities were very much on the radar screen at the governor's office.

9

⑥ ⑥ ⑥ ⑥ ⑥ ⑥ ⑥ **Liquidating the Storehouse of Value**

More Deals and Deal Makers

Its [St. Joe's] strategy is simple:
Sell what can't be developed and develop the rest.
Jack Snyder, *Orlando Sentinel*, July 1999

AS RAPIDLY AS IT MOVED into real estate, the new St. Joe Company divested itself of business units that did not fit into its new strategic plan. The moves left no doubt the "new" St. Joe was eager to shake off the dust of its industrial past. Sales of unwanted business units raised working capital that could be pumped in to help get real estate projects off the ground and to acquire new property.

As it retooled into a highly earnings-conscious conglomerate, St. Joe's new mantra was to "extract the maximum value out of its non-strategic assets."[1] The leadership at the new St. Joe found plenty in what it called its "storehouse of value" to offer in something akin to a duPont estate sale.

With the paper mill and container plants already sold off, the company moved to part with its Everglades sugarcane farm and other long-held properties in lucrative land conservation sales. St. Joe made a failed bid to acquire Florida East Coast Industries outright. Then St. Joe spun off its equity interest in FECI while retaining considerable influence over that Ed Ball–originated holding company. In September 2000, the IRS approved the spin-off as tax exempt after protracted deliberations. The agency would not release records to shed light on its rationale for granting the tax exempt status, a crucial element for the deal to go through. Peter Rummell hailed the spin-off as an important milestone in St. Joe's tightening focus on real estate.

By 2001, the only remaining industrial operations at St. Joe besides its Timberland division, headed by Clay Smallwood, was the ninety-six-mile Apalachicola Northern Railroad from Port St. Joe to Chattahoochee. That railroad, although a relic of St. Joe's industrial past, seemed like a keeper because of its potentially strategic role in the future economy of fast-growing Port St. Joe, especially as the town's port business increased. However, even this portion of the business had been operating in the red, and the Company in 2002 leased the operation to regional short-line railroad magnate Earl Durden of Panama City while maintaining ownership of the right-of-way, track, and related facilities.[2]

A $152 Million Deal

In December 1998, St. Joe made a sweet deal for its stockholders. With the assistance of Florida governor Lawton Chiles and The Nature Conservancy, the company sold off its roughly 50,000-acre Talisman sugar plantation in the Everglades to the federal government for $133.5 million in cash. In addition, the company reaped another $19 million by leasing out its right to farm the land to other sugar companies for another five years.[3]

Beginning in the late 1980s, St. Joe had unsuccessfully tried to unload Talisman.[4] But by the late 1990s, the status of the Everglades had become critical. After years of hand wringing over the deteriorating state of Florida's vital and wondrous Everglades ecosystem, the federal government in 1996 ponied up $200 million from the farm bill to begin a restoration program. The Talisman property was the first big acquisition in a multi-billion-dollar effort to "re-plumb" the Everglades.

St. Joe signed its initial agreement in December 1997 for the $133.5 million purchase price, but the deal did not close until a year later. In the meantime, sugar growers, environmentalists, and the federal and state government all became involved in politicking over the controversial deal. Sugar growers, an immensely powerful lobby in Florida, were concerned about losing farming ground. Growers favored complicated land swaps that would consolidate restoration lands while freeing other areas for continued sugar production. They also wanted to allow sugar cane growing to continue on lands slated for restoration until bureaucrats and engineers were ready to go ahead with the re-plumbing.

The Talisman settlement that the parties ironed out did include land swaps. In addition, Talisman was allowed to continue to farm its acreage rent-free for another five years. Instead it chose to sell the farming rights to other sugar companies through 2003. The politically powerful and wealthy Fanjul sugar family and their competitor, the U.S. Sugar Corp, had lobbied vigorously to farm the arable Talisman land. One critic likened the sale and rent-free use of the land to selling one's car, then having its free use for another several years.[5] In 1996, St. Joe had contributed $2.5 million to fight a proposed penny sales tax on sugar that would have helped fund Everglades cleanup.[6]

By all accounts, St. Joe walked away from Talisman in very good shape. "By selling our 50,000-acre sugar farm and the retained farming rights for a total of $152.5 million, we are exiting the sugar business at a good price," the company told stockholders in its annual report.[7] The sale netted the company $40 million after taxes.[8]

St. Joe topped off its financial success with good publicity. The Florida Audubon Society honored the St. Joe Company with its top award for corporate responsibility to the environment in 1997. St. Joe and the Jessie Ball duPont Foundation have been corporate sponsors of Florida Audubon, and the Jessie Ball duPont Foundation is an especially generous donor. According to Charles Lee, a senior Florida Audubon official, St. Joe deserved the environmental award because it was constructive and helpful in the effort to preserve the Everglades. "They cooperated more than anyone else by being willing to sell," he said.[9] This was the same Charles Lee who had tangled with Ed Ball more than a quarter century earlier over his use of Wakulla Springs.

St. Joe trumpeted its environmental award, telling stockholders that by "working with The Nature Conservancy and the federal government, we are proud to demonstrate it's possible to do what's in our shareholders' interest and the public's interest."[10] Although the company's willingness to sell helped to advance the public land acquisition necessary for Everglades restoration, Talisman's environmental record prior to the sale, like those of most sugarcane farms, was hardly eco-friendly.

On top of their damaging effects on the Everglades natural waterworks, the Everglades sugarcane companies polluted air, water, and soil. According to a state official who preferred not to be named, Talisman was no exception: "Talisman Sugar routinely had the poorest environmental regulatory compliance history, on a consistent basis, for a variety of medias [air, water, and land] in comparison to all of the other sugar mills. The other mills have had problems but in general they all corrected the problems pointed out to them and didn't repeat them. Talisman seemed to never learn from their mistakes. . . . Every time we went to Talisman, there was an environmental problem. If it wasn't one thing, it was another—unauthorized landfills, illegal burns, etc. . . . Other mills didn't seem to have this broad pattern."

With lingering environmental contamination a concern, St. Joe took responsibility for cleaning up the mill site where sugar cane was converted to raw
sugar. More than $5 million was held in escrow pending completion of the
remediation.[11]

As for the cane lands themselves, by the time St. Joe sold Talisman to the
government, most of the acreage was overwrought, according to one official familiar with the property. With the exception of parcels that other sugar companies coveted, "[much of] the land was not valuable for sugar farming any longer.
The muck was all gone; what's left is bedrock [in some parts]. On the southeast
side of Talisman's land [the terrain] was rocky muck." For St. Joe, selling its land
for Everglades restoration was a timely and profitable way out.

In the fall of 2000, the large-scale Everglades restoration plan of which Talisman was a part won overwhelming bipartisan support in Congress. The measure called for recapturing huge quantities of fresh water that currently flow out
to the Atlantic by reworking the maze of manmade canals, pumps and levees
that had been installed with much effort decades earlier to "reclaim" the wet
Everglades. The old Talisman farm was slated for conversion to a huge recharge
reservoir. Overall, the massive federal-state effort was expected to cost over $8
billion and take as long as three decades to complete.

As the restoration effort plodded along in its political and budgetary minefield, St. Joe moved quickly to pump its proceeds from the sale into its new real
estate engine. "They made a wise business decision," conceded Audubon's
Charles Lee.[12]

Other Conservation Sales

Although the Talisman sale dwarfed other land sales, St. Joe sold off more than
80,000 additional acres of other environmentally important lands in Florida
during its first few years, as well as land in Georgia, bringing its overall conservation sales to more than 100,000 acres. These sales contributed mightily to
company earnings. One of its first sales after Talisman was to southern media
mogul Ted Turner, who bought a 3,620-acre forest parcel in Capps, Florida,
twenty miles east of Tallahassee, near where he already had a large spread.
Turner purchased the property for $11 million for use as a private wildlife pre-
serve for its prime turkey and quail habitat. Turner was an ardent conservationist committed to protecting habitat for the red-cockaded woodpecker.

The biggest customer for its rural lands was a familiar one to St. Joe—the
state of Florida, which purchased tens of thousands of Green Empire acres for

conservation. The state was an eager customer because St. Joe in 2000 owned ten of the top fifty parcels on the state's Florida Forever priority land purchasing program that replaced the Conservation and Recreation Lands (CARL) program as of the year 2000.

The state's first purchase after Talisman was for 13,275 acres in the Tate's Hell Swamp area in Franklin County, for which it paid $9.9 million in July 1999. The next year, the state paid $16.2 million for 8,840 acres around the wildlife-packed Wacissa River in Jefferson County. In April 2001, St. Joe sold the state 10,681 acres on Snipe Island, an important natural area between two rivers in Taylor County, in the Big Bend. That land went for $10 million; less than $1,000 per acre. (A February 2003 report by the state Auditor General's office concluded that the state may have overpaid for all three St. Joe parcels included in its audit of the state land acquisitions program. DEP refuted those claims.)[13]

The conservation sales continued at a steady pace. In the early fall of 2001, St. Joe sold one of Bay's County's most pristine spots of ground, an undisturbed wet prairie at the head of Deer Point Reservoir, known as Hobbs Pasture. The 1,011 acres of land sold for $3.64 million, or $3,600 per acre, this time to the Northwest Florida Water Management District. That state entity was interested in the land partly for its location, at the confluence of two creeks leading into the freshwater reservoir that supplied 45 million gallons of water daily. The next day, St. Joe dignitaries gathered in Franklin County, not far from Apalachicola Bay, to celebrate another conservation land sale. The state bought another 3,406 acres of land there for $6.4 million, in a purchase negotiated by The Nature Conservancy. The purchase would further add to the state's Tate's Hell forest holdings and protect the rich Apalachicola estuary at the watershed's end.

A few months later, St. Joe and the Water Management District announced yet another transaction, St. Joe's sale of a 2,600-acre tract known as Devil's Swamp in Walton County, on the fringe of Choctawhatchee Bay. The Water Management District paid $3.7 million for the mixture of bay swamp, dry sand hills, and pine flatwoods interspersed with wetlands, averaging roughly $1,400 per acre. The state's initial outlay would be only part of its investment, however. Before selling, St. Joe logged accessible portions of the land, leaving a condition that one observer described as "nuked."[14] Another $3 million in taxpayer funds from the state Department of Transportation, earmarked to mitigate damage to wetlands from expanding roadways, would have to pay to restore the denuded areas. As one official involved in the deal noted, restoration funding was as important as funding for the land itself.

St. Joe parted with some of its southwest Georgia holdings when it sold 15,105 acres of the Chickasawhatchee Swamp to TNC for $30 million. George Willson described the area as Georgia's "last, best swamp."[15] The Nature Conservancy's national magazine praised St. Joe for its willingness to sell its ecosystem gems for protection. One such place was the 7,048-acre Sweetwater Creek Ravines parcel in Liberty County, with its remaining botanic rarities, which St. Joe contracted to sell the state for $7.2 million in December 2001.

In reality, St. Joe was not willing to sell every ecologically valuable parcel if it was possible to develop it. According to a state employee who did not wish to be named, St. Joe was deciding which parcels it was willing to let go: "We'd rather be able to determine which high priority parcels to negotiate for, but they're calling all the shots. . . . So the state figures getting these lands less endangered by development is better than getting nothing."

Dozens of other varied habitats belonging to St. Joe were on the state's wish list for acquistion, subject to the company's willingness to sell and the availability of state funds. By 2003, the state and TNC closed on conservation purchases including the Wakulla Springs Protection Zone, a buffer north of Ed Ball's treasured springs in Wakulla County, other land along the Apalachicola River, and Bald Point at the mouth of the Ochlockonee River. Later that year, St. Joe offered for sale large tracts of land in Gulf and Franklin Counties, including land around Lake Wimico and the Box R Ranch. The company also agreed to sell more tens of thousands of acres of conservation land along the St. Marks River and western Bay County.[16]

As at Devil's Swamp, on some other St. Joe lands potentially in the pipeline for conservation sales, St. Joe's Timberland division carried out gung-ho harvest operations one last time before selling. In December 2001, St. Joe was simultaneously celebrating the company's contribution to the preservation of Tate's Hell on the east side of the biodiverse Apalachicola Valley, while on the west side of the valley, the Timberland division of St. Joe was rapidly removing large tracts of biodiverse bottomlands hardwoods. The near-clear-cutting operation took place north of Lake Wimico, the picturesque lake through which the Intracoastal Waterway passes west of Apalachicola Bay, and which the state had on its list for future acquisition. The market for hardwood pulp was making such operations at least marginally profitable, and Timberland head Clay Smallwood was fulfilling his promises to shareholders.

An area resident and hunter was shocked when he observed the scale of the timber operation taking place. Ironically, these were on the Ed Ball Wildlife Management Area, St. Joe lands that were still leased to the state to allow hunting. The timbering took down sweetgums, blackgums, red maples, bays, and other trees in the rich variety of species for which the Apalachicola Valley area is known. At the same time, St. Joe took out cypress that were mixed in. Officials from agencies including the Florida DEP, the U.S. Fish and Wildlife Service, and the Northwest Florida Water Management District were aware of the timbering but could do little to stop it. "It looks bad and it's all legal," said Hildreth Cooper, a biologist with Fish and Wildlife .[17]

Even though the timbering nearly amounted to clear-cutting, it met the standards of so-called Best Management Practices, or BMPs as they are known in Florida forestry. Timber companies can legally cut out all but 5 percent of trees and still comply with these BMPs. With Lake Wimico on the state's wish list for conservation purchases from St. Joe, it could one day end up as state property in need of costly restoration to return it to something approximating its circa 2001 condition.

For St. Joe, conservation land sales were not only good deeds, but fiscal winners. One example was the Snipe Island sale, which brought in $10 million, representing a gain of $9.4 million.[18] The sum was quite a nice return on Ball's "sand and mud." On several parcels, including Talisman and Devil's Swamp, some critics questioned whether the state's purchase prices were too high. The state continued to walk the same fine line it had on conservation buys since its land-buying programs began. It had to make competitive offers on the ever-shrinking bank of Florida's undeveloped lands, knowing that prices would inevitably go up, while also trying to avoid jacking up those very prices with overly generous purchases.

Conservation sales served other underlying purposes in addition to helping the state to maintain some wild and ecologically important lands. They also offered a buy-out option to landowners who might be denied permission to develop environmentally sensitive lands. As noted in a speech by St. Joe's top lawyer Robert Rhodes, the availability of a pot of state money helps ease the clash between the contrary ideologies and legalities of property rights and environmental protection. He noted the value of CARL for preserving sensitive lands, providing recreation, and taking land off the market that might otherwise engender sprawl. But he also observed, "These programs can also provide a constitutional safety valve for stringent regulation of particular property."[19]

All told, the St. Joe Company sold more than $200 million worth of real estate for conservation purposes in Florida and Georgia in its first five years, with the state of Florida alone (in its various entities) buying more than 89,000 acres and spending more than $182 million. Looking ahead, St. Joe planned to put up more than 170,000 additional acres for conservation sales by the year 2006, according to St. Joe president Kevin Twomey. If those plans are realized, St. Joe will take in hundreds of millions of dollars more from the state.

As St. Joe refined its focus and scope, the executive ranks experienced considerable turnover. Kevin M. Twomey came on board to replace Charles Ledsinger as president and chief financial officer (CFO). Twomey later acquired the additional title of chief operating officer (COO), putting him in charge of day-to-day operations at St. Joe.

Kevin Twomey, the second in charge in the lineup, was a veteran of Texas banks, Beverly Hills, and Wall Street. His career demonstrated an affinity for financially aggressive organizations. According to his company biography, Twomey had a "proven track record of shaping merged businesses and melding the best of their cultures and systems to create shareholder value." Twomey got off to a brilliant start with St. Joe, where earnings shot up 47 percent in 1999 over the previous year. Twomey later won praise for helping arrange the tax-free FECI spin-off and an $111 million "forward sale" of equities that put ready cash at St. Joe's disposal.

After earning advanced degrees in administration and business from George Washington University and Duke University and serving in the U.S. Navy, Twomey went to work at MCorp. MCorp was a twenty-five-bank chain formed by the merger of two large Texas banks in 1984. In 1989, the FDIC declared twenty of MCorp's banks insolvent, another in the slew of bank failures of the day. Texas banks made many risky and questionable investments and were particularly hard hit by failed commercial loans for real estate and energy ventures. MCorp stood out in Texas and nationally as one of the country's costliest bank failures with losses of $20.2 billion.[20]

One postscript to the MCorp bankruptcy was a set of loans described in a 1992 congressional report as "golden parachute" forms of executive compensation totaling $8.5 million given to MCorp executives, including Twomey. By 1992, none of the recipients had paid back loans due four years earlier.[21] The next year, more than two dozen loan recipients settled claims with regulators, but Twomey, who received $187,500 in October 1985, was not listed among them.[22] Repeated attempts to interview Twomey for this book in person or by telephone were unsuccessful.

After MCorp's collapse, Twomey went to another Texas bank, First Gibraltar, where in July 1989 he became executive vice president for finance and administration and chief financial officer.[23] Like MCorp, First Gibraltar was the product of a merger, this time of five S&Ls. The formation of First Gibraltar was aided by a plan in which the federal government absorbed billions in losses to give the banks a clean bill of health. Investor and corporate raider Ronald Perelman purchased the five banks that formed First Gibraltar for a fraction of the value of their good assets.[24] According to information from the St. Joe Company, "At First Gibraltar, Twomey worked to combine five failed thrifts into a high performing financial institution and expanded its operations through successful mortgage and depository acquisitions."[25]

In an interesting coincidence, both the MCorp banks and First Gibraltar did business in south Walton County during the heady days of high risk loans to buy and develop St. Joe's valuable Topsail land. MBank-Houston loaned developer Robert Corson $7.3 million on New Year's Eve 1987, with the loan backed by a mortgage on south Walton property.[26] Corson was the founder of one of the S&Ls that financed the joint venture's initial Topsail purchase. Corson's purchase of the S&L, itself subsequently bankrupted by the failed Topsail purchase, was also financed with a loan from MBank Houston.

The loans to Corson coincided with Twomey's time with the MCorp organization, although not in Houston. Twomey's biographical sketch indicates he was employed with MCorp, the parent holding company, based in Dallas. First Gibraltar did business in south Walton later, in 1991, when it had a transaction with the Resolution Trust Corporation while Twomey was First Gibraltar's chief financial officer.

Twomey's affiliation with two banking groups that did business in south Walton County in the 1980s and early 1990s may have given him some familiarity with the vast St. Joe holdings from the outside perspective of buyers and investors. As second-in-command at the new St. Joe Company, he was on the opposite side, in charge of attracting favorable investor attention to the assets of the entire Green Empire.

After First Gibraltar sold most of its Texas branch network in 1993, Twomey gained what St. Joe touted as "extensive Wall Street experience" at Bank of America and the New York holding company called MacAndrews and Forbes, also owned by Ronald Perelman. Later that same year, Twomey went to California as CFO of Ahmanson and Company, where he contributed to a doubling of the company's profits through an aggressive restructuring. In addition, Twomey managed the disposition of Ahmanson's investment real estate portfolio, described as "extensive" in St. Joe material. This experience was a perfect prelude to his joining the land-happy St. Joe Company.

Growth Management Guru

Besides the financial wizardry of Kevin Twomey, St. Joe's hiring of Robert M. Rhodes as general counsel added top-tier expertise in the vital areas of growth management and land-use law. Not only did Rhodes know Florida's land law back and forth, but he was also a well-respected figure in planning and government circles. Rhodes's credentials showed an extraordinary breadth across the political and philosophical spectrum. For example, Rhodes had ties to both the cutting-edge New Urbanist movement and the more conservative and populist property rights movements, rounded out by ties to power brokers in state government and academia. Rhodes had memberships in organizations as diverse as the Seaside Institute, 1,000 Friends of Florida, and Defenders of Property Rights.

Rhodes was one of the key persons making it possible for St. Joe to boast in its company literature about its strong background in "the complex Florida entitlement process"[27] other words, gaining development permits. Rhodes knew his way around development law because in several important instances, he helped to write the laws. Mediation was another talent of Rhodes, who put his negotiating skills to work almost immediately to help work out the Talisman cane farm sale after lawsuits from competing sugar interests threatened to sour the deal.[28]

Rhodes began his career in Florida as an aide to Democratic house speaker Richard Pettigrew in the early 1970s. Rhodes headed Florida's Bureau of Land and Water Management, which oversaw real estate regulation in the state, before going into private practice. While in state government, Rhodes helped get Florida's growth management program off the ground, including drafting regulations for the Development of Regional Impact (DRI), which are strict review standards for major projects that St. Joe must now navigate.

Rhodes stayed involved in Florida's evolving growth management program. In 1982, he chaired the influential Environmental Land Management Study Committee (called ELMS II). Three ELMS committees over the years offered guidance on changes to growth management law. The ELMS II committee that Rhodes chaired called for the state to engage more in growth management, which had not amounted to much more than unenforced planning documents to that time. The recommendations of the committee led to the adoption of a state comprehensive policy plan and ultimately to the milestone Growth Management Act of 1985. That law elevated the importance and state enforcement zeal regarding planning at the local level.

ELMS III, in the early 1990s, conversely scaled back the state role. One out-

come of ELMS III was a weakening of the controversial "concurrency" requirements. Concurrency is the spottily enforced requirement that necessary infrastructure like adequate roads and water service be in place before planned new
development is approved. After the state failed to establish a funding mechanism to pay for concurrency requirements, enforcement became a problem. In
1987, a commission reported that financing Florida's orderly growth would cost
$52.9 billion over the following decade. This figure must have given pause to
lawmakers bound to a balanced state budget if they looked to state monies to
properly pave the way for new development.[29]

Without a clear formula to spell out a means for either public or private
funding to pay for all the public facilities supposed to be in place in conjunction
with development, concurrency remained little more than a good idea.
"Concurrency should have been field tested," Rhodes said.[30] In late 2001, concurrency, and who should pay for it, was still an unresolved issue. In the inter-
vening years since the 1987 study, concurrency deficits have continued to
mount. A 1999 statewide survey by the state's Department of Community
Affairs showed that citizens still favored making the link between support services and development; Floridians overwhelmingly supported keeping and
even expanding the state's concurrency requirements.[31]

In his private law practice, Rhodes represented Arvida for years before signing on as Disney/Arvida's senior vice president and general counsel in 1985,
similar to the role he took on at St. Joe when he came aboard in early 1997. At
Disney/Arvida, Rhodes pushed for allowing counties with good planning staffs
to bypass the usual state DRI process. The concept seemed to be gaining support fifteen years later with the introduction of new planning concepts such as
"sector plans" and more liberal standards for when DRIs should be applied in
rural Panhandle counties.[32]

Rhodes stayed with Disney after it sold Arvida, then left Disney to work as
partner in the Tallahassee law practice of Steel, Hector, and Davis LLP, a firm at
which former FSU president Sandy D'Alemberte also was a partner.

Rhodes was instrumental in crafting a landmark piece of state legislation relating to land use, the Bert J. Harris Private Property Rights Protection Act.
Rhodes served on the ad hoc committee of stakeholders that drafted the bill,
which Florida lawmakers adopted in 1995 with only one dissenting vote and
which Governor Chiles signed into law. The new statute gave property owners
recourse when they were "inordinately burdened" in use of their land
because of state regulations imposed for the benefit of the public at large.
Named for a Highlands County citrus farmer and longtime property rights advocate, the Bert J. Harris Act opened the way for landowners who were "unable

to attain reasonable, investment-backed expectations" for use of their property to receive just and expeditious review and compensation. The law gave statutory authority for a landowner to sue local government or a state agency when a property's value depreciated by 40 percent or more as a result of a new zoning, growth management or environmental decision. It applied only to laws put on the books after 1995.

The Harris Act was well received in northwest Florida, where the property rights movement was strong, and where the requirements to comply with the Growth Management Act were sometimes viewed as a police action. One group whose central mission included protection of private property rights included the Tallahassee-based James Madison Institute, which from its origin during Jake Belin's era to the present has counted among its board members a number of top St. Joe executives. North Florida organizations were among the strongest property rights voices in Florida, joined by corporations individually and as members of the nonprofit Florida Legal Foundation of which St. Joe was a prominent supporter.

In an article in the FSU law journal shortly after the act's passage, Rhodes and coauthors and colleagues David L. Powell (later a St. Joe lobbyist) and Dan R. Stengle (listed as the principal drafter of the legislation and later a St. Joe lobbyist) predicted that Bert Harris would not "prompt an explosion or a rash of damage awards. Rather, it will produce a sense of caution on the part of the regulators who are entrusted with the responsibility of protecting Florida's environment and managing its growth." The authors argued that the Harris Act "was not intended to chill all new regulation" but rather to restore public confidence in government.[33]

Yet the Harris Act was not without critics. A representative of the Florida League of Cities, who had also served on the drafting committee, testified on Capitol Hill, "This legislation was so heavily greased that I think Mazola probably should have had some type of stock price jump, and I feel I was successful in at least obtaining one negative vote." She told a congressional committee that the Harris Act was having a "deep and chilling effect on governmental actions for the public good." She maintained that while the act protected individuals from the cost of societal decisions, it did not address the problem of having society bear the cost of an individual's gain.[34]

When the Harris Act went into effect, some consumer groups worried about its financial implications. It had not included a mechanism to fund compensation claims. As of 2003, the state had not been overburdened by costly compensation claims. One reason was a dispute resolution process that accompanied the Harris Act. Arguably, another reason was that the Harris Act had indeed created a serious chilling effect, preventing new regulations and even enforcement of old ones that would give rise to costly claims for compensation. In northwest Florida at least, the Harris Act quickly assumed almost mythical proportions. At public meetings, city and county officials threw in routine references to the Harris Act and takings law when discussing zoning and land-use issues.

As the legislature and governor attempted to revisit Florida's growth management laws again in the years 2000 to 2002, Rhodes remained a sought-after expert on growth management topics. Rhodes called for a rewrite of state growth laws to replace inflexible rules with incentives. At present, he said, Florida's programs more focused on "achieving regulatory compliance than on desired results." He favored rewarding good new development, which he called "smart growth," with "bonuses, tax and other economic incentives, priority government program funding, accelerated project review, and appropriate regulatory variances and waivers." The private sector, he said, should be challenged to work with government to achieve goals. "These strategies will be far more effective than simply prohibiting someone's definition of 'dumb growth,'" he said.[35]

Rhodes acknowledged that Florida's growth management program had many plusses but also called for the state role to shrink in some key areas, for example, overseeing the Development of Regional Impact process. DRIs, abhorred by developers, provide a wealth of information about proposed major projects, along with clear provisions for public review. Rhodes urged decision makers to consider eliminating DRIs altogether, while ensuring that local governments protect significant state interests. After twenty-eight years, Rhodes observed, "DRIs remain lengthy, expensive, duplicative, and avoided."[36] The 2000–2001 growth management study commission appointed by Governor Bush also recommended repealing the program. Although it was clear that Rhodes and others were ready to toss out some of the irksome regulations that they had worked under in the past, what they would be replaced with was less clear.

As top planner and land-use lawyer for the state's largest private landlord, Rhodes's views on growth law mattered. Based on his past influence over state growth management policy, his views even stood a good chance of eventually becoming law. Over the several years during which the Jeb Bush administration sought to retool growth management, Rhodes's ideas were in sync with the rhetoric of Jeb Bush's first-term Department of Community Affairs chief Steve Seibert. His growth management notions also jibed with the free-market ideology that dominated a study commission handpicked by Governor Bush (which did not include Rhodes). The emerging policy, still nebulous in many aspects by 2003, called for a continued diminution in the role of the state in favor of local control and cost-benefit studies of new development.

As the contentious effort to reshape Florida's growth laws continued, Rhodes would be well-situated to use another of his skills—his tested ability at behind-the-scenes mediation and consensus building, skills that he had applied in his leadership roles on the ELMS committees and bill-drafting commissions. One observer noted of the Bert J. Harris bill writing effort, "The group's political muscle showed; what could have been a bloody political battle became a smooth political compromise."[37]

St. Joe's Gatekeeper and Image Shaper

Another crucial member of St. Joe's management team from the start was Alabama native Jerry Ray, senior vice president for corporate communications. As a child growing up in southern Alabama, Ray visited the same Florida Panhandle beaches that St. Joe is now developing. Ray brought to St. Joe not only a strong background in public and government relations but also firsthand knowledge of the territory.

Ray's job was to oversee the information the company generated for shareholders, opinion leaders, and the media. He also tracked the reception the company got with audiences as varied as Walton County newspaper readers and Wall Street financiers. Along with Rummell and Twomey, Ray traveled to stir investor interest and build excitement about quarterly earnings reports. He organized conference calls and oversaw production of SEC reports, press releases, and St. Joe's slick marketing materials. Ray also met with public officials as St. Joe's top public relations guru.

As information gatekeeper for St. Joe, he guarded company officials from unwanted media intrusions while providing information that was in bounds because St. Joe is a publicly traded company. He dispensed comments on topics ranging from economic development to DRIs to the company's timbering methods. Ray bristled at questions about St. Joe's impact on sprawl, taxpayer subsidy of infrastructure, and on negative interpretations of its "place-making" marketing push. He labeled as possible "Luddites" those who questioned St. Joe's place making. He got the feeling that some journalists he dealt with believed "it is in the best interest of the broader good that this region remain poor, uneducated and backward."[38]

Ray was naturally bullish on what St. Joe could do for the Panhandle, especially with cooperation from the public sector on infrastructure and economic development incentives. "The number one strength is the quality of life," he said in an interview after the May 2000 annual meeting in which he took stock of the challenges facing St. Joe.[39] If Florida could match the kind of incentives that Alabama used to attract industries such as Mercedes, Honda, and Boeing, he said, exciting things would follow. He especially had his eye on the potential for high-tech broadband installations along the I-10 corridor.

Ray carefully distinguished between the old St. Joe Paper Company and the post-1997 company. He acknowledged that the old St. Joe's extensive greenbelts were a part of the reason behind northwest Florida's constrained economic development. "That was when Mr. duPont was alive," he pointed out, making it sound like "old" St. Joe died in the 1930s with duPont. At the same time, he appreciated the bargain $100 average per acre of land acquired during the ancient regime of the duPont-Ball years.[40]

Ray was a seasoned media relations professional. Before coming to St. Joe in 1997, he spent many years in Washington, D.C., where he helped to found Powell Tate, the company that handled public relations for Rummell on the proposed Disney's America project. Before that, Ray was with the Washington, D.C. office of Burson-Marsteller, a large, international public relations firm that over the years has represented clients dealing with serious environmental issues, such as Exxon after the Valdez accident in Alaska and Union Carbide after Bhopal, India. Ray went to Washington in 1981 as press secretary to U.S. senator Howell Heflin of Alabama, a conservative Democrat.

Ray held communications positions for the U.S. Senate Committee on the Judiciary and Ethics, and for the Senate Iran-Contra Committee, on which Heflin, one of many Contra supporters, served. Ray is accustomed to being, if not in the hot seat, in the seat behind the hot seat.

Other Rising St. Joe Stars

Some of the polish for the new St. Joe came from young executive Chris Corr, vice president of public affairs, who, like Jerry Ray, was at St. Joe's public relations forefront. Corr started at St. Joe in 1998 in the position of "vice president of strategy and new ventures." By the following year he was promoted to corporate vice president of public affairs. Corr's role, as stated on the St. Joe web site, included "directing federal and state government efforts for St. Joe, as well as coordinating the company's local public affairs."[41] He reported directly to Robert Rhodes.

Corr was a darling of the Florida conservative establishment, as evidenced by his seat on the board of directors of the James Madison Institute, the think tank dedicated to promoting limited government, property rights, and economic freedom, among other politically conservative ideals.[42] Corr also claimed a coveted spot on Governor Bush's Growth Management Study Commission in 2000, a position even Bob Rhodes applied for but did not receive. Corr brought a free-market and property rights perspective to the Growth Management Study Commission. "Property rights is the basis of the [smart growth] argument," he said in an interview. "We need to hold that value sacred and make decisions from there."[43]

Corr grew up in Apollo Beach on the southeast side of Tampa Bay. His grandfather purchased 6,000 acres there in the 1950s, but it took decades for his family to develop the wetlands-filled property. In a newspaper interview Corr nostalgically recalled how he would fall asleep to the sound of the dredge pump at work converting the area into usable real estate. "It was like a heartbeat," Corr said.[44] Apollo Beach grew from "bay front swamplands into what is now a thriving town of 10,000 people," according to his St. Joe writeup.[45] His family's experiences with the bureaucratic hold-ups in developing their swampy land gave him the fire in the belly to tackle the state's growth management rules.

After managing his family's development company, Corr won a seat in the Florida House of Representatives in 1990, before he had reached the age of thirty. From there Corr got a job with the Walt Disney Company, working for Peter Rummell at Celebration. Corr is careful to describe himself as a "community developer," not just simply a real estate developer, someone who considers schools, transportation, and more along with constructing residential dwellings.[46]

Also in the public eye was Panhandle native Billy Buzzett, who before joining St. Joe headed the state's constitutional revision committee.

One of the few St. Joe executives bridging the old and new companies was Clay Smallwood. A native of Panama City who was born at Tyndall Air Force Base, Smallwood started at St. Joe's Timberland division in 1978 as a young forester right out of college. Even as St. Joe deemphasized forestry, Smallwood's experience in Port St. Joe gained him a promotion supervising St. Joe's growing business interests in Gulf County, including real estate. In a long interview at his Port St. Joe office in the Apalachicola Northern Railroad building near the tracks, Smallwood courteously answered a variety of questions, ranging from how IRS rules help determine the timing of hardwoods harvest to the company's interest in master planning and revitalizing downtown Port St. Joe. "I chase a lot of rabbits, don't I?" he grinned.[47] Smallwood by 2003 had served several terms on the planning and review board of Gulf County, the voluntary body of citizens that issues development orders and considers consistency of proposed developments with the county's comprehensive plan.

Smallwood displayed a keen loyalty to the company and dedicated himself to finding ways to keep the timberlands turning a profit, even in a prolonged industry downturn. Smallwood was a proponent of scientific forestry and viewed private forests as being all about business, whether that business took the form of paid hunting or timber harvest. A forest left alone, in his view, was not fulfilling its highest purpose. "Most foresters will take the position that preservation is a very, very poor way to manage your lands. . . . Forests are not static, they're dynamic." Whether dealing with trees or St. Joe's new real estate ventures, Smallwood was clear about his focus. "Our mission is to maximize shareholder value, however that is."[48]

While Smallwood has spent his professional life cultivating trees, so in a different way, has George Willson, the former top-notch negotiator for The Nature Conservancy in Florida. St. Joe lured Willson from the well-regarded environmental group in 1999. Most viewed Willson's hire as a good thing for Florida and St. Joe. Certainly, it was good public relations for St. Joe to have on their staff someone who worked for a notable conservation organization. As a skilled negotiator intimately familiar with the value of various wild lands for preservation-minded organizations and government, Willson brought a wealth of on-the-ground knowledge to the company. Willson was in the U.S. Marine Corps for a few years in the early 1970s, serving in both the United States and Vietnam. A graduate of FSU with both a bachelor's and master's degree, he went on to work in state government at the Department of Environmental Regulation before going to TNC, where he helped acquire 900,000 acres of land over his time there.[49]

Willson's hiring demonstrated the cordial rapport between St. Joe, owner of so much of Florida's remaining undeveloped lands, and TNC, an organization dedicated to helping purchase land for conservation. The two organizations' missions made them natural business partners, with one on the selling end and the other on the buying, or at least, brokering end. TNC's Florida director at the time, Bob Bendick, described his organization as "nature's real estate agent," serving a different role than other advocacy-oriented environmental groups. It receives a small fee for purchases it brokers, but, said Bendick, "Our work on acquisition doesn't cover our cost."[50]

Another new hire at St. Joe in early 2000 took on the job of beefing up the Panhandle's underdeveloped economy. Neal Wade had previously worked for a private-sector economic development consortium in Alabama, his home state, where, aided by favorable state incentives, he helped bring 43,000 jobs and forty companies to Alabama in the 1990s. In hiring Wade, St. Joe demonstrated its commitment to taking a leadership role to help fill the gaping voids in north-west Florida's economy. As if by script, Wade's hiring announcement came the day before the Florida Coast paper mill (formerly the St. Joe Paper Company mill) declared its permanent closure. But three years later, Wade left the St. Joe Company to once again take a job as an economic developer in Alabama, this time working for the governor of Alabama.

Meet the Board of Directors

Whereas the power of the old St. Joe often radiated from just a few men, the far-reaching power of the St. Joe of the twenty-first century was more the result of collective experience and street smarts. Nowhere was this more apparent than in the assemblage of skills and connections found on the St. Joe board of directors.

Going into the year 2002, the old guard still on St. Joe's board included Winfred Thornton, head of the A. I. duPont Trust, St. Joe's largest stockholder, as well as John Uible. Uible had joined the board in 1994 having worked for many years with Charter Financial Company, a subsidiary of Charter Oil, then running Florida National Banks after Ball was forced to divest them. He was one of several bankers/investors in St. Joe's board.

The same year that Uible came on board, so did Walter Revell, a native north Floridian who has lived in Miami for decades. Revell called himself a "public policy nut" and had his share of political accolades, having served as secretary for the Florida Department of Transportation under Governor Reubin Askew and in various other capacities for most of Florida's recent governors, including chair for two study commissions under Governor Jeb Bush. Revell also was CEO of the engineering firm Post, Buckley, Schuh and Jernigan (PBS&J), a consultant to both St. Joe and the state of Florida. Revell most recently headed an engineering and architectural firm in Coral Gables, Florida.

St. Joe augmented its board in 1995 with Tallahassee developer and investor Frank Shaw. The *Tallahassee Democrat* once named Shaw one of the eight most influential people in Florida's capital city, labeling him the one "who decides who runs for office and helps sway our votes."[51]

Shaw also served on the board of directors of the James Madison Institute, a perpetual intellectual watering hole for St. Joe movers and shakers. Shaw knew Belin and Ed Ball. He recounted with amusement an early run-in he had with Jake Belin, before Shaw became involved with the company: "One of the ways I met Jake was after they [St. Joe Paper] had clear-cut near St. Teresa. I've had a house down there for many years. I said to him it was none of my business, but it would seem to me that for PR you should leave a buffer. He said, 'You're right. It *is* none of your business.'"[52] Eventually Shaw and Belin became friends and the company did adopt a policy of leaving small buffers when they clear-cut.

By the year 2002, St. Joe had added four new directors. One was Michael L. Ainslie, a private investor and former CEO and director of Sotheby's Holdings, where he served from 1984 through 1994.[53] Earlier in his career, Ainslie was president of Palmas Del Mar, a real estate company owned by Charles Fraser, Peter Rummell's mentor. Ainslie had a director's seat on the boards of a number of elite institutions in addition to Lehman Brothers Holdings, which became a note holder of the Florida Coast Paper mill.

Herbert Peyton was a duPont trustee before being named to the St. Joe board, and was a key element in reshaping St. Joe in the mid-1990s. He also was one of the most colorful of St. Joe's dignitaries. Peyton's Gate Petroleum is a privately held company that in 2000 ranked as the twentieth largest in the state of Florida.[54] In his autobiography, *New Boy,* Peyton writes about how he came to think of himself as the perennial new kid on the block. His family relocated almost every year when his father changed jobs or was transferred in his positions with Spur Oil. When he was sixteen, he and his older brother built a flat-bottom rowboat with a cabin, and along with two friends in Kentucky, made their way down several rivers to the Mississippi and all the way to New Orleans.

Peyton's "new boy training" created an indomitable fighter, a gutsy outdoorsman, and, briefly, a rodeo rider. He became a business person who viewed his entrepreneurial exploits as "military campaigns." The underdog Confederate army appeared especially dear to Peyton, whose book included a thumbnail sketch of what went wrong for the South in the Civil War.

Peyton incorporated Gate Petroleum in the summer of 1960 and opened his first gas station in a high-crime area of Jacksonville. Nearly forty years later, Gate had expanded to 150 service stations in seven southeastern states.[55] Peyton's interests also grew to encompass cement plants, asphalt plants, and commercial real estate, including the lucrative and expansive commercial holding in Jacksonville now called Deerwood Park, where St. Joe built at least four office buildings. Peyton also served on the advisory board of First Union National Bank. He was a member of the board of directors for the James Madison Institute and served as director of the Nemours Foundation.

Punctuating the separation of the old and new eras of St. Joe was the passing of Jacob Belin on May 31, 2000. Belin held a seat on St. Joe's board from 1952 until his death. Friends and co-parishioners admired Belin, business partners respected him, yet many who worked for him or tried to challenge him in his business capacity found him a hard-nosed opponent. Longtime friend Floye Brewton eulogized Belin at his funeral, held at the Baptist church Belin had helped start in Port St. Joe, his hometown for seventy-five years. "I really believe Jake Belin never lost touch with the working man," Brewton said. He shared several of Belin's management insights. Besides stressing the importance of loyalty, Belin had emphasized to Brewton the importance of working the phone to do business: "The phone allowed that no one would know what had been said."[56]

Attendees at the funeral included only a handful of the hundreds of non-managerial former mill workers who had known Belin for years. Yet lots of brass from the "new" St. Joe company were there, along with Mary Roberts, the widow of Supreme Court Justice B. K. Roberts, an old friend of Ed Ball's as well as Jake Belin's.

Interviews with residents of Port St. Joe reflected a mixture of cynicism and distrust of St. Joe and Jake Belin and yet an odd fondness for the man, since, unlike Ed Ball, he was so much a part of the community. Some of the affinity for Jake Belin might have stemmed from his role in disbursing funds for churches and other community causes as chairman of the Nemours Foundation. Into the year 2002, many needy families in the Port St. Joe area still received monthly checks from Nemours. Belin also was in a position to influence disbursements from several other duPont-related foundations. The steady stream of checks may have contributed to a kind of passivity in the company town.

Apart from Nemours, St. Joe supported community good works in the Panhandle through its Northwest Florida Improvement Foundation, which reaps its funds from transfer fees of half a percent of the sales price each time an Arvida home is sold or resold. The funding thus came from the pockets of St. Joe's home buyers and not from company largesse. Begun in 1999, the foundation awards grants for a variety of civic improvements from community gardens to libraries to lighthouse preservation. The company is careful to label these contributions "investments" in the region, not simply gifts or grants. In 2002, the foundation granted more than $1.16 million to Bay, Gulf, Franklin, and Walton Counties.

The Charities at the End, Revisited

There was perhaps an uncomfortable but unavoidable vestigial alliance of the A. I. duPont Trust and the new St. Joe. In the year 2000, the proportion of shares controlled by the Trust had slipped to just under 60 percent, down from as much as 75 percent in 1981.[57] Still, St. Joe and all its entities were very much under the auspices of duPont interests into 2002, although some St. Joe executives appeared uncomfortable discussing the relationship of the Trust and St. Joe. The two entities did share a mutual interest in making the company's stock valuable and cooperated on a stock buy-back at the end of 2000 to increase the value of each share while the Trust maintained a controlling majority in St. Joe. By the summer of 2002, the Trust's ownership slipped to just under 50 percent. The duPont Trust's willingness to give up majority interest was an historical turn.

The Nemours Foundation seemed to have benefited from the remaking of the St. Joe Company. Over the years, the A. I. duPont hospital and clinics have provided health care to thousands of children and others. With St. Joe's new push for profits, contributions to Nemours rose markedly—with amounts on the order of $70 to $80 million a year in the late 1990s versus $40 to $50 million through each of the years 1991 through 1995.[58] In 1998 alone, Nemours received $80 million from the A. I. duPont Trust.[59] Thus, it was fair to infer that the Testamentary Trust was worth more than $2.6 billion since it is legally required to distribute 3 percent of its worth to charity. Under the new regime at St. Joe, Nemours began to receive considerably more funding from the A. I. duPont Trust than it had previously. Still, as St. Joe marched boldly ahead, Alfred duPont's charitable intentions for the entity he endowed seemed almost lost in the heady rush to prove that an aging Florida empire could reinvent itself.

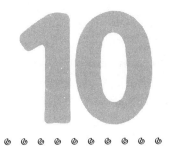

⑥ ⑥ ⑥ ⑥ ⑥ ⑥ ⑥ ⑥ ⑥ ⑥ **From Trees to Towns
and Grits to Godiva**

*It doesn't take a rocket scientist to see that if you own
a million acres in Florida, and you've got about 700 to
800 people a day moving into the state, there's a need for
places for those folks to live. It makes a lot of sense to
make a transition to a real estate development company.*
Clay Smallwood, president, St. Joe Timberland Company

THE NEW MANAGEMENT TEAM at St. Joe knew that to succeed, they had to
turn the backwater image of the Florida Panhandle on its head. A map the company released in its early days as a real estate company literally turned the state
upside down, inflating the Panhandle as the state's most prominent feature in
the foreground with the peninsula trailing off insignificantly behind it. Fanciful
script proclaimed "The New Florida," and bold, carefree sketching depicted a
reclining beachgoer amid palms and pines.

With around a million acres of rural land to reinvent, St. Joe began to sys-
tematically roll back the greenbelt, employing a variety of development strategies that would, as it told stockholders, extract the best return from what it
called its "storehouse of value." St. Joe set aside the choicest land to develop itself—tracts along the scenic coast and rivers or near desirable urban areas. Over
the coming decades, these tracts would be converted to resorts, year-round
communities, and commercial and industrial sites.

Developing its inland rural holdings would take more imagination and patience. The company experimented with the best ways to turn land to cash,
whether on its own or by selling outright. After some fine-tuning, St. Joe found
unexpected success at this, too. Rural land would be sold for conservation or
rural retreats. The lure of hunting and fishing as well as the ever-present draw of

well-sculpted golf courses would direct buyers away from the water in a fashion similar to the growth pattern of Hilton Head Island, South Carolina, where Peter Rummell cut his developer teeth.

Some acres would be consumed by the very infrastructure needed to support the conversion of trees to towns. By strategically donating land for roads, schools, water pipelines, a hospital, and an airport, St. Joe increased the value of surrounding holdings.

Several years after Rummell joined St. Joe, the plan was going great guns. By 2002, St. Joe/Arvida had more than a dozen northwest Florida communities in various stages of development, and its commercial branch had four projects underway or planned from Tallahassee west. Its rural retreats were selling like johnnycakes. Already, the architecture of trees was giving way to a new human-designed architecture that ranged from multi-million-dollar beach homes to middle-class housing. Seemingly overnight, Ed Ball's treasured pinelands changed from a crucial fiber reservoir to potential real estate land.

St. Joe's new tack paid off. Net income jumped from $28.8 million in 1998 to $124.4 million the next year and $100.3 million in year 2000.[1] The year 2001 got off to a good start, with second-quarter profits of $24.3 million, an increase of 71 percent over the same period the year before.[2] First-quarter profits in 2003 were $14.4 million.

The company took pains to roll back the greenbelt in stages, assuaging fears of creating a land rush that would unleash unfavorable development. It was eager to sell off acreage, but not at the peril of diminishing the value of its surrounding holdings. Company officials spoke of being careful not to "soil the nest." With a huge inventory of debt-free land, and the minimal greenbelt taxes in effect on much of it, St. Joe could afford to be choosy.

"The worst enemy of any community is a guy who owns one acre and that's his only investment, and his goal is to maximize that acre and get the hell out," Rummell pointed out in an interview. "That's trouble because he doesn't care what happens. If he's a rational animal, he's going to maximize the value on that land and then he's gone. Well, if we maximize the value of the first acre and it screws up the two thousand surrounding it, then we've just done the shareholders as well as west Florida a disservice."[3]

Fate of the Rural Lands

One of the fundamental tasks that St. Joe took on at the outset was trying to unload large parcels of forest land. An early attempt to auction 100,000-acre parcels failed to attract buyers, so in late 1999 the company created the St. Joe

Land Company. The new venture identified some half million acres to sell gradually in smaller acreages. By early 2001, the Land Company had mounted an all-out push to sell parcels as small as five acres, which buyers could check out on its web site. The marketing effort met with tremendous success, surpassing the company's sales expectations. The company ran ads in area newspapers, inviting buyers to enjoy their piece of the land that had previously been closed to almost all offers. St. Joe found that it could more than triple its return by selling plots for ranches, quail plantations, and hunting and fishing retreats instead of as timberland. The Land Company sold $105.6 million in land in 2000 as compared to $3.9 million in 1999.[4]

Deep consumer interest led the way to other marketing maneuvers, such as the rural RiverCamps that cropped up in St. Joe's 2000 annual report. Rummell described RiverCamps as sets of "high-quality finished cabins" convenient to a variety of forms of outdoor recreation, from fishing and hunting to horseback riding.[5] Company spokesmen Billy Buzzett described the idea as "Lewis and Clark meets Ralph Lauren."[6] The first of the RiverCamps was slated for the tiny town of West Bay along St. Andrew Bay, and on the other, eastern side of Bay County, near Sandy Creek and Mexico Beach. Other potential locations for RiverCamps were near the St. Marks, Ochlockonee, and Chipola Rivers.

The success of the Land Company division pointed to a future Panhandle with low-density development, in the form of rural homesites or getaways, replacing many timberlands. The company's transition was part of the Panhandle's ongoing shift from a resource-based economy reliant on fishing and forestry to a diversifying regional economy with pockets of eco-tourism. In keeping with the appeal of its rural lands for natural attributes, St. Joe took steps to groom some forest lands for aesthetic and wildlife values to serve future markets.[7] Areas featured in its Land Company ads were select forests with widely spaced pines that did not represent its typical slash pine plantation.

As St. Joe found a paying market for rural recreation on its lands, the company ended its longstanding policy of allowing locals free access to its forests. New orange construction mesh and locked gates blocked off dozens of fire lanes and logging roads across the Green Empire that locals had used for decades for access to hunting, fishing and party spots. Traditionally, the company's open access policy was an appeasement necessary to prevent its valuable timber from going up in flames due to resentful arsonists. After the company reorganized, the new managers finally cracked down. "We felt like our exposure was so great we needed to close our lands," St. Joe executive Clay Smallwood said.[8] The sad truth was that in many areas, open access had meant the company's lands had been strewn with refuse.

The closing of the dirt roads seemed to mark the end of an era. Although the move may not have been a boon for local public relations, it improved the bottom line by making most of the company's forest land available for hunting leases. In 2000, the company leased 600,000 acres to private hunting clubs. It also leased 300,000 acres to the state for Wildlife Management Areas, but that figure was likely to drop over time as St. Joe adopted a more financially aggressive approach. Hunt clubs won exclusive rights for access to company land across the far-flung Green Empire. The clubs were responsible for cleaning up litter and keeping roads locked.

In addition, St. Joe itself managed hunting access on certain choice areas. One of these was the M-K Ranch in northern Gulf County. After a previous lifetime as a rice and crawfish operation, converted not too successfully to a pine tree farm, St. Joe reconstructed old levees and flooded the area with a generous diversion from a tributary of the Apalachicola to create a 1,000-acre duck-hunting compound that was an almost instant success with well-heeled sportsmen.

In the meantime, forestry continued as an interim, but dominant land use on upward of 800,000 acres of St. Joe lands. St. Joe signaled its new, more tentative commitment to forestry in 1997, when it went from owning to leasing vital forestry components, including fire-fighting equipment. St. Joe continued supplying softwood fiber by rail or truck to existing markets, including its biggest customer, the Smurfit-Stone paper mill in Panama City. Smallwood said the company would continue its intensive forestry methods similar to row-crop agriculture, including planting of carefully bred seedlings, use of herbicides to give plants a head start over competing vegetation, and bedding in wet areas. The planting mix would consist of slash pine for most areas (85 to 90 percent of St. Joe's timberlands), sand pine for especially sandy areas, loblolly for clay soils, and a smattering of longleaf pine, which in recent years amounted to about 3,000 to 4,000 acres annually.[9]

To Market, to Market

While fine-tuning its divestment strategy for rural lands, St. Joe's main focus remained on its 50,000 coastal and near-coastal acres, as well as on real estate in prime growth areas like Tallahassee. St. Joe was pulling out the stops to capture some of what Peter Rummell has labeled "a mass internal migration on the scale this country has never seen" as baby boomers prepare for an active retirement.[10] At the May 2000 company annual meeting, Rummell laid out a promising string of facts.

Swelling numbers of wealthy baby boomers were interested in buying vacation and second homes and were just starting to reach the prime buying age of fifty-four; more of these boomers were choosing Florida than any other state. Over the next decade, 10 percent of the nation's growth would be in Florida, where 80 percent of the population lives within ten miles of the coast. Then the clincher: St. Joe, with its ownership of 256 miles of near-coast waterfront and five miles of white sand beaches, was the single largest holder of remaining developable shoreline property.[11]

The facts sounded fantastically promising for business, yet at the same time ominous to those who worry about things such as wetlands, traffic snarls, and demands on regional resources. If its marketing engines were successful, the company could expect to attract legions of aging baby boomers to its newly discovered coast.

St. Joe relied upon the expertise of Arvida to help turn trees to towns. Since the early 1970s, under the direction of former Arvida chief Charles Cobb Jr., Arvida has taken a sophisticated approach to planning and marketing its communities. For thirty years, the company has relied on market surveys and analyses before bringing in the heavy equipment. "I don't think you'll find anybody in the country, in fact I'm very confident of this—that really understands the market the way Arvida does," Arvida Capital Area president Tim Edmond said.[12]

To the extent that economic development efforts were successful, St. Joe would experience a mushroom effect as its commercial and industrial development catalyzed demand for housing. "We're just not coming in here to slug it out for our share of the existing market. Our goal here is to try to grow the entire market, which will accrue to our benefit, but also to others," Peter Rummell said in a 1998 interview.[13]

The company's approach at SouthWood, its large development on the southeast edge of Tallahassee, illustrated its way of gauging a potential buying audience and simultaneously publicizing a city or region. In marketing SouthWood, St. Joe/Arvida sent out 26,000 surveys to state employees as well as alumni from both Florida State University (FSU) and Florida Agricultural and Mechanical University (FAMU) that it thought might be enticed to return to the master-planned outcrop of the capital city. To further help target its marketing, the company also paid people to check license plates at various Panhandle beaches to see where people were driving from. Ohio and the Midwest were especially well represented.[14]

The signatures of Arvida developments were good schools close at hand, immaculate golf courses, and beautiful landscaping. The new St. Joe/Arvida "place-making" approach was a marketing strategy that mined the existing attributes of a locale and added instant cachet through the built elements to create a distinctive atmosphere. The company aimed to "create" more places with the kind of unique appeal found in Santa Fe, Nantucket, or Napa Valley. The Disneyesque place-making approach included selecting the right name.

A beachfront project in Gulf County went through several labels before St. Joe settled on WindMark Beach. At first it was informally called Dixie Belle, the name locals use to describe the area. For a while it was the "Point at Sabal Beach." Apparently not enough people knew whether the sabal was a fish, a furry animal or a palm (the correct meaning), so St. Joe at last settled on the trendy, not geographic-specific name of WindMark Beach. (The less than propitious name for a coastal development was especially ironic considering the hurricane that dealt a death blow to the old town of St. Joseph back in 1844.) Recounting the brainstorming session where St. Joe/Arvida executives came up with WindMark, John Hendry of Arvida noted Peter Rummell's assertion that naming these places is harder than selling them. "When is the last time you've been to a place and said, 'What a great place! But what a lousy name!'?"[15]

In several venues, St. Joe is employing New Urbanism mainstays such as village greens and walkable neighborhoods with small commercial centers. Many people are tired of their cars, or at least ready to loosen the dependency, and Arvida is taking note of this dissatisfaction.

Arvida, however, was slow to embrace New Urbanism. James Howard Kunstler is a journalist and author of several books, including *The Geography of Nowhere,* an account of the decline of cities and towns and how worship of the automobile has marred the American landscape.[16] By Kunstler's account, Andres Duany, the South Florida architect who, along with his architect wife Elizabeth Plater-Zyberk, helped to pioneer the New Urbanism concept, had a hard time convincing Arvida of the desirability of New Urbanism.

"He [Duany] wanted badly to convert them to a New Urbanism viewpoint," Kunstler said during an interview while at a speaking engagement in Tallahassee. Some years back, a former Arvida executive gave Kunstler a tour of Celebration, Disney's community in central Florida. The executive told Kunstler that when Arvida was given an opportunity to adopt these New Urbanism concepts, such as walkability, mixed-use zoning, and higher residential density, Arvida rejected them.[17] Arvida has since come to adopt these concepts, though selectively and with modifications such as bigger feeder roads and use of cul-de-sacs instead of the standard grid street pattern.

Although St. Joe saw New Urbanism as a marketing enhancement and a way to build more livable communities, the company was not about to push the envelope. Peter Rummell explained that St. Joe was not as interested in innovating as in applying proven ideas that would appeal to its market. For example, he doubted whether the buyers for whom he was building would prefer that their carpets be made from recycled soda bottles. "I don't think we have anything on the drawing boards now that says this is going to be the prototypical environmental community. . . . We are continually looking around for what works and what doesn't work, but I would think philosophically you're going to find that we are early adopters as opposed to inventors."[18]

"We don't offer a solar option now," Rummel said, "although we've talked about it. This is true of Arvida statewide. There hasn't been the interest or willingness to pay for it." He added that he wasn't willing to take the risk involved in creating a solar village and telling consumers "you've got to do this if you want to buy a home from us."[19]

The Places Being Made

It was no accident that the reinvented St. Joe, now with the experienced community builder Arvida in its fold, cut its teeth in south Walton. Of all the corners of the Green Empire, this was the one that was already best attracting the high-end consumer St. Joe sought. A survey conducted for the South Walton Tourist Development Council in 1999 found that visitors there tended to be college-educated and of a wealthier set than visitors only twenty miles away in Panama City Beach.[20]

Well-heeled vacationers were the kind of people St. Joe/Arvida had in mind as second-home buyers when it unveiled its first round of casual but pricey properties in south Walton County. The Retreat, a project already underway when Rummell came aboard, spanned the westernmost holdings that St. Joe retained after the Topsail Hill transactions. Buyers snapped up ninety beachside lots there, at prices averaging $400,000 each.[21]

Success at The Retreat was an opening act for the master-planned Water-Color project, built on 499 acres around Seaside. St. Joe anticipated the intense scrutiny that would attend WaterColor by virtue of its proximity to Seaside, and it tailored its design to meld harmoniously with its famous, and finicky, neighbor. At WaterColor, St. Joe launched its "place-making" marketing concept, highlighting southern relaxation, natural beauty, and art.

At full build-out, WaterColor would contain 1,100 single and multifamily residences, mostly second homes that could be leased for long-term rentals. In addition, WaterColor was expected to eventually fill 100,000 square feet of commercial space. Other key parts of the plan were a hotel, tennis club, bike trails, boathouse and lakefront park.[22]

In accordance with the consent agreement hammered out between the state and St. Joe in the Topsail Hill settlement, WaterColor's building footprints would stay far from one of south Walton's biggest freshwater lakes, the 220-acre Western Lake. St. Joe left a 100-foot buffer of native vegetation around its share of the lake and pushed back any buildings to a distance of at least 300 feet. Even though the consent agreement legalized housing density up to eight units per acre, St. Joe kept density to 2.5 units per acre, a move that eased opposition of nearby residents to the massive new project.

With WaterColor, Arvida took on its most painstaking New Urbanist project to that date. Company officials and consultants labored over decisions, down to how to artfully conceal air conditioning units and what kind of native plants would create the best hedges. Ideas that downplayed cars and emphasized walkability were evident, including alleys, back-entry garages, and sidewalks and gravel trails. However, WaterColor made more allowance for cars than at pioneering Seaside, something quickly apparent in its wider streets. Perhaps its most functional New Urbanist move was to connect several WaterColor streets with existing streets at Seaside.

Buyers were expected to select their homes from pattern books, choosing looks that were similar to Seaside but with fewer ornaments and more hints of Louisiana Creole and the Caribbean. They could choose their own builder from an approved list but had to abide by a voluminous list of covenants, codes and restrictions (CCRs) that specified allowable facades, paint colors, porch locations and myriad other details.

Like Seaside, WaterColor does not allow lawns at individual homes, restricting them to the town commons and parks. The on-site horticulturist, Stephen Greer, was available to help residents select appropriate plantings. Greer tended a nursery full of plants that were both attractive and suited to the desertlike beach conditions, including those salvaged from construction sites.

Meanwhile, St. Joe hired biologist Jim Moyers to fulfill its promise to protect the Choctawhatchee beach mouse, whose critical habitat the WaterColor project impinged upon with its beach-side structures. One key protection would be a ban on cats at WaterColor, an item written into the CCR. In addition to actively protecting the WaterColor beach mouse population, including rounding up stray cats that failed to abide by the rules, the mitigation called for attempting to introduce a new population down the beach at another St. Joe development. Moyers also presented naturalist programs to residents on the

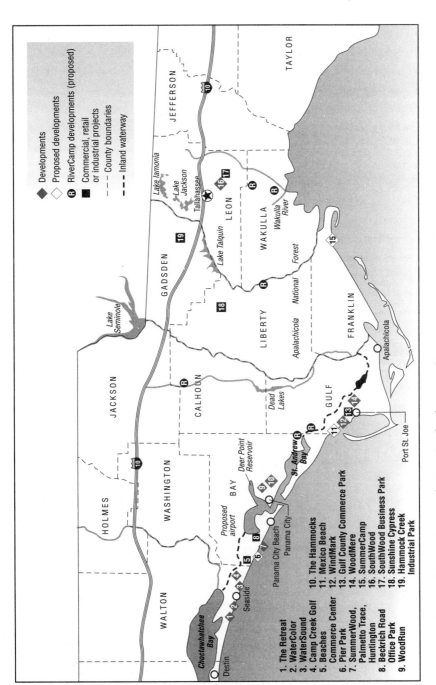

MAP 4. Trees to towns: St. Joe Company's emerging developments in 2001.

Legend:
- ◆ Developments
- ◇ Proposed developments
- Ⓡ RiverCamp developments (proposed)
- ■ Commercial, retail or industrial projects
- - - - County boundaries
- – ▪ – Inland waterway

1. The Retreat
2. WaterColor
3. WaterSound
4. Camp Creek Golf
5. Beaches Commerce Center
6. Pier Park
7. SummerWood, Palmetto Trace, Huntington
8. Beckrich Road Office Park
9. WoodRun
10. The Hammocks
11. Mexico Beach
12. WindMark
13. Gulf County Commerce Park
14. WoodMere
15. SummerCamp
16. SouthWood
17. SouthWood Business Park
18. Sunshine Cypress
19. Hammock Creek Industrial Park

area's ecological features. Adding to the cultural amenities implied in the name WaterColor, Arvida also promised to have a resident artist.

Biologist Moyers went to work on another serious task when a mishap sent sediment-laden water into Western Lake during construction, an incident that local watchdogs and news outlets noticed. St. Joe responded by beefing up floating turbidity barriers and hay bales and assigning Moyers and Greer to closely monitor water quality. In the end, WaterColor's storm-water retention area resembled a natural wetland, thanks to appropriate and abundant native plantings.

The issue of protecting the quality of the sterling dune lakes, including Western Lake, was an important one in the final stages of WaterColor's Development of Regional Impact approval. Concerned Seaside residents joined others to create a dune lake task force whose daunting goal was to protect the county's rare lakes as development by St. Joe and others ratcheted up the impacts. As the accident at WaterColor showed, impacts could occur even when developers had the best of intentions.

WaterColor opened to brisk sales—more than thirty sites sold within the first two months, mainly to buyers from the drive-in southern market, which would include Atlanta and Birmingham, as well as "a lot from the Midwest."[23] By the close of 2000, St. Joe had made gross profits of $18 million at WaterColor on the sale of sixty-six lots and nine condos at the nascent resort, even with stiff competition nearby from other new developments, including Andres Duany and Elizabeth Plater-Zyberk's award-winning Rosemary Beach.[24]

Close to home, WaterColor won over some tough hometown critics. Barbara Weidrich of the South Walton Community Council citizens' group, said she "came in ready to do battle" over the company's plans and came away from its September 1999 groundbreaking pleasantly surprised at St. Joe's willingness to pare density and make other concessions.[25] As WaterColor began taking shape, Seaside's vice president of real estate, Beth Folta, relayed that "in general, with some reservations, the homeowners in Seaside have reacted positively." St. Joe's willingness to tweak its initial plans to set aside more natural areas and adopt a native landscape scheme similar to Seaside's was a big plus. When WaterColor is completed, St. Joe officials expected it to blend seamlessly with Seaside.[26]

Seaside's Folta viewed the 24,000 acres in south Walton's state park and forest land mostly created in the Topsail Hill era as an adequate bulwark against wall-to-wall building. That land will ensure that south Walton retains its natural appeal, she said. As for St. Joe's remaining acreage, Folta argued that Seaside residents "always knew it would be developed in some way."[27] It was a good

FIGURE 7. Sign posted at the WaterColor groundbreaking ceremony, September 1999: "Please Do Not Disturb the Vegetation." Photo by Kathryn Ziewitz.

thing that Seasiders generally approved of WaterColor because St. Joe planned two other major pods of future development at WaterColor.

Several miles east of WaterColor, St. Joe chose the shores of Camp Creek Lake for its WaterSound community where sticker prices for homes began at $1 million. The location offered one of the most dramatic views of dunes in the state, dunes that the resident pedestrians would cross without harming by way of a wood suspension bridge. The beach side would offer a little-used mile of gorgeous beach, to be shared perhaps with biologist Moyers' newly seeded colony of endangered Choctawhatchee beach mice, if they successfully began to reproduce there on their own.

WaterSound is bounded on the west by Deer Lake State Park, one piece of land St. Joe sold to the state along with Topsail Hill while keeping the parcel next to Camp Creek Lake. That tradeoff provided a park buffer that helped make WaterSound "exclusive and secluded," in the words of Arvida's former president for Northwest Florida, James Rester.[28] St. Joe/Arvida would ensure exclusivity by making the enclave a gated community, thereby capturing the portion of the upscale market that insisted on gated security. Newspaper ads pitched WaterSound to elite consumers as "the perfect refuge from the outside world." Buyers in this protected paradise could enjoy a lakeside swimming pool, nature trails, nearby golf, or boating in nonmotorized crafts—the stipulation against motors was in effect both at WaterSound and WaterColor to protect the coastal dune lakes.

The first phase at WaterSound offered fifty condominiums and six homesites on a fifteen-acre tract with direct Gulf access. According to the "building value inland" philosophy, two later phases would cover several hundred more acres inland across Highway 30-A and include a mix of residential units, from multifamily to individual homesites, as well as a retail cluster. Altogether, WaterSound comprised 256 acres.

Rounding out its early south Walton developments, St. Joe wasted no time in adding a brand-name golf course to the mix. Set in a generous wedge of more than 1,000 acres between U.S. 98 and Highway 30-A, the Camp Creek Golf Club is a private club for Arvida property owners only. The first eighteen holes were designed by golf pro Tom Fazio to cover 220 acres, a spread much larger than most golf courses, partially due to the abundance of lakes and high-quality wetlands that blanket south Walton County. Fazio worked these natural features into the design of the links and relied heavily on native plants, while targeting wetlands already tarnished by St. Joe's silviculture activities for fill and construction.

Still on the drawing boards in 2001 for Walton County was another eighteen-hole Tom Fazio course, along with plans for two clubhouses. Golf course homes were not part of the plan, but St. Joe/Arvida planned fifty golf "cottages." St. Joe constructed a new road that would provide access to the golf amenity for both beach-dwelling Arvida residents and those farther north on the additional expanse of company land that it could develop someday. St. Joe's insistence on golf proved to be a successful hunch. Only months after its opening, St. Joe credited the golf club with "driving sales" in south Walton beyond expectations.

The luxury concept carried over to Bay County where in the fall of 2002 St. Joe announced its plans for the 360-unit "WaterSound East" along Lake Powell, near a golf course designed by pro Greg Norman. Earlier, the company had stated plans to build 1,900 units in the area west of Lake Powell near the Walton County line.

In the year 2001, St. Joe owned more than 191,000 acres of land in Bay County, more than in any other region except the former industrial fountainhead of Gulf County.[29] Whereas Jacksonville was the company's brain center, Bay County was the epicenter of St. Joe's on-the-ground activities and the location of its Northwest Florida offices. St. Joe's ambitions for Bay County were big and varied. Plans included housing developments and retail centers, as well as possible future golf communities and beachfront projects. In addition, St. Joe hoped for an international airport built on its land around West Bay, with associated industrial and commercial sites and villages to accommodate a population of roughly 70,000 persons. The plan also included a conservation area of about 37,000 acres. The total area for this West Bay sector plan, including the airport, comprised 78,000 acres, almost all of it St. Joe land.

Bay County presented St. Joe with a mosaic of existing development, from chic to shabby, divided into fiefdoms of eight municipal governments—seven cities and the county—that tended to squabble over matters like annexations and sewage treatment. Until recently, St. Joe's greenbelt hemmed in the outer bounds of development over much of the county. As St. Joe launched development, the lack of unity in local governments presented a situation ripe for St. Joe to exert a strong leadership role, and to court those governments under which it preferred to build. If the people in Bay County could not coordinate planning, then St. Joe would be "calling the shots," Jerry Ray said.[30]

Annexations increased, among them several controversial requests made by the St. Joe Company. The effort of municipalities to acquire acreage outside their existing boundaries steadily shrank the amount of land under county control while boosting acreages of eager-to-grow cities. Annexations enlarge a city's power and tax base while at the same time obligating it to supply vital, and costly services including water, sewerage, police, and fire fighting. Annexations also change which comprehensive plan a developer must abide by, including allowable density. In most cases in Bay County, city "comp plans" are not as stringent as the county's rule book for developers. In Gulf County as well, St. Joe proposed annexation for much of its land by the city of Port St. Joe, even extending to include WindMark Beach two miles to the north.

Two cities at the forefront in Bay County were Panama City, the older urban area sheltered from the open Gulf by St. Andrew Bay, and its condo-dotted tourist counterpart on the Gulf, Panama City Beach. The company drew a sharp distinction between beach and nonbeach areas, and lavished its best attention on the latter city.

The project that best expressed St. Joe's early high-energy expectations for Panama City Beach was Pier Park, a joint venture between St. Joe and the city of

Panama City Beach. Pier Park would remake a ho-hum city fishing pier and a little-used adjacent state park into a hub for fun and spending stretching only a few yards from the beach to busy Highway 98. Plans called for a huge makeover to the existing pier and the busy beachfront road and development of 160 acres across the beach into half park, and half shops, eateries and attractions. An outlet center abutting Highway 98 would replace eighty acres of sand pines with a Disney store, The Gap, and scores of other discount shops. A hotel was also part of the plans floated.

St. Joe saw Pier Park as both a destination and a "gateway" for future development in the area. The project began after Panama City Beach officials approached St. Joe to ask about using their adjacent land for overflow parking to serve an annual seafood festival held at the existing state park. Those discussions launched a formal public-private partnership. The city got an opportunity to build itself a dynamic, master-planned centerpiece and St. Joe got the benefit of having the local government on board as a full-fledged partner in the project. One councilman saw Pier Park as a chance to "turn the beach around, image-wise."[31] In recent years some residents have grown weary of the Beach's annual Bacchanalian spring break scene and have pushed for better representation for year-round residents as well as hotel interests.

The partnership between St. Joe and the city went from concept to reality under a new mayor, Lee Sullivan, a former Marine and Panama City Beach police chief known for his cowboy boots and quick wit. Mayor Sullivan approached the partnership with St. Joe expressing a wary but hopeful view of what the arrangement could do for his small, strategically positioned city. In an interview at city hall, he explained that he was looking out for his own "stock-holders"—the citizens of Panama City Beach, and that his decisions would be based on how well St. Joe's plans meshed with the city's own goals.

The mayor took office with the municipality already well on its way to a formal partnership with St. Joe—a situation Sullivan described as akin to having signed a prenuptial agreement. Under Sullivan's term the beach city proceeded to exchange vows and ride off into the sunset, after overcoming some reluctance on the part of the state to approve the union. The state at first balked at the partners' request to buy back at cost the forty-nine-acre state park that was central to the project; however, in August 2001 the state okayed the deal with a provision that a share of the former park land remain in permanent use for recreation.

The land at Pier Park had vestiges of the natural appeal that once blanketed Panama City Beach in the same fashion as neighboring south Walton. In the past, the pine forest there supported red-cockaded woodpeckers and gopher tortoises, as well as carnivorous sundew plants around tiny seeping springs, according to some locals. However, St. Joe's timber operations took a toll. Biologists who surveyed the site for Pier Park found evidence of past gopher tortoise use, but like the woodpeckers, none survive. Several rare plants were present, along with trash heaps, in the sandy woods. Planned nature trails would help visitors enjoy the wild landscape that remained.

The partnership agreement left the city with eighty acres of park land and St. Joe with the other 197 acres. The city obligated itself to float revenue bonds to pay for park improvements and half the costs of roads, sewers, and other necessities; St. Joe agreed to pay the other half of infrastructure costs and assume the role of developer. St. Joe reserved the option of developing housing on the site in the future, but only if necessary to make the project pay off.

While arrangements for Pier Park were coming together, the city of Panama City Beach stayed busy with several other St. Joe/Arvida projects in its borders. These included a twenty-four-acre office park where St. Joe/Arvida would house its office and whose anchor tenant would be a telecommunications company. Also, St. Joe unveiled the beach's first light industrial park, by 2001 housing a batch cement plant along with five other tenants, with plenty of room for more businesses on its 180 acres. City officials viewed the facilities as a means to broaden the local economic base beyond tourism.

Future elections might test how well citizens think the city walked the fine line between watchdog of and partner with St. Joe Company. As of late 2002, the honeymoon between St. Joe and the city appeared to be lingering. St. Joe showed its fondness for the city by piling up requests for its lands to be annexed into the city; in the year 2000 alone the requests covered some 800 acres.[32]

As owner of most of the land in the Panama City Beach area and near the proposed airport, St. Joe had plenty of room to grow there. By the fall of 2002, Panama City Beach sought to annex from the county 2,000 additional acres of coastal scrub and pine along U.S. 98. The annexation would require a comp plan amendment to allow for residential, tourist and mixed uses instead of forestry.

Across the Hathaway Bridge in Panama City, longtime mayor Gerry Clemons pursued a strategy for joining forces with St. Joe by means of gutsy annexations. Annexations offered a way for the city to grow into the greenbelt that had confined it for so long. Within the older urban areas of Panama City and adjoining smaller towns, St. Joe/Arvida showed little interest in undertaking major projects.

Quite the opposite, it had "for sale" signs on other tracts, including 368 acres of pine forest just east of Panama City, close to the urban core. The land was near a major highway and seemingly suitable for a multitude of uses. Clearly, though, St. Joe was selective about where it would itself choose to develop within existing urban areas, and greenfields in older areas were of little interest. One possible drawback was its location within a few miles of the local paper mill. Although the mill was handy as St. Joe's biggest pulp buyer, its smell hurt the value of surrounding real estate.

As the county seat, Panama City could have been content to enjoy secondary benefits that came its way as an established regional center for trade, law, health care, education and cultural opportunities. Or, it could more aggressively seek a piece of the pie. Mayor Clemons chose the latter path. Under Clemons, the city began to annex a northern extension that had swelled to more than 6,850 acres by fall of 2001. Eventually, this area could expand to meet the new inland highway that St. Joe proposed to link Bay and Gulf Counties.

Panama City had achieved some success in its older areas, being recognized as an outstanding "Small Arts Town" for its lively theater, music, and art scene. Modernization of two downtown marinas and other investments brought the city recognition in both the "Main Street" and "Waterfronts Florida" programs. With these efforts and more like them underway, the idea of growing Panama City's borders bothered some residents. It was uncertain how Bay County's older city centers and neighborhoods would hold onto their vitality as growth began to spin outward.

The future city boundary lines on the Bay County map would no doubt change as the county's competitive cities vied for a larger share of St. Joe's action. Among the cities that found favor with St. Joe was Lynn Haven, the Yankee-founded old town a few miles north of Panama City whose growing suburbs were popular with home buyers. Soon after Peter Rummell's hiring, St. Joe sited there a stand-alone subdivision of fifty-one homes called WoodRun. The development's spacious model homes tempted buyers with their snappy interior décor and enclosed pools with gurgling fountains. Prices were in the $200,000 to $300,000 range. But Arvida suffered a public relations blow when local television station WMBB aired a segment covering new WoodRun homeowners' dissatisfaction with construction flaws.[33]

In 2001, St. Joe launched The Hammocks, also in booming Lynn Haven. Buyers flocked to purchase townhouses starting at $90,000 and homes priced starting in the mid-$130,000s. The subdivision was next to an existing high school adding further appeal to the family market. Its 189-acre site included wetlands and forest hammock, some of which were preserved in natural areas in keeping with the project's name.

The City of Lynn Haven spent $826,373 to extend a road, Mosley Drive, that provided the only access to the project. At the time, the city was facing a budget crisis. Commissioner Frances Wittkopf, who voted against the expenditure, thought the cost of the road would have been more fairly shared between the city, the developer, and the school board, which benefited because the road provided new access to the neighboring high school. Instead, she said, "The city paid every dime." Wittkopf, who is an advocate of walkable communities, also objected to the lack of sidewalks along the narrow, winding road, which she likened to a "pig trail."[34]

City manager John Lynch, who joined the city after the road was underway, did not view the project as a fiscal drain. He noted that St. Joe donated nearly sixty acres of land to build the road, with a taxable value of $744,920. He said the road would pay for itself over time through impact fees, water fees, and ad valorem taxes.[35]

East of Bay County lies Gulf County, where St. Joe owns the lion's share of land, more than 240,000 acres. In the wake of the paper mill's closure, local leaders rallied to recruit newcomers such as wealthy boat owners who might be attracted to a gleaming new marina paid for mostly by state and federal grants. The rapid change in focus challenged Gulf County government. Droves of people visited county offices to find out about flood zones and to look at maps. "We almost feel like we're a real estate office. We've never seen this many people," said harried Gulf County administrator Don Butler in June 2000.[36]

The whole area was poised to boom. St. Joe's first project near its old industrial center was the WindMark Beach project, an eighty-acre, single-family subdivision of 110 units on a scenic jut of St. Joseph Bay northwest of Port St. Joe. The first twenty lots sold within a month, at prices from $90,000 to more than $400,000. A later phase, called simply "WindMark," would plant another 1,500 homes just inland. Ad copy for WindMark touted the area's natural beauty and location on "an undiscovered part of Northwest Florida's Gulf Coast."

The ad proclaimed, "It's not what we created. It's what we left alone." Indeed, WindMark Beach left intact a thirty-acre conservation area. The community also featured a series of community docks amid the coastal dunes. According to the editor of Port St. Joe's *Star* newspaper, this one development would generate $1.2 million a year or 10 percent of Gulf County's tax base.[37] With the closure of the mill, county officials were thrilled to have other sources of tax revenue, although they did not seem to fully consider the infrastructure costs of the new development.

But the early phases of WindMark were only the beginning of St. Joe's plans to help newcomers discover the hitherto "Forgotten Coast." After several years of laying groundwork, focusing on roads to serve the area, the company announced vague plans to develop behind another 3.7-mile stretch of beach and an area stretching a whopping five miles inland. According to an April 2001 company press release, the planning area encompassed an astounding 27,000 acres. That was the same size area on which Walt Disney World sits, or roughly 60 percent the size of Washington, D.C.

St. Joe's reception in Franklin County, the heart of "Florida Wild" country, was tepid. At a meeting in Bay County in 2001, economic development chief Neal Wade joked that Franklin County, which as of 2001 had only one blinking light in the whole county, was the place to go for those who did not embrace development. With the Apalachicola River Valley the anchor of biodiversity for the region, St. Joe's hands-off approach was fitting. St. Joe owned almost 70,000 acres in the county.[38]

Still, St. Joe/Arvida had several Franklin County projects in the works. The first, Driftwood, was a joint endeavor between Arvida and local real estate company Anchor Realty. Driftwood consisted of twenty-seven lots on the Gulf six miles east of Carrabelle and forty-eight miles south of Tallahassee. A second, much larger project, SummerCamp, was slated for a few miles east of Driftwood. In August 2001, the assistant planning director for the county was unaware of St. Joe's intentions near the coastal hamlet of St. Teresa, about forty-five miles from Tallahassee, where it planned to build SummerCamp. "The land is still zoned for agriculture," assistant county planner Mark Curenton said. "They have never come to us. . . . They should have started years ago. The county commission is not going to just push it through overnight."[39]

St. Joe planned for SummerCamp to be a major second-home cluster with a beach club, a sixty-room inn (later reduced to fifty rooms), a restaurant, and a marina set on the tranquil marsh near St. Teresa. SummerCamp would provide recreation for its own residents as well as for inhabitants of St. Joe's SouthWood community in Tallahassee. SummerCamp would offer a canoe area and a "sunset beach," which would have to rely on trucked-in sand because of the marshy coast.

St. Joe also hoped to offer a marina at SummerCamp—a contentious feature of the resort, given that SummerCamp would flank the ecologically sensitive Alligator Harbor, a state aquatic preserve. For St. Joe, a marina would enhance the value of its properties over a wide area. At the same time, a marina, and the boating activity it would engender, would have an inevitable impact on the bay. Even the cleanest commercial marinas affect the surrounding environment. Accidental discharges of oil and gas, destruction to sea grass and other resources by inexperienced boaters, and impacts of construction itself can do damage. With some 1,600 species of marine life in the dense sea grass beds and sheltered marshes of Alligator Harbor, the stakes were high.

The number of dwellings fluctuated from an early 250 units to more than 600 before ending up at just under 500 units when the development won approval from the Franklin County Commission in March 2002, minus the marina.[40]

The county's nod of approval came only months after St. Joe officially introduced the project for consideration. The zoning change associated with the development meant the land would go from one permitted dwelling each forty acres under the old agricultural zoning to as many as 499 units on 784 acres, a leap in building density of more than twenty-five times. The fluctuation came in part from new state legislation to raise by 150 percent the threshold for which a laborious DRI analysis would be required in the eight Panhandle counties labeled "rural areas of economic concern." Along with a few counties in South Florida, eight Panhandle counties met the criteria for less stringent application of the DRI analysis. At 499 units, SummerCamp fell just one unit short of the scale that would require a DRI. For rural Franklin County that until recently issued only 100 new home permits a year, this was a drastic change.[41]

The St. Joe Company denied initiating the legislation to change the DRI threshold, which passed in a provision tacked onto an economic development measure in the spring of 2001, but that did not prevent state workers from calling it the "St. Joe Relief Act." The bill was sponsored by Quincy Representative Bev Kilmer, who argued that the provision would help stimulate distressed counties' economies by reducing red tape. The bill drew fire for its content and its eleventh-hour appearance. "This gives a blank check for St. Joe to do its development in northwest Florida in the counties that don't have the staff to deal with large-scale developments," said American Planning Association lobbyist Marcia Elder.[42] At the same time the DRI legislation was passed, the *St. Petersburg Times* disclosed that a land-use attorney working as a consultant for St. Joe was also working as a paid advisor to Florida Senate president John McKay on growth management issues. The consultant, Edward Vogler II, said his work for St. Joe concerned a condominium project in southwest Florida and that none of his work for McKay was "specifically directed to a particular private interest."[43]

Even with the helpful legislation, St. Joe's plans hit a pot hole when it was disclosed that much of the coastal terrain that SummerCamp would occupy was subject to flooding and the soil in areas was inappropriate for construction.

The state's Department of Community Affairs would not approve SummerCamp as proposed, at least not until Franklin County amended its comp plan. Or so it seemed.

In the climate of considerable local opposition to the project, St. Joe was forced to sit down with 1000 Friends of Florida, the Apalachee Ecological Conservancy, Apalachicola Bay and River Keeper, Inc., as well as the Florida Wildlife Federation and agree to more than a dozen changes that would reduce the ecological impact of the project, although without giving up the building density that St. Joe desired.

Franklin County commissioners, notably Cheryl Sanders, sister of state representative Will Kendrick (D-Carrabelle), had insisted on these changes before giving approval. It was Sanders's opinion that St. Joe would have been better off if the company had undergone a DRI. By changing state legislation, the company made the SummerCamp decision more openly political, causing delays and raising the ire of locals.[44]

The company's biggest concessions were giving up plans to relocate a segment of U.S. Highway 98 and agreeing to set aside buffer zones, protect wetlands, and build an advanced wastewater treatment plant. The company also agreed not to develop the land seaward of the Category One Hurricane Surge Line—surprisingly not a given.

On January 21, 2003, the Franklin County Commission unanimously approved the modified SummerCamp project by adopting an amendment to its outmoded comprehensive plan. Sentiments from speakers at the meeting ran two to one against approval of the 784-acre project before the county had rewritten its comprehensive plan. Moreover, it was not clear whether the company had fully resolved concerns about coastal flood zone mapping and soil analysis.

Critics also sought but did not get detailed answers about other matters associated with such a large-scale development, including disaster mitigation, the added costs of police and fire protection, and affordable housing—issues that are typically addressed in a DRI. The Sierra Club and the American Red Cross along with the Panhandle Citizens Coalition (PCC) remained opposed to the project. PCC vowed to challenge SummerCamp as it wended its way through state review.

Even those who had granted conditional approval to the project anticipated continued vigilance. As one person involved in crafting the conditions for endorsing SummerCamp noted, the concessions were just a start; the company would have to be "bird dogged" to make sure they became reality.

Affordable Housing

Alfred and Jessie Ball duPont spoke of "rehabilitating" the Florida Panhandle and its residents. Their noblesse oblige contributed to their plans to build the Port St. Joe paper mill to provide decent-paying jobs. Today's inheritors of the Green Empire also view themselves as rehabilitators in the economic development sense. But, as during Ed Ball's era, the St. Joe Company fell short of enthusiastically providing affordable housing, especially on-site along with its higher-end housing "products."

Even the company's inland and moderate homes were not available for less than the $90,000 range (for a townhouse in Bay County), with single-family homes starting around $115,000. Instead, St. Joe/Arvida, like most developers, supported affordable housing largely to the extent it was compelled to, and in Florida, community developers were rarely required to include low-income housing on site. Local governments considered themselves blessed if they could get a developer to voluntarily contribute to an affordable housing fund to help low-income families with the down payment for a home, which is what St. Joe did in Leon County.

Yet the need for affordable housing in the Green Empire is as keen as it was in the day of Alfred duPont. Many residents find prefabricated "mobile" homes the only affordable option. In Bay County, for example, permits issued for mobile homes exceeded permits for site-built homes during much of the 1990s. The search for affordable housing forced many residents to buy small acreages out of town and to adopt a commuter lifestyle that further taxed the household budget with additional transportation expenses. This trend in housing at the lower end of the market spectrum contributed to sprawl and accentuated the spread of population to rural but non-agricultural settings.[45] Besides the many social impacts of this settlement trend, more homes planted around forests also meant increased difficulties in carrying out prescribed burns.

Coastal communities such as those in southern Walton, Santa Rosa, Bay, Gulf, and Franklin Counties have an especially dire need for reasonably priced housing. Walton County alone needed 7,147 affordable homes by 2010.[46]

Large-scale developers are required in the DRI process to demonstrate to local and regional authorities that sufficient low-income housing already exists near their proposed development. Otherwise, they are required to build affordable housing or subsidize it off site. The review also calculates how many lower-paying jobs any proposed commercial space will generate.

St. Joe hired Georgianne Ratliff, a vice president with the Tampa firm Wilson

Miller, to conduct the affordable housing analysis for SouthWood as she later did for WindMark in Gulf County. Susan Caswell, a state affordable housing expert with the East Central Florida Regional Planning Council, was told by a consultant not working for St. Joe that the company instructed its SouthWood consultants to "tear the methodology apart until their numbers worked."[47] Ratliff's team first tried to expand the radius of the affordable housing boundary, taking issue with the boundaries set by the local regional planning council. When the council hung tough, the consultants made concessions and adjusted downward the available supply. Ratliff also maximized the price of an affordable home by using a property tax half of what it actually is in Leon County and not including consideration of Private Mortgage Insurance, which would amount to $45 to $50 per month in most cases.

On that basis, Ratliff's analysis concluded that a family making up to $22,950 could afford a $80,777 home. The calculation applied 30 percent of income for mortgage, taxes, and insurance. The city challenged these assumptions. Ratliff conceded only that the tax estimate was low, changing to $73,572 her "good faith" estimate of an affordable home in Tallahassee.[48] With this adjustment, the unmet need for affordable houses came out to forty-eight units at build-out, just two units short of the threshold above which a developer would have to help with housing.[49]

The East Central Florida Planning Council later changed its methodology, used throughout the state, to explicitly include Private Mortgage Insurance in its calculation. Subsequent state legislation that made PMI a required consideration might have forced St. Joe to build on-site affordable housing at South-Wood, had it been on the books at the time.

In a close vote, the Apalachee Regional Planning Council determined that St. Joe/Arvida would not be required to make provisions for affordable dwellings to go forward with SouthWood, in spite of the best efforts of affordable housing advocate Jaimie Ross of 1000 Friends of Florida to convince the planning council otherwise. St. Joe's "wriggling around" the methodology was not all that unusual, Caswell said.

"The model almost never results in houses being built anywhere," according to Michael Parker of Tallahassee's affordable housing program.[50] Instead, the methodology is most useful for demonstrating to local government in broad terms what the housing impact of a project is, rather than precisely deriving a number of needed low income homes.

In Caswell's opinion, a promising approach to cover affordable housing needs is to assess a dollar amount per square foot for all development, as is done in Boston. A number of states and cities have developed programs that link affordable housing to more expensive development.[51] Since approval of SouthWood, Florida has moved toward allowing local governments to adopt ordinances or other measures such as "inclusionary housing" mechanisms to increase the supply of affordable housing to meet local needs.[52]

At the SouthWood groundbreaking ceremony two years later, Ratliff defended the methodology, saying the responsibility for affordable housing should not fall just on developers of new communities. "After all, they bring jobs," Ratliff said, inadvertently underscoring the need to have some reasonably priced housing near the newly created jobs. "The community as a whole should be responsible for providing affordable housing," she concluded.[53]

Instead of getting a bricks-and-mortar solution from St. Joe, Tallahassee, and Leon County, which also had to sign off on affordable housing provisions, asked that St. Joe/Arvida contribute $160 for each dwelling built at SouthWood to go into a housing assistance fund. St. Joe/Arvida agreed to make this "voluntary" mitigation, starting with $150,000 after the first unit at SouthWood was occupied. The sum at the end of twenty years was projected to be $550,000, enough to help fifty-five or more families receive up to $10,000 for house down payments.[54] The money would help ease low-income families into home ownership. Just not at SouthWood.

In Gulf County, St. Joe pointed to lots for sale at Woodmere on Avenue A as its contribution to affordable housing in the company's namesake town of Port St. Joe. The company offered the lots for sale at cost, according to Clay Smallwood. St. Joe Land Company hired the engineering firm of Preble-Rish to run water and sewer lines to the land in north Port St. Joe, close to where St. Joe Paper in the 1950s and 1960s filled in lowland with boiler ash to create the Mill View development. Woodmere initially offered lots at $14,000 each for fourteen homes, an effort that County Commissioner Nathan Peters applauded as his predominantly African American district had few options for home ownership.[55] Yet only a small number of qualified buyers came forward.

After Jaimie Ross appeared at a Gulf County commission meeting in September 2002 to present an inclusionary housing ordinance proposal to the county, Clay Smallwood stood up (after Ross had left the meeting to drive back to Tallahassee) and warned against having outsiders from Tallahassee dictate what the county should do about addressing the affordable housing issue. County officials were very much in agreement with Smallwood, expressing confidence that the DRI mechanism for WindMark as carried out by St. Joe and its consultant Wilson Miller was sufficient to deal with affordable housing. County Administrator Don Butler went so far as to label the inclusionary housing proposal as "dangerous."[56]

In south Walton County, St. Joe took yet another path to satisfying affordable housing requirements. That resort area already had a large deficit of low-priced housing before St. Joe began any of its projects. Beth Folta of Seaside acknowledged how difficult it is to bring affordable housing to the heart of south Walton. At Seaside, dwellings on Ruskin Place originally were conceived as affordable housing, Folta said. When Seaside took off beyond all expectations, the values there escalated as well. No formal pricing restraints were used to maintain affordability, and the market kept driving prices skyward. "We didn't realize early enough we would run into these issues with such intensity," Folta said.[57]

In 1999, St. Joe had to jump through hoops on affordable housing to gain approval for WaterColor. The company promised to address affordable housing in three years. But that commitment at the time was not in writing, prompting one Walton County planning commissioner to ask that the development be tabled until there was a concrete agreement. Another commissioner pointed out that other nearby developers had not committed anything to affordable housing. Walton County eventually approved the formation of the Walton Community Development Corporation (CDC), a nonprofit group empowered to obtain grants to subsidize affordable housing.

By this time, St. Joe had secured its development order and voluntarily agreed to finance construction of fifty affordable units.[58] The company chose to have the homes built on land it owned in the fishing town of Freeport, about a dozen miles from WaterColor. St. Joe conveyed the land to a developer who placed there factory-built homes that local realtor and affordable housing advocate Don Curenton called a "trailer-type product."[59] But Lee Perry, the developer of the affordable Bear Creek development, explained they have had to overcome the stigma of factory-built homes. "Our whole focus is so that when a person looks at these, they won't know they're seeing homes that weren't site built. Anything we build in the future will have to be factory built for it to be affordable [in south Walton County]," Perry said.[60]

What is it about on-site affordable housing that makes developers flinch? It is a combination of things: inaccurate perceptions that affordable housing is synonymous with public housing projects, old-fashioned snobbery, tying up land that cannot appreciate in value as rapidly as it otherwise might, and fear. Fear on the part of would-be inhabitants of crime or people who are different, and developers' fear that mixed income levels could reduce the marketability of their "products." Affordable housing advocate Jaimie Ross concedes that there are lots of people who just "want one-third of an acre to mow, a gated community, and people just like them."[61]

The maids and busboys typically live far away from the developments, inns and restaurants. Indeed, realtor and affordable housing advocate Don Curenton already was paying twenty-three dollars per hour, much of that to a jobs broker, to have a maid clean vacation rentals. Up the road, Destin hotels bus in Jamaicans living almost an hour away.[62] Service workers could not maintain a foothold on the coast.

Community Development Districts and Redevelopment Areas

As trees gave way to towns, who would bear the costs of the development was a central question. The developer, government, existing residents, and incoming residents together share the burden of new development. The proportion of such costs borne by each party can vary surprisingly from place to place. Every profit-conscious developer strives to minimize its share of the burden through a variety of means, from simply encouraging governments to fund and build infrastructure to passing on costs to the newcomers in its communities. One way St. Joe/Arvida is minimizing its own debt share is by making use of special financing tools for several of its larger projects, including SouthWood and Pier Park. The most aggressive of these tools is the Community Development District (CDD).

Through CDDs, St. Joe and other large developers can balance the financing for a portion of the internal infrastructure on the backs of the homeowners over the course of thirty years. A community built without a CDD passes on the developer's infrastructure costs to the home buyer directly in its sticker price. In a CDD, however, costs for certain infrastructure, such as parks and other recreational amenities, rights-of-way, storm-water ponds, and other open spaces, are financed by bonds which are paid back gradually through assessments on incoming residents. CDDs give developers more money to work with up front.

Although CDDs must be approved by the local jurisdictional government and technically are supposed to operate in the Sunshine, the blurring of public-private interests is such that citizens may have trouble obtaining information, including the composition of the governing board. An award-winning series in the *Orlando Sentinel* found that in reality, documents pertaining to CDDs are often in the law offices of the developer and not easily or willingly provided,[63] a finding consistent with research for this book.

Governed by board members initially appointed by the developer, CDDs in effect create towns within towns that often are essentially proxies for the developers' interests. Often developers receive a generous payment for land from the district governments.[64] In the case of SouthWood, four of the five board members in 2001 were Arvida executives.

As statutorily mandated, after eight years, homeowners elect their own board members and the governance reverts to the residents, but this is long after the developer has made irrevocable decisions. Developers promote CDDs as a way to guarantee maintenance and improvements in a community and to market communities as quality places, but are rarely candid about their profit maximization potential.

Although CDDs have many benefits, some observers have also raised concerns that they turn over an inordinate degree of control of public space to the developer and can cause an antagonistic relationship between the CDD and city governments.

In Bay County, St. Joe sought to employ a complementary special financing tool—the CRA, or Community Redevelopment Area, to help pay for improvements to its new Pier Park project in the name of redevelopment. St. Joe asked the city of Panama City Beach to "partner" with it and its proposed CDD, the Pier Park Community Development District, to take the unusual step of declaring the entire 265-acre project, most of it sand pine forest, as an area of "slum and blight." Whereas typically CRAs are used to uplift areas of urban decay, city planner Mel Leonard saw it as a way to "clean up a run-down area and by doing that achieve a downtown and a town center."[65]

Although only a small portion of the land along the beachfront road could be considered "blighted" by a layman's conventional definition of the word, state law allowed local governments to designate CRAs based on a variety of measures, including presence of deteriorated structures, tax delinquency, transportation inadequacies, or social factors.

The legal definition turned into a political issue and threatened to derail the whole project when Circuit Court Judge Glenn Hess refused to validate the project's bonds based on his interpretation of the applicability of the CRA mechanism. His ruling in December 2001 sent shock waves across Bay County. He questioned the use of the CRA for property he called "by and large vacant land begging to be built on."[66] After Hess ruled that Pier Park did not qualify as a CRA, he did give his approval to validate $48 million in bonds without that finance tool. By February 2002, the project was moving forward, with the City of Panama City Beach agreeing to contribute proceeds from its city sales tax to help pay off the bonds. Meanwhile, St. Joe and Panama City Beach sought an expedited Florida Supreme Court audience on the applicability of the CRA.[67]

The Difficult Task of Managing Growth

Reasonable people often disagree on what constitutes a fair share for a developer to pay to buy into a community. One popular means for communities to defray the costs of infrastructure needed for growth is to impose "impact fees." Many communities in Florida, including a number of those in the Green Empire, levy impact fees on new developments to help pay for infrastructure needed for growth—especially for roads and sewers. But impact fees are estimated to cover only about one-third of the costs of growth requirements, not taking into account the externalities of increased air and water pollution and even road rage.

Past growth management legislation has tried to offer a framework for quantifying impacts of new development and getting developers and newcomers to contribute their fair share. By law, development orders may be held up if a proposed development can be proved to strain local services. But when the rules are applied on-the-ground, high-minded ideals like concurrency—planning infrastructure needs ahead of growth—can become lost in a technical battleground. To a layman, it appears that standards of concurrency and "sufficiency," such as those requiring a certain level of service for roads, are often subject to manipulation.

Developers reserve special antipathy for the DRI program, still in attenuated effect in 2003. The DRI requires developers to supply extensive analysis about how roads, water, sewer, and other services would be affected by new construction. The upside of the DRI is that it provides technical assistance and state oversight to communities not equipped to independently evaluate development proposals, aiding both bureaucrats and citizens. DRI review also ensures consideration of impacts on wetlands and rare wildlife species and brings a number of agencies into the review, at the developer's cost.

St. Joe described the DRI process as "lengthy and costly" and warned stockholders, "The DRI approval process is expected to have a material impact on the company's real estate development activities in the future."[68] It was no surprise that St. Joe favored legislation that passed in 2001 raising the threshold at which a DRI was required in certain economically lagging counties, including key Green Empire counties.

St. Joe was particularly well equipped to navigate, if not change, Florida growth management law with its experienced in-house executives and consultants. The very presence of Robert Rhodes on the St. Joe team inspired hope among some that St. Joe would voluntarily set a new standard for planning in the area. Terrell Arline, a trial lawyer by training and into 2001 a lobbyist for

1000 Friends of Florida, expressed this view: "If we can ever see good development, it's with St. Joe. . . . I've got a lot of faith that St. Joe will do the right thing.
That group understands smart growth. Most developers don't understand
smart growth. Most developers want to develop to suit the automobile."[69]
Arline's view of St. Joe more than a year later was decidedly more cautious, in
light of St. Joe's support for weakening the applicability of DRIs.

When all is said and done, it may not be the jaded DRI process or concurrency or the traditional paradigms that provide hope for managing growth
in the Florida Panhandle. "The only way we're going to change our land development patterns is if developers realize they can make money in a new way . . .
[and] convincing the market that they can make money by doing it," according
to Arline. Slowly, they seem to be convincing even conservative Wall Street
financial underwriters who are more comfortable with the known profitability
of well-located strip malls that New Urbanism and other aspects of truly smart
growth are profitable.

As it geared up its "place making" efforts, St. Joe was showing itself to be willing to take some risks while forgoing pursuit of truly cutting-edge ideas. St. Joe
was in some ways raising the bar for development in the Green Empire. Most
important though, the scope and range of the company's development plans
affected the region to an extent that the old paper company never did. Through
its own vigorous efforts and the inevitable ripple effects that would follow, St.
Joe was indeed transforming the Panhandle from a backwater to a destination.

11

Breaking Ground

SouthWood as a Case Study

*We want to be good corporate citizens, but . . . at the
end of the day, I have to go back to my board of directors with a number that makes sense financially.*
Tim Edmond, capital region president, St. Joe/Arvida

ST. JOE'S SOUTHWOOD DEVELOPMENT was slated to become the largest and
most comprehensively planned community in all of northwest Florida,[1] eventually planting 4,250 or more residences amid the rolling hills and live oaks of
Ed Ball's stately old Southwood plantation. SouthWood essentially grafted a
whole new town to Tallahassee's southeast side just five miles from the state
capitol. Model homes opened for viewing in the fall of 2001, and building was
set to continue for more than a decade. Later phases on contiguous St. Joe property would add even more homes, amenities, and workplaces.

St. Joe's reasons for making one of its first big splashes in Tallahassee were the
"fantastic land" they had to work with, in the words of CEO Peter Rummell, and
the fact that Tallahassee was a relatively undiscovered place.

"I'll never forget the first time I drove onto SouthWood," Rummell said. "I
didn't know there were hills in Tallahassee. You drive up that rolling landscape
with the lakes and the clear vistas, the naturally cleared areas that have been
clear for 100 years; that was one of my first kind of surprises."[2] Rummell told
Arvida's Tim Edmond, who would oversee development of the site, not to be
"stingy" with the beautiful land.[3] The city had the right components for success,

in the opinion of company spokesman Jerry Ray. It was a university town, not too large, with a good airport, fairly good climate, and huge broadband potential for tapping into e-commerce. St. Joe thus used the phrase "a wired college town" to describe SouthWood's "place-making" attributes.[4] The focal point of SouthWood is a town center with a park adjacent to a lake. Restaurants, retail shops, professional offices and community facilities were slated to fill this hub. Several dozen luxury loft apartments will top storefronts, and two additional neighborhood village centers will serve SouthWood's phase one neighborhoods.

The company targeted considerable acreage for commercial development— 5.6 million square feet approved by the end of 2000. Of this, 250 acres were certified as appropriate for a wished-for semiconductor facility. A 90,000-square-foot building was intended to "leverage FSU's research and development and to incubate businesses," according to St. Joe Spokesman Jerry Ray.[5] South-Wood lured local software company DataMaxx Corporation as one of its first commercial clients.

Planners and business persons were willing to lower the already low level of service on nearby roads so as not to miss the opportunity for economic development. Already having won concessions on traffic concurrency, St. Joe then sought reductions in permitting fees to attract commercial occupants. Several Tallahassee leaders disapproved, arguing that the incentives were meant for truly depressed parts of Tallahassee's south side.[6]

SouthWood adjoined the state government complex built on land St. Joe donated after the first failed SouthWood attempt in the 1980s, a location that made SouthWood especially convenient to state workers, although few who could afford the homes.

The much-vaunted "learning village" at SouthWood includes FSU's Developmental Research School, the K-12 lab school nicknamed "Florida High," along with John Paul II Catholic High School, and community college classes taught in the evenings at the office complex adjacent to SouthWood.

For entertainment and recreation, SouthWood offers a designer semiprivate golf course, and eventually will feature a community center, athletic fields, an aquatic center, health clubs and tennis courts. The town will have playgrounds and interconnected parks with fountains and other "water features." Company literature advertised a "backyard that includes miles of coastline on the Gulf of Mexico," a plan the company presumed to fulfill by offering SouthWood's residents special access to recreation at St. Joe's planned SummerCamp beach resort less than an hour's drive away. SouthWood even hired an "Art of Living

Director" to help foster the sense of community and create "a vibrant atmosphere within SouthWood." A town with a cruise director.

The architecture at SouthWood has a southern accent, emphasizing the north Florida "vernacular," based on a library of 2,000 photos of homes in the region. There will be porches galore, but not the "gingerbread," the fancy trim that Celebration and Seaside homes sport.[7]

SouthWood's covenants and design restrictions lay out "things such as no tin foil in your windows, no chickens in your back yard, or parking your RV on your curb," Tim Edmond, who oversaw SouthWood, quipped. But the many CCRs cover much more to assure tidiness in the new village: You have to keep your garage door closed at all times unless entering, exiting or actively using the garage. Permanent basketball goals are not allowed to be visible from the street; portable hoops are okay, but have to be stored away from public view when not in use.[8] The Bronx this is not.

Putting Together the Widgets

Arvida itself was constructing most of the buildings at SouthWood in an efficient bulk production mode. Asked about the quality of materials for these production houses, Edmond responded, "It's not so much the materials. It's the craftsmanship of putting the widgets together." The issue of quality was sensitive for both Edmond and Arvida. Tim Edmond was president of the Florida division of Town and County Homes,[9] one of the two building companies that did most of the construction at Disney's Celebration, where construction problems took home buyers by surprise, given the Disney aura of perfection. Those problems left him with what he called "scar tissue."

Edmond said SouthWood's construction would be enhanced by Arvida's painstaking choice of subcontractors. "We have met with every trade known to man in this town," Edmond said. We have seen their work. We've spoken to their customers. . . . We're familiar with their financial wherewithal. We have forged those relationships and have not turned a spoonful of dirt. And that's what we have not had the time to do in my other lives."[10]

One of Edmond's challenges was that the type of construction that Arvida has traditionally done—production homes built by the hundreds or thousands —was not the typical mode in Tallahassee, which, like other existing Panhandle communities, has a large proportion of custom-built homes. "The cost of labor is just killing me," Edmond said. "It's higher in Tallahassee than south Florida because there hasn't been a machine created here for production houses."

Only the most expensive, custom-built homes will be overseen by a handful of select local builders. Arvida will market and sell these $250,000-plus estate homes on large lots. In addition to single-family homes, the housing mix at build-out will include luxury apartments and 300 or more townhouses, many rentals. In the first phase, St. Joe sold land to an apartment developer to build 240 units.

New Urbanist Comparison

SouthWood hits the New Urbanism market in the marketing sense, but relatively low density overall makes it a combination of New Urbanism and traditional golf course community. "It's a good hybrid," Edmond said. SouthWood meets the walkability and sustainability criteria of the Congress of New Urbanism, the definitive body headed by Seaside's developer, Robert Davis. Town and village centers were carefully located to place essential services within easy reach. "Research has borne out that Americans typically won't walk more than about 1,500 feet. It's a terrible thing unless you're heated and cooled and entertained [during] the walk." People will be able to walk to school, and to work at the adjacent government office complex or in new commercial space.[11]

In reality, there were few government workers who could afford to buy at SouthWood due to the prohibitively high housing prices, although the addition of luxury apartments was an attractive feature for singles, couples, and small families. By 2002, the company advertised townhouses starting at roughly $120,000, with most considerably more. The situation was ironic, given the argument that St. Joe/Arvida had made in the approval phase that people would be able to walk to and from the nearby Capitol City Office Complex. "The majority of the state workers can't afford it, and I work with a bunch of lawyers," said Diana Swegman, an administrative secretary with the state Department of Health nearby.[12] Swegman and others attended SouthWood's open house in September 2001, complete with clowns, a trolley ride around the grounds, and tours of model homes decorated to exquisite detail, including fake martinis on a silver tray in the living room of one of the models. The more reasonably priced town homes had just about sold out, and the company was planning on building more than originally anticipated.

Architect and planner Andres Duany might not find SouthWood compact or dense enough to meet strict New Urbanist ideals. In addition, street patterns include cul-de-sacs as well as the traditional grid pattern. "Guess what? Some people want cul-de-sacs. So we have some of those in there. It's the best of both worlds," Edmond said. "Duany is an absolute purist, but you have to react to a market."

SouthWood's 3,200 acres of rolling hills will have plenty of green space, about 40 percent of its total acreage. Under some of this green space will lie the remnants of earlier residents, the Apalachee Indians who flourished there at the time the Spanish reached Florida's shores. St. Joe's cultural research on the site, as part of the DRI, revealed that SouthWood has more than sixty sites, ranging from burial mounds to pre-ceramic lithic "scatters" to the remains of what likely was a large Spanish mission.[13]

Ed Ball arguably never intended for his Southwood "sanctuary" to be developed beyond use for cattle ranching and hunting. A covey of quail to this day may appear before a visitor as tokens of that foregone intent. In addition to the cattle and watermelon that were thriving on the site well into the year 2000,[14] SouthWood is home to plenty of wildlife, including several threatened animals, or state "species of special concern." These include gopher tortoises, the Florida pine snake, eastern indigo snake, and kestrels, as well as Sherman's fox squirrels. The occasional wood stork, bald eagle or Florida black bear also is known to wander the variegated terrain that includes 270 acres of wetlands.[15]

State and local authorities required mitigation for wildlife species. St. Joe satisfied these requirements through a variety of measures. For instance, landscaping around the school sites left intact existing habitat, helping both native animals and plants. St. Joe also set aside 160 acres on-site as a natural preserve, part of which was the longleaf pine area the company cut after withdrawing its initial plans to develop Southwood.[16]

Planning officials also required St. Joe to provide mitigation to compensate for disruption to the venerable gopher tortoises that remained at SouthWood in numbers of about one per acre. St. Joe agreed to provide a conservation easement of roughly 260 acres it owned across the county next to the Apalachicola National Forest.[17] These keystone animals are themselves developers of sorts for the animal world by dint of the burrows they make that shelter so many other forms of wildlife. The conservation easement would then become part of the Apalachicola National Forest. St. Joe's approach to meeting wildlife needs showed the advantage of working with large-parcel development, and the flexibility a willing landowner could exhibit to incorporate native wildlife into the scenery.

St. Joe had wanted to use many of the existing wetlands on site for stormwater treatment and retention, making the point that they were already degraded and therefore suitable for alteration. Years of cattle ranching and silviculture had indeed diminished their quality. But Tallahassee's definition of wetlands looked more prospectively at how they function. If there was a chance that a wetland could be restored, it was still treated as viable. St. Joe reluctantly agreed to excavate a large basin south of its residential property to accommodate the storm water, and most of the wetlands on site were improved or left intact. Other counties in the Panhandle are less particular.

Groundbreaking

St. Joe/Arvida broke ground at the old Southwood Farm on a warm September morning in 2000, in an event as carefully orchestrated as the WaterColor groundbreaking had been a year earlier. Driving down the lovely canopy road into SouthWood, invitees passed a series of placards: "Another special place designed by Arvida" . . . "3,200 acres of modern southern living" . . . "Neighborhood of the past" . . . "123 acre central park and lake" . . . "Custom designed homes. . . ."

The festivities took place in front of Ed Ball's former occasional residence, now SouthWood's sales center. Cottages for prospective buyers would soon pop up behind the old house where Ed Ball had left a large stock of bourbon that new St. Joe executives found covered in dust. A few dozen head of cattle grazed in the pasture just north of the white-columned estate. Several even seemed to low on cue as Tim Edmond spoke, welcoming the assembled dignitaries. Present were the city and county commissioners, planners, Tallahassee's mayor, the Leon County School Board Superintendent, state politicians, and staff from the Department of Community Affairs. A phalanx of realtors flashed their Arvida nameplates as they roamed the premises. Also present were the major St. Joe/Arvida players. CEO Peter Rummell was quietly proud but seemingly uncomfortable with the hoopla. Host Tim Edmond recognized SouthWood's master planner from Sasaki Associates, Dick Galehouse, down from Boston, and lauded David Powell, St. Joe/Arvida's primary consultant from the firm of Hopping, Green, Sams, and Smith, with whom Edmond said he had spent more time of late than with his own family.

The long list of people Edmond thanked included Tom McGurk, former head of the Department of Management Services (DMS), Cynthia Henderson, then secretary of the Bureau of Professional Regulation and soon-to-be-anointed state special liaison to St. Joe and head of DMS. He acknowledged longtime St. Joe board of directors member Frank Shaw, a well-connected Tallahassee developer whom he credited with helping win approvals. He reserved special praise for the late governor Lawton Chiles, whom he said took time to

FIGURE 8. The open house at SouthWood, September 2001, showing Ed Ball's former farm-house. Photo by June Wiaz.

meet with Peter Rummell and Bob Rhodes in 1997 to help them create a "model community."

"Without him, this would not have been possible," Edmond said, also acknowledging the presence of Lawton Chiles's widow, Rhea, in the front row. But Edmond carefully added that now the company is working with the "wonderful Bush administration."[18] Bipartisanship is key to savvy developers.

Also key for St. Joe/Arvida is marketing, performed to the hilt at this event with the help of hired thespians. As guests arrived, forty local actors strolled around them attired with the paraphernalia of the suburban good life—a man with his hefty golf bag here, a woman in a tennis outfit there, a bicyclist, a boy with a football, a jogger or two. Rounding out the fetching Disney-like cast of characters were kids in a little red wagon and an obedient chocolate Labrador on a tether.

Edmond's boss at Arvida, Jim Motta, took his turn at the microphone. "Tomorrow is today," Motta said surreally. "Our pledge is that SouthWood will be a true place," he said, one that would benefit from the culture, the fine schools, health care, and other amenities of Tallahassee. SouthWood would embody three simple foundations: authenticity, community, and value, Motta said.[19] Behind him, the actors smiled perfect, if not authentic, smiles. Even the mound of dirt for the simulated ground breaking seemed immaculate with bright blue metal shovels all in a row.

At the end of the remarks and the ritual turning of dirt, guests were treated to a reception. A small band of students from Florida A&M University softly played jazz tunes. A catered spread that fit the declared theme of "Southern Plantation Days" offered guests southern fare, including fried chicken tenderloins, Virginia ham on biscuits, and boiled peanuts, with sweet tea and lemonade to wash it down. Dessert of watermelon wedges, pecan tarts, and pound cake sat on a table under a quaint sign, "SouthWood Bake Sale."

The groundbreaking festivities were just one manifestation of St. Joe/Arvida's creative marketing for SouthWood. In addition to more conventional advertising, the company had planned to erect on the perimeter of SouthWood thirty-foot billboards of sweet suburbia—kids playing sandlot baseball, others on swings; also, a construction worker with shovel in hand. The company said the "pastoral cutouts" were art and requested a variance to post them, but eventually withdrew its request after negative public reaction.[20]

One much-discussed element of SouthWood was its public school. St. Joe/Arvida did not begin construction until it secured Florida High as the core of its "learning village." Forced reliance on existing schools near SouthWood could have been a deal breaker. Initially, some educators and planners had hoped students from SouthWood would attend existing south-side schools, bringing socioeconomic balance to the minority-dominated schools there. But St. Joe/Arvida wanted a school right within its ungated borders, and not just any school—it sought the innovative K-12 FSU laboratory school, "Florida High."

"The school was linchpin without question," Edmond said. "Tallahassee is so focused on education. Like the Austins, Raleighs, Boulders, and competing-type cities . . . lifelong learning for everyone, cradle to grave, is of paramount importance."[21] As Disney did at Celebration under Rummell, St. Joe/Arvida managed to leverage public dollars to locate a new, innovative school on its grounds as a fundamental marketing draw.

St. Joe and FSU formed a public/private partnership to accomplish the relocation. St. Joe donated fifty acres at SouthWood, valued at roughly $5 million, for the Florida High campus. FSU reimbursed St. Joe, which then contributed that amount in turn to start a construction fund. The Florida legislature eased the way to raise additional monies by agreeing to spend $10 million in state funds for the relocation and passing a law allowing university lab schools (like charter schools) to issue bonds for financing school construction—$23.3 million in this case. Haskell Construction, the builder based in Jacksonville, helped structure the deal.[22] Of the thirty-nine states with charter schools, Florida is one of three that give these schools construction money.[23]

Many saw the transaction as win-win: St. Joe would secure a magnet to draw residents to SouthWood, and the lab school (that essentially functions as a charter school) would get a whole new facility on a site twice as large as its prior home. The land that the Florida High lab school vacated at the downtown FSU campus would be used to build a basic sciences building for FSU's new medical school in another advance for FSU and St. Joe, which also had an interest in boosting medical care in the region.

One downside of the relocation was that the progressive school would be prohibitively far to reach for some returning students, especially children of farm workers who lived on the west end of town. Glenn Thomas, then director/CEO of Florida High, stressed that efforts would be made to maintain a diverse student body that previously had been required to mirror the community.[24]

Besides the children of SouthWood, for whom 500 slots were reserved, others among the 1,600 students might be children of parents employed at the nearby Capitol City Office Complex. Sandy D'Alemberte, FSU president at the time, touted the state offices as "really a wonderful asset if you're trying to have diversity in your laboratory school."[25] Even so, Thomas acknowledged that the school would have to recruit minorities from the community.

The school, which opened on time for the 2001–2002 academic year, enlisted help from FSU and other universities, plus nonprofit organizations and businesses, to help design the curriculum.[26] At the high school level, students must choose one of four career tracks: hospitality, health services, engineering technology, or business technology. The vocational tracks coincide with St. Joe/Arvida's economic development objectives, seemingly providing a training ground for people to work at upscale coastal developments or fill positions at medium-tech companies it hopes to lure to Tallahassee. However, the mandatory "academies" did not necessarily mesh with the educational desires of some students, who opted to attend other high schools because of what they perceived to be a deemphasis of the college-oriented curriculum at Florida High.

The approach at Florida High appeared comparable to the school at Celebration, which also was high-tech, similar in physical layout, and keen on multi-age grouping. Whereas the Celebration school's bumpy beginnings were compounded by a brand-new staff, Florida High from the start at SouthWood retained the staff experience and cohesiveness that the Celebration school lacked. Still, some critics questioned the transitions at Florida High. One long-time former Florida High teacher, former Tallahassee city commission member Dorothy Inman-Johnson, was especially concerned about the mandatory vocational tracks.[27]

Glenn Thomas, who left Florida High to head another lab school in south Florida, was prepared to take some risks to make Florida High stand out. "Our purpose is to be really different. If we're not going to be unique, it's not worth it," Thomas said.[28] The director/CEO added that the requisite vocational-technical training opens up scholarship opportunities for students who are not bound for four-year colleges and allows all postsecondary students to acquire skills that will increase their earning potential while still in college.

Rummell hoped the SouthWood school would turn into "a real lab school where the kids aren't lab rats, where they get the benefit of some real forward thinking." Director Thomas cited the success of academies elsewhere and noted that students can accelerate when necessary. St. Joe also donated land next to Florida High for a second smaller private school, John Paul II Catholic High School. Adding a second school on-site further diluted the impetus for the higher- income families at SouthWood to use existing schools on the south side of Tallahassee, a premise that had been laid out hopefully in the city's 1998 amendments to its comprehensive plan.

In the summer of 2001, traffic was backed up for miles near SouthWood, even before residential and commercial occupancy at SouthWood. Tim Edmond said he knew it would be problematic at first but expected significant improvement by the end of the school year upon the completion of another entrance into SouthWood.[29] The entrance still was not completed well into the 2002–2003 school year.

For higher and continuing education, SouthWood residents could attend classes at the nearby state office buildings, where Tallahassee Community College made use of spaces that would otherwise be vacant at night. Edmond, current FSU president T. K. Wetherell (then president of TCC and at the same time behind-the-scenes lobbyist for St. Joe), and Tom McGurk, then secretary of DMS, developed the idea to make use of the 1,500,000 square feet of state office buildings that were heated and cooled anyway. St. Joe/Arvida offered to help pay the additional maintenance costs. Once again, the company apparently crafted an apparent win-win arrangement for its "learning village."

Overall, Tallahassee's reception of SouthWood was positive. St. Joe took a drastically different approach to working with citizens and local government than it had in its first failed attempt. "There really was not much consensus built as we've hopefully done, to really understand the market place and to be sensitive to the needs of community," Edmond said. This time, St. Joe worked hard to gain public buy-in for its already-crafted plans. By May 2000, Edmond estimated he had had more than 250 meetings with various organizations to gather support.[30]

In response to civic input, the company altered some plans. It agreed to provide a connection from SouthWood to the St. Marks Trail and to set aside additional conservation areas. The company also agreed to preserve more wetlands and include a storm-water master plan, although much of this was not so much volunteered as required by the local government.

At the crucial April 1999 meeting, at which the Tallahassee and Leon County commissions assembled to vote on SouthWood, the majority of officials and citizens present endorsed the project. SouthWood won development approval with only one dissenting vote on the county commission. Many citizens took the floor to praise SouthWood. "I feel like I won the lottery," enthused Penny Herman, realtor and former mayor of Tallahassee, citing the ample green space and absence of gates as pluses. "The benefits outweigh the negatives." The head of the local Chamber of Commerce gave the project his blessing for its expected economic benefits. Edmond projected SouthWood would create 12,000 temporary and 13,000 permanent jobs.[31]

Other activists and watchdog individuals and groups gave at least qualified endorsements. Former city commissioner Inman-Johnson, who had been critical of the original Southwood proposal, and later weighed in about Florida High, expressed overall optimism about the new version. "I think it will be wonderful," she said. "It's not far from the urban core. . . . My biggest concern is that government does not cave in on its responsibility to fully investigate the impacts on the community now and into the future, and fully attribute a share [of the costs] to the current developer."[32] At the meeting, the nonpartisan growth watchdog group 1000 Friends of Florida also endorsed the project, although Executive Director Charles Pattison said he would like to have seen more detail, especially on how SouthWood's plans would affect the existing southeast part of town.[33]

Some citizens objected to plans for SouthWood based on concerns about traffic and who would foot the bill for roads and other infrastructure. County Commissioner Bob Rackleff, the lone dissenter in the final vote, expressed the opinion that SouthWood was not being made to pay for the things required for concurrency. Enforcing concurrency is a political challenge that falls to local governments.

"I really object to the point of view that SouthWood has no impact on our roads," Rackleff said. "All roadwork is being tilted to accommodate South-Wood."[34] Democratic mayor Scott Maddox, a huge supporter of SouthWood, curtly jumped in: "We're not going to charge SouthWood for needs we already had."[35] (According to Leon County Florida election records, Maddox's mayoral campaign in 1997 received considerable contributions from St. Joe board member Frank Shaw and several St. Joe lobbyists, as well as influential Republicans from Bay County, Charles Hilton and powerful state representative and road builder Allan Bense.)

City Commissioner Debbie Lightsey clarified that the issue is the cost imposed by new development. But no such cost data were provided at the meeting, a point that Rackleff said contributed to his negative vote, even though he supported SouthWood in principle.[36]

One irate citizen who spoke at the meeting found the proceedings disturbing. "I discovered a roomful of adults treating Tallahassee like it was a business to be liquidated. . . . I felt like I was an intruder in a party between a developer and state government. When local government either purposefully or unintentionally hides the cost of growth, it does citizens a disservice," he said.

Yet another citizen expressed concern that SouthWood would seal construction of a controversial road, the Blairstone Extension. The northern portion was to push through a wetland and bisect several neighborhoods to link three other major thoroughfares. Although not exclusively or officially tied to SouthWood, the road was seen by local traffic experts to be crucial for accommodating SouthWood's additional traffic. Indeed, the new southern portion of this controversial road now hooks right into Southwood.

For its part, St. Joe/Arvida provided rights-of-way and footed the bill for several interchanges, turn lanes and some road widening at SouthWood—costs amounting to $9 million of the estimated $14 million for SouthWood's required phase I roadwork. But St. Joe/Arvida could have faced even more severe "exactions" for roads. One analysis found that just the first phase of SouthWood would push thirty-four major roadway segments beyond capacity. Another analysis by a city traffic engineer estimated $85 million in road improvements would be necessary as a result of St. Joe's development. Edmond said the estimate was unrealistic and that it would add $17,800 to the cost of every home in SouthWood, "ruining all chance of creating affordable housing."[37] SouthWood homeowners already were paying surcharges to help finance internal structures and amenities via the Community Development District vehicle.

For all the hoopla surrounding SouthWood, some observers saw room for improvement. Staff in the joint city-county planning department said they felt the development should have been more compact, especially at the town center. Some would have preferred more dispersed village centers over the fewer, larger shopping centers that ended up in the plan. "As good as it is, it could have been a whole lot better," one local planner said.

Tallahassee architect and professor Larry Peterson, found SouthWood "good, as far as it goes." As director of the Florida Design Initiative at Florida A&M University, Peterson has seen the range of development in Florida and elsewhere. Peterson saw room for improvement through enhanced transportation connections with existing roads and non-Southwood neighborhoods nearby. Ideally, SouthWood could be "connected to a new network of streets, walkways, bikeways and mass transit lines surrounding the development," he wrote in an editorial for the *Tallahassee Democrat*.[38] So far, SouthWood depends on several arterial roads not friendly to pedestrians or bicyclists and only assumes New Urbanist transportation features inside its own boundaries.

When local planners attempted to exact money from St. Joe/Arvida for two new bus lines, the company rebuffed the city's efforts. Smaller U.S. cities have had a hard time getting people to use mass transit. Part of the problem is that commuting and parking are too *in*expensive. Higher parking rates downtown and charging for parking at the Capital City Office Complex could provide economic incentive. Drivers pay only a fraction of the costs of road building and maintenance via gas taxes.

"People are not riding the bus," Edmond said. "I'm a very big advocate of mass transit . . . [but] we're not going to buy three buses to see 18 riders on them a day."[39] Still, transportation analysts affiliated with FSU's college of business concluded that, given the scale of SouthWood, "the developer could do much more to support the transportation system and mitigate the project's traffic impacts. . . . The developer has elected to ignore these recommendations [relating to mass transit] and in so doing is ignoring a vital part of the transportation system."[40]

In response, St. Joe agreed to provide an on-site transportation coordinator who would work with businesses to establish car pools, van pools and flextime programs. In addition, St. Joe offered to donate land from its properties along area roadways for development of park and ride lots.[41] These concessions, along with the extensive pedestrian and bicycle trails at SouthWood and the fact that the community will be wired to facilitate telecommunication, allowed the company some credit toward trip reduction, and therefore reduced its obligation to pay for further road improvements.

"St. Joe can afford to do good things," said Wendy Grey, then the director of the frenetic Tallahassee–Leon County Planning Department. Grey saw South-Wood as a good complement to urban infill, which alone could not possibly accommodate the county's population growth. Grey generally supported St. Joe's ungated, mixed-use community, but felt some trepidation. "I have a little anxiety that it won't meet the hopes we have of bringing more benefits to the south side," she said. "On the one hand, [St. Joe/Arvida] has made investments in education and cultural resources, but clearly they are a business that owes stock-holders."[42]

In May 2000, City Commissioner Debbie Lightsey viewed SouthWood as a mixed blessing. While it would undoubtedly be an attractive development, she said, "SouthWood is not going to help us solve our existing community prob-lems. They've held themselves apart. They're building their own schools so their children don't have to use our schools."[43] One of the big downsides, in her opin-ion, is the drain on the city road budget. "We've been using our infrastructure dollars to run roads and sewers out to new development. . . . So we don't spend our money on our urban core," she said. The veteran commissioner also pointed out that commissions often approve projects not consistent with earlier planning attempts: "Citizens have become active in getting us to follow the comp plan because they don't trust us. Bless their hearts, they're right."[44]

Perhaps SouthWood's gentle critics will have success in pushing for im-provements later. The 3,200 acres that St. Joe initially is developing is just the tip of the iceberg, or to use a more appropriate analogy, a longleaf pine in its grass stage. St. Joe's Leon County holdings are a subset of an astounding 200,000 acres crossing four county lines down to the coast twenty-eight miles away.[45]

12

A Company Town in Flux

> *[The town of Port St. Joe] is extraordinarily*
> *important to our future strategy.*
> Arvida project manager John Hendry, February 2001

IN THE 1990S, as the St. Joe Paper Company underwent a radical transformation, the town that had been its industrial center since the late 1930s also faced a crossroads. The paper mill that had been the town's primary employer for six decades closed for good in 1998. Now Port St. Joe could continue to emphasize industry or, alternatively, build on its coastal beauty to attract tourists and newcomers. Or it could try for both—the path that town leaders chose.

Approaching Port St. Joe from the east in the year 2001, travelers emerged from the pine forests to capture the vista of an expansive and placid eleven-mile-long and four-mile-wide blue-green lagoon—St. Joseph's Bay. Stately homes and churches with white Doric columns sat on one side of U.S. Highway 98, while on the other side, the Gulf lapped below the road's edge. Just ahead on the rim of the bay lay the dormant behemoth of the old mill, no longer pumping sulfurous clouds into the sky. Past the tracks, Arizona Chemical Company still emitted a sauerkraut-like smell, putting unaccustomed noses on full alert. Less than two miles beyond the Arizona plant was the southern edge of St. Joe's incipient coastal WindMark development that is a beachhead for a potentially gargantuan project.

The town of Port St. Joe was surprisingly well suited to state representative Bev Kilmer's nickname for it, "Mayberry on the Beach." Three traffic lights served the whole county of about 15,000. There were no traffic snarls or strip malls, no department stores, either, although there used to be. Local mortician Rocky Comfort observed that if a Port St. Joe man, living or dead, needed a suit in a hurry, his best bet was the Methodist Care Closet.[1]

The gorgeous bay also seemed untouched by time. It supported fisheries for shrimp, spotted sea trout, flounder, mackerel, succulent blue-eyed scallops (in good years), clams and much more, as it had for eons. The locals said the water cleared in the open bay when the mill closed. The fisheries had not seemed terribly affected by the mill when it operated, thanks to the cleansing action of tides at the bay's mouth. But the path of sewage effluent from the wastewater treatment plant was one ongoing problem area, a large swath of seabed from which shellfish harvest was banned. Few locals realized the ban was in place or heeded it. Just as easily overlooked were bay sediments that harbored industrial pollutants from years past, in spite of the "pristine" label some boosters used for the bay.

But now Mayberry on the Beach was changing, and not just because of the mill closure. Downtown's Reid Avenue had a new look, thanks to recent revitalization efforts. Another addition was a spiffy new marina, complete with dry dock storage and a ship's store, and nearby a new Piggly Wiggly on the main drag. These investments in Port St. Joe enhanced the town's image, a step civic leaders hoped would usher in a new, prosperous era.

But without the high salaries from the mill that once seemed to smooth over the town's shortcomings, some residents began to gaze at their surroundings and reflect on the St. Joe Company's corporate legacy. Where was the civic center? Where was the land for public parks, donated from the 240,000 acres St. Joe had long owned in the county? Mayor Frank Pate said that he once asked a St. Joe executive why his company made their money in Port St. Joe but spent it elsewhere.[2] The company official never answered his question, but the truth, in retrospect, was that the old St. Joe did not spend much anywhere off company property.

Meanwhile, the environmental legacy of the town's past cast a shadow on efforts to turn a new leaf. In more than one instance, officials and leaders appeared eager to sweep the remnants of the town's industrial past under a rug.

Death Throes of a Giant

When Florida Coast Paper (FCP) took over the mill in 1996, it reduced the work force from 754 to 412.[3] The company also drew up a drastic new contract with a

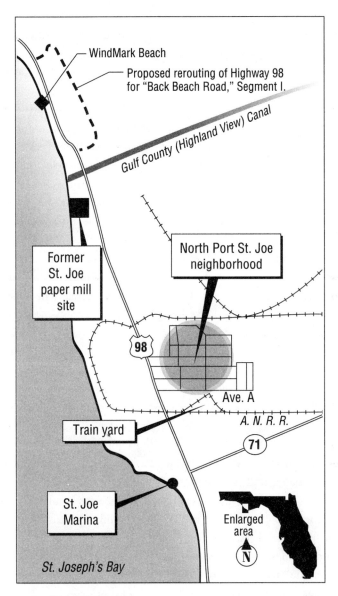

WindMark Beach

Proposed rerouting of Highway 98
for "Back Beach Road," Segment I.

Gulf County (Highland View) Canal

Former
St. Joe
paper mill
site

North Port St. Joe
neighborhood

98

Ave. A

Train yard

A. N. R. R.

71

St. Joe
Marina

Enlarged
area

N

St. Joseph's Bay

MAP 5. Port St. Joe.

foreboding average pay cut of $5,000 per worker.[4] Still, when the plant shut down in August 1998, Florida Coast insisted it was a temporary closure.

The year had started poorly for FCP partner Stone Container Corporation. Uncertainties multiplied after November 1998, when Stone Container Corporation merged with Jefferson Smurfit, creating Smurfit-Stone, one of the world's largest paper and paper-board packaging companies with 300 facilities worldwide. The merger was part of ongoing consolidation in the industry.

In December 1998, the plant was still closed and the company laid off seventy to eighty mill workers, though Ferrel Allen, general manager of the mill, publicly maintained that Florida Coast still intended to recall workers before the year's end.[5] In the meantime, the unions and management held frantic meetings in an attempt to resuscitate the dying business. But on February 5, 1999, Florida Coast submitted to the state a Worker Adjustment and Retraining Notice (WARN), a federally required formal notification that employees were to be terminated.

Several workers insisted that *they* never received an official, final lay-off notice and were adamant that they each were owed two months pay under provisions of the WARN Act. "We never did receive official notice. They just didn't talk to us," union representative Duke Jones said.[6]

Despite the willingness of the union to do whatever it would take to keep the mill operating, financial coroners pronounced the mill moribund. Florida Coast also gave formal notice of termination of health coverage for the laid-off workers. The health insurance cut-off later launched workers into a class-action lawsuit that they had hoped to avoid. They sued for vacation pay, holiday pay and continued health coverage that management had promised.

Continued health insurance was especially important. Many of the former workers suffered from a variety of ailments from years of exposure to the chemically rich paper mill environment. One chronic condition that plagued the mill workers was the lung disease asbestosis. Asbestos insulated the intestine-like steam lines throughout much of the mill. The disabling disease afflicted uncounted workers, as well as family members exposed to the asbestos fibers on work clothes. "We walked through it every day," said boilermaker and millwright Charlie Aman, who worked at St. Joe's mill for thirty years but found himself without health insurance after Florida Coast's closure.

Most of the plaintiffs in the class action lawsuit were requesting between $5,000 and $15,000,[7] not a greedy sum considering that workers at other idled paper mills had been given severance agreements worth $30,000 to $40,000.[8] As it stood, the workers were to be paid only two-thirds of their vacation time and no severance pay, since, Smurfit-Stone argued, the workers technically had never worked for their company.[9] By April 2001, the workers had received only 12–14 percent of their unused vacation pay and did not have their health coverage reinstated, according to Duke Jones.[10]

Bankruptcy proceedings kept creditors and bondholders at bay and continued almost another year before Florida Coast formally announced its closure. A staff reporter for the *Panama City News Herald,* the paper of record for the issues surrounding the mill's closure, labeled the idled mill workers "hostages" to a "morally bankrupt and financially fat corporation."[11] Neither St. Joe nor the new and changing mix of corporate owners accepted the fate of its workers as their responsibility.

It was not only mill workers and private institutions that were out their money. So reliant were local governments on the tax revenue from the mill that the closure hamstrung basic services—police, fire, schools, the wastewater treatment plant, and other county services. The Gulf County tax assessor sued Smurfit-Stone, the corporate entity that owned the mill postbankruptcy, to recoup its tax obligation from 1997 to 1999. The overdue bill amounted to $5 million plus interest and attorney fees.[12] Local officials went begging to the state. They found a sympathetic governor and a legislative delegation that was able to secure several million dollars to keep basic services operating, as well as to supply resources to beleaguered Gulf County employees for job retraining.

An annex to the Gulf County prison opened in 1998, as did a new satellite campus of the Panama City–based Gulf Coast Community College, where former mill workers trained to become prison guards. The commercial fishing net ban of 1996 already had reduced jobs in coastal communities, initiating job retraining programs. Thus, Gulf County had a safety net of sorts already cast into the roiling economic waters when the mill shut down.

Reflecting back on that time, a paper union official expressed the view that mill manager Ferrel Allen, who had made the leap from St. Joe to FCP, was earnest in his efforts to keep the mill running. Allen's heart was in the mill, having worked there for more than forty years.

For his part, company man Allen said that when Florida Coast closed in August 1998 he honestly believed it was for a "short maintenance." But he noted that on top of the poor global markets, the mill incurred fiscal stress from the high costs for labor and fiber supply, high local taxes, and an oil and gas supply regime that had been negotiated by the previous owners, St. Joe.[13] The town was unwilling and unable to reduce the tax burden for its biggest employer, then under new management based in New York. Another fiscal stressor resulted from a huge bond FCP needed to pay off because the deal was so highly leveraged.

The final bankruptcy reorganization plan included a payment by Stone (as Smurfit-Stone referred to the company in this transaction) of $123 million into a trust fund to satisfy the claims of all creditors and pay expenses.[14] Yet through the wonders of limited liability corporations' special status and tax write-offs, the Florida Coast bankruptcy had no effect on the indebtedness of Stone, according to an April 5, 1999, news release by the company. Thus, Stone was able to buy and shut down one of its major competitors in the Southeast without suffering financial damage.

In May 1999, the bondholders that had come together to finance the Stone and Four M Corporation's joint venture to acquire the mill alleged in a lawsuit that the owners of the joint venture had purposefully allowed the paper mill to go down to benefit their own mills. Neither Florida Coast Paper nor its joint venture owners had made the $10.5 million interest payment due on the loan the previous December.[15] The question in many people's minds in Port St. Joe was whether the closure was part of a larger plan.

In the 1990s, other large companies, such as International Paper, were buying out competitors only to shut them down—sometimes just several days after the purchase—thereby gaining market share and tax write-offs. Stone, around the time of its purchase of the St. Joe facility, took a number of mills off line—some because of the costs of meeting the new "cluster rules" for environmental controls, and a lot due to overcapacity. "We had another mill close by in Panama City and another in Alabama," Steve Hamilton, Smurfit-Stone regional environmental services manager explained. "That was more capacity than was needed for the Southeast," he said, unintentionally raising questions about why Stone bought into the mill venture in the first place.[16]

Out-of-state bankruptcy proceedings, the lack of severance agreements, and a general dissatisfaction with the way St. Joe had seemingly fobbed its workers off on a fragile limited liability corporation also provided pulp for the local rumor mill. It is difficult to find residents of Port St. Joe, other than those still affiliated with or vested in the St. Joe Company, who do not think there was some kind of an agreement between St. Joe and Florida Coast Paper to not operate the mill long term. In July 1999, an article in the international edition of *BusinessWeek* magazine noted how St. Joe opposed the reopening of the facility it had sold three years earlier. "St. Joe now plans and builds upscale communities and doesn't want a smelly paper plant nearby," reporter Jane Tanner wrote.[17]

The *Panama City News Herald* quoted another longtime mill worker saying, "They knew Florida Coast wasn't going to run that mill," and that St. Joe sold the mill at below-market price to avoid the bad publicity of shutting it down themselves.[18] In underscoring his belief that Florida Coast Paper and St. Joe had an unwritten understanding, another longtime employee of St. Joe noted, "They work in 20-year increments. It's pretty neat because a pine tree is pretty much useable within that time."[19]

Allen, on the other hand, when asked about whether there was some kind of a deal, said, "I would have extreme difficulty subscribing to the theory [that St. Joe and Florida Coast Paper had a deal]."[20] The president of St. Joe's Timberland division, Clay Smallwood, who clearly had heard the question before, brushed it off. "If there was a deal, it was above my level. I'm not aware of anything."[21]

"We were a Mom and Pop organization in a Wal-Mart environment," Smallwood explained. "We couldn't survive. The only way [was] to sell. Instead of selling to Wal-Mart, we sold to Mom and Pop and they couldn't make it either. That's an over-simplification of what happened, but we didn't have enough market share in any product that we could hold on when Wal-Mart got ready to cut the price and run us out of business. That's what happened to Florida Coast. They were in the same environment that our guys were in."[22]

"We talk about Port St. Joe far more than the sheer [business] volume would allow," said St. Joe CEO Peter Rummell. "The closure of the mill, which we were tagged with, was not our fault. We got tarred with that brush. I frankly think the best thing that happened to that town was the mill closing."[23] Here was something that image-conscious developers and people concerned about the impact of industrial pollution had in common. Without a doubt, the new St. Joe Company was better off without a paper mill in operation near its planned large-scale Gulf County developments.

If There Is a Mess, Whose Is It?

A Limited Liability Corporation, or L.L.C., differs from other corporations in that profits go directly to the member corporations instead of to shareholders. With Florida Coast, the shareholders were Stone Container (by 1998, Smurfit-Stone) and Four M. As with a traditional corporation, the members, or shareholders, are not responsible for outstanding taxes or other liabilities.[24]

As part of the sales agreement, St. Joe Forest Products (a subsidiary of the St. Joe Paper Company) and Florida Coast entered into a mutual cleanup contract which divided financial responsibility among the parties for contamination found by May 30, 1999. St. Joe informed stockholders that it had set aside $10 million in a contingency fund. However, that contract was not necessarily recognized by the Florida Department of Environmental Protection or U.S. Environmental Protection Agency. "You don't sell the statutory liability," explained an attorney with DEP's Office of General Counsel.[25]

When Florida Coast Paper was liquidating in the fall of 1999, management indicated the company's desire to sell the Port St. Joe plant "free and clear of any environmental liabilities." However, FCP's disclosure statement in conjunction with its initial declaration of Chapter 11 (reorganization) bankruptcy struck the federal Department of Justice as "very vague," according to internal EPA correspondence.[26]

The EPA's Region 4 in Atlanta objected to the idea of "selling liabilities free and clear" since FCP's indemnification of St. Joe probably was not legally valid. EPA inquired as to the Superfund status of the site, but at the time took no action otherwise. For the EPA to take a lead in the investigation, the agency must have had strong suspicion or evidence of hazardous contamination at the site. If the buyer, FCP, was willing to let the seller, the St. Joe Forest Products Company (SJFP), off the hook for the cleanup, so much the better for the seller.

In this case, the buyer, Florida Coast, had gone bankrupt. Another complication was that the subsidiary of the St. Joe Paper Company that directly owned and operated the mill, SJFP, no longer existed after the 1996 sale. St. Joe liquidated SJFP and distributed the sale's proceeds to stockholders.

The Stone official dealing with the environmental aspects of the mill closure, Steve Hamilton, was not with the company at the time of the purchase and said he did not know whether any kind of environmental assessment was done at that time. "Even if there were, we wouldn't rely on that," Hamilton said.

Hamilton had a background in heavy industry. He'd seen serious, long-lasting contamination from synthetic organic compounds at other sites. "Historically, paper mills have spilled weak black liquor," Hamilton said. Black liquor is the complex chemical cocktail left over after cooking wood chips in a caustic solution. Hamilton minimized the likelihood of serious residual chemical threats at the mill, noting that one key sulfur compound in black liquor also naturally occurs in seawater.[27]

Paper mills are major polluters of air, water, and soil due to the large amounts of water, energy, and chemicals necessary to break down the stubborn lignin fiber in wood. A series of studies by EPA in the mid-1980s demonstrated that black liquor from bleached kraft paper mills could sometimes also contain very low levels of dioxins and other hazardous chemicals.[28]

As one international paper industry analyst wrote in 1995, "The pulp and paper industry should . . . realize that . . . environmental concerns could one day lead to the consumption of paper being seriously questioned. The industry must mount a common defense."[29] This assessment came out around the time EPA put into effect its new "cluster" rules that called for examination of a mill's total emissions to air and water.

FIGURE 9. The paper mill in Port St. Joe in 1999 after its permanent closure, with St. Joseph Bay in the foreground. Photo by Kathryn Ziewitz.

The mill at Port St. Joe was probably no worse than paper mills elsewhere in the United States with respect to its environmental record. Research and development (R&D) spending by the paper industry averages only about a third of other manufacturing industries.[30] R&D investment is the typical measure of capacity to innovate, and the U.S. paper industry was ill-prepared to meet changing world markets and demands for less environmentally damaging processes.

To its credit, St. Joe had taken some steps to reduce its pollution over the years, notably lining its on-site waste lagoons and retooling its bleaching process. In contrast, some European and Canadian mills have been more innovative, doing away with chlorine bleaching altogether. In fact, kraft mills of the type that existed in Port St. Joe are prohibited in Germany.[31]

A Hough and a Puff

Several miles northeast of town, over the Intracoastal Waterway in White City lives an indomitable woman named Marion Hough. Hough was born in Kissimmee in 1937 and moved to Gulf County in 1984, making her a relative newcomer in a close-knit community. Hough supported a three-pack a day cigarette habit on a tight budget by rolling her own, popping in a filter each time. Hough herself was a further epidemiological quagmire from years of working as a wallpaper hanger and cleaning windows with lacquer thinner, on top of a dozen years of inhaling the emissions from Port St. Joe's industries. She shared her sagging bungalow with mountains of documents and a pair of frisky chihuahuas.

Hough was a curious political crusader who defied labels—Ralph Nader mixed with Phyllis Schlafly. She once went to court to win the right to teach her children at home because she objected to what she perceived as communist, anti-Christian doctrines in Florida textbooks. She also ran for the Florida legislature on the American Party ticket. She was an Air Force wife until her first husband committed suicide after Vietnam. Yet her patriotic convictions remained powerful.

Surrounded by huge stacks of documents "filed" on her sofa, Hough pulled up her knees like a schoolgirl and explained why she filed suit May 7, 1999, against the St. Joe Company and Florida Coast Paper Company, L.L.C. Her case was simple. On behalf of the citizens of Gulf County, she alleged that St. Joe (and then Florida Coast) had for years emitted cancer-causing compounds into the air and water and onto the land, and should therefore be compelled to restore the air, water (including groundwater) and land to a clean state. She also posed a legal challenge to DEP for not enforcing state environmental laws, and had for years tried to get local officials to take action against mill pollution.

Hough brought the case in the Fourteenth Judicial Circuit Court after reading the fine print in the St. Joe Company's 1998 annual report. In the end matter of the report, following the feel-good photos of children on beaches, she found the nitty-gritty on revenues, expenditures, corporate acquisitions, and such "contingencies" as the mill site cleanup contract between St. Joe and Florida Coast Paper.

The report stated that as a condition of the sale of the linerboard mill and container plants, the St. Joe Company "remain[ed] contingently liable" for up to $10 million "relating to On-Site Environmental Liabilities, as defined in the sales agreement, as long as they were discovered within three years of the closing date of the sale."[32] The company's liability was carefully outlined, excluding any pollution off the mill property. The tab for cleanup was divided between St. Joe and the buyer, with each part to alternate payment in steps. The buyer would pay as much as $7.5 million, to remedy "on-site environmental liabilities." In addition, the report showed the company had set aside another $1 million "for certain remediation activities at the linerboard mill [in Port St. Joe], if such activities were required under environmental laws."

The report reassured stockholders that "based on information presently available, Management believe[d] that the ultimate disposition of currently known matters [would] not have a material effect on the financial position, results of operations or liquidity of the Company."[33] After reading the report,

Hough wondered if any government entities had positioned themselves to re-coup expenses for an eventual cleanup, especially given the apparent agreement between the buyer and St. Joe that contamination must be found within three years of the sale of the plant for St. Joe to contribute to its cleanup. That anniversary—May 30, 1999—was swiftly approaching. As it turned out, no one besides Hough seemed to be concerned, including Smurfit-Stone, which had made no publicized effort to assess the contamination of the site. The clock was ticking. Hough brought this to the attention of local officials. Nothing happened, so she hurriedly filed a pro se lawsuit on behalf of Gulf County citizens.

St. Joe's response to Hough's eleventh-hour lawsuit was terse. St. Joe's attorneys noted Hough's failure to demonstrate a breach of contract, and called her other counts vague and ambiguous. Their motion also pointed out that St. Joe, having "sold and conveyed its interest in the Port St. Joe paper mill to a third party," no longer had any interest or control. St. Joe requested an award of their "reasonable attorney's fees and court costs" in dealing with the suit.[34] The company knew that indigent, self-trained attorneys cannot afford to reimburse corporate lawyers for their time.

Hough's lawsuit survived a motion for dismissal as a frivolous case after a federal attorney filed a motion in a federal district court in Gainesville. Within two weeks of Hough's complaint, the Florida DEP had filed a motion to "quash" her case. DEP's response stated, in part, that the Department "cannot be held liable for peculiarly governmental functions such as environmental permitting."[35] Otherwise put, you could not take the government to task for not doing its job.

The federal magistrate in Gainesville dismissed EPA as a defendant party, but remanded the case with the remaining defendants back to the local circuit court. Hough then voluntarily dismissed the case in the hope that her actions at least had established a basis for a future class-action suit.

The Environmental Legacy of the Mill

Mill general manager Ferrel Allen seemed surprised by a question about how Smurfit-Stone would deal with the contamination at the mill as it went about undoing itself. It was almost a given that a bleached paper mill of 1930s vintage would have at least a modicum of contamination. Yet Allen responded, "I don't know that it's contaminated."[36] In fact, the most concentrated contamination likely at the old site was the parcel still owned by St. Joe that was used as a disposal area for a variety of mill wastes and chemical drums.

Robert Nedley, former president of the St. Joe Paper Company, also downplayed any contamination worries. "I don't think there's any big, gray skeletons that would be of any concern," he said.[37] Nedley had a continuing interest in the former mill site because of his then-role as chairman of the Port St. Joe Port Authority. Nedley had chaired the Port Authority at the time of the sale of the mill and supported plans to remake the site as a port facility for oceangoing ships.

Others intimately familiar with the mill were its former workers. Former mill workers interviewed for this book said that the land the mill sat on was grossly contaminated with heavy oil (that Smurfit-Stone agreed to clean up) and black liquor as well as other substances. Black liquor may not be the most toxic concoction, but many said it was present in vast quantities under the mill.

Around 1992, the maintenance supervisor at the mill asked a well driller to sink a shallow well to provide water for a flowerbed near the guard station at the box plant's entrance. The driller, who asked that his name not be used, was confused by the request, since there already was a spigot nearby. But he proceeded. At less than twenty feet down, the one-and-a-half-inch pipe began producing what he described as "pure black liquor," with a characteristic sulfurous stench. "It wasn't something I'd really want to waller in," he said. He sank the well far beyond the typical depth of a "shallow well" until it reached ninety-six feet, still sucking up crud. The driller received $250 and the pipe remained in the ground.

Other former mill workers corroborated another ominous anecdote. In June 1996, the flooring around one of the paper machines at the mill sank into the ground. When the company pulled up the floor, they saw a pool of black liquor. They pumped for two weeks, but at the end of pumping, the hole filled up once again. They filled in the void with dirt and concrete.[38]

In an interview at his Port St. Joe office, Ferrel Allen said he had no recollection of this event, even though he was in charge of the entire mill operation at the time. "Never heard of it," Allen said when asked about the sunken paper machine and black liquor episode.[39] One former mill worker asserted that as production manager at the time, Allen would have overseen the remedy of that situation.[40] Allen himself said that black liquor used to be found when one would dig a few feet into the soil at the mill, but he concluded that the contamination had long since made its way into the Gulf.

Other workers talked of payloaders flattening unwanted chemical drums on site and large tanks leaking or having had their bottoms corroded out.[41] On the day that Smurfit-Stone and St. Joe were scheduled to report preliminary sampling results at a county commission meeting, DEP officials at last took the opportunity to meet with a group of former millworkers to find out after the fact if they'd targeted all the potentially contaminated areas.

Workers told officials about a variety of practices that may have left an environmental footprint over the years. They told of sulfuric acid tanks lined with lead; a PCB transformer storage area where fluids from the transformers would leak into the ground, now paved over; and a drum disposal area behind the bleach plant where a mix of chemical drums were crushed and buried, sometimes still containing residual liquids.

The workers also discussed other areas where they alleged there were spills of petroleum products, degreasers, defoamers and other chemicals, about a dozen sites in all.[42] Longtime employees at the mill said that up until a few years before the mill was sold, a variety of wastes were routinely dumped on the ground. Former mill worker Mark Gay, who suffers from a rare form of leukemia, called the site "just a lot of jury-rigged mess" of dilapidated and corroded machinery. Plus, when they knew an inspector was coming, Gay said, they would slow down the high-pressure wood-chip digester "so the stacks would be in compliance."[43]

A state inspector characterized a portion of the St. Joe facility in 1991 as "a sloppy operation."[44] That year, chemicals spilled near a fiberglass shop on the plant, prompting groundwater monitoring that turned up solvents in the shallow groundwater in 1993. St. Joe Forest Products, which then ran the mill, initially resisted setting up monitoring wells. By May 1995, St. Joe's contractors reported that no more contaminants had turned up above drinking water standards.[45]

The Voluntary Cleanup Begins

The cleanup at the idled mill began without much fanfare or regulatory supervision. However, DEP was monitoring the combination industrial-municipal wastewater treatment plant, owned and operated by the city of Port St. Joe. Without the pulp and paper mill waste that had made up 96 percent of its waste stream, the plant could not operate according to design.[46] After the mill shutdown, the plant limited discharges to several times a month, when it sent out a particularly potent waste stream. The plant had failed toxicity tests since late 1998, and a DEP inspection in November 1999 found the plant "significantly out of compliance." In June 2000, DEP issued a warning letter to Port St. Joe Mayor Frank Pate about "possible violations of the law."

The St. Joe mill was one of only thirteen paper mills in the United States that discharged effluent to a publicly owned wastewater treatment plant. The plant was classified legally as a "publicly owned treatment works," and operationally as an "industrial wastewater treatment plant." An official from EPA's Atlanta office was of the opinion that St. Joe supported this arrangement as a way of "shielding [itself] from compliance."[47]

With the mill no longer operating, building a new, strictly municipal treatment plant or modifying the existing one seemed a logical solution. But a new plant would cost an estimated $6 to $8 million, an expense the city was in no rush to incur. City attorney William Rish informed DEP in June 2000 that fiscal concerns made that difficult inside of a five-year time frame. In addition, he said, the plant was needed to serve the mill during its shut-down operation, and Arizona Chemical thereafter.[48]

The existing facility limped along out of compliance with respect to disinfection until it resolved what to do about a new or retooled treatment plant post mill closure. The Gulf County Health Department appeared unconcerned about pathogenic organisms making their way into the Gulf County (Highland View) Canal that was such a popular fishing spot. Indeed, locals confer the label "turd hustlers" to the mullet that make their way from Lake Wimico to the Gulf County Canal.

The DEP allowed the Port St. Joe wastewater treatment plant a dozen "mixing zones"—areas extending into St. Joe Bay where chemicals, including heavy metals and oxygen-demanding organic substances, could be diluted into the clean bay water. The facility had a "mixing zone" for mercury, along with aluminum, copper, iron, nickel and silver.[49] Mixing zones save polluters money by allowing them to avoid treating or to minimally treat chemical wastes before dumping them into public waters.[50] Assuming that the plant met its permit requirements, literally thousands of pounds of heavy metals could be legally released into the environment.

An incident on August 14, 2000, alarmed local citizens about waste being discharged into the Gulf County Canal. They were concerned about a slug of dark reddish, foamy liquid that had been discharged into the canal, material they suspected was tied to the decommissioning mill. Marion Hough contacted DEP, which sent out an inspector. The DEP official met with city treatment plant manager Larry McArdle and confirmed that the city wastewater plant had conducted a scheduled discharge during the time in question.[51] One DEP official soon after referred to the release as a "substantiated public health threat," but there were no fishing advisories posted along the canal.[52]

Ferrel Allen had mentioned in a July 2000 interview that Smurfit-Stone was getting rid of its process chemicals and that "it has done so periodically using the wastewater stream." The mill had always purged process chemicals in this manner when starting up after an extended closure, he said. In a later telephone interview, after the reddish discharge had caused concern, Allen revised his earlier statement and denied use of the wastewater treatment plant. He said all the chemicals from cleaning out the parts of the mill were legally shipped elsewhere.[53] However, a June 1, 2000, letter from the Port St. Joe attorneys to DEP backed up Allen's original statement. It mentioned that "they [Smurfit-Stone] are trying to complete the clean-up of their tanks and other facilities. At the present time, they are discharging approximately 2 MGD [million gallons per day] to the wastewater plant."[54] Allen was adamant that the waterborne waste or "influent" going to the city plant from the mill was "strictly in accordance with [the] permit. . . . I know of no toxicity."

Clean Water Network's Linda Young called the DEP's Panama City field office after hearing about the problems with effluent. One of the things she and others were wondering was whether there had been attempts to sample the waste stream that the mill was piping over to the quasi-municipal plant. Neither she nor the authors received a definitive answer from DEP or the local wastewater treatment plant official. By law, responsibility for monitoring what comes into a wastewater treatment facility falls on the operator of that plant. What comes out of the pipe after treatment is generally under the state's purview. The state authority did not seem compelled to see for itself if the mill was living up to its pre-treatment permit requirements for the waste stream it sent to the city treatment plant.

Another waste product from the wastewater plant was the voluminous sludge that accumulated in the plant's settling ponds. When the wastewater plant was built in the 1970s, it was good news for the bay, which until then had been the direct receptacle for pulp waste. But what was once a water quality problem became a land disposal issue, as the waste had to be put somewhere.

In the early 1990s, when St. Joe still operated the mill, it leased land to the city of Port St. Joe to dispose of the sludge. Florida Coast later exercised its option to buy the sludge disposal site north of town in Highland View, which then passed to Smurfit-Stone as a result of the bankruptcy. In addition, the city applied sludge on another permitted site in Gulf County, which was also the place where sludge from Panama City ended up.

Sludge from bleached paper mills in general contains dioxin and heavy metals. One EPA report noted that because of the tendency for chlorinated organic compounds—including dioxins—to bind to solids, "wastewater treatment sludge has generated the most significant environmental concerns for the pulp and paper industry."[55] However, sludge was not the subject of DEP investigation in the decommissioning process.

A September 30, 1999, letter to David Struhs, secretary of the Florida DEP, from the Florida Wildlife Federation expressed concerns about deficiencies in the state's testing methodologies that had found little dioxin in sludge predominantly from a paper mill in Bay County—the same deficiencies allegedly present in the sludge sampling at the Port St. Joe wastewater plant. The Federation estimated that the actual "total harmful dioxin Toxicity Equivalents (TEQ) concentration" for the Bay County sludge ranged between 300 and 1,500 parts per trillion (ppt), tens of times in excess of the EPA guidelines for sediments. The letter pointed out that mammals are sensitive at levels of 25 ppt.[56] More than one year later, David Struhs had not responded to Florida Wildlife Federation's letter.

One former mill worker said that pine seedlings absolutely thrive in the applied sludge that conserves soil moisture. However, Clay Smallwood of St. Joe Timber, noting the high quantities of some heavy metals, said the company did not apply sludge to its timberlands, but conceded that "there's probably some stuff from the mill that ended up in the woods."[57] As of this writing, the extent of sludge distribution in Gulf County beyond the two permitted facilities was unclear.

Taking Apart a Behemoth

As parts of the mill were disassembled and shipped off to plants elsewhere, some Gulf County residents raised alarms about the fate of other materials from the mill's industrial past, including asbestos, lime mud, and contaminated soil. Their watchdog efforts seemed to increase state oversight beyond the city-owned wastewater plant to the mill itself.

Smurfit-Stone's environmental official, Steve Hamilton, provided to DEP in the fall of 2000 his company's plans to hire a contractor to do the voluntary cleanup that would in the end cost the company several million dollars. The request for proposals for "the removal of hazardous materials" specifically mentioned twelve transformers containing the cancer-causing chemical PCBs or polychlorinated biphenyls, more than 4,000 barrels of asphaltlike No. 6 crude oil from three tanks, and thousands of square feet of friable asbestos-containing materials, as well as the need to clean out tanks and other parts of the deceased mill.[58]

Around the same time, Marion Hough contacted DEP to express concern about what she perceived as a general lack of oversight during the mill decommissioning. A DEP official informed Hough, "DEP does not get into dismantling unless there is asbestos, causes other air problems, has storm runoff problems or debris disposal is not legally performed."[59] The official's response indicated that up until that time, DEP apparently had not taken steps to oversee asbestos removal. Hough promptly informed the official that asbestos was on site. After the communications from Hamilton and Hough, DEP did provide oversight. Two months later, Port St. Joe's weekly newspaper, the *Star* assured its readers that the asbestos removal was occurring under the "watchful eyes of state regulators."[60]

The next month, DEP officials from Pensacola, Panama City, and Tallahassee toured and inspected the defunct mill. One official commended Smurfit-Stone for its "prompt action in removing the hazardous materials and wastes." Tons of materials already had been shipped off site, with proper documentation, according to DEP's postvisit report. "SS [Smurfit-Stone] has apparently complied with all requirements of the Resource Conservation and Recovery Act and Florida State Statutes for hazardous waste management," the hazardous waste inspection report concluded.

Smurfit-Stone's Steve Hamilton was adamant that the company was doing the right thing at the mill. "The liability of doing that stuff [wrong] is not worth it, and I don't have a passport," Hamilton jested.[61]

Clean-up Legalities

In September 2000, DEP officials completed the first step in the assessment of the site for the federal Superfund hazardous waste program, a site screening report submitted to EPA's regional headquarters in Atlanta. The preliminary report noted that there was a potential that contaminants were on the old mill site and recommended that a full-blown Preliminary Assessment, or PA, be completed as a priority.[62]

Attorneys for Smurfit-Stone and St. Joe, claiming that there was no evidence of contamination at the mill site, put pressure on the Florida Department of Environmental Protection in December 2000 to halt its environmental assessment work. Smurfit-Stone dispatched a team of lawyers to DEP along with a St. Joe legal representative to challenge the accuracy of DEP's preliminary site screening assessment and prevent EPA Superfund involvement. They claimed that the department's work would interfere with "sensitive negotiations for long-term rehabilitation of the site in ways that would be beneficial" to the economically depressed area.[63] Even placing a property in the Superfund database of sites that are potentially contaminated places a legal cloud over the property.

Stone's lead attorney in this matter, Terry Cole, had in previous years represented St. Joe. Cole served as an assistant secretary and general counsel of Florida's environmental agency before passing through the revolving door, along with others in his firm, to represent industry. Cole demanded that DEP withdraw its recommendation for listing the mill site in the Superfund database. He also asked for a sixty-day delay in forwarding a revised report to EPA in Atlanta. St. Joe's letter, too, requested that DEP not forward the preliminary assessment report to EPA.[64] St. Joe was involved because of its prior ownership of the mill site and also because it retained the adjacent site that had been an unlined waste impoundment area.

Their lobbying paid off. On April 4, 2001, DEP backed off its staff recommendation to conduct a full-blown PA. DEP deputy secretary Kirby Green wrote the EPA in Atlanta urging the agency to delay a PA study. Green echoed Smurfit-Stone's point of view, noting, "The land on which the site is located is projected for redevelopment that should help improve the economic conditions. The stigma of a site undergoing CERCLA [Superfund] screening will have an adverse affect [sic] on redevelopment." Green proposed letting Smurfit-Stone and St. Joe conduct the assessment.[65] DEP secretary David Struhs said his agency had never before done a favor such as this for a Florida industry.[66] Later that year Green left the agency to head up the St. Johns River Water Management District, a body of strategic importance to developers in northeast Florida, St. Joe among them.

After long consideration, EPA supported Green's desire to keep the site away from the claws of Superfund, as long as there was a "binding agreement" with the state environmental agency. One Superfund staffer kidded that EPA now stood for the "Economic Promotion Agency."

The DEP also called for strict governmental oversight of sampling, including splitting samples so that DEP or EPA could have their own set of soil, sediment, and groundwater data to compare to Stone's and St. Joe's. Neither company wanted to sample bay sediments, but St. Joe more readily agreed, since in the past they indisputably had waste directly flow into the bay.

Smurfit-Stone, St. Joe and DEP conducted limited sampling of groundwater, soil and bay sediments off the dock of the old St. Joe Paper mill in October 2001. Smurfit-Stone finished its study first. Consulting firm Malcolm Pirnie, Inc., reported that the sampling of soils found a number of contaminants, but only one, a polynuclear aromatic hydrocarbon (PAH) associated with fossil fuels, was above EPA's site screening levels, or amounts that trigger further testing. The groundwater at the same site—the former location of a paint shop—also contained two contaminants two to three times above EPA's maximum contaminant levels for drinking water, the volatile organic chemicals trichloroethene (TCE) and vinyl chloride. Other chemicals were present in groundwater, but in concentrations below levels that would require further action.[67] Malcolm Pirnie concluded that the contamination detected in the well was of "no immediate concern" because the chemicals did not appear to be migrating across property boundaries.

At a marathon December 11, 2001, Gulf County Commission meeting, Smurfit-Stone and St. Joe summarized their preliminary results. Smurfit-Stone's consultant reported its finds of localized contamination and noted that a separate regulatory program would be overseeing an area of potential petroleum contamination around the site's old tank farm. Clay Smallwood said that St. Joe's testing yielded a similar result to Smurfit-Stone's. He added that the dioxin levels that they had found were about the same as the background of dioxin three to four miles away, although there was one sample that did not quite "make sense," and they were retesting. Smallwood did not present actual data at the end of this drawn-out meeting, although he mentioned that his laptop computer for projecting the data was in his truck parked outside the court house.

Smallwood concluded, based on this ethereal data, that they had not seen anything that merited concern. A bleary-eyed Commissioner Billy Traylor distilled, "That's good news for Gulf County," and the *Star* newspaper ran with the upbeat, albeit tentative news, "Mill Tests Look Good: Early Data Indicates Superfund Designation Very Unlikely."[68]

Later research at DEP in Tallahassee showed the sample in question was for dioxin in one of the groundwater wells and was nearly five times greater than recommended standards.[69] St. Joe's consultant PSI tossed out the dioxin data because it did not meet the quality assurance parameters for data. PSI retested the well without DEP oversight and incorporated the new, much lower data into the final report that it produced several months later.[70]

St. Joe and Smurfit-Stone had followed the agreed-upon work plan, according to an official in DEP's hazardous waste program. "It's a large site and it would have been nice to sample more, but we picked the area we thought most likely to be contaminated." He seemed satisfied with the outcome, although he acknowledged that there might be call for more testing in light of information supplied by former mill workers. No further government supervised sampling of these sites occurred at the time.

Thus there remained lingering environmental concerns. The quality of Gulf County's near-shore groundwater was an open question in early 2002. Local health official Doug Kent seemed sure that tidal action had removed any of the subsurface contamination from the mill. The general flow of ground water in southern Gulf County was south-southwest, away from the drinking water intake wells but toward the "pristine" bay. However, the four municipal water wells were situated on the water treatment plant property with its unlined sludge lagoons, three-quarters of a mile from the mill site.[71] The city and Northwest Florida Water Management District in 2001 decided to shift the town's drinking water supply from groundwater to surface water from the Chipola Canal.

Linda Young's prediction held. In 1999, with the mill newly shut down for good, she had speculated, "Regulators [EPA and the state] will relieve the responsible parties of responsibility as much as possible. They'll go and cap it and do a minimal cleanup. It will be as if the mill never existed."[72] The mill appeared a likely candidate for a "brownfields" approach that encourages new businesses to use sites that have real or perceived contamination without inheriting the liability and costs of an extensive clean-up. In March 2000, Bobby Cooley, district director for DEP, thought the final disposition of the land could be "something pretty easily dealt with under brownfields."[73] Peter Rummell, too, concluded that the "classic brownfields" approach would come into play for the mill site. When asked about cleanup responsibilities, Rummell alluded to the liability provisions in the sales contract with Florida Coast Paper.[74] As predicted, the old mill site and the adjacent parcel formally entered Florida's Brownfield Redevelopment Program by early 2003. This designation meant that state funds would to some degree help pay for the rehabilitation of the site. Further testing was planned along with any required cleanup to make sure the sites would meet the standards for residential development, should Smurfit-Stone and St. Joe pursue that route.

Stepchildren and Public Health

Perhaps out of a combination of fear and indebtedness, only a handful of Gulf County citizens took an activist role in pursuing contamination issues. An undisclosed number of low-income families in Gulf County still received monthly $200 to $300 checks from the Alfred I. duPont Foundation, another offshoot of the Alfred I. duPont Trust. Many of the area's churches also were recipients of funds from the various St. Joe–affiliated charities.

As one longtime resident of Port St. Joe said, "St. Joe owned the bank, the telephone [company], the mill. They owned the people. . . . We feel like stepchildren; every time we make a move, we get stepped on."

Health problems and suspicions about their origins fueled antipathy toward the former industrial company. According to data from the Florida Department of Health for 1996 to 1998, Gulf County had the second highest age-adjusted rate for all cancers in the state of Florida, exceeded only by Union County, the location of the state prison hospital where many terminally ill convicts go to die.[75] An important caveat is that in a relatively small population, just a few cancers out of whack can lead to misleading extrapolations, so the data was not necessarily definitive.

Still, according to the available data, in the late 1990s Gulf County had, by far, the highest death rates for colorectal cancer: 47.51 deaths per 100,000 population versus the next highest of 31.42 per 100,000 in Hamilton County. Gulf County also had almost twice the state average for deaths attributable to lung cancer. From 1996 to 1998, the county had the second highest rate of fatalities in the state from chronic liver disease and cirrhosis, and in that same period, well over twice the state average for age-adjusted fatal strokes.[76] Diabetes also was considerably higher than the state average.

According to the Environmental Protection Agency's Toxic Release Inventory (TRI) the paper industry ranked third (behind chemicals and primary metals manufacturers) in total releases of 300 reportable toxic chemicals and second for air emissions.[77] The Port St. Joe mill was labeled a "major source of hazardous air pollutants," according to its 1996 air-permit application.[78] Paper mills also generate heavy metals such as mercury and arsenic, and a large variety of other chemicals such as chloroform and dioxin.

A database called Scorecard, assembled by the Environmental Defense Fund, listed the paper mill at Port St. Joe as the eighth highest cancer risk in the state, mainly due to air emissions of chloroform that ceased to occur when the mill shut down.[79] But the score was based on 1997 data, a year that produced considerably less product and emissions compared to previous ones. By then, Florida Coast Paper had taken over operation and production was curtailed. So over the lifetime of the St. Joe paper mill, the hazardous air emissions easily were among the worst in Florida by Scorecard's reckoning.

Epidemiologists caution about jumping to conclusions about cause and effect where environmental contamination is concerned. Yet for years the population experienced the intense smokestack emissions from the mill's many processes. Lifestyle also must be factored in, along with likely routes of exposure to environmental toxins, possible genetic propensities in the exposed population, income and education levels, and the quality of health care. Port St. Joe has more than its share of poor lifestyle practices with heavy rates of fried food consumption, drinking and smoking. Quality health care facilities also are lacking and early detection of cancers and other illnesses may not be the norm. In retrospect, a Nemours clinic in Port St. Joe would have been a real boon to the community. Peter Rummell's push for better rural health care and doctors to these settings—a necessity for luring monied baby boomers to the Panhandle—will help those already in Gulf County.

Doug Kent, the county health officer, said that much of the disease in this coastal county related to lifestyle, especially to smoking. More than one-third of the adult population in Gulf County smoked cigarettes, according to Kent. In 1997, the mortality rate for those aged thirty-five and above due to tobacco in Gulf County was estimated to be 22.6 percent, versus the state average of 18.9 percent.[80]

Deaths attributed to diabetes were 75 percent above the state average and the eighth highest in Florida for 1996–98. Interestingly, recent studies of Vietnam vets exposed to dioxins in the defoliant Agent Orange also show a link between dioxin exposure and diabetes. Dioxins are byproducts of bleached paper mills, the most potent forms of which are thought to be associated with a variety of illnesses. However, much of the elevated diabetes and cardiovascular disease may also be explained by their overrepresentation among African Americans in general; Gulf County is nearly 30 percent African American. Nevertheless, the rate of cancers and other diseases such as diabetes at least *appeared* extraordinarily high.

County health officer Kent was not readily willing to place environmental causes as a leading factor. "There has to be a balance somewhere. What is an acceptable risk?" he asked rhetorically in an informal interview in the summer of 2000. "I think we're getting to a point where people want zero risk. [Yet] we pass each other going 70 miles per hour 20 feet apart . . . or less."[81]

Barbara Oksanen, who manages one of the larger healthcare practices in Port St. Joe, did not view the town's people as disproportionately beset by disease. However, Oksanen cautioned, their practice does see a considerable number of hepatitis cases that she attributes to the consumption of shellfish contaminated from the flushing of boat toilets.[82]

For years, Gulf County activist Marilyn Blackwell wrote to numerous state and federal environmental health officials imploring them to consider a study of Gulf County. Blackwell and Hough had endeavored to piece together information to determine whether "cancer clusters" existed in the county. Officials Blackwell contacted referred her to an endless loop of databases and experts.

But the disclosure of mill waste deposits in a residential area forced the issue, at least for a limited area of north Port St. Joe that appeared to be a classic example of environmental injustice. In the 1940s and 1950s, the St. Joe Paper Company used lime grits and boiler ash (residuals of combusting a brew of black liquor, number 6 crude oil, and tree bark) to fill in wetlands north of the Apalachicola Northern rail yard and east of the mill. The St. Joe Land and Development Company then sold this land as residential lots to African American mill workers for the Mill View development. The Florida Department of Health characterized the ash deposit site at Mill View as an "indeterminate public health hazard." There were anecdotal reports of a variety of health problems,[83] although pinpointing any environmental causes would be difficult given the industrial facilities nearby—a rail yard, wastewater plant, Arizona Chemical and the former mill site.

Problems first surfaced in the mid-1980s, when, after complaints from citizens, the Florida Department of Environmental Resources (DER) found evidence of spills of chemicals and heavy oils as well as improper storage of chemicals at the Apalachicola Northern rail yard. DER cited and fined the company several times before entering in a consent order whereby ANR was required to conduct groundwater monitoring and upgrade its facility.

Mill View residents gardened fifty feet from the edge of the contaminated property. Children played in the ditches connected to a waste lagoon contaminated with petroleum and solvents from cleaning the locomotives. "The railroad was in continual operation with little or no deference to the environmental standards," according to Tracy Moye, an attorney formerly with the Andrews and Walker, P.A. law firm in Tallahassee that represented the citizens in a later suit. "They [ANR] were operating in 1985 as they would have in 1940," Moye said.[84]

Groundwater samples showed that a contaminated plume of solvent had migrated from the rail yard south toward downtown. Arsenic contamination existed north of the rail yard. ANR's contractors, Alvarez Lehman and Associates (which later changed its name to ALA Environmental Services) claimed they could not pinpoint the source of the arsenic contamination. As Andrews and Walker prepared to file a motion for punitive damages against the railroad, the firm discovered documents suggesting that Lehman and his St. Joe clients did not disclose another possible source of the arsenic contamination—the boiler ash that had been used for fill.

A 1989 letter from Robert Nedley, then the president of the St. Joe Paper Company, to technical consultant Mel Lehman, explained that the company had deposited boiler ash north of the rail yard into the 1950s.[85] Attached to the memo was a handwritten note from Ferrel Allen, the long time paper mill manager, providing the same information. Another handwritten internal memo from the Alvarez Lehman files read: "Attached is confidential map of the 'fill' area—This information was provided by St. Joe Forest Products Company to help us interpret the recent CAP [Contamination Assessment Plan]. Please do not release this information to agencies at this time."[86]

The Andrews and Walker law firm argued in a March 2001 court complaint that ANR should have disclosed the existence of the ash deposits. But in a deposition conducted by Andrews and Walker, Melvin Lehman said he did not know the ash could be hazardous.[87]

By August 2001, results of DEP testing of soils at Mill View showed that eight of thirty-two samples were above health-based screening levels, although likely not high enough to cause disease. However, a consultation by the Florida Department of Health (DOH) recommended sampling for additional contaminants besides the arsenic, cadmium, lead, mercury and nickel for which they already had tested. The DOH recommended sampling of irrigation wells and areas where mill waste was visible.[88] A subsidence problem also cropped up. About half a dozen homes were beginning to sink into the sodden earth and fill. Their plumbing systems were failing, walls cracking, and raw sewage pooled in the center of Mill View, especially after a soaking rain.[89]

As the case stood at the beginning of 2002 with more data pending, the focus had broadened from concern about human health effects to encompass issues of public safety and property value. Even if the results did not turn up high levels of contaminants, the question remained, as Moye asked, "Would you want to live there?"[90]

Dioxin

One of the most talked-about potential contaminants at Port St. Joe is a class of compounds called dioxins. Dioxins are generated in many ways, including municipal and medical waste incineration, power plant production, plastics manufacturing, and petroleum processing. They are also produced at paper mills by the interaction of the chlorine used for bleaching wood pulp with carbon-containing compounds in wood pulp, and are found mainly in the sludge from the wastewater effluent. The dioxin threat from paper mills stems mostly from the residual sludge. Once in the environment, dioxins bind tightly to carbon and can "bio-magnify," or become more concentrated, going up the food chain. The most damaging of the dioxins are among the endocrine-disrupting chemicals that can cause a wide array of health problems from cancers to diabetes, skin ailments, and more. A number of studies have documented abnormalities and reproductive failure among animals that have lived in dioxin-contaminated environments, even at extraordinarily low levels.[91]

Sampling studies by the U.S. Fish and Wildlife Service, EPA, and private contractors during the 1990s turned up very low levels of dioxin widely distributed across the St. Joe Bay bottom and higher levels in catfish from the Gulf County canal. The dioxin found in St. Joe Bay and in fish tissue from the bay and canal has not been definitively linked with any particular sources.

In 1990, the EPA determined the paper mill at Port St. Joe was one of twenty bleached paper mills nationwide deemed to cause a risk of one or more additional cancers in 100,000, given "reasonable worst-case" characterizations. The EPA suggested that states consider imposing fish consumption advisories.[92]

One Gulf County resident who was concerned by the issues addressed in the EPA report was attorney and historian R. Wayne Childers. Like his more widely known distant cousin, former state senator W. D. Childers of Pensacola, the Port St. Joe native was prominent in his community, and county commissioners appointed Childers to a "Save the Bay" committee in 1990. However, when Childers broached the possibility that dioxin was a threat to St. Joe Bay, he was booted from the committee. Childers opposed loosening effluent standards for the wastewater treatment plant, one possible pathway by which dioxin could reach the bay. He was concerned about the condition of marsh grass and sea grass, as well as the possibility that some locals were ingesting high levels of dioxin from the seafood they frequently consumed from the bay.

A study in 1991 by the National Council of the Paper Industry for Air and Stream Improvement (NCASI) concluded that the EPA report had overstated the risk, partially due to conservative assumptions. People do not eat fish *just* from affected waters, and they do not typically spend a whole life in one place, the industry study pointed out. Yet on most days, you could find predominantly low-income residents of Port St. Joe—many who *had* spent their whole life in this town—fishing the canal. This was especially true for individuals from the African American community in north Port St. Joe. Their exposure was probably far greater than the NCASI study assumed.

The most toxic form of dioxin in fish taken from the Gulf County Canal was 0.5 parts per trillion, a low level but still a possible concern for people who frequently eat the contaminated fish.[93] The Food and Drug Administration traditionally has used the 1.0 ppt value as representing a significant "level of concern." However, EPA's decade-long dioxin study released in 2001 suggested that dioxin may be more dangerous than thought previously.

In 1996, the EPA and a contractor cooperated on a study for the city of Port St. Joe to analyze fish tissue of a number of species found in and around the Gulf County Canal. Their analysis of catfish samples showed that the toxicity of the most potent form of dioxin (2,3,7,8 TCDD), combined with the related class of chemicals called furans, amounted to six times the EPA maximum acceptable tissue concentration. These levels were "associated with a high level of risk to aquatic life and associated piscivorous [fish-eating] wildlife," the study concluded.[94] Still, no fishing advisories were posted. Late into 2002, DEP had not rendered a final decision on the dioxin data in the mill site's vicinity. A state official said the agency was in a "holding pattern" pending further review of the toxicity of the various dioxins present.

Dioxin was not the most pressing concern in the bay, it turned out. A U.S. Fish and Wildlife Service study released in 2001 found other classes of dangerous chemicals in much larger quantities: PCBs, the cancer-causing fire retardant chemicals found in the lubricating and insulating oil of some electrical equipment; and PAHs, toxic compounds found in crude oil, refined petroleum, and coal. The FWS sampling found both classes of chemicals in "values that greatly exceed the sediment quality guidelines," along with arsenic and mercury, all at levels that FWS said warranted further evaluation.[95] The most striking finding perhaps was that the water found in deep sediments just off the dock of the paper mill—"pore water"—was extremely toxic to each of three species tested: the sheepshead minnow, mysid shrimp and Florida clam.[96]

The Port Rises Again

Despite confusion and muted concerns over the health of the water in Gulf County, Port St. Joe was beginning to blossom at the start of the twenty-first century. The town's mayor, the Port Authority, and the St. Joe Company shared high hopes that three key seaport facilities in various stages of construction would energize the local economy. The first to take shape was the pleasure-boat marina; the second was a ten-acre barge facility, chiefly for St. Joe to transport forest products; and the third and foremost was a planned deep-water port for oceangoing ships. St. Joe played an important role in each of the port efforts.

The beautiful new marina in downtown Port St. Joe was a surprising juxtaposition to the rusting paper mill a stone's throw away. In October 1997, when DEP issued the marina permit, the mill was experiencing difficulties but still in operation, making placement of the marina controversial. One of those opposed was then-mayor Johnny Linton. "The reason I voted against it was because you couldn't have both [the mill and marina] down there," Linton said. He added, "I firmly believe that St. Joe knew that the mill was going to close."[97] A former manager with the state's Department of Community Affairs reached the same conclusion.[98] The city commission approved the project with a vote of three to two.

The $3.3 million state-of-the-art marina opened in July 1999 as a cooperative venture between St. Joe/Arvida, the city of Port St. Joe and Brandy Marine of Tampa. Government economic development funds paid for most of it. The land had been used for decades as an oil terminal, first by Pure Oil and Gulf Oil, then by Amerada Hess. After it sat vacant for some years, Amerada Hess "sold" the land to the city for $10, and Port St. Joe had the soil tested for contamination before construction.

The old tank oil farm, like other facilities of its kind, was a likely site of contamination. One citizen said the tanks were bled every day to remove the water condensate. "They would open the valve until pure fuel ran out," said Billy Howell who worked at the paper mill for decades and had a buddy who worked at Hess.[99] A fuel-soaked drainage ditch also reportedly existed on site. For months after construction of the facility, a pile of discolored soil sat just off the marina property. Eventually the city allowed it to be used as fill elsewhere. Mayor Pate, who himself owned a Shell station in town and once did business with Pure Oil, figured that whatever contamination might have been there had long since washed into the Gulf of Mexico. "Same with the mill site," he said.[100]

Several residents expressed surprise when the company hired to test the soil found no contamination. They suspected that Amerada Hess's virtual giveaway of the land was in lieu of cleaning up the site. The city's engineering company, Preble-Rish, a firm that also does extensive work for the St. Joe Company, chose to use a Panama City–based company—The Water Spigot—to conduct the sampling at the site.

The Water Spigot initially conducted the wrong tests on the samples submitted to them by Preble-Rish late in 1998, testing for oil and grease rather than petroleum.[101] An engineer with Preble-Rish a few days earlier had assured a state DEP official that "the samples [would] be checked for petroleum contamination as required by permit."[102] A subsequent round of testing found no evidence of petroleum contamination. However, according to an official in DEP's laboratory program, The Water Spigot was primarily geared to do water sampling and did not officially have soil testing listed in their capabilities. "They just didn't have the necessary approvals as expressed by rule, [which] might be a reason to suspect the data," the official said. "It's not automatically bad," he added, "but it's a big trigger [for further inquiry]."[103]

A regulatory loophole also may have helped to expedite the marina construction. Hess used the terminal mainly to store crude oil, which is not considered an oil *product* or a "pollutant" under the Florida Administrative Code, Chapter 62-762. "Since crude oil does not meet Chapter 376, Florida Statue's definition for petroleum products, this eliminates the need for the Hess facility to meet the regulatory requirements of Chapter 62-762, Florida Administrative Code (F.A.C.)," Douglas Kent, then Gulf County environmental manager, wrote to Mayor Frank Pate in 1996. Kent's approach essentially obviated the need for Hess to conduct any kind of soil or water testing before unloading the property to the eager city officials.[104] The city could have opted to use an alternative petroleum cleanup rule, but it did not. The letter was forwarded to DEP, and no regulatory body ever conducted the full-blown "closure assessment" that was standard practice for shut-down oil and gas storage tank facilities, according to state officials.

The marina became a dramatic contrast to the closed paper mill. It had 120 covered and uncovered wet slips, air-conditioned showers, and dry storage for up to thirty-foot boats, a key feature for boaters who live in Florida only part time. The marina also had a store, a restaurant, and pump-out facilities to deal responsibly with human waste—not a given at Florida marinas. It was a beautiful facility with room for expansion, clearly a major draw for folks St. Joe hoped would buy properties up the road at WindMark and elsewhere. A rising tide would lift all yachts.

However, when the city sought bidders to assume the operation of the marina, few came forward, though the lease was based on a municipal bond interest rate of less than 5 percent to pay off a $2.5 million loan from the federal Rural Development Agency.[105] The lack of interest was odd, given that as early as 1995 the offices of both Governor Chiles and Lieutenant Governor Buddy McKay were putting tremendous pressure on DEP to approve the Port St. Joe Marina permit.

St. Joe stepped forward to assume the job, paying $12,000 per month for the first five years toward bond indebtedness, with the lease subject to renewal in subsequent five-year increments.[106] In the first couple of years of operation, St. Joe lost money on the marina but foresaw a bright future for boating on St. Joe Bay, an outcome that others apparently could not envision.

The local newspaper, the *Star,* generally sympathetic to the St. Joe Company, noted that the Port St. Joe Marina was "the hub of the company's future development plans." St. Joe also planned for a hotel and other mixed uses near the marina.[107] At the marina ribbon-cutting ceremony in the summer of 1999, after a meeting with Gulf County politicians, Rummell said, "There is a huge, enormous vacation, resort, ecotourism, use-the-natural-resources opportunity that we are going to go after as hard and as fast as we can."[108]

Several years later, St. Joe's strategic sale of two key parcels of land represented the first concrete step in the much more ambitious project of constructing a full-fledged deepwater port. There was little deepwater port space left between Pensacola and Tampa. Governor Bush talked about using Port St. Joe, one of only fourteen deepwater ports in Florida, as a conduit for import and export with the South American countries with which he was attempting to forge economic ties. The business potential was huge, given that the value of shipped products using Florida seaports more than doubled from 1990 to 1999, when the figure reached $45.5 billion.[109] The resurrection of Port St. Joe was a rare opportunity to do it all right from the ground up, to simultaneously create a modern port—at a cost exceeding a remarkable $550 million by the year 2015 for the most extensive reconfiguration—and serve tourists in a manner similar to Port Fernandina in northeast Florida.

St. Joe sold two parcels of downtown Port St. Joe land to the Port Authority in March 2001: a four-acre site next to the ship channel, and a twenty-two-acre parcel on U.S. 98 suitable for a cargo staging and storage area. St. Joe and local leaders hailed the transaction as a step toward "putting the port back in Port St. Joe," in the words of Port Director Tommy Pitts.

The front page of the March 22, 2001, edition of the *Star* included a photo of Clay Smallwood shaking hands with Robert Nedley to seal the deal. "St. Joe finally agreed to sell us land to berth one ship," he said. "If we acquire the dock [associated with the St. Joe parcel], they will have the opportunity to buy back the land with improvements," Nedley said about what appeared to be a good deal for St. Joe waiting in the wings.[110]

When St. Joe sold its aging mill property in the mid-1990s that through bankruptcy came into the hands of Smurfit-Stone, it also parted with most of the length of its hugely valuable dock. This action seemed inconsistent with both old and new St. Joe, a company that typically had not been inclined to get rid of its most potentially lucrative parcels. Steve Hamilton of Smurfit-Stone remained close-mouthed about prospective buyers of the much larger mill property.

Most people assumed that the Port Authority was the front-running prospect to purchase the mill. Preliminary data indicated only minimal contamination at the site. It seemed that port facilities would be the most logical use for the postindustrial site, especially with all the state monies being pumped into surrounding projects in the name of port revitalization. In late March 2002, the Gulf County Commission passed a resolution endorsing the purchase of the former mill site by the Port Authority.

In a twist that took some locals by surprise, the *Panama City News Herald* reported the following month that Smurfit Stone and St. Joe were working together to decide what would take the place of the mill. A spokeswoman for Smurfit-Stone mentioned the possibility of a resort while St. Joe officials said that other unnamed options were possible as well.[111] In an interview, Jerry Ray said tantalizingly that the St. Joe company was trying to get the "best kind of industry there," and that could mean using the land for more than port facilities for shipping.[112] Ray's comments hinted at the possibility of the cruise or resort industry at the old mill site. The port seemed likely to have straw hats and umbrella drinks in its future as well as "rolling stock."

By mid-January 2003, the *Star* reported that not only were Smurfit-Stone and St. Joe considering a joint venture to develop the old mill site, but that St. Joe was seeking to have the port facilities on its property just to the north.[113] It was the best possible outcome for the shrewdly managed former paper company.

Around the time that Smurfit-Stone announced a possible recreational use for the land, Smurfit-Stone's Steve Hamilton said that DEP's data as well as its own indicated that the mill and north Port St. Joe ash sites "did not represent a threat to human health and environment." Hamilton also mentioned that the Port Authority had made an offer "sometime ago" for the land, and that Smurfit-Stone had rejected it since the price was "far below the value of the property."[114] Port Authority head Tommy Pitts wasn't quite sure what to make of the new developments. "I don't know what it means," Pitts said. "Those who own the land apparently are influencing the future of that land," Pitts said.[115]

A reinvigorated port was of clear economic importance for the town and the St. Joe Company. Yet according to port consultants and some other observers, St. Joe the company and Port St. Joe the town, as represented by its port authority, did not always agree on how exactly the new port town should function or what the best use would be for the old mill site. The tourist-oriented St. Joe Company wanted to be sure that there were not highly visible piles of coal and ore. The Port Authority seemed more inclined to put function over form.

In January 2001, the Port Authority of Port St. Joe had shared *its* notions for redevelopment in a public workshop. "Do You Want Jobs?" screamed the *Star*'s headline in sepia ink, which the weekly used on special occasions. The Port Authority highlighted the port's strategic location for imports such as coal and iron ore from South America and vehicles from Mexico, balanced by Midwestern grain exports. Truck, rail and barge facilities also were part of the planned system to move bulk goods. The old paper mill site was slated for coal and ore storage.[116] The success of the port very much depended on the availability of the mill site, which was looking less and less likely. Robert Nedley, the former St. Joe Paper Company president and then-chairman of the Port Authority, called the parcel "crucial" for revitalizing the port,[117] a facility that would yield anywhere from several hundred to several thousand new jobs, depending upon the development scenarios.

After three public workshops, port consultants quietly drafted a new Port St. Joe master plan dated March 2002 that was not released for public comment for another six months—just before the county planning and review board and county commission approved it. The public had virtually no opportunity to review the new port plan before its approval by local government. The report made no mention of cruise ships, nor did it address how the U.S. Army Corps of Engineers, having been convinced of the economic justification for dredging, would deal with the dredge spoils from deepening and widening the fourteen-mile-long channel and turning basin. (The price tag for the dredging alone of a 700-foot-wide and forty-foot-deep channel well exceeded $50 million.)[118]

Under the new master plan, the total area of the port increased fourfold to a 1,600-acre area encompassing the former mill site, marina, the wastewater treatment plant, area industries, and considerable St. Joe land. With a price tag of at least half a billion dollars, this grandiose public works project would surpass even the $200 million Bay County airport. However, by 2003, it was not at all clear how these ambitious port plans would square with the plans of St. Joe and Smurfit-Stone, the owners of the most strategic parcel for port revitalization—the former mill site.

As the plans for the port jelled, ancillary businesses along the gulf-front dock and Gulf County Canal were already popping up. The new Gulf County Canal Commerce Park had found its first tenant. Downtown, a sparkling new Piggly Wiggly grocery store with palm trees in the parking lot and attached retail space claimed a choice spot on former industrial land near the new marina.[119] Other small businesses opened, too, all hopeful signs of economic renewal. Property taxes were rising rapidly commensurate with rising property values, creating a financial burden for many residents.

Good things were in store for Port St. Joe, but because of the manner in which the change came about, there were lingering questions and cynicism in the community with respect to the "new" St. Joe. However, time, ambition and new blood would soon heal those wounds. Leaving behind concerns about the lingering impacts of six decades of industrial pollution, the metaphorical train had left the station in Port St. Joe, a town with dollar signs on its horizon.

The Wish List

Concepts such as moving airports or sections of federal highways—as in Gulf County—can prove as simple as having a plan, some well-connected friends and the sway to make things happen.
Tim Croft, *Panama City News Herald*, March 2000

WHEN NEWLY ELECTED President George W. Bush paid a visit to Panama City on March 12, 2001, his presence in the small city brought national attention to the area. The chief of state strode across the stage at Panama City's Marina Civic Center to garner support for his federal tax cut and came to a stop at the podium behind a banner welcoming him, not to Panama City, but to "Florida's Great Northwest."

This label, which later that night flashed across TV news screens nationwide, was the very marketing description that St. Joe had unveiled to replace "Florida Panhandle," a term the company considered pejorative and associated with the even less appealing "Redneck Riviera" brand. The new name mirrored an emerging consortium of economic development councils, colleges, and corporations spearheaded by the St. Joe Company and called Florida's Great Northwest, Inc. (FGN). Beaming "Florida's Great Northwest" to the nation, however briefly, was a marketing coup.

The specially invited crowd gathered for the president's speech found St. Joe's Chris Corr, vice president for public affairs, seated front and center, next to Florida's top Republican lawmakers of the day, House Speaker Tom Feeney and Senate President John McKay. After being introduced by his brother, Florida governor Jeb Bush, the president thanked the "economic development folks" for making his visit possible. Although the president did not elaborate, the St. Joe Company was central to the area's economic development initiatives and not unknown in the president's family orbit.

Besides his brother Jeb's past partnership in the state's leading commercial real estate firm the Codina Group, now half owned by St. Joe, there were other ties between St. Joe and the Bush family. The governor still maintained a vested interest in Codina via his Savings and Protection Plan (401k) worth more than $257,000 at the end of 2000.[1] Bay County attorney William Harrison, who co-chaired George W. Bush's campaign in northwest Florida and went to Washington to help with the transition, represented St. Joe/Arvida among other clients. (He also went on to head the local reelection campaign for Jeb Bush in 2002.) Political insiders placed credit for the presidential visit squarely at Harrison's feet. And on the campaign trail in south Florida, George W. Bush had stayed at the Coral Gables home of former Arvida chairman Chuck Cobb, where he raised hundreds of thousands of dollars.[2] Cobb described himself as being "very, very close to the Bush family."[3] He served as Ambassador to Iceland under George H. W. Bush and later helped direct Jeb Bush's "transition team" as the governor segued from his first to his second administration.

The event in Panama City illustrated not only how highly placed the company could count its friends, but also how subtly and successfully the St. Joe Company achieved its objectives in a short time frame. Many of its wishes appeared to be sanctioned as a broad community vision, or to be fulfilled by sheer inevitability. In reality, the company worked hard at achieving its goals and was an updated, sophisticated machine that called to mind the empire-shaping days of Robert Moses in New York City and the Walt Disney Company in Florida.

The company was forthright about many items on its wish list as it set about marketing and developing the region: chiefly, infrastructure of all kinds, from roads to schools to a new airport; and economic development incentives to sweeten investment in the area. As CEO Rummell told stockholders in May 2000: "Infrastructure improvements fuel growth," and infrastructure "enhances the value of land holdings."[4] Assistance to help St. Joe fulfill its infrastructure wishes cropped up in budgets at the local, state, and even federal level, often with help from state economic incentives.

As in the days of Alfred duPont, the St. Joe Company was at the forefront as the Panhandle struggled to strengthen its economy. Attracting new residents in large numbers to St. Joe/Arvida's emerging inland communities necessitated creating new workplaces, and here the company faced the economic downside of its own green curtain. In two counties at the heart of the Green Empire (Bay and Gulf), unemployment was consistently higher than the state average and annual incomes were lower. The resource-based economy in place from the time of Alfred duPont was precarious, and the region had yet to develop a mature economy.

Globalization and corporate takeovers continued to rock the forest products industries, dampening the future for the patient business of growing trees and all the secondary jobs dependent on forestry. Agriculture in the former plantation belt struggled to maintain its position through years of drought and remained only a small part of the economy. The traditional fishing industry, like agriculture as much a way of life as a business, clung to survival. Many fishermen left the business after Florida voters in November 1994 passed a constitutional amendment to ban commercial fishing with large nets in state waters, a ban backed by an odd alliance of environmentalists and developers. As St. Joe began its push in real estate, more and more fishing boats were left to rot—forming scenes that appeared picturesque to tourists but were painful reminders to locals of a vanishing way of life. In the transitional economy, prisons became one of the largest sources of rural Panhandle jobs.

Government, tourism, and services, along with the military, were the region's biggest employers at the cusp of the new millennium. Outside of the capital city of Tallahassee, the Green Empire was only slowly displaying signs of entering the prosperous New South economy typified by Atlanta, Nashville, Chattanooga, and other leading southern cities. Yet the momentum was building.

Marketing the Region

In early 2000, St. Joe put newly hired vice president Neal Wade to work as a business booster who hoped to diversify the region's economic base beyond tourism as St. Joe worked its way inland. Wade served on the board of directors of the statewide group Enterprise Florida, Inc. (EFI), a state-agency-level public-private business development group. He also served as chair of Florida's Great Northwest; in fact, one of Wade's early tasks was helping to form this public-private partnership whose mission was to "market" the sixteen counties of northwest Florida.

The members of Florida's Great Northwest included the St. Joe Company, Gulf Power, Touchstone Energy Cooperative of Northwest Florida, county and multicounty economic development councils, the area's community and junior colleges, FSU, the University of West Florida, and businesses. Members paid a minimum of $10,000 to join. St. Joe and Gulf Power each kicked in $100,000, and Touchstone Energy gave $50,000.[5] The official regional planning councils, however, were not participating with this powerful region-wide group.

After a survey by the organization showed that 85 percent of corporate site-selection managers knew next to nothing about the Florida Panhandle, FGN began its efforts with a campaign to "brand the region."[6] Once the area started to gain the kind of attention it won during the presidential visit, Wade and others hoped the I-10 corridor would give rise to high-tech industries tapping the fiber optic cable passing by. Tallahassee was especially promising because of the presence of Florida State University, Florida Agricultural and Mechanical University, and the prestigious National High Magnetic Field Laboratory—the only research facility of its kind in the United States and one of only nine in the world.

The southeastern United States could be the next Silicon Valley of the nation, according to one consultant to FGN who said chip manufacturers were looking at several southern states.[7] Aviation-related industries, too, were a natural for the wide triangle between Alabama's Ft. Rucker and the Panhandle's Eglin and Tyndall Air Force bases. However, since the presence of an educated workforce was one key criterion for success in these high-tech industries, workforce development was needed to bring such industry to the heart of the Green Empire. "Bay County is not ready for a semi-conductor plant," Wade noted.[8]

By the spring of 2001, the group had raised half a million dollars and was on its way to hiring a staff of three and opening its headquarters. After considering an office near I-10, the group instead settled on a Destin location. In June 2001, Al Cook, formerly on the staff of the Montgomery, Alabama, Chamber of Commerce, became the first executive director of Florida's Great Northwest.

Florida's Great Northwest launched a web site (brandnewflorida.com) and set up exhibits at trade shows at Hanover, Germany, the Paris Air Show, and a semiconductor show in Singapore. Closer to home, FGN members met with site selection consultants in Atlanta. The group sought to enhance those factors that, according to its statewide counterpart, Enterprise Florida, make a place more appealing for new businesses: available, affordable energy; highway, port, and airport accessibility; broadband telecom services; and skilled and unskilled labor. Other plusses listed were a "low union profile" and favorable environmental regulations and tax structure.[9]

Even early on, there were successes in landing businesses. In spring of 2001, Nextel Partners, a wireless communications firm based in Kirkland, Washington, committed to lease a customer support facility in Panama City Beach in a business park being developed by St. Joe. Nextel had approached Bay County's Economic Development Alliance (EDA), one FGN partner. The company appeared to be a good match for the area—delivering jobs that did not require college degrees yet with above-average pay. The company expected an eventual work force of 600. Nextel said it chose the location over other areas not because of tax breaks or other special concessions but because the company felt "this community wanted it more."[10]

Other new businesses that located in the Panhandle took advantage of several state rural economic development carrots designed to nudge along the region's economy. In 1995, Florida implemented its Enterprise Zone (EZ) program to attract businesses to economically disadvantaged communities. Businesses that located in these zones received a variety of tax credits and exemptions. In addition, state programs granted money for infrastructure through organizations such as Enterprise Florida, the decision-making body that allotted state funds and tax forgiveness to new businesses. Special "Net Ban Zones" afforded even greater tax relief to areas affected by the fishing net ban, including areas on or near St. Joe's holdings. Early in 2002, the governor's Office of Tourism, Trade and Economic Development (OTTED) nearly quadrupled the size of an Enterprise Zone in the Port St. Joe area, further helping the company to increase the value of its Gulf County holdings.[11]

On top of these programs, Governor Jeb Bush signed an executive order declaring eight Panhandle counties "areas of critical state economic concern." Among the extra benefits of the 1999 designation was "fast-track" funding from the Florida Department of Transportation (FDOT) worth $70 million in road subsidies statewide and expedited environmental permitting from DEP. The cluster of counties included Calhoun, Franklin, Gadsden, Gulf, Holmes, Jackson, Liberty, and Washington.[12] Most of these counties were the location of significant St. Joe holdings, where the incentives helped give the St. Joe Company an edge in attracting enterprises to its land along with helping locals get jobs. Paradoxically, one rationale for the assistance program was to counter the effects of the closure of St. Joe's former mill.

Liberty County, about thirty miles west of Tallahassee, was one of the least populated counties in the state and one of the first to take advantage of fast-track permitting. An aide to state representative Bev Kilmer was proud to say that by "fast tracking" licensing and permitting, the state was able to pull together a meeting of DEP, FDOT, and others to establish the Sunshine State Cypress saw mill on St. Joe property in Liberty County. Sunshine created sixty jobs after it was incorporated in April 1999, with St. Joe signed on to maintain a steady supply of cypress to keep production of its saw timber humming. The company benefited from fast-track permitting, a road subsidy and tax breaks worth $360,000,[13] benefits that accrued to St. Joe when the company bought out Sunshine State in 2001 in part to have a direct supply of cypress for its upscale Arvida homes.

Then, in 2001, the state announced that Georgia Pacific hoped to buy a 700-acre parcel of St. Joe land for a $150 million Oriented Strand Board (OSB) facility that would be close to a rail line, gas pipeline and the Interstate highway, I-10, also in Liberty County.[14] OSB is made of wood particles imbued with resin and steamed into a strong, composite product. The process creates some formaldehyde emissions; still Clay Smallwood, president of St. Joe Timberland, called it a "good clean, industry" as well as an economic "home run."[15] Certainly, it would be a welcome employer in Liberty County, where forestry jobs had otherwise tapered off, and the average household income in 2000 was $43,757, or roughly two-thirds the family income in wealthier Leon County.[16] The state offered up more than $1.3 million in incentives to Georgia Pacific.[17]

Elsewhere in the Green Empire, state grants from EFI, and its related state funding arm, OTTED, helped to pay for the groundwork behind "putting the port back in Port St. Joe." Two state awards totaling $4 million went to rebuild docks, berths, and bulkheads at the disused seaport at the waterfront edge of the old mill site in Port St. Joe. The state awarded one $2 million grant from EFI less than one week after the St. Joe Company sold two parcels, totaling twenty-six acres, to the Port Authority.[18] Additionally, the U.S. Army Corps of Engineers set aside $800,000 for a port study and proposed dredging. These investments were a fraction of the estimated half-billion dollars the local Port Authority sought to revamp the port.

St. Joe would share in the rewards of a reinvigorated port through increased demand for ancillary businesses on St. Joe sites and the general upswing in the economy of the county it dominated like no other. Statewide leaders knew that Gulf County could not rely just upon the tourism lure of "sand in your shoes" to boost the local economy, according to John Ray, legislative director of Enterprise Florida (and no relation to St. Joe's Jerry Ray). EFI's interests went beyond aiding the St. Joe Company, but at the same time were compatible, he said. "Our goals and their goals have a lot in common," according to Ray. "They want to build a more sustainable type of growth. . . . We're after the same kind of business recruitment that they are."[19]

In Bay County, too, EFI contributed to infrastructure improvements that enhanced possibilities for St. Joe, among others. One EFI grant for $1 million helped fund a water transmission line serving Tyndall Air Force Base and Mexico Beach, on Bay County's eastern fringe. With a development in the offing for Mexico Beach, St. Joe had a direct interest in the public water supply of Mexico Beach.

Another EFI member organization that sought state funding for St. Joe–related ventures centering on Gulf County was Opportunity Florida, an economic development consortium of eight Panhandle counties chaired by Bev Kilmer. This agency in 2002 received state funds of $3.45 million to pay for studies of new roads in Gulf and Bay Counties.[20] The funding brought to at least $10 million the state investment in the Gulf County area between 1999 and early 2002—a drop in the bucket relative to the public funds that would be needed to bring the projects to completion.

In some corners of the Green Empire, St. Joe's economic development goals were not eagerly embraced. At a meeting of the Chamber of Commerce in Apalachicola, Neal Wade felt out the audience about their attitudes toward growth. "I came here because it was small and backward and I kind of liked it that way," one owner of a jewelry shop informed Wade. Her views were countered by another who pointed out, "There's a lot of people in Franklin County that need a good job."[21]

In April 2001, two dozen Tallahassee business and education leaders experienced a taste of what their hometown could become when they joined Neal Wade on a tour of another capitol city, Austin, Texas. Tallahassee's Chamber of Commerce and executives in St. Joe's commercial real estate division were working hard to attract new high- and medium-tech companies to Tallahassee. Austin offered an example of a city whose economic development incentives landed high-tech firms, including Motorola, IBM, and half a dozen others. But Austin's growth had a downside too; the city had trouble keeping pace with infrastructure needs, and not all segments of the population experienced an upswing in living standards. Then, some of Austin's high-tech industries had setbacks during late 1990s.

As St. Joe opened its corporate arms—and land—to enterprises, just who would get the new jobs created was a sensitive point. Without the skills base to qualify for technically demanding jobs, locals could watch newcomers snap up the best positions.

Another uncertainty was the hidden environmental price tag that might accompany "fast-track permitting." Fast-tracking gave the government carte blanche to waive a host of regulations. The eased guidelines ranged from wetlands protection to meeting minimum requirements for eligibility for tax refunds, especially for locating business on "brownfields" of already-used commercial and industrial lands. The Department of Management Services, headed by Cynthia Henderson, who also for a time was the state's official liaison to the St. Joe Company, was authorized to designate "Quick Permitting" Counties. Yet there was no explicit requirement that a county have any kind of technical expertise in evaluating the environmental impacts of a new business, even though the Quick Permitting authority allowed counties to issue wetlands and environmental permits. The state embraced a process that was quick and dirty, perhaps literally.

Courting Infrastructure

St. Joe argued that new infrastructure was crucial to attract and serve commerce that would uplift the area as a whole. "If you want to bring economic development, you must have infrastructure," company spokesman Jerry Ray pointed out. "This area has been neglected. [It's] probably at the early 1980s in terms of infrastructure."[22]

St. Joe executives spoke about expensive infrastructure it desired as sure things, although on an uncertain time line. To stockholders, the company pointed out instances where it had "worked diligently with community leaders," to locate infrastructure on or near its land. Such enhancements would surely add value to the land. Maps company executives shared with stockholders and area business leaders and politicians depicted a sweeping regional transportation plan that included widened or whole new roads carved into the pine lands and increased use of the existing deepwater ports and the Intracoastal Waterway. By virtue of owning so much land and seeking to use it for other than tree farms, the St. Joe Company became a de facto regional planning agency and even proclaimed its role in "regional planning" in corporate literature.

Unlike a government agency, however, the company's plans were proprietary. Company executives usually kept their plans close to the vest. As the company's intentions changed, so did details in the maps. Caught in the box of protecting its interests while also needing to build support for its many infrastructure needs and appear good-spirited, St. Joe alternated between disclosure and secrecy.

At times, citizens expressed frustration in their attempts to pry maps and plans for their hometowns from the company. At a League of Women Voters meeting in Panama City in May 2001, one questioner asked if St. Joe was developing its plans in a vacuum, ignoring existing comprehensive plans and visioning efforts that had already taken place. "We can't just come in and dictate what happens," Wade replied.

In contrast, St. Joe board of directors member Herbert Peyton, when asked how long the new airport for Bay County had been in the works proudly said, "Ever since Rummell came. That was one of his projects."[23] Other St. Joe executives also were frank about going after infrastructure they considered vital.

St. Joe was keenly involved in pushing for the expansion, construction, or relocation of half a dozen highways in the eastern and central Panhandle. Road building across Florida got a big boost after Governor Jeb Bush took office and launched his Mobility 2000 program, which allotted $4 billion to improve road capacity statewide after traffic tie-ups stranded motorists trying to flee Hurricane Floyd in 1999. The Florida Department of Transportation district encompassing the northwestern part of the state received an additional $198 million over and above its normal transportation budget.[24] Most of the road segments targeted by the governor for improvement in the Panhandle nicely served St. Joe's up-and-coming projects in Walton and Bay Counties.[25]

Panama City's Allan Bense, elected as the state District 6 representative in 1998, focused on transportation improvements from the start. He worked with new Governor Bush to redirect more than $8 million in spending from the bullet train for transportation projects centered on Bay County.[26] Newly funded projects included the four-laning of Highway 98 all the way from Tyndall Air Force Base west to Pensacola. The project would greatly benefit travelers all along the Emerald Coast, including where new St. Joe/Arvida projects were popping up. The additional funding also sped four-laning for stretches of north-south highways 79 and 77 in Bay and Walton Counties.

Representative Bense's hardworking pursuit of improvements for his home district helped to advance infrastructure goals held by St. Joe, including relocation of the Bay County airport. However, in a telephone interview in April 2002, Bense said his actions in the legislature had little to do with the St. Joe Company. "I'm thinking of my constituents," he said. "I want to see Bay County grow. I want to see good, high-paying jobs come, and they won't until we get the infrastructure." Bense, whose array of business interests included development and asphalt companies, saw no conflict of interest in expanding the asphalt arteries in his own legislative district. Indeed, Florida House ethics rules allow legislators to vote on measures that benefit them personally as long as there is no "special gain" to themselves or family members—in other words, as long as they are sharing the pie. Bense said he was convinced that the combination of four-laning existing north-south roads in Bay County and siting an airport with associated industrial park would help industry "flock to Bay County."[27] Bense even referred to himself as a "rainmaker" who would help rev up the area economy.

Bense became a hometown hero when he secured $83 million in state funds in 2000 for replacing the Hathaway Bridge between Panama City and Panama

City Beach. Bay County leaders had struggled for years to find solutions for the traffic bottleneck created by the aging bridge and its approaches. Just a few years earlier, the county hired Panama City attorney and later St. Joe lobbyist William Harrison to seek bridge funding at the state and federal levels. Harrison rounded up support for some, but not all, the necessary funding. The bridge was not even listed on the Metropolitan Planning Organization's five-year work plan because of the lack of identified funding. That too changed once St. Joe/Arvida bluebirds began to fly over northwest Florida. Northwest Florida would likely see its influence over the state budget grow, as Representative Bense was slated to become speaker of the Florida House in 2005–2006.

St. Joe vice president for communications, Jerry Ray, acknowledged that St. Joe did its part to push funding for the bridge replacement, a vital link between its housing and commercial developments on Panama City Beach and shopping and business in Panama City. "We pushed the bridge very, very hard," Jerry Ray told Steve Bornhoft, then executive editor of the *Panama City News Herald*.[28]

St. Joe also quickly responded by giving up land in Walton County to facilitate the four-laning of U.S. Highway 98. "We told them [in Walton County] to take the money they would have paid us and spend it on speeding up the project," Ray said.[29] The donation of road easements kept up a company tradition that began in the days of Alfred duPont and the Highwaymen. The state saved many millions of dollars, as the value of the rights-of-way often exceeded the cost of road construction itself, while the company benefited in increased land values. The long history of dealings between St. Joe and the Florida DOT was a definite two-way street with no stop signs in sight.

Fiscal year 2001–2002 brought continued infrastructure funding that aided St. Joe. Three out of twenty-four Transportation Outreach Program (TOP) priority projects statewide (winnowed from an applicant list of 205) funded infrastructure that benefited St. Joe.[30] That represented 100 percent of the monies for FDOT's District 3 and roughly 14 percent of TOP allocations for that year. The TOP funding paid to study relocation of the Panama City–Bay County airport and plan for two new highways in Bay and Gulf Counties. Upon completion, FDOT expected to spend $70 million for the airport and $23 million for the shorter of the two highways.[31]

Another boost was a $3.3 million economic stimulus package for the six-county Big Bend region that Governor Bush signed into law in 2001. Covering a considerable area of St. Joe's eastern Panhandle holdings, the package further accelerated road projects and allowed the Florida DOT to issue contracts for road design and design-build phases even before obtaining easements and rights-of-way.[32]

One of the most expensive infrastructure items to be publicly broached was a new interstate connector, at a cost of about $10 million per mile, for sixty to seventy-five miles. Lack of a north-south interstate in the Panhandle tacked delays and extra expenses onto trucking and other transportation relative to metropolitan areas. Major firms insisted on ready access to interstates, St. Joe's Neal Wade explained. The three magic words for companies looking for sites were "limited access highway," he said.[33] (St. Joe's draft strategic plans dating from the 1990s and obtained by the Panhandle Citizens Coalition watchdog group labeled the existing two-lane Route 20 west of Tallahassee as an apparent northwestern extension of the "Florida Turnpike.")

When the Florida DOT unveiled alternative corridors for an interstate that would connect Dothan, Alabama to Panama City Beach, the selected route was St. Joe's top choice. The favored route also happened to skirt the St. Joe land where the company hoped to site a new regional airport in rural north Bay County.

Critics of the proposed route questioned the wisdom of carving a brand new swath of interstate roadway into rural lands instead of simply adding capacity to existing north-south routes or even converting them to limited-access highways. Hurricane evacuation could be improved by adding lanes—an improvement that was already unfolding by early 2002—but that would not satisfy the limited-access ideal sought by site specialists.

As the powers-that-be in Florida and Alabama mulled over the interstate proposals, they would have to come to terms with another highway proposal for northwest Florida, this one connecting to I-65 and terminating in Pensacola. Deciding whether there were resources to go around for both and where one or more "magical" limited access highways would be located promised to keep politicians busy for years.

Meanwhile, the proposal for a brand-new "Gulf Coast Parkway" moved from a St. Joe concept to a plan backed by the economic development group Opportunity Florida. The regional group, of which Representative Kilmer was chair, obtained state funds to study placing the new four-lane, limited-access highway connecting U.S. 98 in Gulf County with U.S. 231 in Bay County, a road it said would "enhance the economic growth and competitiveness of Gulf County."[34] The proposed highway followed the same general route that surfaced years earlier in St. Joe Company drawings depicting a new "St. Joseph Parkway."

Rerouting the Old Gulf Coast Highway

St. Joe's plans for another road, the so-called Gulf to Bay Highway, generated a firestorm of opposition that moderated over time. St. Joe proposed to replace the scenic stretch of two-lane Highway 98 hugging the shore of St. Joseph's Bay north and west of Port St. Joe with a thoroughfare set back roughly one-half to one mile from the shore, a new "Back Beach Road."

By late 2001, the plan for the twelve-mile-long Gulf to Bay Highway was proposed in three phases, which would eventually stretch from north of Port St. Joe to near Tyndall Air Force Base. The first hotly debated phase would move 3.7 miles of highway near St. Joe's new WindMark Beach development along an idyllic sweep of St. Joseph Bay. St. Joe offered to provide the right-of-way and partially finance construction of the new road farther inland offsetting "a substantial share" of the costs, according to spokesman Jerry Ray.[35] Initially, Gulf County officials and St. Joe touted the road rerouting as necessary to improve hurricane evacuation. Yet this new road segment would have only 35 percent of its length outside the influence of a category III storm.[36] Otherwise put, 65 percent of this road could be underwater in a severe hurricane. Soon it appeared that the impetus was actually the economic benefit of securing a large chunk of beachfront. The land was extremely valuable to St. Joe, more so without a major highway chopping it up.

Five hundred Gulf County residents showed up at the first informational meeting about the road proposal in the fall of 1999. Many voiced skepticism about the public benefits of the proposal. With the beginning of the indefinite mill shutdown less than a year behind them, some were still brimming with anger at the company that had once owned the mill and still owned most of the undeveloped land in the port town. They booed the consultant hired to conduct a question and answer session when he tried to bring the meeting to an end. Others wrote pointed letters to the DOT. All in all, it was a public relations fiasco for St. Joe.

A second meeting was less heated. A host of hired consultants and St. Joe representatives stationed throughout the high school meeting room displayed maps and listened to all public comment. The more accommodating approach seemed to defuse the controversy. With no focal point of discussion, the meeting was a sort of thematic cocktail party without the booze.

The long-awaited third and final public hearing took place in December 2001. One of the outspoken citizens then was Sally Malone, who questioned whether the county was giving away valuable public property in the proposed relocation. Six months after the inflammatory first public meeting, Malone had met with DOT district secretary Edward Prescott in his office in Chipley. According to Malone, the district director made clear to Malone there was little she could do to stop the Highway 98 project. "At that time, he said it was a 'done deal,'" Malone alleged.[37]

By September 2000, DOT's district counsel, Bob Deal, a former south Walton County developer who reported directly to the district director, had drafted a "Right-of-Way Exchange Agreement" in the event that St. Joe got its way.[38] Neither that draft agreement nor the final agreement presented in May 2002 made mention of the total acreage St. Joe would get in the swap.

Dissatisfied with Prescott's response that there was nothing she could do, Malone continued to copy right-of-way maps and contact higher-level government officials including Governor Jeb Bush and Lieutenant Governor Frank Brogan. While Malone's discussion with the governor at a public forum seemed to go nowhere, shortly after Malone spoke to Brogan, Prescott called Malone, apparently to explain the status of the project at the instruction of Brogan's office. "He went overboard with niceness," Malone said. "He kept saying there never was a done deal," Malone said.[39]

After Prescott spoke at a commission meeting, the indefatigable Marilyn Blackwell stood up attired in her usual work clothes and hair bandana, wanting to know ultimately whose decision it would be to give a portion of Highway 98 to St. Joe. Five minutes of dog-chasing-tail discussion yielded the bottom line owing to Blackwell's insistence on a straightforward answer: the DOT had the final decision. In response to public pressure, Gulf County commissioners had earlier voted to put the matter to a public referendum, but they later rescinded that resolution.

Many locals—hopeful about economic development benefits tied to the new road—thought rerouting would be acceptable if the present route were maintained as a scenic highway with at least limited continued beach access. St. Joe agreed to the latter but did not embrace anything less than an all-out swap of its inland swampland for the coastal right-of-way.

By the company's estimates, the value of the right-of-way it proposed to donate for all three segments of the new Gulf to Bay Highway, as well as the design and construction that St. Joe would undertake for the first most controversial segment, amounted to $24 million, roughly $15 million of that for the value of 266 acres of coastal swamp.[40] In contrast, Clay Smallwood and John Hendry of St. Joe/Arvida estimated the value of the 3.7 miles of old roadbed that St. Joe would receive at $9.2 million. It totaled an estimated forty-six acres, based on a right-of-way of 100 feet. According to St. Joe Beach dweller Rich Brenner, who studied the price of comparable parcels, St. Joe's valuation of $200,000 per acre for the coastal land was on the low side.[41] The company's estimate created the appearance that St. Joe was giving much more than it was getting in the bargain.

One important factor in the valuation, the size of the easement to be granted, was a matter of controversy. The old, shoreline-hugging roadbed had a right-of-way that was 200 feet for much of its length, according to right-of-way maps obtained from the DOT district office in Chipley. Ed Ball had donated the generous right-of-way in the 1950s in exchange for the land that WindMark Beach now sits on. In April 2002, lawyers from St. Joe and DOT were working out the details of the right-of-way instead of the surveying and mapping office that generally provided such information for deeds.

"Common sense tells me that you don't give away prime beach front for swamp," an emotional Sally Malone asserted at the December 2001 meeting.[42] Hundreds of people attended the final public meeting that began with presentations by St. Joe/Arvida's Clay Smallwood and John Hendry, as well as John Pollard of PBS&J, the engineering consultants for St. Joe and Opportunity Florida. PBS&J also did plenty of engineering work for Florida DOT, so approval of the road swap with all the subsequent phases and tie-ins could mean future coins in PBS&J's pocket. As dual consultant to the state and St. Joe, PBS&J played a prominent role, and at this particular meeting was more conspicuous than the DOT itself. In fact, DOT district director Edward Prescott directed specific inquiries to PBS&J.

At this important gathering, which looked like a public relations event for St. Joe in the estimation of a number of attendees, St. Joe Company officials said its plans would push development back from the shoreline, preserve the scenic view, and even improve public access. "We believe that what you see in South Florida can be avoided. [We] can preserve beauty for everyone," John Hendry said reassuringly. He said the existing roadbed would become a public boardwalk with green space. The company would provide limited public beach access and provide amenities such as dune walkovers at either end of the development.

Roughly three-fourths of the many speakers at the meeting (not counting those working directly for St. Joe/Arvida or its consultant) expressed outright support for St. Joe/Arvida's proposal to reroute the road. Some of the skeptics were starting to find St. Joe's proposals if not welcome, at least acceptable and certainly better than the condo canyons of Panama City Beach and Destin to the west. It appeared that St. Joe had figured out a way to maximize its profits while accommodating at least some of the major concerns of locals. But many citizens' acceptance of the project hinged on having a legally binding agreement in writing that assured public beach access.

The resulting written commitment—which did not emerge until the following month in a surprise resolution introduced by St. Joe's Clay Smallwood—was short on detail. Smallwood presented this resolution during the public comments portion of the commission's first meeting in 2002. "I've taken the liberty of preparing a resolution, and I'd like you guys to pass it," Smallwood said.[43] The resolution called for realigning three segments of Highway 98 to create the Gulf to Bay Highway, including the swap of St. Joe property for the coastal Highway 98 right-of-way.

The much-discussed matter had not been on the advertised agenda. Earlier in the day Smallwood had provided a binding agreement to the commissioners executing his resolution for the "Gulf County Strategic Roadway Plan."[44] With virtually no public notice that the commission meeting would consider a matter that would greatly change Gulf County, Smallwood's resolution and "Roadway Plan" passed by a three-to-two vote at a meeting attended by perhaps fifteen to twenty citizens, many of whom were from the local business community and had an interest in Smallwood's resolution. Commissioners had less than a day to review the proposal.

The agreement did not include the explicit promise not to develop the beach, a commitment made verbally on several occasions and affirmed by company spokesman Jerry Ray in a later interview. It appeared that this most divisive road issue became a "done deal" in a whimper of a county commission meeting.

Unbothered by the lack of specifics in the "Strategic Roadway Plan" that Clay Smallwood had provided, Commissioner Billy Traylor said it did not matter since it and the resolution were not binding and all the contractual agreements would come after the state approved the road swap. However, small print at the end of the roadway agreement said it *was* binding on the parties that signed—St. Joe and the county.[45]

Traylor said he was fine with or without a binding agreement. He had known Clay Smallwood most of his life, having met him on the ball fields of Wewahitchka as a young man. "I'm gonna take his word and what he's saying as good faith," Traylor said.[46] Around the same time, the county reappointed Clay Smallwood chair of its Planning and Review Board for his tenth year of service on that local regulatory body.

For his part, Smallwood was of the opinion that failure to move Highway 98 would result in crawling traffic and aesthetic problems. "It's going to be ugly. And the speed limit is going to be twenty miles per hour instead of fifty-five through that stretch, and people aren't going to be happy with that. . . . You don't have to build anything between where the highway is currently and the waterfront to still enjoy the extraction of value from that property if you do the development right inland," Smallwood concluded.[47]

Rich Brenner of St. Joe Beach was displeased with the decision-making process. He had barely one hour's notice that the county commission meeting would involve some kind of proposal from Smallwood. Brenner in various public forums had seemed an astute voice of reason, and mainly was a supporter of the project, with certain provisions.[48] Brenner rushed to the meeting and addressed the commissioners. "I think the resolution needs to go further and say that they really provide us with a guarantee that the beach will be kept open," he said. "That they are trading swamp for beach would be negated if you're not going to build [on the beach]," Brenner added, noting the absence of commercial value in that case.[49]

In a later interview, Brenner had said he was still concerned about only having two public access points at either end of the WindMark development. "If there's only two openings, what prevents them [an eventual homeowners association] from taking ownership of the beach then the internal roads?" Brenner pondered.[50]

The later phases of the Gulf to Bay Highway would cut through miles of wetlands between Mexico Beach and the Port St. Joe Beach area. Once again, St. Joe offered to donate the right-of-way. Still, it and the Gulf Coast Parkway would cost the state tens to hundreds of millions of dollars once they were deemed feasible. Local historian and attorney Wayne Childers made clear his concern in an article in the *Franklin Chronicle* that there were backroom dealings on roads issues. One month after DOT officials from the district office in Chipley had attended a Gulf County Commission meeting where they denied any knowledge of new highway projects for Gulf County, Childers found the Gulf to Bay project listed on DOT's TOP projects list along with preliminary funding for the Gulf Coast Parkway.

"Development is coming to the area whether we like it or not," Childers wrote. "As this area becomes the 'Yuppie Coast,' perhaps there will be a reservation left for the locals. An enclosed area of marginal land where the tourists and new residents can ride by and see us in our natural habitat with prominent signs that say, 'Do Not Feed the Natives,'" Childers quipped.[51]

Throughout the discussions, environmental issues never seemed much of a concern. At the December 13, 2001, presentation, PBS&J glossed over the environmental effects of the preferred routing alternative for the Gulf to Bay Highway mentioning that of the eighty-five acres for the new right-of-way, there were nineteen acres of impacted wetlands and eighteen acres of floodplain. Pollard mentioned only the gopher tortoise as a species among several that would be affected by the new road.[52]

The environmental impacts of new roads in Gulf County would be heavy.

The Florida Fish and Wildlife Conservation Commission noted that the proposed corridor for the first phase of the Highway 98 bypass would cut through undeveloped lands consisting of wet forests of bay, hardwoods, and cypress that support rare wildlife including black bears, bald eagles, and wading birds. A bird rookery was also present, as was a meander with the evocative name of Panther Creek. While panthers have long passed from that "Florida Wild" span of coast, bears are still very much present. The state wildlife agency was especially concerned about bears as there were already documented cases of bears being killed by cars on Highway 98 in the vicinity.[53] If new roads are built, with other development to follow, St. Joe's ballyhooed "Florida Wild" will be a lot less wild.

The bear was just one of seven sensitive wildlife species the FWCC identified in these coastal wetlands that the agency also has labeled as "Biodiversity Hotspots" and "Strategic Habitat Conservation Areas."[54] Florida Wild or not, Jerry Ray downplayed the environmental impacts. "I've driven that way lots of times and never seen a bear," he said in an August 2000 interview in Jacksonville.

From the beginning, Peter Rummell described the road relocation as a "regulatory problem" that would be solved in time.[55] In May 2001, Neal Wade said the company approach was to get Gulf Countians to change their minds. "I think we're going to work to get citizen backing for moving Highway 98."[56] Paradoxically, Wade's remark about changing the citizens' minds in Port St. Joe followed closely after a statement about the company's need for sensitivity about local preferences.

The bottom line is that road improvements were necessary to serve anticipated growth, Ray said. Better roads into Port St. Joe were necessary if there was to be new industry there, and many locals were behind the changes in hopes that the new roads would bring jobs for themselves and their children.

Bluebirds at the Schoolhouse Door

Education was another critical infrastructure need for the St. Joe Company. In the long run, the availability of an educated work force was key for industry recruitment. In the nearer term, availability of good schools was a must to attract buyers to above-average priced St. Joe/Arvida communities. "We're going to do what we can in terms of getting schools built," said Rummell, who invested time as a volunteer in Jacksonville-area schools. Half a dozen new schools—several of them for-profit charter schools—opened in locations convenient to St. Joe developments in the Panhandle and beyond. Indeed, one of Arvida's many subsidiaries was the for-profit Education Partners, Inc., a school and curriculum design company.

In south Walton County, a new high school went up on onetime St. Joe land, later carved out of Point Washington Forest, several miles north of Seaside and WaterColor. It served students across the southern half of the county, including any permanent residents at the resort developments being constructed by St. Joe and others.

In Bay County, a new high school on Panama City Beach opened its doors in the fall of 2000 to its first freshman class. The school was built on former St. Joe land that the company sold to a longtime Panama City Beach resident who thereafter donated the land to the county school board. The school boasted a college-like campus and innovative programs. It was located near the St. Joe/Arvida developments of Summerwood, Palmetto Trace, and other emerging projects, although its location did not initially present safe access to students by bicycle or foot. It was adjacent to Highway 98, an artery with four lanes of speeding traffic.

The new home of the fighting Marlins was sited in an area surrounded on all sides by forest, which had severe development constraints because of its wet nature. Twenty-one acres of wetlands had to be filled to build the school, a figure representing more than a third of the acreage for the facility and grounds. St. Joe/Arvida came forward to mitigate the wetlands loss by providing a sixty-three-acre conservation easement around the school. Rules on wetlands impacts for schools, as for highways, differ from other types of development. The opening of the school marked a milestone in the overall growth and development of Panama City Beach as a community independent of Panama City. Beach-dwelling students could now complete their education without crossing a bridge into the older, more heavily urbanized areas.

The new school would be useful as St. Joe developed its other Panama City Beach holdings—an area in which the company was particularly active. Construction was made possible by passage of a half-cent countywide sales tax in 1998 that freed other school dollars to bond the new $40 million high school just in time for St. Joe/Arvida's development push. A coalition of parents and citizens backed the tax to try to address the dilapidated condition of many of the county's older schools, another plus for upgrading quality of life in the heart of the Green Empire. Some observers credited St. Joe/Arvida with behind-the-scenes support for the tax referendum, which passed by a whisker.

Another St. Joe Company housing development in Bay County, a 189-acre mix of homes and townhouses called The Hammocks, was located adjacent to an existing high school. St. Joe offered ten acres near The Hammocks as the location of a charter school getting off the ground in 2001, but then sweetened the deal to Bay Haven Charter Academy by offering a spot three times larger in a more remote location near other as-yet undeveloped St. Joe holdings. By 2003, Bay Haven had not chosen its permanent location.

The initial organizing effort for a charter school in Bay County was "given a little impetus" by Arvida, said principal Tim Kitts, although Bay Haven came to fruition under the umbrella of another management company, Ft. Lauderdale's Charter Schools USA.[57] Bay Haven expected to enroll up to 700 students in its second year and eventually take students in kindergarten through twelfth grade.

As for higher education, the company became involved in some way with most of the region's colleges and universities via Florida's Great Northwest. That group's web site offered high praise for the region's places of higher learning, informing visitors that "the region is home to some of the country's most prominent universities." While that prose was overreaching, the Green Empire's educational offerings increased greatly in recent decades. Besides the state universities in Tallahassee and Pensacola, there was Panama City's academically recognized Gulf Coast Community College and a branch campus of FSU across the street. In addition, there were community or junior college programs in nearby Pensacola, Marianna, Blountstown, and Port St. Joe as well as technical colleges.

The "new" St. Joe Company built on a tradition of close connections to Florida State University that harked back to the days of Ed Ball. More recently, during Jake Belin's era, the Nemours Foundation ended the mission of the Ed Ball Wildlife Foundation by turning its assets over to FSU to create a chair in international law. St. Joe and FSU had many mutual empire-building objectives. Cooperation between the real estate company and the university seemed logical in order to coordinate educational offerings with prospective new industry and anchor a high-tech corridor.

"I believe the university can be a very important part of the economic development plan," said FSU president Talbot "Sandy" D'Alemberte during in an interview in May 2001. "We've tried to keep St. Joe closely informed about what we're doing." In November 1999, the Florida Board of Regents appointed St. Joe CEO Peter Rummell to the board of directors for Florida State University's Research Foundation.

Florida State had strong ties with several St. Joe board members and business partners. Frank Shaw, a St. Joe board director, was a longtime friend of D'Alemberte, who had been in Frank and Sarah Shaw's wedding. D'Alemberte had also known St. Joe director Walter Revell for at least twenty years. Another indirect tie was with Cliff Hinkle, who served with Peter Rummell on the FSU Research Foundation and happened to be a director of Commercial Net Realty, Inc. (CNL), a real estate investment trust that partnered with St. Joe on commercial projects in Orlando.

St. Joe appeared to be in a position to go beyond passively tracking the public university's research agenda to wielding some influence over how its considerable endowment would be spent. FSU's D'Alemberte said he frequently briefed Tim Edmond, St. Joe/Arvida's vice president in Tallahassee, on "what we're developing by way of additional research facilities, grants, and so forth."[58] The alliance continued uninterrupted with the appointment to the FSU presidency of T. K. Wetherell, a former legislator and sometime St. Joe lobbyist.

It was hard to find a downside for improved education. As much as any of St. Joe's infrastructure wishes, it appeared to meet the genuine needs of the existing population. A case in point was the new Gulf Coast Community College campus in Port St. Joe. The branch campus was built after the mill shutdown with a specific mission to retrain workers displaced in the wake of the paper mill closure; offerings there started out emphasizing training for prison guard jobs, the most convenient and abundant source of nearby employment. Students could also receive training in the trades, including welding and plumbing.

Still, schools, like roads and airports, are growth magnets and someone has to pay for them. In its 2001 and 2002 sessions, the Florida legislature considered bills that would start to address the problem of lack of school service for new development by calling for school planning as part of overall comprehensive plan requirements.

Health Care

St. Joe also played a part in upgrading medical services. In south Walton, the company donated 35 acres along Highway 98 in Santa Rosa Beach to the Sacred Heart Health System for a $45 million, 50-bed hospital that could be expanded fivefold into the future. The small hospital filled an urgent need in the area, providing care for babies to seniors, including heart surgery. In Tallahassee, St. Joe's provision of new quarters for Florida High opened up facilities on the FSU campus for use in a new medical program geared to training doctors to offer primary care in medically underserved areas.

Water Supply

To develop its land into resorts, subdivisions, and commercial parks, St. Joe/ Arvida needed a ready supply of clean water. Relative to central and south Florida, the Green Empire was awash in water. However, the prolonged drought that began in 1998 and continued into the summer of 2001 exposed the weak spots in the region's water resources and served as a reminder that even abundant resources have limits. Around the region, well drillers in 2000 could not keep pace with the requests to deepen household wells because of the sinking drinking water table. The Apalachicola River, heavily tapped from upstream farmers and the swelling demands of Atlanta, recorded its lowest annual flow ever in 2000 since record keeping began in 1929.

In Bay County, the crystal clear karst lakes in the Sandhills region shrank down to nothing in some cases, and large lakes dropped noticeably. The community of Inlet Beach, just over the Bay County line in Walton County, placed a moratorium on new water meters after it began exceeding its permitted pumping levels. The biggest problems in the Green Empire were along the coast. Destin, south Walton County and Port St. Joe were among the places where overpumping to date created "cones of depression" that led to saltwater intrusion. The communities abandoned coastal pumping and turned to wells farther inland.

On Memorial Day 2001, a new well field at Rock Hill in central Walton County began supplying water to the coast via a pipeline across Choctawhatchee Bay. The water service was made possible because of a twenty-year agreement that allowed South Walton Utilities to tap into a pipeline operated by Florida Community Services Corporation, commonly called Regional Utilities. The agreement put an end to lawsuits among water utilities in the area and removed a huge obstacle to growth for St. Joe and others in booming south Walton.

Over the long term, the Northwest Florida Water Management District predicted continued water shortfalls for growing south Walton. The draw of the emerald beaches was expected to more than double the coastal population by the year 2020, forcing further measures to supply drinking water. Buyers at St. Joe developments would make up the majority of these newcomers, according to company projections.[59]

Among the choices to ensure water availability are conservation and reuse, new wells farther north, or agreements to tap into water sources of other counties, most likely Bay County. Officials also tossed around other more grandiose ideas such as construction of a new reservoir or even building a desalination plant.

At its WaterColor resort, St. Joe employed some water conservation measures, including high-efficiency plumbing and rain sensors that automatically shut off lawn sprinklers.[60] Where pumping groundwater was prohibitive because of either supply or regulation, St. Joe installed wastewater re-use systems to irrigate its golf courses and other landscaping areas, another environmentally sound, and in central and south Florida often legally necessary, measure. At SouthWood, St. Joe/Arvida planned to do the same, but the cost of "virgin" well water was less expensive than re-used water. St. Joe executive Tim Edmond said the company proposed to pay Tallahassee the cost equivalent of drilling new wells if it could install a re-use system. "It's environmentally the right thing to do. Cities, counties, and other regulatory authorities have to make a commitment to do it. There are many of us who would like to use that water." Edmond cringed at the thought of using drinking water to water a golf course, calling it "a blasphemy."[61] Another Arvida official, Keith Dantin, noted, however, that "while the cause is noble, the bottom line will remain money."[62] Tallahassee and St. Joe ultimately worked out a plan to facilitate water recycling at SouthWood.

Before its new Regional Utilities pipeline went into service, Walton Countians eyed another nearby water source—Bay County's amply supplied Deer Point Reservoir. Bay Countians rejected overtures to sell Deer Point water. They were backed up by a state law dubbed "Local Sources First," which protected municipalities from unwanted requests for water from outside their borders.

The reservoir remained a rare source of stored surface water in the region. The reservoir fills what was once the uppermost arm of St. Andrew Bay, where springs large and small along Econfina Creek spill sparkling cool water into the 69,000-acre bay estuary system. Water flows in at an average rate of about 600 million gallons per day. In the 1950s, a dam was built to hold back the Perrier-quality water, which a local bottler sells under several labels, including Econfina, Emerald Springs, and Modica. The Panama City paper mill was the reservoir's biggest customer, but Deer Point Reservoir also served most of Bay County's non-well-water-drinking population. It represented one of Bay County's biggest, and most coveted, long-term assets.

Within Bay County, any concerns St. Joe might have had about water supply were put to rest for the foreseeable future after the county constructed several new water lines tapping the reservoir. A new pipeline that runs from a distribution point in Southport in a seventeen-mile loop around West Bay was constructed in the year 2000 at a cost of $12.5 million. When the city of Panama City

Beach finished the final leg of the pipeline, St. Joe was assured plenty of water to serve its properties around Panama City Beach and West Bay.

As more pumps and pipelines went into operation to supply the near-term freshwater needs of the human population, ecologists wondered how much fresh water could be removed from the St. Andrew Bay system without destroying it. Continued diversions from the bay itself threatened to upset the bay's salinity balance and thus the basic living conditions for the bay's aquatic life.

Meanwhile, with Gulf County facing water quantity and quality problems, the city of Port St. Joe got state dollars to buy the canal owned by Smurfit-Stone that carried fresh water from the lower Chipola to the old paper mill site. The surface water that St. Joe Paper once had tapped to process pulp became an important source of drinking water. The city paid Smurfit-Stone $700,000 for the canal, helped by grants from the rural infrastructure fund administered by the governor's office as well as a grant from the Water Management District, leaving only $168,000 to be financed via a Rural Community Development Revolving Loan.[63]

In eastern Gulf County, St. Joe Timberland also secured from the Water Management District a nearly threefold increase in the amount of water it was withdrawing from the Brothers River, a tributary to the Apalachicola.[64] St. Joe used the diversion to expand a duck hunting compound in eastern Gulf County on the former M-K Ranch, renamed the Tupelo Bend Waterfowl Area. St. Joe had takers lined up for pricey duck-hunting rights.

Gulf County resident and its foremost advocate for the Apalachicola River, Marilyn Blackwell, opposed the drastic increase from the Brothers River, which was already low from drought conditions. But district staff concluded that when water levels were low, the pumps would be unable to remove water from the Brothers. As a precaution, the permit forbade withdrawals during low water conditions.

Across the region, better stewardship of water resources, such as water reuse programs now being implemented in several Green Empire communities, could help bridge the difference between supply and demand. Politics, however, was guaranteed to become a staple feature of water supply issues just as it is in south Florida.

As for sewer, inadequate sewage treatment has been one of the Panhandle's most intractable environmental problems. Sewage spills and septic tanks are a known source of pollution for coastal water bodies including Choctawhatchee Bay, St. Joe Bay, the Apalachicola River and the Gulf of Mexico. Leakage of improperly treated wastes causes a variety of problems; it is even suspected to be a contributing factor to recent severe red tide outbreaks and algal blooms that create a spinachlike growth along the beaches of Bay and Walton Counties and hurt the shellfish industry.[65]

Fortunately, new state-of-the-art sewage treatment facilities recently went on line and others were in the works. As of 2003, though, Port St. Joe still awaited a much-needed new wastewater treatment plant to replace its combination industrial-municipal plant.

Nevertheless, septic tanks continued to serve a large percentage of dispersed homes in the Green Empire's rural areas. More than half the homes in Gulf County were on private septic systems, and the same proportion of Gulf County residences were within 500 feet of a water body.[66] Septic systems have a high failure rate—about one-third fail to contain human wastes because of poor maintenance or placement in sandy soils that are prone to permit wastes to leak out.

Yet the state Department of Health issued permits for St. Joe, among others, to build septic-reliant homes. These included the Oakmont subdivision on the shores of Deer Point Reservoir, where St. Joe/Arvida offered twenty-six lots to be served by wells and septic tanks. There, the septic tank drain fields could start at 100 feet from the water. St. Joe also initially proposed septic tanks for several hundred RiverCamp homes slated for the mostly undeveloped shores of West Bay, a plan later replaced by a hook-up to a wastewater facility. In Franklin County the setback distance from water bodies was 150 feet, and the assistant county planner said that the county is moving toward more centralized treatment facilities.[67] Such a move would help to preserve the high-caliber aquatic ecosystem there.

Amenities

Other forms of infrastructure St. Joe sought for its waterfront properties were seaports and marinas. Seaports were needed for the bread and butter of commerce, while recreational marinas such as the one in Port St. Joe were the icing on the cake for ritzy coastal communities. Besides helping make a go of the recreational marina at Port St. Joe, the St. Joe Company expended a great deal of effort to try to land a marina for its SummerCamp development.

A small marina already existed in the immediate area there, as part of the FSU Marine Laboratory at Turkey Point. Ed Ball donated to FSU the seventy-acre tract on which the lab was sited in the late 1960s. The lab became a locus of aquatic research and "Saturday-at-the-Sea" hands-on programs for area middle school children. As St. Joe geared up for development, discussions took place between FSU, the state, and St. Joe about ways that St. Joe might reclaim that

FIGURE 10. Signs of infrastructure improvements:
water pipes awaiting installation in Bay County. Photo
by Kathryn Ziewitz.

which Ed Ball gave away. FSU and St. Joe tossed around the possibility of sale or relocation of the facility or even a joint-use approach.

The FSU lab had a pier and a three-mile channel to deep water recently dredged at several million dollars of state expense. It could be easily converted into a commercial marina with plenty of space for the lucrative dry dock storage business as well. However, marinas other than for research purposes are discouraged in marine sanctuaries such as Alligator Harbor. FSU was allowed to dredge and blast the channel in the 1960s because of its research function.

State guidelines for development within aquatic preserves were strict, at least on paper. The state holdings in the preserve were to be "set aside forever in their essentially natural or existing condition for the benefit of future generations," according to the management plan for the Alligator Harbor preserve. Private noncommercial docks were permitted for homes along Alligator Harbor, but commercial facilities were discouraged.

A group of FSU faculty and community representatives calling itself the FSU Marine Lab Advisory Council recommended making the lab into a venue for eco-tourism with nature trails and boardwalks, a small exhibit center, classrooms and docents. The group also suggested asking St. Joe to donate a generous buffer zone of 1,200 to 1,500 acres in an arc spanning east and west of the marine lab but advised against making the facility into a commercial marina.

The plan died after the group turned it over to top administrators at FSU. Dr.

Ray Bye, vice president of research for FSU, expressed the opinion that given the land's value for coastal development, St. Joe was "not likely to want to give this [adjacent land] to us."[68] D'Alemberte intimate and St. Joe director Frank Shaw, himself an owner of more than twenty acres in nearby St. Teresa,[69] said that he thought "nothing would be presented until the marina is all worked out."[70] The eventual compromise that led to the state and county approval of Summer-Camp set aside only a three-acre buffer of St. Joe land for the marine lab, along with an agreement to let FSU have access to nearby Turkey Creek for research.[71]

At the early stages of considering a marina location for SummerCamp, Bye, lab director Nancy Marcus and D'Alemberte were among those who took a helicopter tour with St. Joe officials, including conservation lands specialist George Willson, to check out other locations that might be suitable for a relocated marine lab. After reviewing all the possibilities, the advisory council confirmed the existing location as the top choice. Some FSU faculty thought the lab itself might not fare well into the future if development led to decline in water quality. Others thought FSU should stay put and strive to safeguard the natural resources at Alligator Harbor and challenge what one observer labeled "corporate arrogance."

In the spring of 2001, bow-tied FSU president D'Alemberte displayed an openness to compromise. "We care about natural resources, but we also are willing to work with St. Joe with some reasonable proposition on the table," he said in his wood-paneled office replete with law books and biographies of notables such as Benjamin Franklin, John F. Kennedy, and Justice Hugo Black.[72]

While university administrators seemed willing to consider a commercial marina at Alligator Harbor, St. Joe met with staunch local opposition. St. Joe then sought permission to install a scaled-down twenty-four-slip marina with a boat launch and additional storage for 200 boats elsewhere on its own land. In the face of stiff local disapproval, Doug Delano of Arvida withdrew the request to build even the scaled-back marina for SummerCamp. When the Franklin County Commission approved the SummerCamp development of 499 homes, stores, a restaurant, and beach club, it was with the caveat that any marina associated with SummerCamp in the future would require approval of the county commission.

In the 2002 legislative session, a measure especially pertinent to Franklin County cropped up in a late-breaking addition to growth management legislation. The Florida House approved a provision to lift DRI review of marinas under certain conditions and specifically exempt from state agency review new marinas west of 84 degrees 24 minutes west longitude. That line happened to fall just a few miles east of the proposed marina at SummerCamp. The bill

passed in the state house, but by the time it went to the state senate, the longitude wording clearly favorable to St. Joe and other Panhandle coastal developers
and boating lobbies was removed, largely due to the efforts of state representative Will Kendrick. St. Joe denied that it was pushing for the language.[73] The bill
that passed lifted DRI review for counties that had marina siting plans, which
Franklin County did not. At least for a time, any new marinas there would be
evaluated under existing DRI rules.

Representative Kendrick, a sixth-generation Franklin Countian, gave an im-
passioned speech on the floor of the Florida House in opposition to the late-
breaking language. He was told by a DCA official that the push to lift DRI review of marinas came from the governor's office.[74]

Kendrick was adamant that the inserted language would take away local control in Franklin County and provide "an open gate to one company"—St. Joe—
while undermining protection of delicate coastal resources. Kendrick's very visible opposition to the new marina language on the floor of the Florida House
provoked threats from a number of lobbyists to withdraw financial support for
Kendrick. "Their support pays for my ear, not my vote," Kendrick insisted.
"When the time comes to where I can't represent the people, then it's time for
me to take it back to the house—and I mean the house in Carrabelle," Kendrick
said.[75]

In general, Kendrick was supportive of the SummerCamp development and
the opportunity it represented for enhancement of Franklin County's tax base.
However, Kendrick felt strongly about the siting of the marina. He recalled telling St. Joe's Chris Corr that a much better marina site existed ten miles away in
Carrabelle. Corr told Kendrick that the company had paid for studies that
showed people would not drive that far to use a marina.[76]

In the fall of 2003, three years after making its initial proposal to locate a
marina at SummerCamp, St. Joe finally found a site for a full-scale marina—
near Carrabelle, as Kendrick and others had urged. It would be built at the
mouth of the Carrabelle River on Timber Island, a 49-acre property the St. Joe
Company had bought from the state for $6.8 million. At SummerCamp itself,
the only boating structures approved were ten community piers with no boat
slips and a single ten-craft dock.[77] Along with other concessions it made to win
approval for SummerCamp, St. Joe issued a "warranty" that there would be no
adverse impacts on water quality or shellfish harvesting at Alligator Harbor.

One Panhandle resident who followed the marina issue from the start, biologist and FSU adjunct professor Anne Rudloe (who also operated a marine
specimen laboratory nearby with her husband, Jack Rudloe), challenged St. Joe
to follow up its lofty words with low-impact development that would "reinvent

how people live on the land." Rudloe said, "If they can get public money to build airports, I challenge them to get the money to improve water quality."[78]

Greasing the Skids

From the basics to the amenities, at the beginning of the twenty-first century, the St. Joe Company seemed well on its way to fulfilling its biggest wishes. Hundreds of millions of dollars' worth of promised infrastructure appeared on the scene, just in time for the flood of newcomers St. Joe expected to flock to its newly marketed Green Empire. It was publicly funded concurrency on a massive scale. The airport, pipelines, roads, marinas, schools and, hospitals would add greatly to the region's built environment and impress the most lasting transformation yet upon the region, on a scale even more broad than the advent of Disney to Orlando.

The combination of St. Joe's political muscle, savvy corporate knowledge both in-house and in the form of hired consultants and lobbyists, and a cooperative stance from regulators converged to smooth the way for the St. Joe Company to develop the region. Some viewed the company as propelling long-overdue change and economic development. They assessed the company's wish fulfillment as win-win. Others saw a proprietary vision being developed at public expense, but with little public scrutiny, and sometimes at a cost to quality of life for existing residents and the environment.

14

🪙 🪙 🪙 🪙 🪙 🪙 🪙 🪙 🪙 🪙 **An Airport Taxis for Takeoff**

*The relocated airport, with significant expansion
capacity, will unleash the economic growth potential
of northwest Florida, especially serving to enhance
economic development in counties designated by
Florida as an Area of Critical Economic Concern.*
**Airport Authority Transportation Outreach Program
2001 Proposal**

ONE BIG-TICKET ITEM on St. Joe's wish list, a new regional airport, moved
from the conceptual stage to the planning stage at warp speed once the local
airport authority and St. Joe discovered a shared objective. The Panama City–
Bay County Airport Authority for years had been concerned with deficiencies at
its present location within the city limits of Panama City, according to Airport
Manager Randy Curtis.[1]

The airport was sited on 745 acres of attractive land surrounded by residential neighborhoods, a state highway, and St. Andrew Bay. The airport's longest
runway, at 6,308 feet, could accommodate some regional jets but was too short
for existing jets used in nonstop domestic flights or the wide-body jets for international travel that the airport hoped to attract in the distant future. The airport lacked an adequate safety buffer at the end of its runway and operated under a waiver from FAA for overruns. Among its other deficiencies, Curtis noted
that the air strip was affected by hurricane storm surges and was too short to
land Air Force One—a factor that might seem of little consequence because of
the nearby presence of Tyndall Air Force Base. In addition, nearby residents
complained of noise and potential safety risks.

As of 2002, the airport operated well under capacity and had lost, rather than gained, commercial airlines. Bay County's push for a new airport came at a time when the airline industry was suffering from its worst fiscal stress in more than a decade. Airlines were halting marginal routes or curtailing flights, as well as flying smaller jets to cut losses.

After building a handsome new terminal in 1995, the airport proposed to lengthen the runway into the bay to solve its overrun problem. This proposal required the destruction of dozens of acres of some of the healthiest seagrass in St. Andrew Bay. As opposition to this plan by area residents and environmentalists swelled, the Airport Authority solicited support for its expansion, going to area companies including St. Joe. "We had general information that they had reorganized," Curtis recalled in an interview from his office overlooking the air traffic control tower, with St. Andrew Bay glimmering in the distance.[2]

At first, the new St. Joe Company was receptive to the airport's desire to expand on site. Officials felt a "strong, viable airport" was important to their new corporate mission and agreed to put their support behind a runway extension, Curtis said. Further discussions ensued, during which St. Joe then "tossed out" the idea of starting a whole new airport from scratch, Curtis said. With the runway extension snagged on the environmental quagmire of seagrass, the idea of a whole new site became an increasingly attractive option, and airport officials began working with the state DOT and FAA to begin studies. St. Joe supplied the Airport Authority with a pledge to donate 4,000 acres of silvicultural land north of West Bay, worth an estimated $25 million. Managers at large, congested airports could only dream of offers of 4,000-acre tracts on which to expand or build from the ground up.

Consultants hired to research the feasibility of a new airport presented their findings in July 2000 to an excited standing-room-only crowd in an airport meeting room. Representative Allan Bense addressed the group. "Besides education, the number one issue in this community is jobs," he said. The combination of a thriving port and an enhanced airport, he noted, would be two of the area's strongest assets, creating new jobs. "If both of these are in place, I think we could have a great boom here," he said. Employment that could be created would go beyond service jobs to include "welders, mechanics, and boilermakers."[3]

Bechtel Infrastructure Corporation, one of the companies under the umbrella of the worldwide engineering and construction giant Bechtel, won the job of lead consultant. Airport manager Curtis said initially the airport wanted to select a company to do a limited scope of study, but after discussions with the FAA and others decided instead to "put together a development team that could go through to construction." Rather than seek competitive bids, the Airport Authority examined applicant companies' track records and qualifications and narrowed the field accordingly. Bechtel came out on top. In some institutions, hiring the same company to do a needs assessment with a prospect for future work on design and building of said project would be avoided as a potential conflict of interest. Curtis stated that contracting procedures were in accordance with state and federal laws.[4]

Bechtel had built many major engineering projects around the world, including pipelines, mines, power plants, refineries, and hydroelectric dams. It also had close ties to the upper echelons of the Republican Party and listed Reagan administration Secretary of State George Schultz on its board of directors. It was not common for one company to work from concept all the way to construction, but Bechtel could claim two examples of "soup to nuts" airport construction: King Khaled International Airport and King Fahd International, both in Saudi Arabia.[5]

In Bay County's case, Bechtel concluded that relocating the airport was a better, less costly option than trying to expand at the current site. Bechtel determined that a new airport could be built by 2006, at a cost of between $200 and $218 million, whereas acquiring more land around the existing airport to make a longer air strip would cost $276 million and displace a large number of homes.[6] A subsequent site selection study costing another $1 million homed in on the St. Joe land above West Bay as the preferred location—in the same area that had been identified in the first, $2.4 million feasibility study. The new location was about seventeen miles from the current airport location.

Bechtel's determination of economic viability for the proposed Bay County airport hinged on eventual demand from an increased permanent and tourist population, along with cargo such as FedEx and UPS express delivery services.

Bechtel's findings mystified some in the community. A retired Delta engineer, Don Hodges, whose credentials included helping to design the Atlanta airport, was among the most vocal and informed of critics. He went on to pursue a county-appointed seat on the Airport Authority, but was among several candidates for that seat who were passed over in favor of an incumbent who had already served multiple terms. Hodges charged that Bechtel's feasibility study was "selective in assumptions, based on very imprecise cost estimates, and either ignored or was not concerned with economic justification."[7]

Hodges' own independent analysis turned up no justification for constructing a new airport within the twenty-year planning horizon. The existing airport was operating under 50 percent of capacity as of the year 2000, with the overwhelming activity consisting of general aviation. FAA guidelines suggest considering expansions once 60 percent of capacity is reached and beginning construction at 90 percent of capacity. Hodges said the data showed the present airfield capacity would be adequate until the year 2030. As for the constraints at the present airport, including the relatively short runway and the urban location, similar constraints are commonplace at far busier airports, Hodges said.

The Airport Authority responded in written comments to Hodges' critique. Regarding his assertion about need, the response was, "Agreed. There is no need for additional capacity enhancements today. The relocated airport would provide room for such expansion in the future without additional condemnation of land."[8]

Hodges also questioned the public policy ramifications of investing large sums of taxpayer money in airport infrastructure. "I believe the decision on relocating the airport should be made after the alternatives are reconsidered, and the debate should include the distinction between aviation needs and the pressure or desire to relocate the economic nexus of the region to the west. This shift is not certain to accelerate economic development, but it is certain to swallow $250 million of public funds before the private interests risk anything," he asserted. One alternative he raised was construction of an airport as a public-private venture similar to the one that Ross Perot built in Alliance, Texas. That option would require St. Joe and other private sector entities, not the taxpayer, to shoulder the operational expense.

The precise fate of the *existing* airport site of 745 acres was a mystery as this book went to press, although the Airport Authority stated its intentions to sell the land to help provide the local cost share for the new facility. The choice site was being considered for homes and a golf course, and an educational campus, or continued use for general aviation. Officials from both St. Joe and the Airport Authority denied persistent rumors that the company would develop the old airport property once the new one came on line. Nevertheless, the Bechtel feasibility study concluded that the "highest and best use" for the land was development into residential and mixed-use commercial real estate.

Local governments and chambers of commerce were supportive of the airport relocation as proposed. However, critics weighed in at public hearings on the site selection study and fired off a steady stream of letters to the editor over a long period. Several naysayers pointed out that a new airport would guarantee neither more flights nor lower fares. A local travel agency owner, who was also an unsuccessful candidate for a seat on the Airport Authority, questioned whether a new airport could serve the consumer's need for more airlines. The existing airport was capable of servicing regional airlines but was not attracting them, she said. At the heated July 2001 county meeting to fill a seat on the Air port Authority, one citizen summed up the concern: "Is it going to be like 'Field of Dreams'—build it and they will come? They'll still go to Dothan and Atlanta and Fort Walton because the prices are right," she predicted, to an outburst of applause.

The need for improved local air service was important to state representative Allan Bense. "We can't have people drive one hundred miles or pay eight-hundred dollars to fly to Atlanta," he said at the July 2000 meeting. But airport officials later conceded that a new airport would not automatically bring better service. The feasibility study itself noted that an overwhelming percentage of visitors to the area, 84 percent, drove. Since airline deregulation, small cities across the country have competed fiercely for air carrier service, a trend that showed no sign of ending.

The St. Joe Company, however, persisted in citing better air service as part of the airport relocation justification in Bay County. A press release it issued on the heels of the FAA site selection study approval proclaimed, "The new airport provides a substantial opportunity to accelerate responsible economic growth throughout the region and bring improved air service at competitive fares to the entire region."[9] Earlier, in its letter pledging the land donation, St. Joe chief Peter Rummell said the airport would be necessary because of "growth that will accelerate dramatically in the near future."[10]

A common refrain among critics was that the optimistic St. Joe Company was in the pilot's seat for the relocation process. One letter writer even satirically dubbed the proposed airport the "Arvida City–Arvida County International Airport." Airport Manager Curtis insisted that St. Joe had no formal role in the study.

Nevertheless, the overlap between St. Joe's corporate messages and the Bechtel study was remarkable. Both St. Joe and Bechtel used Ft. Myers as a model for northwest Florida's growth potential, focusing on the impact that the Southwest Florida Regional Jetport had there. Bechtel called Bay County "a mirror of Ft. Myers." The St. Joe Company told its stockholders that in terms of number of people and households, Panama City was equivalent to the Fort Myers of 1975.[11]

Graphics used by Bechtel in its July 2000 slide presentation repeated such terms as the St. Joe–derived "Florida Wild" without ever mentioning the St. Joe Company. The feasibility report contained passages that could have rolled out of St. Joe's marketing department, for instance:

> For the time being at least, discontinuity between the image of Panama City Beach and south Walton County remains an impediment to marketing the

Region as one distinct tourism "product". . . . The recent announcement of Arvida/St.Joe and the Town of Panama City Beach to build "Pier Park," however, is one step to unify this image. . . . Pier Park will serve as a physical "focus" of beach activities and present a well-designed space that could become a model for further design improvements along Panama City Beach. It will also help complement the development of high quality tourist offerings as the designer golf courses will bridge the link to south Walton County: while mom and dad attend the convention social at the WaterColor Inn, their teenagers can enjoy high-quality entertainment at nearby Pier Park.[12]

One had to conclude that, whether by accident or design, Bechtel's vision was St. Joe's vision. Even the timing of announcements from FAA coordinated nicely with the St. Joe Company's objectives—FAA approval of the site selection study came April 13, just four days before St. Joe released its first quarter 2001 earnings report.

Another common element to the two companies was that both were represented in Bay County by attorney William Harrison, who is regarded as the person in Bay County most likely to have the ear of Jeb Bush, or, for that matter, President Bush. While Representative Bense was the undisputed king of infrastructure for northwest Florida at the start of the new millennium, Panama City lawyer William Harrison could be justly considered the behind-the-scenes prince of public procurement for Bay County. His work to promote the Hathaway Bridge for Bay County paid him $47,000 over a four-month period.[13] Harrison was involved in securing low-interest loans for a new Advanced Wastewater Treatment Plant (AWT) and he advised local governments about an ill-starred project of laying sewer lines to feed the AWT. For a company in need of infrastructure, Harrison was a natural ally. As counsel to both Bechtel and St. Joe, he was playing a vital role in one of the biggest public works projects to hit the Green Empire.

Whatever St. Joe's behind-the-scenes role in the airport studies, its executives made no bones about their desire for the project to move forward on its own land in West Bay. CEO Peter Rummell called the proposed airport the "centerpiece of economic and infrastructure development."[14]

Even before the airport received final approval from a multitude of state and federal agencies, many local leaders viewed the relocation as a done deal. Some in the business press got that impression as well. Investor publication *Standard and Poor's* in January 2001 pronounced St. Joe stock a "good long-term investment," noting that "enhanced visibility in northwest Florida augers well for St. Joe." The report stated that northwest Florida "has not enjoyed the same type of growth as its southeast counterpart. However, this could change with the relocation of the Panama City airport."[15]

In the view of many area leaders, the combination of the availability of a huge chunk of donated rural land and almost complete funding from state and federal dollars made the prospect of a brand new airport too good to pass up. Bay County commissioner Danny Sparks, who endorsed the status quo by nominating sitting Airport Authority member Don Crisp to a fourth term over the other candidates vying for the position, said, "I sincerely believe building the new airport is the best thing to do for Bay County. . . . We will never see the stars aligned again, with this availability of FAA money."[16]

Bechtel managers, apparently acting as lobbyists as well as analysts, assured Bay Countians at an informational meeting in July 2000 that positive discussions had taken place "to the highest level" in Washington regarding the relocation and the federal government's $70 million share of its cost.[17]

These discussions took place even before the feasibility study had been completed. In addition, state-level support was strong because of hopes an airport would give a broad stimulus to the lagging regional economy.

Any doubts about the viability of the airport post–September 11 were erased on December 18, 2001, when President George W. Bush signed into law the 2002 Transportation Appropriations Act, which included language designating the Panama City–Bay County International Airport as "high priority." The act earmarked $2 million for the project, which was just the beginning.[18]

The Panama City–Bay County Airport Authority expected to seek total state spending of $70 million; the $10 million funded by the state in the 2001 legislative session was a big step forward, thanks to strong backing from Representative Bense and the Florida Department of Transportation. Bechtel project leader Bob Cone met several times with the governor and lawmakers, according to news reports.[19] In an interview, Curtis defended the sessions as more in the category of information sharing than lobbying.[20]

Language in the Airport Authority's 2001 budget request to the state argued that a relocated airport would provide an economic shot in the arm for the region as a whole. While Bay County was not among the counties in the "Area of Critical Economic Concern," adjacent counties with that designation were Washington County to the north and Gulf County to the east, also in the airport's broad service area.

The budget request projected that 1,750 new jobs would be created by the new airport.[21] In comparison, the advent of the Southwest Florida Regional Airport near Fort Myers in 1983 produced "a massive, massive economic impact on

Lee County and Southwest Florida in general," according to Wade Taylor of the Lee County Economic Development Office.[22] It also exacerbated urban sprawl.

Most local politicians were reluctant to quibble over the drawbacks of the proposal lest the opportunity disappear. "Sure Arvida wants it," said then-chairman of the Bay County Commission Mike Ropa. "But just because they gain, doesn't mean we lose.... If we get something out of it, then we gain, too."[23] Ropa voted with the majority of Bay County commissioners to stay the course on the airport relocation when he, like the majority of Panama City commissioners, reappointed the existing county designee to the Airport Authority instead of choosing a new candidate who questioned the move. Economic development was the main reason the commissioners cited for going ahead with the new airport.

The biggest hang-up for the airport relocation would be environmental impacts and permitting, as with airport projects nationwide, and the earlier runway expansion proposal. Early on, the environmental community was largely supportive after the St. Joe Company proposed setting up a huge land preserve to mitigate effects of the airport as well as the growing number of St. Joe's environmental impacts on other nearby land. The prospect of a large preserve in the vicinity of the airport appealed to some local environmentalists when contrasted to visions of all-out development they feared as an alternative, even given the low-density zoning in place at the time for the area. Approval of large-scale amendments to raise zoning densities had been a familiar feature of land use policy in the county in the past. There was no indication that the designation "conservation" land was going to stick any more than previous designations that had been changed to more intensive development.

Also, while some nearby counties had large amounts of land set aside in its natural condition, either in state or federal forests or huge military reservations, Bay County was well below the statewide average of 16 percent of land set aside for conservation.[24] A preserve large enough to become a National Wildlife Refuge or other significant natural area rimming West Bay was compelling.

Before 2001, no mapped boundaries for such a preserve were presented to the environmental community; at the same time, citizens learned that 4,000 acres—or 6.25 square miles—would be turned into what a Bechtel spokesman frankly described as a "moonscape." Some environmentally minded citizens began to wonder if they should have looked more closely at the teeth of this gift horse.

Sparing seagrass destruction was laudable, but large-scale alteration of a significant portion of the West Bay watershed was starting to look like a big price to pay. Wetlands made up 30 to 60 percent of the area, which contained several idyllic black water creeks set in one of the few remaining continuous large forest areas around St. Andrew Bay. Along with destroying 1,000 to 2,000 acres of wetlands, development would remove habitat for rare plants and animals. In addition to the 2,000 to 4,000 acres of all-out destruction, large borrow pits to supply fill material for construction could consume another 1,000 or more acres.

The local Audubon Society chapter sent a letter to the FAA questioning the process by which the National Environmental Policy Act (NEPA) would be carried out. NEPA requires environmental impact studies of federally funded projects. Another group, the Citizens for Enduring Communities, also asked that a broad-based environmental review be carried out cooperatively by the FAA and three other federal agencies. This group expressed concerns that additional lands might be converted to industrial park. If an industrial park of another 4,000 acres were added, the airport and related projects would destroy almost a third of the subdrainage basin, raising the real possibility of impacts to the St. Andrew Bay estuary. In April 2002, the FAA announced it would carry out a full Environmental Impact Statement (EIS) for the project.

Later that year, President George W. Bush issued an executive order that could lift the airport from this stringent review. The executive order created a Cabinet-level task force that would bypass what were described as "inefficient review procedures" required by the National Environmental Policy Act. The lifting of standard federal law would apply to "transportation projects deemed critical to the nation's infrastructure, such as highway widening projects and airport expansions," according to one report.[25]

"By working in close concert with governors and transportation leaders, we hope to identify effective procedures for routinely expediting consideration of environmentally sound transportation projects nationwide," said U.S. Secretary of Transportation Norman Mineta.[26] The executive order appeared to be an especially welcome policy coup for Florida's Great Northwest. The determination of the airport's environmental soundness might now rest with a task force reporting to the White House instead of with the stricter rules of NEPA.

From the start, the original group that had opposed the runway extension threw its support behind the airport relocation, with several caveats, including that no barge port be located in association with a new industrial area. A news release sent out by the Airport Authority announcing the FAA site approval on April 17, 2001, included the prearranged endorsement of respected spokesman John Robert Middlemas on behalf of a grassroots group, the Bay County Coordinating Committee for Sensible Airport Development. Middlemas was quoted saying that mitigation lands associated with the airport "will give us the opportunity to protect West Bay, a buffer of land around the Bay and the principal streams that flow into the Bay."[27] Later, as the planning process for the airport advanced, mapped boundaries for conservation areas were identified, covering some 37,000 acres. Still, St. Joe failed to supply a written commitment for conservation lands. Ten months later, Middlemas waited out a marathon Bay County planning board meeting to offer his comments on the status of the project he had helped along. He protested that St. Joe had failed to make an airtight, written commitment to set aside the conservation lands.

"I think this is a wonderful plan. I've been involved from the beginning. But I wish that there was a real commitment there," he said. "If I were Peter Rummell, that's what I'd do," he said.[28] When the Bay County Commission approved the "West Bay Sector Plan" that included the airport in September 2002, Commissioner Ropa (who had been an early supporter of the airport relocation) objected that the plan still did not contain language sufficient to prevent development of conservation lands in the early stages of the project.

As the airport and sector plan continued to clear regulatory hurdles, it appeared St. Joe/Arvida had struck itself a winning bargain. The company would forego development in the large West Bay Conservation Area, from which it could still reap some conservation dollars after satisfying mitigation requirements. In return, St. Joe would receive permission to plant more than 70,000 people plus industrial and commercial enterprises—a complex several times larger than SouthWood—in the former wilds of Bay County. If successful, the company would sharply increase the value of its vast Green Empire in the Florida Panhandle. By early 2003, a lingering contingent of area citizens continued its opposition to the airport. The Panhandle Citizens Coalition, a small regional growth watchdog group, mounted a petition drive that sought to put the airport relocation to a popular vote among the citizens of Panama City.

St. Joe and the Growth Machine

> *There is literally no other company in the U.S. that has been reborn the same way and has the opportunity that St. Joe has, literally with control over an entire region's destiny.*
> Julie Strauss Bettinger, Tallahassee writer/editor

AS ST. JOE ROLLED BACK its greenbelt, CEO Peter Rummell clearly expected the company to play a leading role in the future of the Panhandle, where it owned roughly 22 percent of the land in its core ten-county stronghold. "If we are smart about it—if we are methodical but aggressive—it is a huge opportunity. We have an opportunity to create a very special kind of region," Rummell told *New York Times* reporter Douglas Frantz.[1]

By early 2002, St. Joe's efforts at remaking the Panhandle were snowballing in what it called a "value creation cycle," depicted in a glossy company handout. This latest corporate buzz phrase described a soup-to-nuts process of turning raw land to valuable real estate, beginning with regional level planning, siting of infrastructure, and the building of resorts, golf courses, and other growth magnets dubbed "accelerators." The diagramed handout showed the cycle continuing with the construction of homes, commercial outlets including "big box" retail centers like Wal-Mart, civic structures such as hospitals and schools, and ending with office and industrial parks.

The comprehensive approach to growth, with St. Joe acknowledging its role in regional planning, seemed to show that what some planners and social scientists call "the growth machine" was going strong in northwest Florida. Economist Harvey Molotch coined the phrase "growth machine" to describe the effectiveness of a cohort of pro-growth interests that fuels growth to its own benefit.[2] Developers, builders, and others in the housing trades, road pavers, consultants, bankers, and others with a financial stake in growth can have powerful momentum that drives political decisions. In the case of St. Joe, others too would benefit from the literal and metaphorical inroads the company was making. Whether or not they were boosters for St. Joe, most Green Empire power brokers wholeheartedly endorsed a pro-growth agenda.

St. Joe's state-level support started at the top with Governor Jeb Bush, the former Codina developer. The Bush–St. Joe relationship appeared to have picked up where the relationship between St. Joe and former Governor Chiles, a Democrat and an early champion of the SouthWood project, had left off. On a warm day in May 2001, a cordial tone prevailed as Governor Bush and CEO Peter Rummell shoveled snow-white sand at the site of the new Nextel building site on St. Joe land in Panama City Beach and hailed the development on hitherto undeveloped beach scrub as "smart growth." The same day, the governor broke ground at the much-needed Sacred Heart mini-hospital in south Walton County, where St. Joe had donated thirty-five acres for the facility.

Under the Jeb Bush administration, the state appeared more often a partner than a watchdog concerning the ambitions of its largest landowner. Through special appointments, public-private partnerships, favorable agency policies and legislation, the state directly and indirectly aided St. Joe in many of its objectives.

Bush named St. Joe executives and board members to a variety of advisory posts in his administration, thereby giving them an opportunity to help steer state policy. St. Joe/Arvida executives and directors were appointed to the Growth Management Study Commission, the Energy 2020 Study Commission, a river basin board, the Florida School Construction Finance Board, the Florida Transportation Commission, and university boards of trustees. Influential state officials also strode through the proverbial revolving doors to work directly for the St. Joe Company. Governor Bush's former communications director, Katie Baur Muniz, assumed a post at St. Joe as public affairs manager, working under Vice President Jerry Ray.

Bev Kilmer, a state representative who chaired the regional economic development group Opportunity Florida and was a director for Workforce Florida and Florida's Great Northwest, met with Governor Bush "on a regular basis" to discuss St. Joe. "I know that the St. Joe Company confers with the governor as well," Kilmer said. "And if the governor has a problem with anything the com-

FIGURE 11. Governor Jeb Bush and St. Joe CEO Peter Rummell breaking ground for Nextel facility, Panama City Beach, May 2001.

pany does, he voices it. They've got a good working relationship and speak openly and frankly."[3]

Peter Rummell was refreshingly open about St. Joe's connections: "It would be naïve to sit here and say that we don't have access to people, because we do. And we have a lot of people who care about what we do, who are hopeful about what we're going to do, who are worried about what we are going to do, who want to help us, who want to make money off us—you pick it. . . . We've got a lot of people that want to be involved and so to the extent that that means we have some power, yeah I guess we do. We're involved politically with people because that's the way the world works, whether you like it or not."

Rummell says the important question is whether the company abuses its power. "I don't think there's any evidence of that yet. I don't think there's anything that we feel that we've gotten away with. We're using our influence to get infrastructure funded and those kinds of things which do nothing but accrue to the benefit of the community. Do they help us? Yes, but it also means that there's less congestion, cheaper airline fares. . . . We've developed a lot of relationships that I feel are very legitimate."[4]

Florida's Government and St. Joe

Jeb Bush was elected Florida's governor in 1998 in the first administration since Reconstruction to have both legislative bodies and the governor aligned with the Republican Party. His administration ushered in a period of state government marked by deregulation, privatization, and pro-business sentiment, all of which created a particularly accommodating climate for developers, including St. Joe. "The business of the Florida Legislature is business," quipped an article reporting on an analysis of the 2000 legislature, which found that Florida senators voted 86 percent of the time in support of the stance supported by the Florida Chamber of Commerce.[5]

The St. Joe Company's plans to remake the Panhandle meshed nicely with Governor Bush's goals to shrink the role of traditional government while enlarging opportunities for the private sector to engage in quasi-governmental functions. Privatization was one cause that was championed by the Council of 100, a by-invitation assembly of elite Florida business executives whose nominations are approved by the governor and that itself seemed to exemplify the blurring of public and private sector lines in Florida circa 2000.[6]

St. Joe CEO Peter Rummell was a member of the Council of 100, as was St. Joe board member Walter Revell and former St. Joe CEO Winfred Thornton, still chair of the A. I. duPont Trust in 2002. Former Arvida head Chuck Cobb chaired the group in 1998. The Council of 100 was yet another dimension of St. Joe's involvement with the state's agenda setters.

At the forefront of privatization was one public-private organization with which St. Joe was affiliated, Enterprise Florida, which between 1996 and 2001 had made awards upward of $8 million for northwest Florida projects from which St. Joe could anticipate direct or indirect benefits. The Orlando-based group, officially chaired by Governor Bush, was the state's largest economic development group and was funded mostly by the state, with a smaller share of its expenses picked up by corporate members, including St. Joe. The company paid between $50,000 and $100,000 in annual fees.[7] St. Joe economic developer Neal Wade was a director, as was state representative Allan Bense, whom Florida house speaker Tom Feeney named to the position in 2001. Although many found EFI's goals for economic development laudable, a 2001 audit report issued by the state Office of the Comptroller seriously questioned EFI's fiscal accountability, pinpointing flaws in the entity's internal financial controls. The comptroller directed EFI and the Office of Tourism, Trade and Economic Development, which made final decisions on EFI awards, to correct deficiencies in the largely taxpayer-funded outfit. Less than two years later, Governor Bush proposed to remove the auditing function from the comptroller's office.

The other regional economic development groups to which St. Joe belonged, Opportunity Florida, Inc., and Florida's Great Northwest, worked both independently and under the umbrella of EFI. Together these groups assumed an important planning-like role in locating businesses and infrastructure in the eastern and central Panhandle.

Along with its ties to government directly and through public-private ventures, St. Joe as a corporation or through the memberships of its executives was affiliated with many nongovernmental organizations too that helped to serve interests of their members behind the scenes through lobbying efforts or issue advocacy. Among them were the Florida Forestry Association, the Florida Homebuilders Association, the Association of Florida Community Developers (AFCD), and the free-market-oriented James Madison Institute, which counted St. Joe executive Chris Corr and Bay County lobbyist William Harrison among its directors.

St. Joe was a financial supporter of Florida Tax Watch, an advocacy organization that is the self-appointed, government-spending watchdog famous for shooting at budget "turkeys." Counter to its typical antitax stance with a focus on accountability, the group endorsed the penny sales tax in Tallahassee and a half-cent tax in Duval County,[8] both coincidentally places where St. Joe needed infrastructure improvements for its properties.

The "new" St. Joe even enjoyed affiliations with select environmental organizations, including The Nature Conservancy, with which it worked on many land sales, and the Florida Audubon Society, to which it was a contributor. The Jessie Ball duPont Foundation also was a major Audubon supporter. The St. Joe/Audubon relationship had apparently mended since the Ed Ball years, given the financial support and the society's award to St. Joe for its Talisman sugarcane farm sale.

For tending its concerns in the Florida legislature and beyond, St. Joe had ten registered state lobbyists in 2001; mostly from the influential firm of Hopping, Green, Sams, and Smith. These included land-use experts David Powell and Dan Stengle, former general counsel to the Department of Community Affairs (DCA), both colleagues of Robert Rhodes; and Frank Matthews, who in 2002 took a leading role in efforts to scale back the ability of citizens to challenge development. Company spokesman Jerry Ray denied any involvement by St. Joe in those efforts.

Another prominent lobbyist who sometimes represented St. Joe was Sam Ard, who gained recognition for leading a year 2000 attempt favored by the state's large landowners to change the state's sovereign submerged land law. In Washington, D.C., St. Joe was a client of the powerhouse law firm Hogan and Hartson, whose other clients included General Motors and General Electric. The cumulative expertise of St. Joe's brace of legal eagles was impressive, especially in the field of growth management and land use, and in 2002 St. Joe added yet another heavy hitter lobbyist, former Florida House Speaker John Thrasher.

Getting A Leg Up from Regulators

At the same time the state's budget tilted favorably to fund infrastructure and economic development projects beneficial to St. Joe, the company also benefited from streamlined access to key state agencies and a general weakening of state regulatory zeal.

Governor Jeb Bush took the rare, if not unprecedented, step of formally designating a state employee as a go-between for a private company, St. Joe. Cynthia Henderson, director of the Department of Management Services, took on the role of official liaison between the state and St. Joe in addition to her other management responsibilities. Henderson's office, in spite of repeated requests, neither responded to questions about her duties as St. Joe liaison nor provided a written description of her official duties relating to the company. Neither would Henderson grant an interview. Her role as liaison to a private business, on a state paycheck, remained largely a mystery to the general public after *Florida Trend* reported her appointment in February 2001.[9]

At DMS, Henderson oversaw retirement and insurance programs for state employees and managed state facilities. DMS was instrumental in helping the governor work toward trimming the state workforce by 25 percent over a five-year period. Of special relevance to the Green Empire, DMS also was chosen to handle "quick permitting" to expedite regulatory approvals for Areas of Critical Economic Concern, including the multiple Panhandle counties.

Prior to heading DMS, Henderson served as Governor Bush's secretary for the Department of Business and Professional Regulation. In that position, Henderson generated enough heat to be dubbed the governor's "most controversial appointee."[10] Her ethics were challenged over a trip she took on a corporate jet to the Kentucky Derby and the hiring of a friend to a state position. She also caught flak when shortly after her arrival at DBPR the agency dropped an ongoing probe of alleged construction flaws by a Pensacola builder.

Henderson first entered the powerful Bush family universe in the 1980s, when she worked as general counsel for a Florida company called Gulfstream Land and Development, one of the directors of which was Neil Bush, brother to

Jeb and President George W. Bush.[11] Neil Bush became a director at Gulfstream after he helped its head, Kenneth M. Good, obtain millions of dollars of loans from Silverado, a Colorado bank on which Neil Bush also served as a director and which racked up huge losses in failed loans during the 1980s S&L crisis.[12] Before she entered state government, Henderson also worked as a regional vice president of a large engineering firm and as a land-use attorney. She was among the early loyal supporters of Jeb Bush. In the mid-1990s she joined the board of directors of the Foundation for Florida's Future, a think tank Jeb Bush created after his failed run for governor in 1994.[13]

Governor Bush chose one of the busiest news days of the year—primary election day, September 5, 2000, to announce that the controversial Henderson would be shifting over to DMS. Within several months, Bush gave Henderson the additional role of St. Joe liaison. After the governor's reelection, Henderson left government service to join the Tallahassee office of the Tew Cardenas, et al. law and lobbying firm. Partner Al Cardenas previously had headed the Florida Republican Party.

In early 2001, another special liaison emerged for St. Joe in the Department of Community Affairs, Bob Cambric. His official title was "Community and Citizen Liaison." In a meeting convened to begin a special planning process for Bay County, he was introduced as the agency's point man for "activity related to St. Joe."[14] One longtime DCA staffer characterized the designation of a liaison to specifically handle the affairs of one corporation as "unique" in the agency's history, to the best of his knowledge.

One of Cambric's first tasks was helping to plan the proposed Panama City–Bay County Airport using sector planning, an experimental and "flexible" planning procedure developed as a prototype for replacing the existing state DRI process. (Cambric's boss, Tom Beck, had expressed great confidence that by working with St. Joe, DCA could "develop a model for other developers to follow."[15] Of St. Joe's plans, Beck said, "If there's a downside, I don't see it." By 2002, Beck had left DCA to take a job with one of the company's consultants, Wilson Miller, and was representing St. Joe on its WindMark development in Gulf County.)

Cambric's job history included a stint at head of the Apalachee Regional Planning Council, where he had played an important role in reviewing the SouthWood project. When St. Joe was working to fit the development into Tallahassee's own city-crafted "Southeast Sector Plan," former legislator T. Kent Wetherell II, husband of the departing DEP secretary, Virginia Wetherell, contacted Cambric. At the time Wetherell was president of Tallahassee Community College and apparently acting as a St. Joe lobbyist under the aegis of the law firm of Hopping, Green, Sams, and Smith, St. Joe's prime lobbying firm. Wetherell (who in late 2002 became president of Florida State University) wrote Cambric regarding an upcoming public workshop on the development order for SouthWood.

"As we previously discussed," Wetherell wrote, "our goal is to resolve any differences over language or presentation in an informal setting and to avoid unnecessary disagreement in a public forum."[16] The communication was evidence of the behind-the-scenes horse trading that goes on before the public at large becomes involved in development issues. St. Joe was adept at making these types of inroads so the public rarely saw any broken-legged horses, Trojan or otherwise.

Environmental Protection in the Age of Voluntary Compliance

The state's regulatory checks—most notably in the arenas of environmental protection and growth management—continued a trend from strict enforcement to voluntary compliance that had begun during the Chiles administration. With some exceptions, at the federal and local levels too, St. Joe's way seemed to be eased by the nationwide trend of deregulation.

One state agency with a key permitting role for St. Joe and any developer was the Department of Environmental Protection. From the vantage of many in the construction industry, DEP was seen as a tough regulator. However, others have criticized DEP in recent years for taking too accommodating a stance toward industry, developers, and others with the potential to degrade the environment. These criticisms came at the same time that the federal government delegated more and more responsibilities for key environmental programs, including the Clean Air and Clean Water Acts, to the states. Despite the common perception that the EPA diligently stands guard regulating air and water pollution to protect the public, the state in fact bears the primary responsibility in these areas.

When Jeb Bush took office, he named an experienced environmental administrator, David Struhs, to head DEP. Struhs came from the Massachusetts Department of Environmental Quality in 1999. A self-described free-market environmentalist, Struhs served under President George H. W. Bush at the Council on Environmental Quality. Apart from being Jeb Bush's appointee, Struhs had separate high-level ties to the White House; his brother-in-law, Andrew Card, became President Bush's chief-of-staff. As a former secretary of transportation under the elder President Bush, Card would appear to have an inside track on transportation matters at the nation's highest levels.

In Florida, Struhs was supportive of voluntary compliance programs for industry coupled with enforcement. Echoing a familiar chord in Florida government at the time, he spoke of the need to protect private property interests in addition to the environment.[17] "More protection, less process," became the agency's motto.

A scathing white paper by the national environmental whistleblower group, Public Employees for Environmental Responsibility (PEER), was highly critical of DEP and its lack of enforcement during the administration of Democratic governor Lawton Chiles. PEER's report led to a 1999 grand jury investigation of the actions of DEP in Escambia and Santa Rosa Counties. The 120-page report was especially critical of the DEP's Northwest District director, Bobby Cooley, saying he had "succumbed to political, economic, and other pressures, allowing regulated businesses, industries and individuals to pollute the area's air and water."[18] The report did not lead to criminal indictments, but made clear that the district director and others working with him were derelict in their duties.

Cooley, in a 2000 interview in his security-conscious office in downtown Pensacola, described the grand jury report as unfair and emphasized that it had turned up no illegal actions. He acknowledged a "culture switch" that took place after Chiles appointee Virginia Wetherell took over the agency. Cooley said this direction was being reversed under Secretary Struhs, who was returning the agency to more emphasis on enforcement and fines while still emphasizing voluntary compliance.

The general climate of environmental regulation mattered to St. Joe as it marketed northwest Florida. The less stringent the regulatory climate, the more marketable were St. Joe's lands to commercial and industrial clients, at least according to some economic development specialists. In addition, St. Joe had a keen interest in having DEP sign off on major Panhandle infrastructure projects it supported, from the proposed airport relocation to new water and sewer facilities across the region.

For its construction projects, the postindustrial St. Joe Company itself needed scores of new DEP permits, for everything from marinas to storm-water outfalls. For the first phase of its WaterColor project alone, St. Joe obtained eight permits from DEP, for items ranging from laying water distribution lines to building a storm-water discharge facility.

Storm-water runoff is one of the biggest pollution problems in northwest Florida and a huge problem to tackle because of its widespread origins. Filling wetlands and paving over vegetated terrain of all types creates storm-water runoff by preventing percolation of rainwater into the ground and forcing water to pile up in unwanted places. Too much water on too much paving not only causes flooding but also washes copious amounts of oils, greases, dirt, and worse into water bodies. Storm-water runoff is directly associated with development. Environmental scientists have a rule of thumb that watersheds are at risk from serious pollution once more than 10 percent of the area is converted to impervious surface, a finding of great importance for the future of the eastern and central Panhandle's generally high-quality water bodies. Without deliberate setting aside of vegetated buffer areas, the water quality of lakes, rivers, bays, and estuaries can be expected to decline and become less capable of supporting aquatic life. To date, St. Joe has been more willing than many other developers to set aside buffers.

Florida became a leader among states in the early 1990s for requiring developers to consider storm-water management before construction. These DEP rules have helped to alleviate the additional burden placed by new construction on top of preexisting problems. The result is the statewide proliferation of swales and man-made ponds, often dug in angular shapes and sprouting cattails behind chain-link fences. However, storm-water management is in some ways more art than science, and failure to maintain manmade structures reduces their usefulness. More and more, scientists and planners are recognizing the virtues of the simpler, and often more aesthetically pleasing, alternative to elaborate storm-water structures—setting aside ample amounts of green space to absorb rainfall. The drawback is that this measure requires developers to give up what they cherish most, buildable space.

At WaterColor, the company took pains to construct systems to pre-treat storm-water for later release into Western Lake. Another key step was establishing a 300-foot buffer around the pristine coastal lake and a twenty-five-foot buffer around other wetlands. Aside from a problem during construction that clouded Western Lake with a surge of untreated water, the system was top-notch. At SouthWood, however, the company's plans initially fell short. The city of Tallahassee required St. Joe to enhance its original plans with manmade facilities instead of relying on existing wetlands alone to absorb the increased levels of run-off that were inevitable after construction.

Under the crush of permit requests, with storm water and wetlands filling among the most numerous, all by law to be processed in a timely fashion, state agencies relied heavily on the findings of consultants hired by developers. For St. Joe, those consultants were frequently PBS&J (Post, Buckley, Schuh and Jernigan), a large engineering firm once headed by St. Joe board member Walter Revell, or, on occasion, Preble-Rish, Consulting Engineers, and others, including Wilson Miller.

From officials at DEP and local planners who reviewed the results, St. Joe got generally high marks for the work presented by its consultants. Panama City Beach planner Mel Leonard noted that St. Joe hired consultants who were familiar with the Panhandle. "They've invested in quality people who will do work and stand behind it," he said.[19] One federal official who visited the site at WaterColor after an accidental storm-water discharge was struck by the state-of-the-art measures St. Joe/Arvida instituted to prevent further siltation of the pristine coastal lake.

In the view of Linda Young, Southeast Regional Coordinator for the organization Clean Water Network, the state's regulatory system was overly dependent on the judgment of consultants, however capable they might be. Clean Water Network is a nonprofit advocacy group with a mission of monitoring enforcement of the Clean Water Act and serving as a watchdog organization over state water resource programs. Young described the permitting process as an "assembly line" where consultants supplied required data and DEP issued permits. "What you have here is a neat little enterprise, all sewn up," she said in a 1999 interview. One downside of the rubber stamping, she noted, was that "the citizens have been effectively shut out of the process."[20]

Beleaguered former Northwest District DEP director Bobby Cooley, who left DEP in 2001, was of the opinion that the grand jury report that came down on him so hard in 1999 was as much an attack on local and state elected officials, and on Florida law, as on him and his agency. "It's not just DEP. If you don't have local government dealing with environmental matters, it just doesn't work" he said.[21]

Cooley added, "If you're looking to DEP to be the sole source of your environmental protection, you're making a major mistake."[22] He said the reason was Florida law. This was one point on which the former district chief and his most severe critics agreed. The grand jury report found that DEP's ineffectiveness in permitting, monitoring, enforcement and restoration efforts "in part reflects problems with state law, and in part stems from flaws in the agency policies."[23] For example, regarding water quality, the Florida code seemed to set high goals but contained lots of "exceptions" and "howevers" that watered down the policy against degradation.[24] Efforts by DEP subsequent to the grand jury report to address storm-water problems held potential for more effective pollution control.

Falling through the Cracks

Some of the Panhandle's most important habitats had little protection as St. Joe geared up its development push. The private forestlands that comprised St. Joe's

Timberland and Land Company divisions were the biggest wild card in the future Green Empire.

Industrial forestry as generally practiced in northwest Florida was as intensive as ever circa 2002. Foresters remained free to reshape their land by forming elevated beds and digging deep trenches to drain away water. They were also allowed to construct logging roads with few restrictions. These practices generally destroy any remaining wiregrass and can upset the hydrology of large areas. Yet forestry companies were permitted to continue with these practices because of "silviculture exemptions" to the federal Clean Water Act permitted by the state of Florida. Florida delegates enforcement of the Clean Water Act for forestry operations to the water management districts rather than to DEP. One loophole is that pine flatwoods forests, even with their preponderance of watery places, are not legally protected as wetlands.

Silvicultural exemptions also ease the conversion of forests to development. Because any wetlands present are already "degraded," they are valued less than a pristine wetland in reviews for development permits. "I would hate to see us keep on saying wetlands are degraded, so we can do dredge and fill," one official said. The cycling of former forests into developable land, with reduced expectations and protection of wetlands involved, was extraordinarily helpful to St. Joe, among others.

The ecological toll of modern forestry was wide and enduring. Detrimental effects of 1980s-era forestry operations on St. Joe lands in Wakulla County still were being felt at St. Marks National Wildlife Refuge in 2001. The refuge was at the bottom of the watershed and reaped the effects of St. Joe's ditched and bedded slash pines upgradient. "The result has been a decline in our fishery and especially in our waterfowl habitat that we cannot address by management of our own existing land base," the refuge manager wrote in a 2001 letter to a St. Joe official.[25]

As pine and pulp markets continued to slump, timber operators continued to harvest more trees, creating a worsening glut. Naturally regenerated bottomlands that contained diverse hardwoods and cypress were also fair game for harvest under the drought conditions that prevailed around the turn of the millennium. And while pine and pulp prices hit rock bottom, prices for hardwood were better.

As noted elsewhere, St. Joe logged cypress and other hardwoods at several locations, including around Lake Wimico and at Devil's Swamp in south Walton as well as near the St. Marks Wildlife Refuge. The refuge manager at St. Marks expressed concerns about the legal, but nonetheless damaging, logging occurring nearby: "On-going cutting and replanting of pines, and especially the recent harvesting of cypress from the ponds on your property, threatens the continued existence of flatwood salamanders on this property. The swallow-tail kite, designated as a species of special concern by the State of Florida, nests in cypress ponds and hardwood/pine drainages on the property north of the refuge. Continued cutting within these areas may reduce or eliminate this nesting habitat."[26]

Despite these concerns, the refuge manager feared that effects on the refuge could worsen under St. Joe's new real estate mission. "As you begin to divest or develop your lands, fragmentation and outright loss of habitat threatens to diminish the value of refuge lands to wildlife disproportionate to the area of lost habitat," he wrote. "In other words, 10,000 acres of St. Marks National Wildlife Refuge is worth more as wildlife habitat now than the same 10,000 acres will be worth if the lands around it are lost to uses less compatible to wildlife than industrial forestry."[27]

For these reasons, the St. Marks Refuge manager hoped St. Joe would consider either selling lands in question or entering into conservation easements that would pay the company for adopting favorable management practices. The outlook for conservation sales to expand the St. Marks Refuge were promising.

Meanwhile, St. Joe appeared less interested than some other timber companies in changing its forestry practices to work around wildlife on the considerable acreage of its remaining industrial forest land. Some foresters sought to retool their operations with an eye toward sustainability, as evidenced by a nationwide "Sustainable Forestry Initiative" sponsored by a major industry association. This initiative added water quality protection and biodiversity conservation to the list of land management goals.

For example, Gulf Coastal Plain Ecosystems Partnership brought together the forestry company Champion International with other landowners and conservation specialists in the western Panhandle to manage a 2-million-acre Panhandle Longleaf Pine Large-Scale Conservation Area centered around Eglin Air Force Base. In the Red Hills region, too, near Tallahassee, landowners increasingly adopted multiple-purpose goals that included longleaf pine and native ground cover restoration combined with selective cutting.

But on St. Joe's timberlands, such practices as selective timbering might have to wait until the land changed hands through conservation sales. A few special areas were out of bounds for industrial forestry, but on the rest St. Joe took a conventional approach to management.

St. Joe, like other foresters, was legally bound to think of conservation values insomuch as they pertained to the Endangered Species Act, which was the most serious impediment to carte blanche forestry. The federal act prohibited outright killing of listed animal species, along with destruction of habitat essential to their survival. On St. Joe lands, the endangered species of concern were red-cockaded woodpeckers and flatwoods salamanders.

St. Joe's Clay Smallwood said he would prefer an incentive program that rewarded foresters for manipulating vegetation to the advantage of rare creatures instead of one that punished them for doing away with their habitat. "As a reward for having a red-cockaded woodpecker on my property, according to the Endangered Species Act, we have to provide three thousand to five thousand foraging trees within a three-quarter mile radius for the birds to have to feed on. . . . If I can't harvest those trees, if I can't relocate the bird and put it in another area, if I can't do certain things to eventually harvest those trees, then in fact, it has seized the opportunity for me to return a profit to my shareholders. . . . So as a reward for having this critter on our property, our property rights are forfeited."[28]

Working under that philosophy, St. Joe's general policy ever since the federal government began to enforce protection of red-cockaded woodpeckers was to harvest pines before they could attain the age to provide habitat for red-cockaded woodpeckers. In addition, 85 percent or more of St. Joe's tree farms were planted in slash pine, which the woodpeckers did not use. St. Joe was also happy to rid itself of some parcels harboring red-cockaded woodpecker colonies through conservation sales. At the same time, St. Joe/Arvida prominently displayed a feel-good nature photo featuring the unwanted but photogenic bird at "The Hammocks," a development in Bay County.

St. Joe Timberland's approach toward red-cockaded woodpeckers reflected its longstanding reluctance to acknowledge rare wildlife that existed on its rural holdings or to share its knowledge with regulators, federal or state. The "old" St. Joe usually withheld permission for biologists to survey its land for rare plants and critters. The "new" St. Joe was sometimes cagey about these touchy issues and sometimes cooperative with researchers. Shortly after Peter Rummell's hiring as CEO, St. Joe took a leading role in derailing state wildlife biologists' efforts to supply regional planning councils with detailed range maps of the habitats of rare species. St. Joe and the Florida Forestry Association feared that the maps would trigger regulatory actions or limit their ability to develop some of their lands.[29]

To environmentalists, St. Joe's unwillingness to enter into agreements to log its lands using management techniques favorable to wildlife was discouraging. At the same time, the extraordinary success of St. Joe's Land Company and the high interest in its "RiverCamps" idea showed that direct consumer demand might cause the company to rethink its forestry strategy. Multiple-use forestry

FIGURE 12. St. Joe Paper Company cypress logging operation in dome forest in Leon County, March 1996. Photo by John Jensen.

with eco-tourism and conservation as a selling point could be just the ticket to marketing rural lands to urban-weary consumers. With decades to go before it could ever sell off its interior lands for development, St. Joe could have new incentive to diversify at least a segment of its forestry operations to meet a wider array of land-use goals.

Wetlands

Wetlands are vital to the quality of life in northwest Florida. They store flood-water, recharge the aquifer, filter pollutants from surface water, and harbor wildlife. In the Green Empire, isolated wetlands are abundant and serve as the first stopping point for migratory birds coming from the Southern Hemisphere.

Yet because of decades of machinations by lawmakers in the northwest Florida delegation, the Panhandle has never given adequate protection to a large class of wetlands, the so-called isolated wetlands, that are not directly connected with a state water body. St. Joe lays claim to a multitude of these.

In early 2001, a much-publicized U.S. Supreme Court ruling led to a nationwide rollback of federal protections for isolated wetlands, causing the U.S. Army Corps of Engineers to stop considering effects of disturbance of isolated wetlands on migratory birds. That effectively limited the corps' jurisdiction over wetlands permitting to non-isolated wetlands that touched navigable waters. In northwest Florida, the ruling left no agency in charge of regulating isolated wetlands outside of Leon and Escambia Counties, which had their own wetlands ordinances.

The ruling set back the corps' nascent efforts to address cumulative wetlands losses in the Panhandle associated with St. Joe's plans. In early 1999, just as St. Joe was unveiling its early projects, the top Army Corps of Engineers official in Florida, Col. Joe Miller, wrote St. Joe CEO Peter Rummell seeking a meeting with company officials to discuss the company's overall plans. "I am aware of the large land ownership of [t]he St. Joe Company in Northwest Florida and the potential for development of that land," he wrote. Miller's comments came as the Bay County School Board sought the corps' approval to fill wetlands in order to build Arnold High School and a related four-lane access road on former St. Joe lands. "Past history has taught us that placement of a school in a relatively undeveloped area foreshadows increased residential development pressure. This brings with it additional secondary and cumulative impacts to the surrounding ecosystem," he wrote.[30]

Miller's letter informed Rummell that he could have pressed for a fuller evaluation of wetlands impacts that included likely secondary and cumulative impacts, but chose not to, partly in hopes that officials from the St. Joe Company would be willing to meet in "the near future." A year later, a St. Joe official reported St. Joe was having "ongoing conversations with the Corps of Engineers," but said the company was not ready to announce its conservation plans.[31]

Almost no one considers cumulative impacts of destruction of wetlands—or other resources—because they are difficult to measure and next to impossible to implement fairly. And as is the case in growth management requirements for concurrency, developers do not want to bear responsibility for preexisting conditions. Yet cumulative impacts are what counts.

One environmental official summed up the difficulties: "Say you've got a lake with one guy putting in a dock. That's okay, right? How about twenty more docks with chemicals leaching from the wood, and the fuel from the boats for which the docks were built. Let's say that puts too much stress on the lake. Where do you draw the line? Number thirteen? What if number five is an especially large dock and boat? . . . How do you determine the straw that breaks the camel's back? And where do you get the scientific credibility to make that decision?"[32]

Other officials also pressed St. Joe to take a "big picture" approach in addressing wetlands impacts. One planner from the West Florida Regional Planning Council noted that projects already in planning stages on recently sold St.

Joe lands in Panama City Beach, when considered in combination with St. Joe's plans for Pier Park, would have tripped certain regulatory thresholds.

A biologist in charge of reviewing St. Joe's plans for wetlands impacts credited the company for going "above and beyond what most developers would do to avoid wetlands."[33] Still, the wetland impacts of St. Joe projects, taken as a whole, were considerable. Besides the losses at the proposed airport, expected to be more than 1,400 acres of wetlands, more wetlands acres were disappearing on St. Joe projects or under the asphalt, pipelines and other infrastructure apparatus that supported the company's growth. Whereas wetlands in silivicultural areas could with effort be restored, those filled and paved over never could.

As the largest private landowner in a soggy state, St. Joe had a curious relation with wetlands. It stood in a position to do the most harm, and at the same time, the most good, to these underprotected wild lands. If its donation of land for a new airport went through, more than six square miles laced with wetlands were slated to be destroyed in a massive clearing, filling, and mining enterprise. At the same time, St. Joe, as of fall 2001, told environmental groups it was willing to set aside more than 30,000 acres of land around West Bay for permanent conservation, if buyers could be brought to the table within five years.[34]

This quid pro quo seemed to fulfill its promise to offer a large-scale wetlands conservation plan. The scope of the package struck most environmentalists as generous. In light of the shrinking protection of wetlands, any plan that conserved as many wetlands as it destroyed seemed appealing. Bay County environmentalists' greatest fear was that the plan would not stick.

Another wetlands quid pro quo resulted in the preservation of the 2,600-acre Devil's Swamp in Walton County. The purchase was prompted by the Florida DOT's legal obligation to mitigate wetlands losses associated with four-laning Highway 98 in Walton County from Highway 331 to the Bay County line. The widening project, which improved travel to south Walton County's beaches, helping St. Joe among others, had a major impact on wetlands, destroying eighty-seven acres of wetlands at stream crossings and lake swamps. DOT mitigated for the losses by allocating funds that allowed the Water Management District to purchase nearby Devil's Swamp from St. Joe. DOT spent roughly $6.7 million to cover land acquisition and restoration costs.[35]

Except for the Tate's Hell area, where a cooperative multi-agency effort was underway with a goal of restoring around 200,000 acres of that remote watery wilderness, there was no master plan for wetlands preservation in the Panhandle.[36] As the wave of growth moved from the coast to the interior, where the isolated wetlands predominated, losses would likely be great, and a regional approach to preserving these was sorely needed. In the face of continued inaction at the state level, it would be left to counties and municipalities to pick up the slack. Yet pro-development interests in Walton and Bay Counties fought to move wetlands protection in the other direction, with Bay County planning commission members even considering lifting a wetlands buffer requirement altogether at one point.

By early 2002, St. Joe was still discussing a broad-scale approach to compensating for its wetlands losses. Craig Pittman of the *St. Petersburg Times* reported that DEP met with St. Joe and TNC in a "quiet workshop" at the Disney Wilderness Preserve—a thriving wildlife area formed to mitigate the many impacts of the Disney operations in central Florida. The company desired to establish a similar preserve in northwest Florida. St. Joe could preserve wetlands in one large area in exchange for many permits to fill wetlands elsewhere. "It could then be sold to the state or a conservation group," the article said, raising the interesting possibility that St. Joe could in the end profit from its mitigation requirements. St. Joe counsel Bob Rhodes referred to this as "The Big Idea."[37] In May of 2003, state and federal agencies announced a "big picture" plan whereby St. Joe would limit wetlands losses over a 60,000-acre area in Walton and Bay Counties through establishment of conservation and mitigation areas.

Building on the Coast

Coastal parts of the Panhandle supported species found nowhere else in the world. Because of that, scientists classify the coastal scrub as "globally imperiled." The same areas might just as well be labeled "universally appealing," because of the draw of the coast to humans, a propensity that in no way escaped the notice of St. Joe. "These remaining natural areas are some of the most endangered areas because of the attraction of people to develop second homes," pointed out Gary Knight, director of the Florida Natural Areas Inventory, an organization that tracks rare plants, animals, and habitats.[38]

Unless the coastal strand contained a federally or state-protected species, it was not shielded from development by St. Joe/Arvida or anyone else. At Pier Park, St. Joe's Dave Tillis dismissed the small portions of that site containing coastal scrub as "unremarkable."[39] Yet even unremarkable scrub was unique and irreplaceable, supporting rare vegetation and offering resting and feeding places for migratory birds and butterflies, among other creatures. Acre by acre, it was disappearing from privately held parts of the Gulf Coast, including on St. Joe lands.

In the area of coastal protection, St. Joe bore more than the usual share of responsibility because of its much-touted possession of 50,000 acres of coastal and near-coastal areas, which it used as a drawing card to attract newcomers. The company's actions showed its reluctance to forgo the profit that went with beachfront development. At WaterColor, St. Joe rejected the option of building no more than beach walk-overs on its choice twenty-four-acre chunk of beachfront between Seaside and Grayton Beach, even though that beach included habitat critical to the endangered beach mouse. The reason: "Without the beach portion of the project, the ability to successfully 'sell' the project could be compromised or less economic benefits realized."[40] So, several acres of beach mouse habitat was given up for St. Joe's beach-side development. Federal approval under the Endangered Species Act came in exchange for St. Joe's commitment to intensively, almost heroically, manage WaterColor and down-the-beach WaterSound for the well-being of endangered beach mice for thirty years, at which time homeowners associations would become responsible.

Even before the construction of WaterColor, state biologists concluded that the Choctawhatchee beach mouse, like other species of native and imperiled beach mice in the state, had below the minimum amount of habitat needed for long-term security.[41] Catastrophic events like hurricanes could wipe out whole colonies.

In Gulf County, St. Joe's machinations to relocate Highway 98 at first appeared intended to open more beachfront buildable space for the company at the expense of the scenic open coast that greeted highway travelers since Alfred duPont and his highwaymen planted the coastal road in the 1920s. By 2001, St. Joe had already planted its first beach-side buildings along St. Joseph's Bay as part of the WindMark Beach project. Assuming the company carried through with its publicly stated intentions of leaving the beach undeveloped and accessible to the public, the development would be extraordinary in its preservation of coastline.

The coastline farther east, around Turkey Point and Bald Point, was highly ranked for its wildlife values, notably for shorebirds and rare plants. The level of shore conservation there would be greatly dependent on St. Joe's land-use decisions, including how many docks and marinas it would ultimately use.

In Bay County, St. Joe made a legal gambit to ease coastal development for its best remaining beachfront, its property near Mexico Beach on the county's eastern extremes. In May 2000, at St. Joe's request, U.S. congressman Allen Boyd introduced a bill that would have exempted this stretch of coast from the strictures of the federal Coastal Barriers Resources System (CBRS). The property was the same area that had been a legal battleground between the company and the Bay County Property Appraiser concerning greenbelt taxes, property that St. Joe sold and repurchased on the heels of a bank foreclosure in the 1980s.

St. Joe argued that it had not been duly informed that its land was part of the CBRS. The designation had serious financial implications because lands within CBRS are ineligible for federal subsidies generally available to homeowners. The federal program attempts to shift the costs of risky and environmentally questionable coastal development to the private sector. Coastal development within specified barrier coasts is not prohibited, but is discouraged by ineligibility for nationally subsidized flood insurance, FDIC mortgages, and other federal programs. Considering the insurance headaches posed by building on hurricane-prone beaches, the value of federal subsidies can be substantial—averaging about $82,000 per developed acre in year 2000, according to the Department of Interior.[42]

Representative Boyd's bill would have deleted St. Joe's property and adjacent land, removing 280 acres of prime coast from the CBRS in the largest deletion ever. St. Joe argued that maps depicting the area were drawn incorrectly to indicate expansions to the CBRS that went into effect in 1990, and that it had not been aware its land was covered by CBRS. The FWS admitted to mistakes in mixing up dotted versus solid lines and did not oppose the change; neither did the agency support the deletion. Boyd aide Chris Schloesser explained that the congressman introduced the legislation, which he said was written by St. Joe's lawyers in Washington. "It's an issue of fairness," he said.[43]

The Washington, D.C.–based Coast Alliance mounted a vociferous protest. "This bill is not a technical correction and is anything but small. This bill represents a political favor to a large corporation that makes all those that came before it pale in comparison," the alliance argued.[44] After a flurry of protests and even an appearance by the act's author, Thomas B. Evans, to testify against it, the bill died. Development there would be without federal subsidies.

Growth Management

After the election of Jeb Bush as governor, the state began to markedly retreat from the growth management program that had guided it since passage of the landmark Growth Management Act in 1985. With St. Joe's top lawyer and land-use expert Bob Rhodes in the background and St. Joe executive Chris Corr an official member of the governor's hand-picked commission to study growth management, St. Joe was close by during the state's attempt to retool its approach to managing growth. After a rocky period during which many Floridians questioned the wisdom of scuttling the existing program, changes emerging by early 2002 seemed made-to-order for St. Joe—a shift to more local control and a retreat from DRIs.

In 2000, DCA secretary Steve Seibert kicked off a campaign to launch his proposed reforms that would give greater control to local communities while reserving state review over features that were of "compelling state interest."[45]

Miami Herald columnist and novelist Carl Hiaasen offered up his stinging take on Seibert's public push to trust local communities. "Trust local communities. Translation: Trust your county commission to do whatever politically connected developers want. It happens time and again in Florida, and that's why the Growth Management Act was passed in the first place. . . . The law isn't failing because of the content," Hiaasen wrote. "It's failing because it is not enforced fairly or consistently. . . . Giving more control to local governments, as the DCA's Seibert advocates, is like giving Robert Downey, Jr. the key to your medicine chest."[46]

In an e-mail from Seibert to Governor Bush, the newly appointed DCA secretary struggled to understand the depth of the public outcry against local control. "This message of local empowerment has generated much discussion and led some to decry our proposed reliance upon the people," he wrote. "Imagine that! Are our local officials either so incompetent or so unscrupulous to exercise a wholesome discretion? If so, Floridians have much more to be concerned about than comprehensive planning. I suggest, then, as the first principle a fundamental trust in the local comprehensive planning process to protect the future of Florida." In response, Governor Bush chided Seibert for putting his thoughts in writing. "First you have created a public record which as you know will leave you open to criticism without recourse," he wrote.[47]

In the wake of the controversy, Governor Bush appointed a study commission to take up the contentious issues that were getting nowhere in the legislature. Luminaries in the field of Florida growth management submitted their names for consideration and were passed over. The make-up of the committee was mostly Republican, including St. Joe's Chris Corr, along with several Democrats who were agency heads and served at the pleasure of the Republican governor. The group's apparent partisan and pro-development tilt diminished its credibility. One former secretary of DCA predicted the group's composition would "cloud the panel in controversy" when its recommendations were forwarded to the legislature.[48]

The panel delivered its recommendations to the legislature in time for its 2001 session, but none of its major recommendations became law. Governor Bush backed two items from the list as priorities: first, linking new development to school facilities as a requirement for comprehensive planning; and second, adopting a "full-cost accounting" measure of costs and benefits of development.

These measures seemed to be steps toward answering the state's decade-plus struggle over concurrency.

The details were sketchy, and the governor called for a new commission to create the fiscal model to be used. A formula that came out of early recommendations did not include hard-to-quantify items like the value of wetlands or, the benefits of affordable housing.[49]

St. Joe's shrewd chief counsel Bob Rhodes advocated giving the budding full-cost accounting method a try, starting with a pilot project to gauge its effectiveness. If a workable model could be devised, he saw the potential for it to replace the concurrency provisions that the state had never found a way to fund.

Concurrency was an extremely important topic for St. Joe, which would not want to assume more than its share of costs to remedy the state's existing infrastructure deficits totaling several billion dollars. The issue was a big concern in places like Bay County, where until the late 1990s, developers were allowed to build homes without having to pave the roads that served them.

Working within existing laws, St. Joe was adept at interpreting concurrency requirements to its advantage. In making the case for state and federal assistance for new roads in Gulf County, St. Joe and Opportunity Florida argued that the near-term projection for level of service showed the potential for restrictions on growth.[50] However, as the company sought approvals for South-Wood, its consultants made the case that poor service levels on affected roads should not be a show stopper. The same was true for the Pier Park development on congested Panama City Beach, where acceptable level of service was simply downgraded.

As for DRIs, the governor's study commission recommended eliminating the DRI process by the year 2003, a direction that Rhodes found more promising than simply tweaking the existing program: "DRI process 'fixes' are useful, but why not again consider replacing the DRI program with greater reliance on local plans?" Rhodes asked in a lecture to growth management experts. He tempered expectations that doing away with DRIs would be easy, noting, "Regulators and regulatory advocates generally do not like to give anything up. So, until we are comfortable relying more on solid, in-compliance local plans. . . . I don't see much prospect for significant DRI change." He pointed to sector plans, such as St. Joe was involved with in Bay County, as worth trying.[51]

As Florida lawmakers considered revamping state growth laws, *St. Petersburg Times* reporter Julie Hauserman disclosed that Florida senate president John McKay hired land-use attorney and St. Joe consultant Edward Vogler II as a paid advisor to him on growth management. Vogler, who had been working for St.

Joe on a Bradenton, Florida, condominium development, claimed that none of his work for McKay was "specifically directed to a particular private interest," and that he had not spoken with any of the "people from St. Joe" about his work for the Senate.[52]

As lobbyists and legislators in the state capital were hashing out the theoretics of growth management, St. Joe was involved in on-the-ground efforts to pursue alternatives to DRIs, starting with a new state "sector planning" process. Instead of evaluating in detail the expected impacts of one particular development at a time, sector planning called for long-range planning over a broad area—in this case 78,000 acres of western Bay County.

Officials described a sector plan as a hybrid between a comprehensive plan and a DRI. Sector planning requires preparation of a general overlay map, followed by more in-depth specific area plans. The overlay and specific area plans are reviewed in similar fashion to comprehensive plan amendments, but once these steps are followed, no further DRI review is required.

The officials involved in getting Bay County's sector plan off the ground acknowledged that they were walking new ground and would have to figure some things out along the way. Whereas developers pay their consultants to do DRIs, the funding and planning process for sector planning was less clear. DCA official Bob Cambric said, "The state is not paying for the sector plan process."[53] However, the Panama City Airport Authority's Transportation Outreach Program (TOP) budget request included large sums for "sector planning." Another point of confusion was who would supervise the study, the Bay County Planning Department or the Airport Authority, which was answerable only to itself and state law.

Even the origins of the sector plan were the subject of confusion. DCA's Cambric said that "Bay County" had initiated the request for sector planning.[54] Yet a Bay County memorandum documented that in reality the plans were decidedly top down—from the very top of DCA, in fact. In November 1998, the same year that sector planning was written into law, St. Joe representatives met with then-DCA head Jim Murley. The parties discussed using Bay County in the largest trial to date of the new "experimental alternative" to a DRI. The memo relayed a request for a follow-up meeting among state and local officials.

"The purpose of the meeting is to discuss the possibility of developing a 'sector plan' for a new Panama City International Airport facility. Apparently, St. Joe met with Secretary Murley last week and this idea was proposed," the memo stated.[55] Although the matter did not come to a public vote with the county commission or planning commission, Jon Mantay, then the Bay County manager, took action early the next year, writing DCA to request that the county receive one of five available statewide slots, and the state granted the request. A subsequent TOP proposal said that the state DCA, the Northwest Florida Regional Planning Council, and the Bay County Planning Department were "all supportive of an amendment to the local comprehensive plan for the airport relocation," although justification for this language was not cited.[56]

Precisely ten days after the news of FAA approval of the site selection study, on April 27, 2001, the state convened a preliminary Sector Plan meeting, activating the planning option that had lain dormant since early 1999. The meeting took place not in Bay County, but at the regional DOT headquarters an hour's drive away in the small town of Chipley. St. Joe's Chris Corr and Bechtel's consultant Bob Cone were on the list of those informed about the meeting; Bay County commissioners were not.[57] Subsequently, the process became more open to citizens and leaders in the area it would affect, including a series of professionally conducted, well-advertised, in-depth visioning meetings concerning the sector plan for the West Bay area.

The outcome of the West Bay sector plan was tied in with approval of airport relocation, plans for future highways and barge ports, set-asides of conservation land, and St. Joe's own proposed mix of development for the sweeping area, all in one of the state's most complex and political planning processes ever. The process had the potential to introduce high-quality planning of a breadth never before seen in the Panhandle. A great deal rested on the golden qualities of St. Joe's planning and its ability to live up to the trust the community placed in it.

All Politics Is Local

At the local level, where many important development decisions began and ended, St. Joe wielded considerable power. In many counties where St. Joe had extensive holdings, the company dangled the carrot of bolstered property taxes if only its plans were successful. Also, many local governments and civic leaders welcomed the St. Joe Company precisely because it employed master planning that brought new professionalism to the table. Quite a few local governments operated on skimpy budgets that did not allow for employment of full-time, in-house lawyers or technical experts. In smaller counties, administrators had to wear multiple hats, carrying out duties of county manager, planner and many other roles, if not quite extending to proverbial dog catcher.

But along with the recognition of St. Joe's professional know-how came the fresh worry that a very sophisticated fox was guarding the Green Empire's henhouse. Walton County resident and environmental watchdog Cynthia Alexander worried that government would go "from the good ol' boys to St. Joe."[58]

By year 2000, "good ol' boy" politics had begun changing. In Bay County, for the first time, commissioners with college degrees took office. In Walton County, the newly constituted commission began taking steps to bring on staff with professional credentials. Yet in this critical time of growing pains, both staff and elected officials depended heavily on the advice of consultants and attorneys, who often had financial ties to the very clients doing business with local government, including St. Joe. Some in appointed volunteer positions too had business interests, including interests in the St. Joe Company.

In several locales, key advisors had overlapping fealties to local governments and to St. Joe. In Port St. Joe, St. Joe Timberland head Clay Smallwood for years chaired the Gulf County Planning and Review Board, of which he had been a member since 1993. In Bay County, St. Joe lobbyist William Harrison's uncle was a partner in a law firm that provided legal services for the school board and several cities, including Panama City Beach. Longtime attorney for Bay County, Nevin Zimmerman, in 2002 left that role to work for William Harrison and St. Joe. And in one case, St. Joe was actually a partner with a municipality, the City of Panama City Beach.

In the Panhandle, the legacy of "good ol' boy" government raised fears about the consequences of the state's move toward more local control. Some residents envisioned a return to the days when the Panhandle was considered Florida's "Wild West" in terms of environmental protection. Nowhere was this legacy more visible than at Panama City Beach, where latter-day Pork Chop politicians ignored the "Coastal Control Line" set up after Hurricane Eloise in 1975 to discourage construction seaward of an imaginary line. Twenty years later, Hurricane Opal wrought an astounding $3 billion in damage to the area, including to structures built where high dunes once stood.[59] If the latest wave of growth brought better protection of public resources than prior development, it would be a major reversal over past events.

Like the Coastal Construction Control Line, other high-minded concepts might be easily amended. In 1999, Bay County had adopted a "comp plan" with a sprawl-containment policy called the "Wide Open Spaces Strategy." The policy called for concentration of future growth and development within its urban core, with service and infrastructure outside of key service areas discouraged. That strategy appeared quixotic at best, given the West Bay Sector Plan, which would center the full complement of development, from residential to industrial, around a new airport in what was currently a greenbelt and hunting ground.

Planning Director Terry Jernigan, who crafted the Wide Open Spaces Strategy, left his job after being criticized in the midst of an acrimonious battle over county land-use codes. Although he had received good evaluations since his employment began in 1992, Jernigan's supervisor told him in mid-December 2000 that he was slated for termination. A memo to Jernigan's personnel record noted that the supervisor informed him that if his termination became "a political issue" it would come sooner.[60]

Jernigan had internally voiced his objection to the Pier Park Community Redevelopment Area in only one, and by far the least public, controversy in which Jernigan was embroiled at the time. Jernigan was also critical of the annexation of around 1,220 acres of St. Joe land along Star Avenue in eastern Bay County into Panama City. In his opinion, the annexation created an illegal pocket. Most public, though, was Jernigan's role as county official in the hot seat over a contentious attempt to rewrite the county's land-use codes, a battle that featured a suggestion by Charles Hilton, an owner of many Bay County businesses and employer of Representative Allan Bense, to list pine trees as nuisances. The missteps that led to Jernigan's termination, as noted in his personnel record and reported in the newspaper, included smoking—in the open air parking lot outside his office—and distributing copies of an article from *Florida Trend* directly to county commissioners. The troublesome article's topic was growth management.

Jernigan, in a telephone interview a few months after quitting his job, contended that questioning Pier Park and the Star Avenue annexation were factors in a sequence of events that forced his departure. Jernigan said Panama City attorney and St. Joe consultant William Harrison called him and "dressed [him] down" for opposing the annexation. Jernigan said that "standing in the way of St. Joe" was one of three reasons he was pressured to resign.[61]

Qualms about how well the public interest would fare under the new statewide push toward local control were understandable, at least based on local politics in Bay County. There at the close of the millennium, twin debacles over water and sewer pipelines raised questions about whether favors to public officials in Bay County routinely influenced their decisions over county business.

The infrastructure in question was essential to the plans of St. Joe in a county where the company held around 40 percent of the land in 2001 and was a prime customer for both kinds of pipeline services. People and firms connected with St. Joe were involved, notably St. Joe lobbyist and local lawyer William Harrison and the Port St. Joe–based engineering firm of Preble-Rish.

The first Bay County pipeline scandal began after a Bay County commissioner and the county manager at the time enjoyed a freebie hunting excursion shortly before a contract was due to be awarded for laying a drinking water pipeline. The men took the invitation of an owner of one of the firms bidding. Reporter Kendall Middlemas of the *Panama City News Herald* broke the story. Commissioner Danny Sparks, who bagged a deer on the excursion, dismissed the notion that the hunting outing would sway him in favor of a bid jointly submitted by the owner of the hunt camp, Port St. Joe resident Ralph Rish. Rish's engineering firm, Preble-Rish, and Lynn Haven's Phoenix Construction, Inc. were partners in the bid. Sparks defended the hunting trip as routine. "Nobody's getting a better deal than anybody else. . . . We do things with all of them. I am an equal opportunity moocher," he told the *News Herald*.[62]

Sparks's frank comments about favors were reinforced by later reports about other commissioners. One commissioner had declined the deer hunt invitation in favor of a competing invitation to dine as a guest of the county's engineering consulting firm. A grand jury investigation determined that yet a third enjoyed favors including use of a beachfront penthouse belonging to Phoenix Construction's flamboyant head, James Finch, who owned a NASCAR racing team and a private jet as well as several construction-related companies in Bay County.

The commission responded to the ethics concerns by dispensing with the subjective portion of bid evaluation based on firms' presentations about how they planned to carry out the job. Instead, the county voted to simply take the low bid, which turned out to be Preble-Rish-Phoenix's by a slim margin. Later, the county skipped the competitive bidding process altogether and awarded the construction of an additional seventeen-mile leg around West Bay to Preble-Rish/Phoenix as an extension of the earlier contract. This contract, worth $12.5 million, was crucial to St. Joe's water needs for western Bay County.

The hunting trip brouhaha only served as a warm-up to another pipeline scandal that enveloped Bay County and contributed to the ouster of all three incumbents in the election of 2000. Engineering failures of major proportions on an underwater sewage line turned what should have been a triumph of intergovernmental cooperation on this vital government service into a fiasco.

Under duress from the EPA to remedy inadequate sewage treatment that had been out of compliance for years, the county and four Bay County cities banded together to win a grant to build a combined $32 million state-of-the-art advanced wastewater plant. This was a need that existed regardless of St. Joe's actions in Bay County, but certainly was a prerequisite for extensive growth to occur. With the Advanced Wastewater Treatment plant under construction, the next step was to lay an underwater pipeline to reach the plant on a peninsula across the bay, near the duPont Bridge leading to Tyndall Air Force Base. The job was not easy. Specifications called for the pipeline to be laid four feet deep into a sea bottom hardened in places with encrusted oysters. Although his company had no prior experience for this type of work, Phoenix Construction owner James Finch won the job with his $1.6 million low bid after assuring county representatives that he would bring on a qualified subcontractor.[63]

The effort went seriously wrong, leaving portions of the pipeline unburied. Phoenix's subcontractor failed to get a dredge and fill permit, destroyed 9,000 square feet of seagrass, and ran a barge into the pipeline, sinking the vessel, before Phoenix terminated its contract. A subsequent subcontractor found a workable technique, but ran out of time to backtrack over problem areas to install line correctly.

About one-third of the pipe remained untrenched, leaving it vulnerable to dragging anchors and scouring from hurricanes or other storms. But rather than ask the state DEP for an extension, officials appealed to DEP to ease its standards. At this point, Panama City attorney William Harrison emerged as a key player in the pipeline controversy. He served as the spokesman for the AWT owners by virtue of serving as city attorney to one AWT partner, the city of Callaway. Harrison met with DEP officials several times to propose that the DEP grant an exception allowing most of the pipe to remain unburied.[64] Later, he recused himself from the discussions to remove any appearance of conflict of interest, revealing that he had represented James Finch on occasion.

A grand jury that looked into the pipeline controversy soon afterward detailed a poorly coordinated process and instances of favors from those doing business with the county, including free meals and greens fees for county officials. However, the favors fell within the $100 a day limit set by state ethics law. The grand jury called for a stricter new county policy against accepting gratuities of any value and more attention to performance history of contractors when awarding bids. There were no criminal indictments.

The Florida chapter of the Public Employees for Environmental Responsibility (PEER) became involved, submitting several legal petitions on the matter to Governor Bush. PEER also requested a special grand jury to look into what it called "serious environmental problems" in Bay and Gulf Counties, similar to the grand jury in Pensacola. The governor did not act on any of the group's requests.

The grand jury presentment made no mention of William Harrison in its findings. In the fall 2000 elections, Harrison helped win Bay County for George W. Bush, after hosting a visit to the county by the former president George H. W. Bush. But all three incumbent county commissioners were voted out.

As the 2002 hurricane season wound up, the pipeline was still not fixed. It was possible the delay might prove a boon to the environment. The DEP suggested using the improperly installed pipe to transport treated water back to the mainland for land application, thus refilling the aquifer. Initially, the Bay County Commission rejected this idea as an added expense.

In early 2002, Daniel P. Meyer, general counsel for PEER, reiterated that the group stood behind its petitions, even though they were summarily dismissed by the governor. Meyer observed that government growth issues, such as ones that PEER found disturbing in Bay and Gulf Counties, often reveal an "iron triangle" at work. The triangle's three points consist of financiers, lawyers, and local business interests of a pro-growth bent. This elite consortium are "very nice people who give to the symphony and hand out the bulletins at church, but who fight very tough and very hard to protect their interests." To them, environmental laws and other regulations are "just transaction costs," Meyer said.[65]

Watchdogs that Bark

Citizen watchdogs, both individuals and groups, were a small but vocal presence in the Green Empire at the start of the twenty-first century. They represented possibly the biggest thorn in St. Joe's side. Individuals such as Marilyn Blackwell in Wewahitchka and Marion Hough, Sally Malone and Wayne Childers in the Port St. Joe area were the Davids with attitude versus the Goliaths with deep pockets, including the St. Joe Company. Groups such as the South Walton Coordinating Council, Beach to Bay, Apalachicola Bay and RiverKeepers (ABARK), Friends of Franklin County, Apalachee Ecological Conservancy, and others were effective voices that often went it alone with little to no funding. National and statewide advocacy groups—the Clean Water Network, Coastal Alliance, National Wildlife Federation, Florida Audubon, 1,000 Friends of Florida, Sierra Club, PEER—had some local involvement. The efforts of watchdogs who scrutinized and sometimes challenged the company's operations in these counties and others seemed to fill a critical void in an otherwise near-total embrace of St. Joe's own vision by government entities.

The summer of 2002 marked the emergence of a group calling itself the Panhandle Citizens Coalition. The group pursued a "pause for planning" to allow the region to properly digest and manage the coming growth, much of it fueled by St. Joe.

After government entities and the St. Joe Company itself failed to warm to a moratorium, PCC took a different tack. As of spring 2003, PCC had twelve petition drives underway in three counties and five cities across the Panhandle. The initiatives were varied but each was designed to "give the citizens the ability to have a say-so over whether and how their areas grow," according to PCC chairman John Hedrick.[66]

The single biggest effort was the drive to put the Panama City airport relocation to a vote. In addition, the group gathered enough signatures in Carrabelle to force a referendum on whether that small fishing town should extend water and sewer outside its city limits—a move that could put a damper on SummerCamp if it succeeded.

The effectiveness of citizens statewide could be gauged by attempts to curb their efforts by legislative fiat. Citizens and nonprofits were subject to strategic lawsuits against public participation ("SLAPPs"), a form of harassment intended to intimidate and bankrupt active citizens as they attempt to defend against them. In addition, citizens can be curbed by being prevented access to administrative hearings. For several years running, Florida lawmakers considered multiple bills that would limit the eligibility or legal "standing" of citizens to challenge development approvals and, at the same time, make their efforts more complicated and expensive.

St. Joe's general counsel, Bob Rhodes, expressed a middle-of-the-road public position on this hot topic in a column he wrote in April 2000, which was carried in the opinion pages of several leading Florida newspapers. He credited public participation with increasing government accountability but also cautioned, "Unrestrained opportunities to sue encourage meritless and harassing challenges, primarily to delay action or build a bargaining position. Such challenges frustrate public officials, alienate the regulated community and undermine the credibility of growth management." The happy medium, according to Rhodes, was citizen "standing" measures that "promote desirable goals without fostering spurious litigation."[67]

The 2001–2002 legislature passed a measure limiting citizen standing that was attached to a bill for Everglades restoration, creating a dilemma for environmentalists. The legislation repealed standing for unincorporated groups, out-of-county groups, single-interest groups, and homeowner associations, among its other features. Representative Larry Crow, a Republican from Palm Harbor, was among the lawmakers who opposed the changes. "If you make the process any more difficult, it is going to unduly limit the rights of the people," said Crow, an attorney who sometimes represented developers.[68]

Panama City's Representative Bense, who was working toward a shot at Speaker of the House in 2005, voted for the stricter standing provisions. He said the new law was needed because "someone from Dade or Broward County could stop a project at the drop of a hat." Bense had no specifics in mind that had affected his district to date, but said he supported the measure on philosophical grounds because of his strong beliefs in "home rule" and property rights. Bense said that Bay County's existing growth management policies were adequate to safeguard the public interest in the wake of rapid growth.[69] Bense's stance on such issues consistently earned him among the lowest rankings by the Florida League of Conservation Voters. Based on that group's interpretation of environmentally related laws, Bense ranked 116 out of 120 in the year 2000 and 110 out of 120 the next year.

St. Joe's fingerprints were not on the standing bills, unlike the legislation that changed DRI requirements the previous year. David Gluckman, a lobbyist for the Florida Wildlife Federation, said he had never heard of St. Joe being directly associated with them. Yet St. Joe was a prominent member of three major lobbies for these bills—the Association of Florida Community Developers, the Florida Homebuilders Association, and the Florida Chamber of Commerce—as well as a longtime client of the Hopping firm. The law firm of Wade Hopping, which represented St. Joe among many other clients, was in the forefront of the effort in 2002, as in years past with lawyer and lobbyist Frank Matthews taking a leading role.

As citizens fought to remain part of the process, there was a recognition that growth was inevitable. The costs of growth and the task of hanging onto an acceptable quality of life appeared to be falling diffusely to the public at large and to a disconnected array of governments, most of them poorly equipped for growth management and hungry for tax dollars. In the face of what appeared to be a wide embrace of a narrow property-rights ideology, summoning up the political will to rein in the excesses of growth would be especially difficult. The oversight and planning apparatus in place at the turn of the millennium was considerably less oiled than the growth machine.

16

The Two Bottom Lines

Profit and Quality of Life

Citizens actively engaged in their communities
will continue to be the strongest force for progressive
change in the new millennium.
Eben Fodor, Better, Not Bigger

THE ST. JOE COMPANY has put a For Sale sign up on its Green Empire. It is clearly the company's intent to develop or sell as much as it can for the highest price possible to meet the ambitious demands of its bottom line. St. Joe's strategy centers on inviting well-off baby boomers to come to Florida's Great Northwest, the company's euphemism for the Florida Panhandle. The irony is that marketing the region's quiet natural beauty, ecological richness, and slower pace of living—in short, its quality of life—is far easier than maintaining it. As the Green Empire grows, will the characteristics that contribute to its agreeable lifestyle be adequately safeguarded?

Six years after the company's makeover into a real estate enterprise, St. Joe's impacts on the region are becoming tangible. It is possible to form some general impressions about the upsides and downsides of the St. Joe Company's sweeping plans and the place-making machinery the company has put to work to grow its Green Empire of northwest Florida. These early results are indicators of the tradeoffs between growth and quality of life that face the region in the years ahead.

High Expectations

By the company's telling, its corporate ambitions for northwest Florida are also in the public's best interest. Time and again in researching this book, the authors heard regulatory officials and citizen observers of St. Joe express confidence in the company. "Everything they do is gold plated." "They're highly professional." "They build nice developments." There was no disputing it: St. Joe had the management and capital to do great things. Peter Rummell and the company's other executives knew people's expectations of them were high, and they promised not to disappoint.

There were many upsides to the changes that were occurring as St. Joe began rolling back its greenbelt. For one, St. Joe was bringing master planning to the region on a scale that had never before been seen. This approach delivers high-quality results that independent patchwork developments on a smaller scale could never match. St. Joe joined the elite ranks of other developers who were bringing a new aesthetic and identity to northwest Florida, one conscious of consumer desires for better planning, not just of dwellings, but their settings.

With its large inventory of acres, St. Joe can go the extra mile on setting aside green space, as it showed at SouthWood. The incredible taxing power of the Community Development District ensures that would-be home buyers at SouthWood and St. Joe's other large communities will help pick up the tab for that attractive common space. This trend points to a future where St. Joe's developments, particularly its largest and highest-end ones, could yield communities comparable to Hilton Head Island or Amelia Island, where large areas of natural and protected landscapes coexist with housing for those who could afford such upscale price tags.

St. Joe's master planning extends to concerns about roads, schools, and other infrastructure, such as medical facilities and fire stations. While needed to serve St. Joe's thousands of would-be home buyers, these facilities serve the larger community as well.

The company's role in economic development, too, is potentially far-reaching. St. Joe is both catalyst and organizer in a quest to strengthen and diversify the region's economy. With the company's help, local chambers of commerce and other economic development organizations landed several important new industries that offered new jobs at better than average pay. St. Joe and its economic development body, Florida's Great Northwest, are inciting the region to set ambitious sights for the future—on aerospace, computer chip, and other high-tech enterprises. In the meantime, St. Joe's own construction projects em-

ploy scores of workers, some local and some from outside the area. St. Joe's recognition of the importance of education is another plus.

St. Joe, with its strong political clout, is winning favor with governments that
are directing an outpouring of taxpayer dollars in the direction of the Great
Northwest. With the impetus of a strategic land donation, Bay County and St.
Joe are beginning one of the largest public works projects ever for Bay County,
in the form of a $200-million-plus international airport. (Spending to revamp
the ports at Panama City and the City of Port St. Joe could exceed even this large
outlay.) If the airport crosses the remaining regulatory hurdles, that would
mean an upsurge in contracts for design and engineering work, paving, and
construction, in addition to its long-term effects on the regional economy.

Increased economic activity will in turn bring a greater abundance and variety of cultural offerings, restaurants and stores. And it will bring new residents
with new ideas and skills.

Not the least of the positives, although tough to quantify, is an upswing in
pride and optimism that comes with greater recognition—extending as high as
the White House—to an area that historically had been "hard up for affection,"
as one Bay Countian puts it.

Tradeoffs

In an ideal world, St. Joe's interests and the interests of the larger public would
blend perfectly. Yet in reality, what is good for St. Joe's bottom line and its stockholders does not automatically translate into what is good for the public at
large. Those with the largest holdings of company stock, apart from the A. I.
duPont Trust, not surprisingly are the company's own executives and board
members. Top-ranking insiders who also hold hundreds of millions of dollars
in stock options thus stand to gain the most from their company's success.

In the real world where government budgets and natural resources have their
limits, there are large areas in which St. Joe's interests do not necessarily yield
the best outcome for the public. Growth, especially rapid growth, is not always
the boon to communities that it is to the coterie of those involved in the so-
called growth machine. Whereas a healthy bottom line for St. Joe means good
quarterly earnings and increases in shareholder value, a healthy bottom line for
the general public is measured much differently. This bottom line has to do with
sustaining a good quality of life, something much harder to achieve or quantify.
For example, marinas—big marketing plusses for St. Joe—create some jobs but

can harm seagrass, spread pollution, and hurt fisheries. Working-class locals are not likely to keep their boats there, either.

In the general spirit of boosterism that seems to accompany St. Joe's endeavors to date, the tradeoffs have been minimized. Among the issues where the company's interests seem to most obviously collide with the long-term interest of the public at large are sprawl, costs of growth, environmental integrity, and social issues including equity and economic sustainability.

Sprawl

Perhaps the most obvious downside to St. Joe's "place making" is its tendency to sprawl. While the larger of St. Joe's new developments might be in and of themselves examples of New Urbanism, their locations on the outer fringes of existing urban areas could hardly be described as other than sprawling. Some St. Joe developments leapfrog beyond existing urban areas to what was once pasture or forest or open Gulf shore. Leading examples of this New Urbanist paradox are the company's projects in Tallahassee and DeLand in central Florida. St. Joe's projected massive plans for its West Bay sector in Bay County also involved a full complement of development from industrial and commercial spaces associated with the airport to residential communities, all roughly twenty miles away from the hub of Panama City.

On several occasions, St. Joe Company spokesman Jerry Ray took offense at the suggestion that the company's plans were sprawling or would engender sprawl. He insists it is "very, very difficult" to articulate a definition of sprawl, and says that sometimes there is an "environmental cost for compactness."[1] Natural constraints can necessitate that development spreads out to spare environmentally sensitive areas like the wetlands all over Bay and Walton Counties, he says. Ray's viewpoint seemed to downplay the issue of sprawl, in similar fashion to materials distributed by the James Madison Institute. The materials labeled sprawl the "all purpose scapegoat for our urban discontents."[2]

Professional planners are of mixed minds about St. Joe and sprawl. Some shrug off the issue, pointing instead to the internal New Urbanist features of St. Joe's projects such as the commercial residential mix and walkabililty. Others, however, worry about the sprawl-related impacts not only from St. Joe, but also from the secondary development that will follow from St. Joe's push to put in place infrastructure like major new roads. It is this secondary development that has wreaked the most havoc and ugliness upon the Orlando region, not the perfectly designed and landscaped Disney properties themselves, as author Carl Hiaasen points out in his expose of the darker side of Disney, *Team Rodent*.

Sprawl adds to the costs of providing government services to far-flung areas. Just as damaging, or more so, sprawl subtracts human and financial resources from existing urban areas. Developing in already-urban areas was one tenet of New Urbanism that St. Joe did not embrace as it made its debut. With the exception of its WaterColor development that it knitted to Seaside, the company had little incentive to embed its projects within existing communities, where its holdings were limited anyway.

One simply could not dismiss the tremendous economic incentive that the St. Joe Company had to sprawl out into its former greenbelt. Because the company had many thousands of "greenfield" acres in its sights for development, its very goal was to seed higher valuations into its outlying acreage as it plainly declared in its motto of "building value inland." The chief tools for increasing the value of its former greenbelt were its own developments and the highways and other infrastructure it sought. Another device by which the company created value for its far-flung lands was by making strategic donations of land.

Since Jake Belin's time at the company's helm, if not earlier, St. Joe has known how to benefit from such strategic donations as the land St. Joe gave for the Capitol City Office Complex in Tallahassee, which helped to literally pave the way for SouthWood. The company's commitment to donate 4,000 acres of land for a new airport, an area larger than that of the Tampa airport, seemed to have a similar purpose. Bay Countians could look to Lee County and the city of Fort Myers to see the combined effects of placing two major pieces of infrastructure there—a new, international airport, and the construction of I-75. Lee County's growth has been dramatic. The combination of the airport and interstate contributed to a fragmented growth pattern that encroaches on former panther habitat and swamp and makes residents heavily automobile dependent. As St. Joe Company officials have pointed out, Panama City today is the size of Fort Myers twenty-five years ago.

The Panhandle can learn from elsewhere in Florida. Michael Busha, executive director of the Treasure Coast Regional Planning Council, has a series of sobering slides depicting the morass of southeast Florida. At an economic development workshop in 2000 in the rural hamlet of Blountstown, he displayed aerial photographs showing how cities and towns in Martin County and Palm Beach County have bled together and the open areas have disappeared along the Treasure Coast. The sprawl into the Everglades thirty miles inland is even worse in Broward County to the south, home of Arvida's Weston. Worst of all, the formless growth happened under the auspices of the supposed checks of existing codes, rules and regulations.

"We didn't want *this* to happen," Busha said to workshop attendees. The meeting was organized by a consortium of state bodies interested in positive growth. St. Joe was invited but declined to attend, according to one meeting organizer. "You have . . . some time to decide what to be when you grow up," Busha said. While generally positive about the return to "old values" in development such as those embodied by New Urbanist principles, Busha cautioned that it is not a given that approach will work. "You can have traditional neighborhood development sprawl, too," he said.[3]

Clearly, sprawl is a complex and subjective issue. It is also an issue that requires solutions on two fronts: setting some reasonable boundaries on growth at the outer limits to stem creeping growth that goes from suburbs to ex-urbs to outer-exurbs and, at the same time, building up urban areas into exciting centers of activity that capture interest and dollars for development and redevelopment.

Costs of Growth

In 2001, the Northwest Florida Water Management District projected growth trends twenty years into the future. The district predicted a 41 percent increase in the region's population by year 2020, a mind-boggling figure when projected into terms like additional cars on roads, boaters on waterways, pupils needing classrooms and teachers, and, of course, water users. The coastal rim would grow even faster, with south Walton County projected to grow 58 percent.[4]

As this tremendous growth comes to the Green Empire, boosters of development, including St. Joe executives, are raising public expectations for widespread benefits in the form of jobs, increased tax base, and new infrastructure. Much less attention is being focused on the costs of growth. Yet a growing body of research shows that these costs are frequently greater than anticipated and can thwart a community in providing an optimum quality of life for its residents as a whole.

Engineer and planner Eben Fodor, a leading national researcher on growth impacts, argues that costs of growth are rarely discussed or recognized, partly because the beneficiaries of growth tend to be organized and politically influential. Nevertheless, Fodor contends that growth does involve real net costs to the community, that these costs can be quantified, and . . . they are quite high."[5] In 1996, Fodor applied methodologies from the existing body of research focusing on growth costs and determined that a typical single-family house in Oregon would require $24,500 in public services: school, fire, police, and the like.[6] Other researchers, too, have determined that residential development typically imposes a net fiscal burden because of schooling costs and other expensive public services associated with housing. Sprawling development carries an even higher price tag than compact development.[7] Some kinds of development can mean a net fiscal plus, but that is the exception rather than the rule.

In contrast, land kept in agriculture or conservation tends to generate more in tax revenue than it requires in taxpayer-funded services, as many studies by the American Farmland Trust have shown. This fiscal reality is the basis of the greenbelt tax discount, which seems to serve the public interest as long as it is not used for land speculation. Farmland only costs governments seventeen cents for every tax dollar it generates.[8] Furthermore, these lands perform a wide array of public services, from recharging the water table to providing recreation. Land held in conservation also tends to enhance value of surrounding developed lands.

Yet in the opinion of Florida law professor and growth management expert James Nicholas, St. Joe/Arvida's upper-crust developments should do better than most at generating property taxes to pay their way. "Some growth does pay for itself. Homes over $300,000 and high-end commercial," he says. St. Joe/Arvida was building luxury homes and high-end commercial structures that fit into this net-gain category, especially along the coast. Nevertheless, plenty of St. Joe/Arvida's other ventures are in a more modest price range and indeed have to be priced more reasonably to serve the preponderance of area residents. As St. Joe seeks to "build value inland," the fulcrum easily could shift to create a net tax drain. "If you're not going to develop problems for twenty-five or thirty years, you tend to be complacent," says Nicholas. "Just go to South Florida where some schools are operating at 200 percent planned capacity. Many governments are more inclined to lower the level of service than deal with the infrastructure deficits. The Florida Panhandle is going to absolutely refuse to learn from South Florida."[9]

"Where growth machines are well-entrenched, citizens may face major barriers to change on growth issues," Eben Fodor cautions. "Many of our local governments are on growth 'autopilot.' Citizens seeking responsiveness and accountability from their governments find there does not appear to be anyone at the controls. These governments have become a part of the growth machine whose primary function is to build roads and infrastructure and to provide development services for an ever-expanding mass of subdivisions, industrial parks, and shopping centers."[10] To a large degree, this generalization fits the Green Empire.

At present, voices that question the costs and benefits of growth are not very evident at the tables where the make-or-break growth decisions are made on such issues as infrastructure funding. Although many public interest groups have become involved in trying to moderate the impacts of the St. Joe Company's development projects, rarely have these groups demanded overall cost-to-benefit analyses. Neither have they outright opposed the projects.

The Panhandle Citizens Coalition was unusual in its attempt to reset the fundamental boundaries of the discussions to challenge the very assumption that growth is inevitable. Chairman of the PCC John Hedrick insisted that it should be left to each community to decide whether it wanted growth at all, and then to decide how much and where it should take place in concert with the community's overall vision. "We think that's where the real debate should be, not just trimming on the margins like has been going on," he said.[11] The PCC's strategy of trying to tame growth through public votes on infrastructure necessary to support that growth was a method that remained to be tested as of early 2003.

As the state of Florida attempts to move to a "full-cost" or "true cost" accounting method of growth management, devising fiscal impact analyses that measure the true costs of growth seem a noble but difficult and politically freighted task. Circa 2003, Florida seems stuck in the boot-sucking mud of dated growth paradigms. Many Florida lawmakers have a vested interest in keeping the growth machine humming. According to the Center for Public Integrity, 21 percent of Florida lawmakers reported ties to real estate companies or investments, while 17 percent worked in commercial banking, huge cogs in the pro-growth railroad.[12] Interested parties speak of reform, but bureaucratic changes to date have mainly streamlined growth.

Until the decision making on growth issues becomes more objective, including honestly estimating costs as well as benefits, the Panhandle faces the peril of losing more than it gains in the long run.

Environmental Integrity

As the St. Joe Company exceeds even its own expectations in attracting newcomers to its Panhandle holdings, the once-endless pine plantations and open stretches of so-called forgotten coasts can no longer be taken for granted. Neither can the natural charm and the abundant and diverse wildlife that are part of the cachet of Florida's Great Northwest. By the time St. Joe's "value creation cycle" goes into full effect, with its attendant new roadways, Wal-Marts, and second-home enclaves, protection of natural features will be in the forefront of the tradeoffs occurring.

Northwest Florida's environmental history offers many poignant lessons about an abundant natural heritage squandered in the interest of short-term profit. Bygone tales of roaming panthers and gargantuan cypress are testament to the results of past land-use decisions that shortchanged future generations. The vanished dunes along large sections of Panama City Beach's shoreline tell a similar tale of more recent lost opportunities, for both wildlife and people.

Biologists predict more casualties in Florida's future unless the environment is well tended into the future. Authors of a 1994 state report titled *Closing the Gaps in Florida's Wildlife Habitat Conservation System* identified gaps in habitat needed to sustain wildlife populations into the future. The report bluntly stated, "Just as we now blame past generations for the extinction of the passenger pigeon, Carolina parakeet, and ivory-billed woodpecker, future Floridians will ultimately hold our generation responsible for the manner in which we conserve the species and natural resources that we inherited."[13]

The same authors propose a means to safeguard Florida's biodiversity for the future: "We must conserve a base of habitat that is capable of sustaining wildlife populations far into the future. This habitat base should consist of preservation areas that are publicly owned and managed primarily for natural conditions, but it must also include private lands where special land-use agreements are arranged that allow natural resources to be conserved without sacrificing all private uses of the land."[14] This twofold plan for conservation—purchasing and managing large chunks of public wild lands, combined with conservation-minded policies including monetary compensation for such efforts on privately held lands—offers a blueprint for retaining the natural heritage of the Panhandle.

St. Joe can hardly be expected to shoulder the burden of preserving the region's environment alone. Yet as self-appointed regional planner, orchestrating the placement of millions of dollars of growth-inducing infrastructure to suit its ends, St. Joe could be expected to take the high road in preserving what could be called nature's infrastructure—viable ecosystems. In the long run, the rules of nature are more unforgiving than those of Wall Street.

The combined results of land-use decisions will also affect the future of St. Joe's own bottom line. Success will be measured by whether the purchaser of St. Joe's last acre or home site be as eager to move in as the first crop of buyers, and whether its annual reports in decades to come still features crystal-clear waters and deep green forests and open vistas.

St. Joe's record as environmental steward was mixed in the early years after its turn to real estate. Depending largely on bottom-line considerations, the company in some cases took huge steps to further environmental preservation and at other times was an agent of destruction. The difference depended on how

FIGURE 13. Coastline owned by St. Joe Company in Franklin County, near Indian Pass and St. Vincent Island. Photo by Kathryn Ziewitz.

environmental objectives meshed with earnings objectives and also on the degree to which its activities were publicly visible.

In terms of the first objective of the twofold plan for environmental preservation—setting aside realms of public land explicitly for conservation purposes—the St. Joe Company was a star, although for pragmatic capital-enhancing reasons. The new St. Joe could rightfully take credit for deeds on par with Ed Ball's permanent conservation sale establishing the Apalachicola National Forest. The company's land sales helped to preserve a healthy corridor around the bounteous Wacissa River, with its otters, ibises, and scores of other species; remake the watery wilderness of Tate's Hell, with its matrix of pitcher plants, dwarf cypress, and teeming wetlands that supported Apalachicola Bay; and preserve several other important large expanses of wetlands and uplands. Even lands the company clear-cut, can, with proper expense and care, be restored to thriving habitats over time.

The importance of the state as a willing and able buyer as St. Joe unlocked its land bank was hard to overstate as well. Without a strong state land-buying program in place, the prospects for both northwest Florida and the St. Joe Company could have been drastically different. For the future, too, in terms of sheer acreage it was willing to keep giving up, or more precisely *sell* at a going rate, the prospects were bright, with St. Joe hoping to sell more than 150,000 additional acres to the state for preservation. In 2001, 13.5 percent of the company's earnings came from conservation sales. Especially with the notion of build-out in mind, the role St. Joe played in selling off lands for long-term preservation was invaluable. Land preservation consistently tops most planners' lists of tools for ensuring environmental integrity and is certainly the most palatable technique given the prevailing strength of the property-rights movement.

As for its stewardship over lands within its possession, St. Joe's record was more mixed. On the lands it was developing for real estate, St. Joe exhibited sensitivity to its environs in its use of native landscaping, set-asides of natural areas, and preservation of wetlands, a sensitivity that sat well with well-heeled consumers. In the words of state planner Tim Cannon, "St. Joe is becoming an example of how to develop land without trashing it."[15] Still, there were instances where St. Joe seemed reluctant to fully embrace the land ethic when the acreage in question was pivotal to its plans, for instance the beach club at WaterColor or the proposed SummerCamp project where St. Joe worked so hard to site a marina. Especially on its valuable coastal and other waterfront properties, St. Joe was reluctant to give up buildable ground.

In Franklin County, the riches of the teeming Gulf Coast led locals to dub the area the "Pearl of the Panhandle." An editorial in the *Tallahassee Democrat* urged St. Joe to seize its chance to be "heroic" by not pressing for a marina there.[16] Until public pressure mounted, St. Joe passed on that opportunity for "heroism." Also, in the area of forestry, St. Joe showed a reluctance to depart from the industrial forestry that treated the land strictly as a commodity.

As development from St. Joe and others sped up the pace of change in the Panhandle, it was clear that there would be plenty of environmental tradeoffs ahead, even with St. Joe's high development standards and the company's conservation sales. Although the state's land-buying program was methodically acquiring St. Joe tracts, there was still more ecologically vital land in limbo than the state alone could buy, from St. Joe or any other landowner. Tracts that were both developable and ecologically sensitive were most at risk.

Florida's initial Preservation 2000 program that had paid for Topsail Hill and Point Washington State Forest added 1.25 million acres altogether to state public lands. Though the figure was noteworthy, it still fell short of the 3-million-acre target that had been set at the program's outset as a minimum needed to conserve functioning ecosystems into the future. By year 2000, 1.75 million acres still remained to be purchased. Most Floridians supported continued land set-asides, as evidenced by a 1998 referendum, when state voters resoundingly endorsed a continuation of the state's land-buying effort. That vote led the way for another ten-year, $3 billion land-buying program called Florida Forever.

However, Florida Forever has a 15 percent smaller budget for land acquisition than the previous program. And for several years running, state lawmakers exhibited a tendency to raid state conservation funds to pay for other mandates. As land prices continue to rise, less of the state's annual $300 million budget was going for large land acquisitions, and more for managing it, along with increased spending for parks and green spaces in urban areas and development of water resources.

Some Panhandle counties already have a large proportion of land given over to military bases and public forests, limiting their opportunities for economic growth, and were unlikely to seek much additional conservation land. Others, including Bay and Gulf Counties, were well below the state and regional average in the proportion of conservation lands set aside. In these counties, where St. Joe holds more land than anywhere else and where it has tremendous ambitions for development, the company's willingness to engage in future conservation sales was tempered by its own development plans and the ability of preservation-minded entities to put up cash.

The cold reality was that for St. Joe, as with most businesses, environmental stewardship comes about largely due to either regulation or compensation.

Social Issues, Economic Sustainability, and Equity

Social equity was another area where painful tradeoffs were quietly occurring in the wave of growth sweeping northwest Florida. Some people would clearly benefit more than others in the transformation of the Redneck Riviera into Florida's Great Northwest. The shake out would be apparent in who got the jobs, homes, and even recreational opportunities.

The big-gun approach to economic development advocated by St. Joe, Florida's Great Northwest, and, at a higher level, Enterprise Florida did not guarantee to yield a bounty of better jobs for local residents. Using incentives to lure major industries is a highly competitive gambit that frequently benefits the industry more than its newly anointed hometown.

John Ray of Enterprise Florida concedes that up-front incentives are a "huge gamble" and much prefers performance-based incentives that are awarded if and when a business stays for a certain amount of time producing a reasonable amount of benefits. However, bidding wars among the states mean incentives are a "very necessary tactical tool," Ray says.[17]

Alternative ways to uplift a workforce are to invest more directly in people, their education, and their entrepreneurial dreams. These forms of economic development may help locals more than trying to lure new major industries. A comprehensive Council of State Governments review of studies on the effects of economic development incentives reveals no statistical evidence that such inducements actually "create" jobs. They mostly relocate them, which means there is no national gain in employment and little local gain because many of these jobs are taken by people who migrate to the community.[18]

One advocate of the home-grown approach to economic development, Ernesto Sirolli, points out that by year 2025, 50 percent of the labor force will be self-employed. He favors efforts that help budding businesspeople to get local enterprises off the ground. Unlike large corporations that may be looking for greener pastures once their incentives expire, local entrepreneurs are likely to stay and even inspire others to create businesses of their own, he says.[19]

In terms of boosting education, St. Joe was making some corporate moves in that direction. Especially laudable was the involvement of its top executives in the Duval County school system. But a deeper and stronger financial contribution was needed to help upgrade the educational systems at the heart of its Green Empire. Its efforts to bring doctors to the hinterlands and encourage programs that would produce workers for the hospitality industry were necessary, but also self-serving, as was the welcome mat it laid out to encourage new schools to locate on or near its developments.

As for who would get the new homes, St. Joe/Arvida's initial developments made it clear that the company was not an advocate of mixed-income communities where the mixture included lower middle-class residents. Arvida has always been an upscale developer, and as a builder of high-end enclaves was not interested in pushing for features that accommodated the "great unwashed masses," in the words of one planner at DCA, such as mass transit links to its communities. Affordable housing seemed destined to remain an unmet need as the Green Empire matured. In addition, existing residents whose incomes could not compete with newly arrived residents could find themselves newly in need of affordable housing if they were displaced by rising property taxes, especially in coastal communities like Port St. Joe.

One of the most noticeable changes as St. Joe revved up its real estate engine was the loss of recreational access for locals. The closing of rural fire lanes and the conversion of formerly public wildlife management areas to members-only hunt clubs was a downside for many locals. As the Green Empire was becoming a busier place, they found fewer places to hunt, fish, and roam freely. The new Green Empire valued its recreation and would charge for it. The rural River-Camps price tags were beyond the reach of most locals.

Other questions of equity stemmed from the disparities between standards of living along the tony coasts and the rural hinterlands. Places like St. George Island, Panama City Beach, and south Walton County brought in the bounty of tax dollars relative to neighboring inland communities. The region needed a diplomatic means to balance income and services for all residents to stave off resentment flowing in both directions.

Toward a Regional Vision

St. Joe, in boldly assuming the role of regional planner, opened the way to a new level of planning that some observers and academics saw as highly promising. A regional approach allows for strategic infrastructure planning, as St. Joe was keenly aware, but also for much more—addressing sprawl, education, diversity, greenway planning, and more efficient and equitable allocation of resources. Regional cooperation can even help adjacent communities view each other more as partners than competitors by using tax-revenue sharing formulas that level the costs and benefits of new development across a multi-jurisdictional areas.[20]

But as of 2003, the regional planning that was occurring was driven almost entirely by St. Joe and the economic development groups with which it was associated in an often-secretive manner. The situation raised warning flags for one self-proclaimed "regionalism junkie," *Washington Post* syndicated columnist Neal R. Peirce, who participated in a sustainable communities conference in Tallahassee in May 2000. Peirce expressed surprise and even discomfort at the notion of a region's economic development being spearheaded by one particular private sector entity. "If I were a mayor or a councilman, I'd feel very uneasy about this economic development and worry whose terms it would be on," Peirce said, questioning how this approach to economic development related to civic leadership, environmental issues, and its effect on existing centers of towns.[21]

St. Joe's place-making approach carried with it an element of hubris that disturbed many locals, among them Don and Pamela Ashley, of the Friends of Franklin, a group that initially opposed the company's plans for SummerCamp after a prolonged period of failed attempts to be allowed to take part in the planning process.

Florida natives who operate a lodge along the Ochlockonee River, the Ashleys maintained at the time that St. Joe was less than transparent about its plans for Franklin County. The company denied it had a master plan for its roughly 55,000 acres inland from SummerCamp—the St. James Island region between Alligator Harbor and the Ochlockonee Bay. But an internal St. Joe e-mail accidentally sent to the Ashleys made reference to "a Master Plan effort underway to St. James Island."[22]

The Ashleys wrote to DCA to encourage St. Joe to engage the community in its plans for the entire county, not just the SummerCamp development that seemed clearly designed to avoid the newly revised DRI radar and bypass intensive multi-agency review. "Just because St. Joe's hand is quicker than the public eye in politics and power, does not justify increasing shareholder value at the expense of community concerns," Ashley said.[23]

By early 2003, Franklin County, St. Joe, and several other parties had committed to a visioning process for St. James Island after persistent demands by Ashley and others. This concession contributed to the ultimate endorsement of the SummerCamp project by several statewide and local environmental groups as well as the Ashleys with several others still dissenting. But vigilance would be required to make sure that the process was true to the grassroots vision.

Many other citizens across the Green Empire were similarly frustrated at their inability to gain a seat at the table where the guiding visions were being formulated. Without a fuller array of stakeholders at the planning table, and a lot more Florida Sunshine on the process, what was being touted as regional planning really amounted to fulfilling St. Joe's many infrastructure wishes to lay the necessary groundwork for growth.

Even the regional planning councils that were technically equipped with the necessary information and planning skills to back up large-scale planning efforts seemed relegated to a service function in the remaking of the Panhandle. Neither the Apalachee nor West Florida Regional Planning Council has a seat in Florida's Great Northwest, for instance.

This trend points to a satisfactory bottom line for St. Joe, but a less satisfactory bottom line for quality of life in the region. As much as Panhandle leaders might like to pretend they are immune to tradeoffs from rapid growth, there is no rational reason to expect the growth boom in which St. Joe had become a prominent force to proceed differently in northwest Florida than similar booms have elsewhere.

Broadening the St. Joe–initiated regional planning into a true, multifaceted effort that paid attention to quality-of-life issues and invited a full spectrum of stakeholders to the planning table was necessary before regional planning could be said to be truly occurring. Considering the public resources being used, more civic participation and a broader purpose seemed more than appropriate.

While there is no cut-and-dried formula to carry out regional planning, broad and meaningful public participation is a central feature to efforts directed at quality-of-life issues. In the Panhandle, "there's a tremendous amount of pressure to develop land coupled with a relatively weak civic infrastructure," observed planner Kim Ogren, a proponent of "smart growth" who travels around the country for the Miami-based Funders' Network for Smart Growth and Livable Communities.[24] As a Bay County native, Ogren is hoping the Panhandle pursues a smart growth strategy as a means to grow while still protecting and enhancing the resources that make it unique.

A balanced approach to planning integrates what Ogren calls "the four E's of smart growth": economic development, environment, equity, and, perhaps most important, engagement, meaning broad civic involvement. "By integrating the four E's of smart growth into a regional planning process, an area like Bay County stands a better chance at a sustainable, livable future," Ogren says.[25]

Planners have long recognized the first three of those E's, but without the addition of engagement, high-minded ideals stand little chance of implementation. Around the country, several successful planning efforts point to the synergistic payoff that can occur when businesses, citizens, governments, and interest groups together chart a course for the future. Revitalized Chattanooga, Tennessee, and fast-growing Utah were two such places.

"It takes civic and political leadership, information on potential impacts of decisions and the commitment of all the stakeholders to bring about a county-wide or regional planning process that embraces the principles of Smart Growth," according to Ogren.[26] It also takes sustained engagement on the part of empowered citizens, who at the turning of the millennium were not often welcomed in the halls of power.

The seeds for a successful collaborative planning effort in the Panhandle existed in the smaller successes of similar visioning and community-based efforts, from the Walton County visioning efforts present and past to Tallahassee's Blueprint 2000, to the Bay Vision project, kept alive by the Citizens Leadership Institute at Gulf Coast Community College and the Bay County Chamber of Commerce. A $500,000 grant from the Doris Duke Charitable Foundation to 1000 Friends of Florida in 2001 also was a promising spark for a cross-section of citizen participation. The money funded a "Panhandle Initiative" to improve local land-use planning, protect sensitive natural areas, and encourage the formation of business and environmental coalitions in several "eco-regions." However, the project omitted large portions of the Green Empire, including Bay and Gulf

Counties. In Bay County, the St. Joe–initiated "sector planning" effort too offered a start at the inclusive, collaborative effort needed to provide a win-win outcome for the Panhandle's future bottom lines.

For a collaborative regional planning effort to be successful, however, the participation of civic stakeholders had to be both meaningful and sustained. Considering the many barriers that confronted citizens who sought real participation, the challenge of improving civic infrastructure was enormous. The answer lay in changing citizen participation from a reactionary to pathfinding mode, complete with a new level of empowerment that held elected officials accountable for making government mean more than the dispensing of infrastructure dollars and development orders.

St. Joe's "For Sale" sign on the Panhandle has challenged its citizens to form a new vision for the region's future, and to campaign for it against the odds in the cases where it clashes with St. Joe's corporate vision. The alternative is a tacit acceptance of St. Joe's master plan for Florida's Great Northwest, a vision firmly rooted in dollars. For citizens fiercely committed to protecting the region they love, preserving its authentic character and quality of life is a difficult but attainable goal.

Notes

Chapter 1. A Slice of Paradise

1. St. Joe Company, 1998 Annual Report, p. 25.

2. Telephone interview with Beth Folta, vice president for real estate, Seaside Community Development Corporation, August 28, 2000.

3. Brooke, *Seaside,* p. 18.

4. Telephone interview with Beth Folta, August 28, 2000.

5. Belin and Ball, *The Edward Ball We Knew,* p. 2.

6. Bennett, *Twelve on the St. Johns,* p. 136.

7. Agreement between Charles E. Cessna and Stella Cessna, Santa Rosa Plantation, Fidelity Company, by William H. Brown and Sons, agent and attorney, and Edward Ball of Delaware, May 11, 1925, Bay County Clerk of Court.

8. Brooke, *Seaside,* p. 14.

9. Douglas Frantz, "A Land Giant Is Stirring: Will Florida Ever Be the Same?" *New York Times,* April 12, 1998, sec. 3.

10. St. Joe Company, SEC Filing, 8-K, May 18, 2000, p. 14.

11. Interview with Jerry Ray, St. Joe Company vice president for communications, Jacksonville, Fla., August 16, 2000.

12. Frantz, "Land Giant," sec. 3.

13. John Finotti, "A Million Acres," *Florida Trend,* August 1998, p. 38.

14. Paul Hawken, *Ecology of Commerce,* p. xiv.

15. St. Joe Company, SEC Filing, 8-K, May 18, 2000, p. 54.

16. Peter Rummell, CEO, St. Joe Company, remarks at WaterColor groundbreaking, October 1999.

17. Interview with Stephen Greer, St. Joe Company horticulturist, south Walton County, May 17, 2000.

18. Bureau of Economic and Business Research, Warrington College of Business Administration, *Florida Statistical Abstract* (Gainesville: University of Florida, 1999), pp. 232–34.

19. U.S. Department of Commerce, Economics and Statistics Administration, Bureau of the Census, *County and City Data Book* 1994, pp. 78, 92.

20. Angela Childers, "Bay Death Statistics Reveal Reckless Habits," *Panama City News Herald,* November 28, 1999.

21. Interview at public meeting with Jim DeVries, Florida Department of Transportation, June 8, 2000.

22. Bechtel Infrastructure Corporation, *Panama City–Bay County International Airport Feasibility Study*, July 2000, p. 19.

23. Robert Davis, background paper submitted for November 8, 1993, meeting of South Walton Conservation and Development Trust, on file at Florida Conflict Resolution Consortium, Tallahassee.

24. South Walton Conservation and Development Trust, "Strategic Plan," December 1994, p. S-7, on file at Walton County Planning Department Annex.

25. The Nature Conservancy, "Celebrating Preservation 2000: A Decade of Commitment—A Legacy for Generations," 2000, p. 24.

26. Interview with Jerry Ray, Jacksonville, Fla., May 9, 2000.

Chapter 2. The Lay of the Land

Epigraph source: Wilson, *Biophilia*, p.86.

1. Wolfe et al., *Ecological Characterization*, p. 24.

2. Nature Conservancy, "Florida Chapter News," Summer 2000.

3. Interview with Robert L. Bendick Jr., vice president, Southeast Division of the Nature Conservancy, Tallahassee, June 21, 2000.

4. Wolfe et al., *Ecological Characterization*, p. 127.

5. Carr, *Naturalist in Florida*, p. 239.

6. Florida Park Service, *Florida State Park News in the Panhandle* 1.2 (Summer 1999).

7. Belin and Ball, *The Edward Ball We Knew*, p. 43.

8. David S. Webb, "Historical Biogeography," in Myers and Ewel, *Ecosystems of Florida*, p. 99.

9. Interview with Angus Gholson, field botanist, Chattahoochee, Fla., May 23, 2000.

10. Myers and Ewel, *Ecosystems of Florida*, p. 110.

11. Katherine C. Ewel, "Swamps," in Myers and Ewel, *Ecosystems of Florida*, p. 291.

12. Remarks by Woody Miley, meeting of Apalachicola Chamber of Commerce, Apalachicola, Fla., June 7, 2000.

13. Cowdrey, *This Land, This South*, p. 51.

14. Ray, *Ecology of a Cracker Childhood*, p. 81.

15. Ibid., pp. 164–65.

16. Paisley, *Red Hills of Florida*, p. 89.

17. Rogers, *Outposts on the Gulf*, p. 4.

18. Sandra Jo Forney, *Cultural Resources Overview, Apalachicola National Forest, Florida* (Atlanta: U.S. Department of Agriculture, Forest Service, August 1984), p. 28.

19. Rogers, *Outposts on the Gulf*, p. 46.

20. City of Port St. Joe, *The Story of the Old City of St. Joseph: Facts of Florida's First Constitutional Convention*, brochure, n.d. (c. 1950s), p. 3.

21. Womack, *Along the Bay*, p. 22.

22. Ibid., p. 27.

23. Ibid.

24. Ibid., p. 23.

25. Interpretive material at Forest Capital State Museum, Perry, Fla., operated by Florida Department of Environmental Protection, Division of Recreation and Parks.

26. Telephone interview with Jerry Ray, July 2000.

27. Womack, *Along the Bay,* p. 8.

28. Derr, *Some Kind of Paradise,* p. 112.

29. Ibid., p. 120.

30. Rogers, *Outposts on the Gulf,* p. 100.

31. Andre Clewell, *The Vegetation of the Apalachicola National Forest: An Ecological Perspective* (Atlanta: U.S. Department of Agriculture, Forest Service) (Contract Number 38-2249, November 1971), p. 24.

32. Quoted in Derr, *Some Kind of Paradise,* p. 114.

33. Ibid., p. 112.

34. Reed F. Noss, Edward T. LaRoe III, and J. Michael Scott, *Endangered Ecosystems of the United States: A Preliminary Assessment of Loss and Degradation,* U.S. Department of Interior, National Biological Service, Biological Report 28, February 1995, Appendix B, p. 50.

35. E. W. "Judge" Carswell, interview in *Historical Remembrances of Choctawhatchee River,* Water Resources Special Report 89-1, edited by George Fisher (Havana, Fla.: Northwest Florida Water Management District, March 1989), p. 2.

36. Interview with Larry Ogren, Panama City, April 24, 2000.

37. Remarks by George Willson, meeting of Citizens for Sensible Airport Development, Panama City, June 6, 2001.

38. Cowdrey, *This Land, This South,* pp. 118–19.

39. Ibid., p. 137.

Chapter 3. Good Ol' Florida Sand and Mud

Epigraph source: Belin and Ball, *The Edward Ball We Knew,* p. 37.

1. Mosley, *Blood Relations,* p. 172.

2. Ibid., p. 186.

3. James, *Alfred I. duPont,* p. 157.

4. Mosley, *Blood Relations,* p. 285.

5. Ibid., p. 319.

6. Belin and Ball, *The Edward Ball We Knew,* p. 17.

7. Hewlett, *Jessie Ball DuPont,* p. 19.

8. Griffith, *Ed Ball,* p. 16.

9. Belin and Ball, *The Edward Ball We Knew,* p. 19; Hewlett, *Jessie Ball duPont,* p. 62.

10. Hewlett, *Jessie Ball duPont,* pp. 65, 68.

11. Belin and Ball, *The Edward Ball We Knew,* p. 34.

12. Rogers, *Outposts on the Gulf,* p. 240.

13. Ibid., pp. 138–39.

14. Interview with Dave Maddox, Port St. Joe, Fla., October 22, 1999.

15. *Golden Anniversary Celebration,* p. 12.

16. Belin and Ball, *The Edward Ball We Knew,* p. 35.

17. Agreement between Charles E. Cessna and Stella Cessna, Santa Rosa Plantation, and Edward Ball, May 11, 1925, on file at Bay County Clerk of Court.

18. St. Joe Company, SEC Filing, 8-K, May 18, 2000.

19. Agreement between Charles E. Cessna and Stella Cessna and Edward Ball, May 11, 1925.

20. Belin and Ball, *The Edward Ball We Knew,* p. 39; Hewlett, *Jessie Ball duPont,* p. 69.

21. Hewlett, *Jessie Ball duPont*, p. 73.

22. Belin and Ball, *The Edward Ball We Knew*, p. 98; Alfred I. duPont Testamentary Trust, *Estate of Alfred duPont and the Nemours Foundation*, report (hereafter cited as "Estate report"), Jacksonville, Fla., Spring 1963. p. 13; Colby, *Du Pont Dynasty*, p. 528.

23. Hewlett, *Jessie Ball duPont*, p. 73.

24. Belin and Ball, *The Edward Ball We Knew*, p. 104.

25. Danese, *Claude Pepper and Ed Ball*, p. 13.

26. Womack, *Along the Bay*, p. 130.

27. Hewlett, *Jessie Ball duPont*, p. 102.

28. Wall, *Alfred I. duPont*, p. 501.

29. Belin and Ball, *The Edward Ball We Knew*, p. 40.

30. Ibid., p. 44.

31. Revels, *Watery Eden*, p. 49.

32. Wall, *Alfred I. duPont*, p. 499.

33. Belin and Ball, *The Edward Ball We Knew*, p. 115.

34. Wall, *Alfred I. duPont*, pp. 505–6.

35. Belin and Ball, *The Edward Ball We Knew*, p. 118.

36. Ibid., p. 48.

37. Hewlett, *Jessie Ball duPont*, pp. 131–32.

38. Wall, *Alfred I. duPont*, p. 612.

Chapter 4. The Era of the St. Joe Paper Company

1. Hewlett, *Jessie Ball duPont*, pp. 113–14.

2. Articles of incorporation, St. Joe Paper Company, on file with the Department of State, Division of Corporations, Tallahassee.

3. Hewlett, *Jessie Ball duPont*, p. 114.

4. Belin and Ball, *The Edward Ball We Knew*, p. 133.

5. "Progress Edition," *Star*, April 8, 1938, p. 4.

6. Hewlett, *Jessie Ball duPont*, p. 114.

7. Ibid., p. 115.

8. Estate report, p. 25.

9. Conversation with Robert Nedley, chair, Port St. Joe Port Authority, and former president, St. Joe Paper Company, Port St. Joe, Fla., May 10, 2001.

10. "Mill Now in Operation," *Star*, April 8, 1938, p. 1.

11. "A Dream Come True," *Star*, April 8, 1938, p. 4.

12. *Golden Anniversary Celebration*, p. 21.

13. Estate report, p. 25.

14. Smith, *U.S. Paper Industry*, p. 116.

15. Hewlett, *Jessie Ball duPont*, p. 130.

16. Estate report, p. 9.

17. *Complete Guide to Florida Foundations* (Miami: J. L. Adams, 1999), p. 57.

18. Hewlett, *Jessie Ball duPont*, p. xiv.

19. "Agreement of Merger of St. Joe Paper Company, Gulf Coast Properties, Inc., and Panama Beach Development Company into St. Joe Paper Company," final copy signed September 28, 1940, pp. 5–10, microfiche on file with the Florida Department of State.

20. Belin and Ball, *The Edward Ball We Knew,* p. 223.

21. Hewlett, *Jessie Ball duPont,* pp. 170–71.

22. Danese, *Claude Pepper and Ed Ball,* p. 62.

23. Ibid.

24. Ibid., p. 178.

25. Ibid., p. 181.

26. Ibid., p. 203.

27. Undated oral history transcription from Dave Maddox, copy provided to authors, September 9, 2000; interview with Dave Maddox and Sarah Maddox, Port St. Joe, Fla., October 10, 1999.

28. Warranty deed for the Maddox parcel, St. Joe Dock and Terminal, Railway Company, Port St. Joe, Fla., November 29, 1939.

29. Mason and Harrison, *Confusion to the Enemy,* p. 151.

30. Ibid., p. 155.

31. Ibid., p. 140.

32. Philip S. Adkins, *The Impact of Government and Technology on Business and Labor in the Pulp and Paper Industry: A Case Study of the Pensacola Paper Firms, 1940–1985,* dissertation submitted to the Department of History, Florida State University, Tallahassee, Spring 1999, p. 81.

33. Hewlett, *Jessie Ball duPont,* p. 149.

34. Revels, *Watery Eden,* pp. 52–53.

35. "Ed Ball," *Jacksonville Today,* December 1985, p. 65.

36. Bill Varian, "Growth Plan Rooted in Farm's Rich History," *Tallahassee Democrat,* April 25, 1999, pp. 1A, 7A.

37. "A Pictorial and Historical Story of Port St. Joe," Florida State Library, Tallahassee, 1963.

38. Estate report, p. 26.

39. George L. Henderson and his wife to W. T. Edwards, St. Joe Paper, December 8, 1947, Tallahassee Historic Trust.

40. "Henderson Property Sold for $81,800," *Daily Democrat,* April 1, 1948.

41. "British Envoy Is Visitor in Capital," *Tallahassee Democrat,* February 17, 1960, p. 1A.

42. Ball, *Around West Florida,* p. 199.

43. Varian, "Growth Plan," pp. 1, 7A.

44. Interview with Tim Edmond, capital region president, St. Joe/Arvida, Tallahasse, Fla., May 25, 2000.

45. Landrum, "Study of the St. Joe Paper Company Land Using Activities," p. 56.

46. "St. Joe's Piney Woods," *Orlando Sunday Sentinel-Star,* Nov. 2, 1952, p. 5-D.

47. Interview with Jim Murphee, Southport, Fla., July 4, 2001.

48. Interview with Jim Barkuloo, Panama City, Fla., September 9, 1999.

49. Ibid.

50. Mason and Harrison, *Confusion to the Enemy,* p. 109.

51. Marlene Womack, "Out of the Past" column, *Panama City News Herald,* March 30, 1997, pp. 4–5C.

52. Interview with Angus Gholson, May 23, 2000.

53. Ibid.

54. Ibid.

55. Interview with Clay Smallwood, St. Joe Timberland Company president, Port St. Joe, Fla., February 8, 2001.

56. Ibid.

57. Interview with Angus Gholson, May 23, 2000.

58. Ibid.

59. Interview with Bruce Means, Quincy, Fla., February 2000; Bruce Means to authors, e-mails, March 2 and December 5, 2000.

60. Ibid, March 2, 2000 email.

61. Interview with Angus Gholson, May 23, 2000.

62. Telephone interview with Ace Haddock, restoration specialist, Florida Department of Forestry, April 2, 2002.

63. Landrum, "Study of the St. Joe Paper Company Land Using Activities," p. 49.

64. Cowdrey, *This Land, This South,* p. 177.

65. "St. Joe's Piney Woods," p. 5-D.

Chapter 5. Pork Chop Emperor

Epigraph source: Robert Sherrill, *Gothic Politics in the Deep South,* p. 141.

1. Colburn, "Florida Politics in the Twentieth Century," p. 361.

2. Belin and Ball, *The Edward Ball We Knew,* p. 121.

3. Griffith, *Ed Ball,* p. 83.

4. Jahoda, *Other Florida,* pp. 187-88.

5. "Ed Ball," *Jacksonville Today,* December 1985, p. 71.

6. Colby, *Du Pont Dynasty,* p. 541.

7. Belin and Ball, *The Edward Ball We Knew,* p. 160.

8. Ibid., pp. 160–65.

9. Telephone interview with Sue Phillips, former receptionist the with St. Joe Paper Company, November 30, 2000.

10. SAC [Special Agent in Charge] R. A. Alt, Jacksonville, to Director [J. Edgar Hoover], FBI, April 17, 1935.

11. John Edgar Hoover, Director, FBI, to the U.S. Attorney General, memorandum, May 14, 1935.

12. R. L. Shivers, SAC, to the Director, FBI, memorandum, February 26, 1937.

13. SAC, Jacksonville, Fla., to the Director, FBI, September 2, 1964.

14. Estate report, p. 26.

15. Ibid., p. 26.

16. Interview with Ferrell Allen, Florida Coast Paper mill manager and formerly with the St. Joe Paper Company, Port St. Joe, Fla., July 25, 2000.

17. Interview with Billy Howell, Port St. Joe, Fla., September 9, 2000.

18. Interview with Ferrell Allen, July 25, 2000.

19. Interview with Patricia Barry Gammel, Nemours Foundation, at Wakulla Springs "Great Floridian" ceremony, October 2000.

20. Hewlett, *Jessie Ball duPont,* p. 168.

21. "Port St. Joe Landmark Jacob Belin Dead at 85," *Panama City News Herald,* June 2, 2000, p. 1A.

22. Colby, *Du Pont Dynasty,* p. 540.

23. *Golden Anniversary Celebration,* pp. 30–31.

24. Marlene Womack, "Time Changes Resulted in Great Deal of Grumbling, Sleepiness for Bay County," *Panama City News Herald,* Sunday, April 2, 2000, p. 2B.

25. Interview with Jim Barkuloo, September 9, 1999.

26. *St. Joe Paper Co. v. Brown* (Fla. App. 1 Dist. 1968), Nos. I-392, I-393, District Court of Appeal of Florida, First District, April 16, 1968.

27. Bill Varian, "St. Joe Dispute with County over Taxes Ends," *Tallahassee Democrat,* April 22, 1998.

28. Ibid.

29. 333 So.2d 527, *St. Joe Paper Co. v. Conrad* (Fla. App. 1 Dist. 1976).

30. 400 So.2d 983, *St. Joe Paper Co. v. Adkinson* (Fla. App. 1 Dist. 1981), St. Joe Paper Co., appellant, versus Hubert R. Adkinson, Property Appraiser of Walton Co., et al.

31. 652 So.2d 907, 20 Fla. L. Weekly D735, *Davis v. St. Joe Paper Co.* (Fla. App. 1 Dist. 1995), Richard Davis, Property Appraiser of Bay County, and Larry Fuchs, Executive Director of the Department of Revenue Appellants, versus St. Joe Paper Company, Appellee. No. 93-3144, District Court of Appeal of Florida, First District, March 23, 1995. Rehearing denied May 4, 1995.

32. Ibid.

33. Ian Trontz, "St. Joe Paper Land Reclassified, Backed by Court, May Hike Tax Bill," *Panama City News Herald,* March 28, 1995, p. 1B.

34. *St. Joe Paper Co. v. Brown.*

35. Telephone interview with Mack Webb, property assessor, Bay County, Fla., August 3, 2000.

36. Nixon Smiley, "Official Mr. Florida, Mr. Ball," *Floridian,* May 5, 1968, pp. 12–17.

37. Griffith, *Ed Ball,* p. 47.

38. Telephone interview with Winfred Thornton, chairman, Alfred I. duPont Trust, December 18, 2000.

39. Hewlett, *Jessie Ball duPont,* p. 261.

40. Colby, *Du Pont Dynasty,* p. 539.

41. Ibid.

42. Griffith, *Ed Ball,* p. 59.

43. Colby, *Du Pont Dynasty,* p. 541.

44. Danese, *Claude Pepper and Ed Ball,* p. 219.

Chapter 6. Challenges to the Empire

Epigraph source: Quoted in John Taylor, "The House that Ball Built," *St. Petersburg Times,* April 15, 1984, p. 1-I. Dent was, for many years, a dissident trustee.

1. Colby, *Du Pont Dynasty,* p. 552.

2. Belin and Ball, *The Edward Ball We Knew,* p. 165; Colby, *Du Pont Dynasty,* p. 542.

3. Belin and Ball, *The Edward Ball We Knew,* p. 99; Colby, *Du Pont Dynasty,* pp. 542–43.

4. Cary A. Everett, Director, Florida First National Bank at Chipley, to Billy Hudson, President, Florida National Bank, Chipley, July 20, 1977.

5. Ibid.

6. Dix Druse, President, Louisiana and Southern Life Insurance Company, to John S. Miller Jr., Roberts, Miller, Baggett and LaFace, Attorneys at Law, Tallahassee, Fla., October 31, 1977.

7. Everett to Hudson, July 20, 1977.

8. Ibid.

9. Barry Stavro, "Running Ed Ball's Empire Without the Emperor," *Florida Trend,* November 1981, p. 57.

10. 380 So.2d 1128, *Mills v. Ball* (Fla. App. 1 Dist 1980).

11. Rush Loving, "Raymond Mason Needs More than Optimism Now," *Fortune,* November 1975, p. 120.

12. Max Holland, "A Luce Connection: Senator Keating, Willliam Pawley, and the Cuban Missile Crisis," *Journal of Cold War Studies* 1.3 (1999): pp. 139–67.

13. Murray Illson, "William D. Pawley, Financier, Dies at 80," *New York Times,* January 8, 1977.

14. Telephone interview with Winfred Thornton, January 8, 2001.

15. Telephone interview with Winfred Thornton, December 18, 2000.

16. Wilkinson, *Big Sugar,* pp. 248–59.

17. SAC [Special Agent in Charge], Miami, to FBI Director [J. Edgar Hoover], memorandum, "Subject: William D. Pawley, President, Talisman Sugar Corporation, Miami (Dade County), Florida, Unknown Victims [item blocked out] Complainant, Iss and Peonage," April 4, 1972.

18. Talisman Sugar Corporation report and tax return, state of Florida, Department of State, March 7, 1971.

19. Wilkinson, *Big Sugar,* pp. 72–77.

20. Mason and Harrison, *Confusion to the Enemy,* p. 102; interview with Dave Maddox, October 22, 1999.

21. Interviews with Billy Howell, Port St. Joe, Fla., September 9, 2000 and December 13, 2000.

22. Interview with John Reeves, union person, Port St. Joe, Fla., June 6, 2000.

23. Mason and Harrison, *Confusion to the Enemy,* p. 103.

24. Ibid., p. 4.

25. Telephone interview with Philip Adkins, June 2000.

26. Timothy J. Minchin, "There Were Two Jobs in St. Joe Paper Company, White Job and a Black Job: The Struggle for Civil Rights in a North Florida Paper Mill Community, 1938–1990," *Florida Historical Quarterly* (April 2000): pp. 331–59.

27. Ibid., p. 346.

28. *James Winfield, et al., Plaintiffs, v. St. Joe Paper Company, et al., Defendants,* Case No. MCA 76-28, U.S. District Court, Northern District of Florida, Marianna Division, Consent Decree, p. 19.

29. *James Winfield, et al., etc., Plaintiffs-Appellants, v. St. Joe Paper Company, et al., Defendants-Appellees,* U.S. Court of Appeals, Fifth Circuit, No. 81-5486, p. 7.

30. St. Joe Paper Company, 1987 Annual Report, p. 13.

31. Interviews with Frank Pate, mayor of St. Joe, St. Joe, Fla., June 5, 2000 and December 13, 2000.

32. "Pair Wrongly Convicted of Murder," AP wire story, July 14, 1998, www.SunOne.com.

33. Mason and Harris, *Confusion to the Enemy,* p. 107.

34. Floye Brewton eulogy for Jacob Belin, Port St. Joe, Fla., June 3, 2000.

35. Mason and Harrison, *Confusion to the Enemy,* p. 101.

36. Griffith, *Ed Ball,* p. 184.

37. Jahoda, *Other Florida,* p. 134.

38. Derr, *Some Kind of Paradise,* p. 334.

39. Mason and Harris, *Confusion to the Enemy,* p. 7.

40. Belin and Ball, *The Edward Ball We Knew,* p. 249.

41. Al Burt, "The Last Resort," *Tropic,* August 11, 1985, pp. 18–22.

42. Revels, *Watery Eden,* p. 60.

43. Ibid., p. 59.

44. Telephone with Madeleine Carr, founding member of the board, Friends of Wakulla Springs, April 2000.

45. Burt, "Last Resort."

46. Revels, *Watery Eden,* p. 74.

47. Ibid., p. 72.

48. Belin and Ball, *The Edward Ball We Knew,* p. 62.

49. Revels, *Watery Eden,* p. 52.

50. Ibid., p. 79.

51. Comments made at the "Great Floridian" reception, Wakulla Springs, October 2000.

52. Griffith, *Ed Ball,* p. 30.

53. Belin and Ball, *The Edward Ball We Knew,* p. 166.

54. Brewton, *The Mafia,* p. 329.

55. Thomas Karnes, *Tropical Enterprise* (Baton Rouge: Louisiana State University Press, 1978), 172, 275–77, quoted in Scott, *Deep Politics,* pp. 96–97.

56. Scott, *Deep Politics,* p. 97.

Chapter 7. A Company in Transition

Epigraph source: Quoted in Robert Frank, "Deal Makers Unsettle the Mysterious Empire of St. Joe Paper Co.," *Wall Street Journal,* October 13, 1994, p. A1.

1. Stavro, "Running Ed Ball's Empire," p. 58.

2. St. Joe Paper Company, 1988 Annual Report, p. 3.

3. Stavro, "Running Ed Ball's Empire," p. 60.

4. Ibid.

5. Paul Thiel, "Different Stock: St. Joe Paper Uses Unconventional Approach to Protect Trust," *Florida Times-Union,* May 30, 1989, pp. 10–12.

6. Telephone with Winfred Thornton, December 18, 2000.

7. Barry Stavro, "Charter Tries a Team Approach," *Florida Trend,* September 1981.

8. St. Joe Paper Company, 1985 Annual Report, p. F-4.

9. "Cleanup of Missouri Toxic Waste Site Complete: Times Beach Superfund Site 1st of Three Toxic Waste Sites to be Cleaned Up That Spurred Creation of the Superfund Law," Press Release 281, July 3, 1997, U.S. Department of Justice.

10. Thiel, "Different Stock," pp. 10–12.

11. Interview with Clay Smallwood, February 8, 2001.

12. Telephone interview with Wayne Mixon, former Florida governor and lieutenant governor, February 2000.

13. St. Joe Paper Company, 1985 Annual Report, p. 10.

14. St. Joe Paper Company, 1987 Annual Report, p. 5.

15. Ibid.

16. Thiel, "Different Stock" (based on map accompanying article).

17. Telephone interview with Pat Seery, coordinator of Grass Roots School and resident of the Grass Roots development, Tallahassee, Fla., August 2000.

18. Telephone interview with Dorothy Inman-Crews [later Inman-Johnson], executive director of the Capital Area Community Action Agency and former Tallahassee city commissioner, April 2000.

19. "Executive Summary: St. Joe Paper," WestCountry Financial; report on Timberland Segment of the company, Original date: October 26, 1995, amended April 1996.

20. Interview with Clay Smallwood, February 8, 2001.

21. Southwood Project Overview, Natural Features Inventory, St. Joe/Arvida Company, L.P., June 1999, p. 1.

22. Comments of Debbie Lightsey, Tallahassee city commissioner, "Civitas" Sustainability Conference, Tallahassee, Fla., May 15–16, 2000.

23. Greg Brown, "The Metamorphosis: St. Joe Company and the Growth Machine in a Global Economy," unpublished research paper submitted to Urban and Regional Planning 5313, Florida State University, Fall 1998, on file with author Wiaz.

24. Bruce Ritchie, "Travel on Capital Circle May Rise," *Tallahassee Democrat*, November 13, 2000, p. 1B.

25. Brown, "Metamorphosis."

26. Bill Cotterell, "Governor, Cabinet OK Deal with St. Joe Co. to Swap Land," *Tallahassee Democrat*, June 25, 1998, p. 5C.

27. Gary Fineout, "St. Joe Will Get Land Back if State Doesn't Use It," *Tallahassee Democrat*, December 9, 1998, p. 4C.

28. Stavro, "Running Ed Ball's Empire," p. 61.

29. John Taylor, "A Deal from the Land of Oz," *Florida Trend*, March 1987, p. 60.

30. Brewton, *The Mafia*, p. 349.

31. St. Joe Paper Company, 1986 Annual Report, p. 19.

32. U.S. District Court, Northern District of Florida, Pensacola Division, *United States of America vs. One Parcel of Real Property Located in Walton County, Known as Sandshore Tract B in Topsail Hill*, Affidavit for Forfeiture of Real Property, October 2, 1991, p. 50.

33. Jackie Halifax, "Governor, Cabinet Waive Rules for Topsail Hill Property Purchases," *Tallahassee Democrat*, May 20, 1992.

34. Bruce Rolfsen and Joyce Pugh, "Topsail Hill Among Land to Be Purchased by State," *Panama City News Herald*, May 20, 1992.

35. Staff and News Reports, "Topsail Convictions Overturned," *Houston Chronicle*, February 27, 1998.

36. Florida Department of State Records, Division of Corporations, www.sunbiz.org.

37. Brewton, *The Mafia*, p. 350.

38. Julie Hauserman and Fred A. Schneyer, "Topsail Hill: Dunes, Deals, and Doomed S&Ls," *Tallahassee Democrat*, September 16, 1990.

39. Ibid.

40. Brewton, *The Mafia*, p. 340.

41. Bay County Clerk of Court, Official Record Book 1064, p. 407.

42. James Russell, "St. Joe Paper and Its Siblings Are in for a Change: New Trustees May Increase Payouts," *Miami Herald*, October 23, 1994, p. 1K.

43. Frank, "Deal Makers Unsettle the Mysterious Empire."

44. Jane Bennett, "Dahl Kick-Started duPont Trust," *Business Journal of Jacksonville* (online), May 26, 1997.

45. Michael Binstein and Charles Bowden, *Trust Me: Charles Keating and the Missing Billions* (New York: Random House, 1993), p. 183.

46. John Finotti, "At Arm's Length," *Florida Trend,* May 1, 1998.

47. Dana Peck, "Dahl Made Millions with Michael Milken. Now He Just Wants Some North Florida Tranquility," *Tallahassee Democrat,* March 15, 1992.

48. Telephone interview with James Dahl, Jacksonville, Florida, venture capitalist, May 16, 2001.

49. Ibid.

50. Frank, "Deal Makers Unsettle the Mysterious Empire."

51. Bennett, "Dahl Kick-Started duPont Trust."

52. Telephone interview with James Dahl, April 11, 2001.

53. Ibid.

54. Frank, "Deal Makers Unsettle the Mysterious Empire."

55. "Executive Summary: St. Joe Paper," WestCountry Financial, original date: October 26, 1995, amended February 1996.

56. Ibid.

57. Interview with Jacob Belin, Jacksonville, Fla., May 9, 2000.

58. Telephone interview with James Dahl, April 11, 2001.

59. Four M Corporation/Box USA Group, Inc., SEC Filing, S-4, July 12, 1996, pp. 20–21.

60. "Objection of Ad Hoc Committee of Noteholders to Motion for Change of Venue to the Northern District of Florida," U.S. Bankruptcy Court for the District of Delaware, In re: Florida Coast Paper Holding Company, LLC, et al., Debtors, Chapter 11, Case No. 99-755 through Case No. 99-758.

61. St. Joe Company, SEC Filing, DEF 14A (Proxy), 1998–2001.

62. Jordan Wankoff, "Stone Container Corporation," in *International Directory of Company Histories,* vol. 4 (Detroit: St. James Press, 1994), pp. 332–34.

63. "Stone Container Settles FTC Charges," Federal Trade Commission press release, FTC File No. 951 00, February 25, 1998, 06.

64. Ibid.

65. 643 F2.d 195 Corrugated Antitrust Litigation, In re: (C.A. 5 (Tex.) 1981), p. 16.

66. Four M Corporation/Box USA Group, Inc., SEC Filing, S-4, July 12, 1996, p. 38.

67. Ibid., p. 2.

68. Telephone interview with L. L. "Duke" Jones, former mill worker, May 2000.

69. Telephone interview with Mark Gay, former mill worker, May 21, 2001.

70. Interview with Ferrel Allen, July 25, 2000.

71. Four M Corporation/Box USA Group, Inc., SEC Filing, S-4, July 12, 1996, p. 37.

72. Telephone interview with Marshall Nelson, emergency management coordinator and former mill worker, Gulf County, Fla., May 1, 2000.

73. St. Joe Company, 1998 Annual Report, p. 64.

74. Telephone interview with Winfred Thornton, January 8, 2001.

75. Ibid.

76. Telephone interview with James Dahl, May 16, 2001.

77. SEC Press Release 2001-49, "SEC Sues Former CEO, CFO and Other Top Former Officers of Sunbeam Corporation in Massive Financial Fraud," May 15, 2001.

78. Finotti, "At Arm's Length."

79. John Finotti, "Agreement on St. Joe/Arvida Deal," *Florida Times-Union,* October 2, 1997.

Chapter 8. The Making of a Real Estate Powerhouse

Epigraph source: Peter Rummell, CEO, St. Joe Company, address to company stockholders, St. Joe Company annual meeting, Jacksonville, Fla., May 9, 2000.

1. St. Joe Company, 1997 Annual Report, p. 2.

2. Ibid., p. 4.

3. Frank, "Deal Makers Unsettle the Mysterious Empire," p. A1.

4. Brent Unger, "As the Economy Blossoms, the Fat Cats Get It All," *Panama City News Herald,* September 12, 1999, p. 1E.

5. Charlotte Crane, "State's Largest Land Company Targets Panhandle for Growth," *Pensacola News Journal,* January 31, 1999, p. 8A.

6. Finotti, "Million Acres," p. 39.

7. Standard and Poors, Standard Corporate Descriptions, Corporations Records, vol. 3, July 2001, p. 497.

8. St. Joe Company, 1997 Annual Report, p. 4.

9. Douglas Frantz, "Florida's Largest Landholder Promises to Develop with a Conscience," *New York Times* on the web, April 12, 1998.

10. Interview with Peter Rummell, Jacksonville, Fla., August 16, 2000.

11. Frantz and Collins, *Celebration, U.S.A.,* p. 5.

12. Interview with Peter Rummell, August 16, 2000.

13. Ibid.

14. McPhee, *Encounters with the Archdruid,* p. 91.

15. Ibid., p. 92.

16. Interview with Peter Rummell, August 16, 2000.

17. Ibid.

18. Frantz, "Florida's Largest Landholder."

19. Interview with Peter Rummell, August 16, 2000.

20. Ibid.

21. Frantz and Collins, *Celebration, U.S.A.,* p. 115.

22. Interview with Celebration resident Ron Dixon on National Public Radio's *Talk of the Nation,* August 10, 1999.

23. Interview with Andrew Ross, author of *The Celebration Chronicles,* speaking about New Urbanism on National Public Radio's *Talk of the Nation,* August 10, 1999.

24. Steve Twomey, "Eisner, Could You Spare a Dime?" *Washington Post,* Monday, January 24, 1994.

25. Richard Squires, "Disney's Trojan Mouse: A Corporate Colony Paid for by Gullible Locals," *Washington Post,* January 23, 1994, p. C1.

26. "Yes, Virginia, There Is a Mickey Mouse," *National Journal,* April 30, 1994.

27. Hugh Sidey, "When Mickey Comes Marching Home," *Time,* March 21, 1994, p. 61.

28. Richard E. Foglesong, "When Disney Comes to Town: From Florida, a Cautionary Tale," *Washington Post Magazine,* May 15, 1994, p. W15.

29. Interview with Peter Rummell, August 16, 2000.

30. Hiaasen, *Team Rodent,* p. 77.

31. St. Joe Company, 1999 Annual Report, p. 15.

32. Interview with Jerry Ray, Jacksonville, Fla., August 18, 2000.

33. *Securities and Exchange Commission, Plaintiff, v. Avida Corporation, Arthur Vining Davis (et al.)*, Civil No. 138-67, U.S. District Court, Southern District of New York, 169 F. Supp. 211; 1958 U.S. Dist. LEXIS 3029; Fed. Sec. L. Rep. (CCH) P90,891 December 12, 1958.

34. "The Time of Our Life," Arvida web site, www.arvida.com/about_timeline_normal.asp, January 16, 2001.

35. Telephone interview with Jerry Karnas, former resident of Longboat Key, November 1999.

36. Stuart Mieher, "Arvida Tries a New Balancing Act Under Disney," *Florida Trend*, November 1984, pp. 74–76.

37. Ibid., p. 75.

38. Angie Francalancia, "Arvida: A Troubled Past," *Palm Beach Post*, May 3, 1998, p. 1F.

39. Mieher, "Arvida Tries a New Balancing Act," p. 74.

40. Jonathan King, Neil Santaniello, and David Fleshler, "Growth and Consequences to Protect the Environment or Grow," *Fort Lauderdale Sun Sentinel*, November 14, 1999, p. 1H.

41. Ibid.

42. Paula Kepos, ed., "JMB Realty Corporation," in *International Directory of Company Histories*, vol. 8 (Detroit: St. James Press).

43. Francalancia, "Arvida," p. 1F.

44. St. Joe Company, 1998 Annual Report, p. 62.

45. Francalancia, "Arvida," p. 1F.

46. St. Joe Company, 1998 Annual Report, pp. 57, 30.

47. Finotti, "Million Acres," p. 34; St. Joe Company, 1998 Annual Report, p. 57.

48. St. Joe Company, 1998 Annual Report, p. 36.

49. Mieher, "Arvida Tries a New Balancing Act," p. 73.

50. Administrative Complaint: Florida Department of Business and Professional Regulation vs. Sanford B. Miot, Respondent, Case No. 93-11955.

51. St. Joe Company, SEC Filing, 10-K, March 22, 2000, p. 5.

52. Matt Moore, "St. Joe Has Stronger Grip on Real Estate Markets," *Panama City News Herald*, April 14, 1999, p. 8B.

53. Associated Press, "St. Joe Co. Makes Deal with Jeb Bush," *Tallahassee Democrat*, June 7, 1998, p. 2B.

54. Robert Trigaux, "Influence and Bailouts a Business Tradition in the Bush Family," *St. Petersburg Times Online*, October 29, 2000, www.sptimes.com.

55. Alecia Swasy and Robert Trigaux, "Make the Money and Run," *St. Petersburg Times Online*, September 20, 1998, p. 5 of 16, www.sptimes.com.

56. Mark Silva, "Milestones in the Biography of Florida's 43rd Governor," *Miami Herald*, January 3, 1999, www.herald.com.

57. "Full and Public Disclosure of Financial Interests 1998, Hon. Jeb Bush, Governor," Form 6, June 30, 1999, on file with the Florida Ethics Commission.

58. Swazy and Trigaux, "Make the Money and Run," p. 6.

59. Ellen Debenport, "Jeb Bush: His Name is Scrutiny," *St. Petersburg Times*, December 20, 1993, p. 1A; Jeff Gerth, "A Savings and Loan Bailout, and Bush's Son Jeb," *New York Times*, October 14, 1990.

60. Stephen Pizzo, "Bush Family Values," *MoJo Wire Magazine,* p. 9 (original piece from *Mother Jones,* September/October 1992, www.motherjones.com).

61. Interview with Peter Rummell, August 16, 2000.

62. Jeb Bush to June Wiaz, e-mail, October 4, 2001.

Chapter 9. Liquidating the Storehouse of Value

Epigraph source: Jack Snyder, "Power to Reshape Florida Will Rest with One Company," *Orlando Sentinel,* July 4, 1999.

1. St. Joe Company, 1998 Annual Report, p. 33.

2. "Money" column, *USA Today,* September 4, 2002, www.marketwatch.com.

3. St. Joe Company, 1998 Annual Report, p. 41.

4. Mark Basch, "St. Joe Paper Co. 'Sitting on Gold Mine,'" *Florida Times-Union,* First Business section, Monday, May 25, 1992.

5. Robert P. King, "Talisman Land Could Be Ripe Plum for Sugar Growers," *Palm Beach Post,* December 15, 1997, p. 1A.

6. St. Joe Company, 1997 Annual Report, pp. 26–27.

7. St. Joe Company, 1998 Annual Report, p. 22.

8. St. Joe Company, SEC Filing, 10-K, March 2000, p. 25.

9. Telephone interview with Charles Lee, senior vice president with the Florida Audubon Society, January 4, 2000.

10. St. Joe Company, 1998 Annual Report, p. 22.

11. Ibid., p. 41.

12. Telephone interview with Charles Lee, January 4, 2000.

13. Report No. 03-115 of the Florida Auditor General, "Department of Environmental Protection: Acquisitions of Lands by the State, January 2000, Through December 31, 2001," February 2003.

14. Interagency meeting on mitigating wetlands affected by Florida Department of Transportation, Camp Helen (Bay County), July 25, 2000.

15. Remarks by George Willson, meeting of Citizens for Sensible Airport Development, Panama City, June 6, 2001.

16. Ibid.

17. Telephone interview with Hildreth Cooper, U.S. Fish and Wildlife Service biologist, December 13, 2001.

18. St. Joe Company News, press release, March 29, 2001, www.joe.com/news/pr/2001/03-29.1.html.

19. Robert M. Rhodes, "Florida Growth Management: Rights, Not Rights, and the Future," printed presentation of speech given for Florida Atlantic University's Joint Center for Environmental and Urban Problems, John M. DeGrove Distinguished Speakers Series, October 3, 2001, p. 9.

20. www.bankruptcy.com.

21. Committee on Banking, Finance and Urban Affairs, U.S. House of Representatives, *MCorp: A Regulatory Case Study,* staff report, 102d Cong., March 1992, pp. 29, 37.

22. Jim Mitchell, "MBank Settlement Reached—Ex-officials Agree to $39.2 Million Tab," *Dallas Morning News* (archive), August 6, 1993.

23. H. F. Ahmanson and Company, SEC Filing, DEF 14-A, April 1, 1996, p. 4.

24. Zepezauer and Naiman, *Take the Rich off Welfare.*

25. Kevin M. Twomey biography, St. Joe Company press release.

26. Walton County Clerk of the Court, Real Estate Mortgage and Security Agreement, December 31, 1987, Official Record 470, p. 103, Filed December 31, 1987.

27. St. Joe Company, 1998 Annual Report, p. 33.

28. Ibid., p. 13

29. Rhodes, "Florida Growth Management," n. 5, p. 16.

30. Remarks of Robert M. Rhodes, Florida Sustainable Communities Network, Statewide Roundtable, Tallahassee, Fla., May 16, 2000.

31. Jon East, "Growing Out of Control," *St. Petersburg Times,* February 25, 2001.

32. "Arvida/Disney Gets a Growth Guru," *Florida Trend,* June 1985, p. 102.

33. David L. Powell, Robert M. Rhodes, and Dan R. Stengle, "A Measured Step to Protect Private Property Rights," *Florida State University Law Review* 23.255 (1995): pp. 277–78.

34. Statement of Jane Cameron Hayman, deputy general counsel, Florida League of Cities, before House Judiciary Committee, September 23, 1997.

35. Rhodes, "Florida Growth Management," p. 14.

36. Ibid., p. 12.

37. Sylvia R. Lazos Vargas, "Florida's Property Rights Act: A Political Quick Fix Results in a Mixed Bag of Tricks," *Florida State University Law Review* 23.255 (1995): p. 320.

38. Telephone interview with Jerry Ray, August 18, 2000.

39. Interview with Jerry Ray, May 9, 2000.

40. Ibid.

41. St. Joe Company News, press release, June 23, 2001.

42. Web site of James Madison Institute, www.jamesmadisoninstitute.org.

43. Interview with Chris Corr, St. Joe Company vice president of public affairs, Tallahassee, Fla., February 13, 2001.

44. Kyle Parks, "A Conversation with . . . Chris Corr," *St. Petersburg Times Online,* Business, August 28, 2000.

45. Chris Corr biography, www.joe.com.

46. Parks, "Conversation."

47. Interview with Clay Smallwood, February 8, 2001.

48. Ibid.

49. George Willson biography, St. Joe Company materials.

50. Interview with Robert Bendick, June 21, 2000.

51. "The Big Eight," *Tallahassee Democrat,* part of the "100 Years in Tallahassee: A Journey Through the Century" series, November 28, 1999, sec. E.

52. Telephone interview with Frank Shaw Jr., August 2001.

53. St. Joe Company, SEC Filing, DEF 14A (Proxy), p. 6, filed April 10, 2000.

54. Eric Cavey, "Pumped About Training," *Business Journal,* Jacksonville (print edition date), June 9, 2000; Office of U.S. Rep. Mark Foley (R-Fla.), "Foley Calls for Details on Talisman Land Purchase Price in Letter to Gore and Babbitt, Congressman Asks if Taxpayers Are Getting Fair Deal," news release, December 12, 1997.

55. Peyton, *Newboy,* p. 160.

56. Floye Brewton eulogy for Jacob Belin.

57. Telephone interview with Winfred Thornton, December 17, 2000.

58. Patricia Barry-Gamel, Director of Business Development, Nemours Foundation, e-mail, April 16, 2001.

59. Ibid.

Chapter 10. From Trees to Towns and Grits to Godiva

Epigraph source: Quotation from authors' interview with Clay Smallwood, February 8, 2001.

1. St. Joe Company, SEC Filing, 10-K, March 22, 2000, p. 23.

2. "The St. Joe Company (NYSE: JOE) Reports Second Quarter Net EBITDA of $0.57 per Share, Up 50 Percent," St. Joe press release, July 18, 2001.

3. Interview with Peter Rummell, August 16, 2000.

4. St. Joe Company, SEC Filing, 10-K, March 20, 2001, p. 20.

5. Robert Trigaux, "St. Joe Co. Goes Pioneering to Develop its Vast Acreage," *St. Petersburg Times,* July 25, 2001.

6. Remarks by Billy Buzzett, St. Joe Company director of strategic planning, meeting in the offices of St. Andrew Bay Resource Management Association, Panama City, Fla., December 7, 2001.

7. Interview with Clay Smallwood, February 8, 2001.

8. Ibid.

9. Ibid.

10. Bill Varian, "Future Retirees Could Fuel Local Real Estate Boom," *Tallahassee Democrat,* September 26, 1998, p. 1C.

11. Peter Rummell, address to company stockholders, St. Joe Company annual meeting, Jacksonville, Fla., May 9, 2000.

12. Interview with Tim Edmond, May 25, 2000.

13. Bill Varian, "Shaping the Landscape: St. Joe's CEO Peers into Future of Leon County," *Tallahassee Democrat,* April 6, 1998, sec. A.

14. Interview with Tim Edmond, May 25, 2000.

15. Interview with John Hendry, Arvida project manager, Port St. Joe, Fla., May 10, 2001.

16. Kunstler, *Geography of Nowhere.*

17. Interview with James Howard Kunstler, Tallahassee, Fla., May 15, 2000.

18. Interview with Peter Rummell, Jacksonville, Fla., August 16, 2000.

19. Ibid.

20. Denise Etheridge, "Researcher Says South Walton Should Develop Its Own Identity," *Walton Sun,* Oct. 16, 1999.

21. St. Joe Company, SEC Filing, 8-K, May 18, 2000, p. 17.

22. St. Joe Company, 1999 Annual Report, p. 20.

23. Interview with Marianne Berrigan, WaterColor, May 17, 2000.

24. St. Joe Company, SEC Filing, 10-K, 2000, p. 23.

25. Interview with Barbara Weidrich, Walton County resident, September 28, 1999.

26. Telephone interview with Beth Folta, August 28, 2000.

27. Ibid.

28. "Arvida Begins Watersound Resort at Camp Creek Lake," *Beach Breeze/DeFuniak Herald,* August 3, 2000, p. 1-A.

29. Telephone interview with Dale Hartzog, Bay County Property Appraiser's office, September 26, 2001.

30. Conversation with Jerry Ray, August 16, 2000.

31. Matt Moore, "'Pier Park' Development Could Be Beach's Future," *Panama City News Herald,* March 25, 1999, p. 1-A.

32. Interview with Mel Leonard, planner, Panama City Beach, Fla., June 9, 2000.

33. Newscast by Lindsey Spear, April 20, WMBB, Panama City, Fla.

34. Telephone interview with Frances Wittkopf, Lynn Haven city commissioner, November 26, 2001.

35. Telephone interview with John Lynch, Lynn Haven city manager, November 27, 2001.

36. Telephone interview with Don Butler, Gulf County administrator, June 30, 2000.

37. Willie Ramsey, "WindMark Beach," editorial, *Star,* August 16, 2001, p. 2.

38. Crane, "State's Largest Land Company Targets Panhandle," p. 8A.

39. Telephone interview with Mark Curenton, assistant Franklin County planner, August 23, 2001.

40. Bruce Ritchie, "Arvida gets OK, Minus Marina," *Tallahassee Democrat,* March 20, 2002, p. 1A.

41. Julie Hauserman, "Landowner Seeks to Alter Development Rules," *St. Petersburg Times,* May 3, 2001, p. 5B.

42. Julie Hauserman, "Advisor's Job Sparks Talk of Conflict of Interest," *St. Petersburg Times,* May 4, 2001, p. 1B.

43. Ibid.

44. Telephone interview with Cheryl Sanders, Franklin County commissioner, February 11, 2003.

45. Bechtel Infrastructure Corporation, *Feasibility Study,* p. 103.

46. The Affordable Housing Study Commission Final Report, State of Florida, 2001, Appendix 2.

47. Susan Caswell, East Central Florida Regional Planning Council, to June Wiaz, e-mail, June 8, 2001.

48. Georgianne Ratliff, Vice President, Director of Planning, Wilson Miller consultants, to Michael Parker, Housing Administrator, City of Tallahassee, October 20, 1998.

49. David L. Powell, Attorney with Hopping, Green, Sams, and Smith, to J. Thomas Beck, Chief, Bureau of Local Planning, Department of Community Affairs, February 4, 1999.

50. Interview with Michael Parker, housing director, City of Tallahassee, April 28, 2000.

51. Susan Caswell to June Wiaz, e-mail, June 7, 2001.

52. "Growth Management Wrap-Up," 1000 Friends of Florida, 2001 legislative summary, updated May 21, 2001.

53. Conversation with Georgianne Ratliff, SouthWood groundbreaking ceremony, Tallahassee, Fla., September 18, 2000.

54. Interview with Michael Parker, April 28, 2000.

55. Telephone interview with Nathan Peters, Gulf County commissioner, August 16, 2001.

56. Videotape recording of Gulf County Board of County Commissioners meeting, September 24, 2002.

57. Telephone interview with Beth Folta, August 28, 2000.

58. Interview with Ken Borick, attorney with St. Joe/Arvida, WaterColor, October 2001.

59. Telephone interview with Don Curenton, Walton County realtor and affordable housing advocate, July 2001.

60. Interview with Lee Perry, builder, October 2001.

61. Telephone interview with Jaimie Ross, attorney, 1000 Friends of Florida, August 23, 2001.

62. Telephone interview with Don Curenton, July 2001.

63. Robert Sargent Jr., Famsey Campbell, and Jim Leusner, "It Takes a Village to Raise a Fortune: Across Florida, People Are Coming Home to Little Tax Districts Set Up by and for Developers Who Wrote Their Own Law," *Orlando Sentinel,* October 15, 2000, p. A1.

64. Interview with Tim Edmond, May 25, 2000.

65. Interview with Mel Leonard, June 9, 2000.

66. Kevin Porter, "Judge Rejects Pier Park Bonds," *Panama City News Herald,* December 8, 2001, p. A1.

67. Kevin Porter, "With Bonds to Be Issued, St. Joe Plans Pier Park Groundbreaking," *Panama City News Herald,* February 22, 2002.

68. St. Joe Company, SEC Filing, 10-K, May 1999, p. 10.

69. Telephone interview with Terrell Arline, attorney with 1000 Friends of Florida, April 6, 2000.

Chapter 11. Breaking Ground: SouthWood as a Case Study

Epigraph source: Quoted in Varian, "Growth Plan," p. 1A.

1. St. Joe Company News, press release, April 17, 2001.

2. Interview with Peter Rummell, August 16, 2000.

3. Remarks of Timothy Edmond, president, St. Joe/Arvida Capital Region, at SouthWood groundbreaking ceremony, September 19, 2000.

4. Telephone interview with Jerry Ray, April 3, 2000.

5. Jerry Ray, "St. Joe Is Preserving the Best While Building the Future," *Tallahassee Democrat,* September 24, 2002, p. 7A.

6. Telephone interview with Henree Martin, Tallahassee Chamber of Commerce, September 2001.

7. Interview with Timothy Edmond, May 25, 2000.

8. SouthWood Covenants and Restrictions, prepared by of Hyatt and Stubblefield, P.C., Atlanta.

9. Frantz and Collins, *Celebration, U.S.A.,* p. 93.

10. Interview with Timothy Edmond, May 25, 2000.

11. Ibid.

12. Interview with Diana Swegman, Tallahassee, Fla., September 22, 2001.

13. Telephone interview with Dan Penton, archeologist with Post, Buckley, Shuh and Jernigan, June 2000.

14. Telephone interview with Karen Mettler, St. Joe/Arvida, June 2000.

15. Southwood Development of Regional Impact, Draft Regional Report and Recommendations, January 8, 1999, p. 9, Apalachee Regional Planning Council; Rick McCann, Biologist with the Florida Game and Fresh Water Fish Commission, to Bob Cambric, Apalachee Regional Planning Council, July 24, 1998.

16. Telephone interview with Rick McCann, biologist, Florida Fish and Wildlife Conservation Commission, March 8, 2002.

17. Telephone interview with Susan Tanski, biologist with the City of Tallahassee, June 2000.

18. Remarks of Timothy Edmond, September 19, 2000.

19. Remarks of Jim Motta, president, Arvida, at SouthWood groundbreaking, September 19, 2000.

20. Bruce Ritchie, "Arvida Withdraws Variance Request," *Tallahassee Democrat*, February 23, 2000, p. 1A.

21. Interview with Tim Edmond, May 25, 2000.

22. Interviews with Glenn Thomas, director/CEO of Florida State University's Laboratory School, April 2000, September 2001; Bill Varian, "Is Proposed Community Answer for South Side?" *Tallahassee Democrat*, Monday, April 26, 1999, p. 1A.

23. Kent Fischer, "Public School, Inc.," *St. Petersburg Times*, September 15, 2002, p. 1A.

24. Telephone interview with Glenn Thomas, April 2000.

25. Interview with Talbot "Sandy" D'Alemberte, President, Florida State University, Tallahassee, May 1, 2001.

26. Glenn Thomas, "Progressive Design, Curriculum Planned for New Florida High," *Tallahassee Democrat*, Monday, November 13, 2000, p. 9A.

27. Dorothy Inman-Crews, "Radical Changes for Florida High Should Be Examined," *Tallahassee Democrat*, Sunday, October 29, 2000, p. 3E.

28. Telephone interview with Glenn Thomas, September 25, 2001.

29. Interview with Georgianne Ratliff, SouthWood Open House, September 22, 2001.

30. Interview with Tim Edmond, May 25, 2000.

31. Tim Edmond, radio interview, *Perspectives*, WFSU, May 27, 1999.

32. Telephone interview with Dorothy Inman-Crews, April 2000.

33. Comments of Charles Pattison, executive director, 1000 Friends of Florida at Leon County/City of Tallahassee joint commission meeting, April 28, 1999.

34. Comments of Robert Rackleff, Leon County commissioner, at Leon County/City of Tallahassee joint commission meeting, April 28, 1999.

35. Comments of Mayor Scott Maddox, Leon County/City of Tallahassee joint commission meeting, April 28, 1999.

36. Bill Varian, "SouthWood Gets the Green Light," *Tallahassee Democrat*, April 29, 1999, p. 1A.

37. Bill Varian, "Southwood Hits a Major Roadblock to Development," *Tallahassee Democrat*, January 19, 1999, p. 1A.

38. Larry Peterson, "Finding a Way to Make Traffic Disappear," *Tallahassee Democrat*, May 27, 2000, p. 1E.

39. Interview with Tim Edmond, May 25, 2002.

40. Tim McPherson, Commuter Services of North Florida, to Dwight Arnold, City of Tallahassee Growth Management, February 15, 1999.

41. Wiatt Bowers, Post Buckley Shuh and Jernigan, to Southwood DRI Transportation Review Agencies, memo and attachments, March 9, 1999, Re: Proposed Transportation Mitigation.

42. Telephone interview with Wendy Grey, director of the Tallahassee–Leon County Planning Department, June 2000.

43. Comments of Debbie Lightsey, May 15–16, 2000.

44. Ibid.

45. Interview with Tim Edmond, May 25, 2000.

Chapter 12. A Company Town in Flux

Epigraph source: Quotation from authors' interview with John Hendry, Port St. Joe, Fla., February 8, 2001.

1. Telephone interview with Rocky Comfort, May 4, 2000.

2. Interview with Frank Pate, June 5, 2000.

3. Interview with Ferrel Allen, July 25, 2000.

4. L. L. "Duke" Jones, "Mill Workers Got Caught in the Crosshairs," *News Herald,* May 1, 2000, p. 1A.

5. Chronology of Activities and Rapid Response Services, Florida Coast Paper Company, Division of Jobs and Benefits Workforce Program Support, Florida Department of Labor and Employment Security, updated March 5, 2000.

6. Telephone interview with L. L. "Duke" Jones, April 24, 2001.

7. Amy Roe, "Idled Workers File Class Action," *Panama City News Herald,* February 16, 1999.

8. St. Joe Company, 1997 Annual Report, p. 25.

9. James E. Dacy, Director of Labor Relations for Smurfit-Stone, to Glenn Goss, Vice President and Regional Director for Region IX of the Paper, Allied Industrial, Chemical and Energy Worker's International Union, Indianapolis, Ind., March 28, 2000.

10. Telephone interview with L. L. "Duke" Jones, April 24, 2001.

11. Tim Croft, "Gulf County Held Hostage over Paper Mill," *Panama City News Herald,* May 8, 2000, p. 1B.

12. Ibid.

13. Interview with Ferrel Allen, July 25, 2000.

14. "Smurfit-Stone Announces Completion of Florida Coast Paper Company, L.L.C. Bankruptcy Reorganization," news release by the Smurfit-Stone Corporation, Chicago, January 20, 2000.

15. Matt Moore, "Motion Filed to Move Mill Bankruptcy Hearing," *Panama City News Herald,* June 11, 1999, p. 1A.

16. Telephone interview with Steve Hamilton, regional environmental services manager, Smurfit-Stone Corporation, May 11, 2001.

17. Jane Tanner, "When the Jobs Just Disappeared," *BusinessWeek* (international edition), July 12, 1999.

18. Amy Roe, "Mill Workers Get the Word and It's Bad," January 16, 2000, www.newsherald.com.

19. Telephone interview with Marshall Nelson, May 1, 2000.

20. Interview with Ferrel Allen, July 25, 2000.

21. Interview with Clay Smallwood, February 8, 2001.

22. Ibid.

23. Interview with Peter Rummell, August 16, 2000.

24. Telephone interview with John Alden, Office of General Counsel, DEP, November 1999.

25. Telephone interview with Tom Beason, Office of General Counsel, DEP, November 1999.

26. Kevin Beswick, Reg. 4, EPA, to Frank Ney, Reg. 4, EPA, e-mail, October 25, 1999.

27. Telephone interview with Steve Hamilton, May 11, 2001.

28. Michael A. Palazzolo, Winton E. Kelly, and Donna Holder, "National Dioxin Study Tier 49—Combustion Sources," Radian Corporation for U.S. EPA, April 1987.

29. Smith, *U.S. Paper Industry,* p. 3.

30. Ibid., p. 43.

31. Ibid., p. 140.

32. St. Joe Company, 1998 Annual Report, p. 73.

33. Ibid.

34. *Marion S. Hough v. John Doe, etc. et al.,* June 9, 1999, Case Number 99-156, Circuit Court of the Fourteenth Judicial Circuit, Gulf County Florida, "Motion to Dismiss or for More Definite Statement," McGuire Woods Battle and Boothe LLP.

35. Motion to Quash Service of Process and to Dismiss Complaint, Case No. 99-156 (*Marion S. Hough, Plaintiff, vs. John doe, etc., et al., Defendants*) Circuit Court of the Fourteenth Judicial Circuit in and for Gulf County, Florida.

36. Interview with Ferrel Allen, July 25, 2000.

37. Telephone interview with Robert Nedley, April 9, 2001.

38. Telephone interview with Marshall Nelson, May 1, 2000; telephone interview with Mark Lamberson, former mill worker, September 4, 2001.

39. Interview with Ferrel Allen, July 25, 2000.

40. Telephone interview with Mark Lamberson, September 4, 2001.

41. "Summary of Conversations with Former Employees of the St. Joe Paper Mill," December 11, 2001, Superfund Site Screening Section, Florida DEP.

42. Ibid.

43. Telephone interview with Mark Gay, May 21, 2001.

44. Ed O'Connell, Inspector, Department of Environmental Regulation, Pensacola District Office, to Bill Kellenberger et al., handwritten memorandum, n.d. but filed with other 1991 correspondence.

45. "Contamination Assessment Report," prepared for St. Joe Products, Company, GTI, August 10, 1993, hazardous waste files of Pensacola DEP.

46. J. L. "Larry" McArdle, Plant Manager, Port St. Joe Industrial Wastewater Treatment Plant, to Douglas K. Lankford, U.S. EPA Region 4 (Atlanta), July 27, 1998.

47. Telephone interview with Marshall Hyatt, U.S. EPA Region 4 (Atlanta), December 1999.

48. William Rish of Rish, Gibson and Scholz, P.A., on behalf of the city of Port St. Joe, to William E. Schaal, Florida, DEP Pensacola, June 1, 2000.

49. Steven Kelly, Panama City Field Office of DEP, to Ms. "Wells," interoffice memorandum, June 23, 2000, "Subject: Port St. Joe WWTF (Wastewater Treatment Facility)."

50. NPDES Appeal Nos. 94-8 and 94-9, In re: City of Port St. Joe and Florida Coast Paper Company, Permit No. FL0020206, Environmental Appeals Board, U.S. EPA, Washington, D.C., July 30, 1997, p. 50.

51. Vic Keisker to Steve Kelly, Panama City Field Office, Florida DEP, internal memorandum, August 15, 2000.

52. Barbara Ruth, Northwest District Office of DEP, to "Greg/Gary" of the Panama City Field Office of DEP, interoffice memorandum, Re: Gulf County/Environment and Pollutants, August 21, 2000.

53. Telephone interview with Ferrel Allen, August 23, 2000.

54. William J. Rish, Attorney, to William A. Evans, Industrial Waste Permitting Section Supervisor, Northwest District DEP, Pensacola, Fla., June 1, 2000.

55. "Sector Notebook Project: Pulp and Paper Industry," U.S. EPA, September 1995, p. 41.

56. Manley Fuller, Florida Wildlife Federation, to DEP Secretary David Struhs, September 30, 1999.

57. Interview with Clay Smallwood, February 8, 2001.

58. Smurfit-Stone Request for Proposal (revised), Steve Hamilton, dated September 21, 2000, supplied to Panama City Branch Office of DEP, October 16, 2000.

59. Barbara Ruth, Pensacola DEP, to Marion Hough, e-mail, Re: Can I get request help/ Re:Papermill [sic], September 25, 2000.

60. "Mill's Final Plans Told, Environmental Issues and Demolition Plans Taking Shape," Star, November 23, 2000, p. 1A.

61. Telephone interview with Steve Hamilton, May 11, 2000.

62. "CERCLA Site Discovery/Prescreening Evaluation," Florida DEP, Sept. 26, 2000.

63. Terry Cole, Attorney for Stone Container Corporation, to John Ruddell, Director, Division of Waste Management, DEP, December 20, 2000.

64. William D. Preston, Attorney for St. Joe, to John Ruddell, Director, Division of Waste Management, DEP, January 3, 2001.

65. Kirby Green III, Deputy Director, DEP, to Mr. Stanley Meiburg, Acting Regional Administrator, EPA, April 4, 2001.

66. Craig Pittman, "Lesson of Millview Is Learned Decades Later," St. Petersburg Times, April 21, 2002, p. 12A.

67. "Port St. Joe Paper Mill: Draft Sampling and Analysis Report," December 2001, Malcolm Pirnie, Inc., Tampa, Fla.

68. "Mill Tests Look Good: Early Data Indicates Superfund Designation Very Unlikely," Star, Thursday, December 13, 2001, p. 1A.

69. "Groundwater Analytical Results (PCDD/PCDF), Former Surface Water Impoundment, Port St. Joe Paper Mill," October 2001, date submitted to Bureau of Waste Cleanup, DEP, by St. Joe's Consultants, Professional Service Industries, Inc., Tampa, Fla.

70. "Sampling Analysis Report for Former Wastewater Impoundment," Port St. Joe Paper Mill, prepared for William D. Preston, Tallahassee, by Professional Service Industries, Inc., Tampa, January 16, 2002.

71. A. James McCarthy Jr., "[Draft] Preliminary Assessment, St. Joe Forest Products, AKA St. Joe Paper Plant, Gulf County Florida," Florida DEP, Division of Waste Management, November 30, 2000.

72. Interview with Linda Young, Florida director, Clean Water Network, Tallahassee, November 10, 1999.

73. Interview with Bobby Cooley, DEP district director, Pensacola, Fla., March 3, 2000.

74. Interview with Peter Rummell, August 16, 2000.

75. "Age-Adjusted Death Rate for Cancer, Florida 1996–98," Florida Department of Health (based on Year 2000 standard population).

76. "Age-Adjusted Death Rate for Chronic Liver Disease and Cirrhosis, Florida 1996–98," and "Age-Adjusted Death Rate for Stroke, Florida 1996–98," Florida Department of Health.

77. Smith, U.S. Paper Industry, p. 3.

78. Title V (air) permit application for the Florida Coast Paper facility, Port St. Joe, Fla., received by DEP Pensacola, June 17, 1999.

79. Environmental Defense Scorecard, Hazardous Air Pollutants, www.scorecard.org/ranking/rank-facilities.tcl.

80. Data from the Florida Department of Health, in Ursula Bauer, chronic disease epidemiologist, Florida Department of Health, to authors, e-mail, April 5, 2000.

81. Interview with Douglas Kent, Gulf County Health Commissioner, Port St. Joe, Fla., June 5, 2000.

82. Telephone interview with Barbara Oksanen, medical office manager, May 2001.

83. Kendall Middlemas, "Former St. Joe Mill Dump Site Feared a Hazard," February 17, 2002, www.newsherald.com.

84. Telephone interview with Tracy Moye, attorney, November 2001.

85. R. E. Nedley, Vice President, St. Joe Forest Products Company, to M. E. Lehman, President, Alvarez, Lehman and Associates, Inc., Re: ANRR Site, November 15, 1989.

86. Internal handwritten memo apparently from Mel Lehman (unclear signature) to "RSD" (Roy S. DeLotelle), Alvarez, Lehman and Associates, Inc., November 21, 1989.

87. Bruce Ritchie, "Residents Fear Hazard Cover-up," *Tallahassee Democrat,* May 20, 2001, p. 1A.

88. Ibid.

89. *Health Consultation: Mill View Subdivision, Port St. Joe, Gulf County Florida,* October 31, 2001, prepared by the Florida Department of Health, Bureau of Environmental Epidemiology, pp. 5–6.

90. Telephone interview with Tracy Moye, November 2001.

91. Theo Colburn, Dianne Dumanoski, and John Peterson Myers, "Hormone Imposters," *Sierra,* January/February 1997, p. 34.

92. Sean McElheny, "EPA Releases Risk Estimates for Eating Dioxin-Contaminated Fish," EPA press release, September 24, 1990.

93. *An Assessment of Exposure to Dioxin from Consumption of Fish Caught in Freshwaters of the United States Impacted by Bleached Chemical Pulp Mills,* Technical Bulletin No. 620, National Council of the Paper Industry for Air and Stream Improvement, Inc., December 1991, p. A-9.

94. EPA–City of Port St. Joe Cooperative Dioxin Sampling Project, Port St. Joe, Fla., EPA, Athens, Ga., September 1996.

95. Michael S. Brim, Diane H. Bateman, and Robert B. Jarvis, *Environmental Contaminants Evaluation of St. Joseph Bay, Florida,* U.S. Fish and Wildlife Service, 2000, Panama City, Fla., p. 58, Publication No. PCFO-EC 00-01, pp. 54–58.

96. Ibid., p. 25.

97. Telephone interview with Johnny Linton, former mayor of Port St. Joe, April 2001.

98. Interview with Susan Anderson, former employee with the Florida Department of Community Affairs, Tallahassee, October 1999.

99. Interview with Billy Howell, September 9, 2000.

100. Interview with Frank Pate, June 5, 2000.

101. Eric Buckelew, Florida DEP, Pensacola District Office, memo to the file, November 10, 1998, "Subject: Port St. Joe Marina."

102. William J. Kennedy, Project Manager, Preble-Rish, to Eric Buckelew, Florida DEP, Pensacola District Office, Re: Port St. Joe Marina Project, November 3, 1998.

103. Telephone interview with Andy Tintle, DEP Laboratory Certification Program, July 2, 2001.

104. Douglas M. Kent, Environmental Manager, to Mayor Frank Pate, Re: Hess Oil Terminal, June 3, 1996.

105. Interview with Paula Pendarvis, city manager, Port St. Joe, June 5, 2000.

106. Ibid.

107. "St. Joe's Vision for Gulf," *Star,* January 18, 2001, p. 1A.

108. Kevin Begos, "St. Joe Sets Sail for New Horizon," *Panama City News Herald,* July 25, 1999, p. 1A.

109. Alex Finkelstein, "Spending New Dollars," *Florida Trend's Business Florida,* 2001, pp. 34–36.

110. Telephone interview with Robert Nedley, April 9, 2001.

111. Mark Kawar, "St. Joe to Level Closed Mill," *Panama City News Herald,* April 10, 2002, p. 1A.

112. Telephone interview with Jerry Ray, February 26, 2002.

113. "Port St. Joe Moves Forward on Brownfield," *Star,* January 16, 2003, p. 1A.

114. Steve Hamilton to June Wiaz, e-mail, April 11, 2002.

115. Tommy Pitts, Port Director, to June Wiaz, voice mail message, April 16, 2002.

116. "Port Strategies Hold Deep Promise," *Star,* February 1, 2001, p. 1A.

117. Interview with Robert Nedley, May 10, 2001 (workshop on port revitalization).

118. Port of Port St. Joe Master Plan, prepared by URS and Foster Wheeler, March 2002.

119. Port St. Joe Paper Mill Voluntary Investigation Plan, Malcolm Pirnie, Inc., Tampa, Fla., September 2001.

Chapter 13. The Wish List

Epigraph source: Quotation from Tim Croft, "Flight Moves: Relocation on Very Fast Track," *Panama City News Herald,* March 20, 2000.

1. "The Honorable John E. and Columba Bush Statement of Financial Condition at Current Values and Amounts," prepared by Gerson, Preston and Company, P.A., on file with the Florida Department of State, Division of Elections, December 31, 2000.

2. Brian E. Crowley, "Gore-Lieberman Visit Kicks Off the Start of Rapidly Growing State Campaigns," Cox News Service, August 23, 2000.

3. Dara Kam, "Florida Council of 100 Blurs Business, Political Lines," *Florida Today,* www.floridatoday.com, December 22, 2001, p. A01.

4. St. Joe Company, SEC Filing, 8-K, May 18, 2000, p. 51.

5. Fraser Sherman, "Regional Self-promotion Won't Transform Economy Overnight," *Destin Log,* October 28, 2000.

6. Staff and wire report, "Panhandle Looks for Business Overseas," *Panama City News Herald,* March 26, 2001.

7. Presentation by Dan Rogers of Rogers Consulting Group, Austin, Texas, to the Energy 2020 Study Commission, July 24, 2001, Tampa, Fla.; St. Joe Company News, press release, April 17, 2001.

8. Remarks by Neal Wade to Bay County League of Women Voters, Panama City, Fla., May 23, 2001.

9. Enterprise Florida, "Site Selection Factors: Area Development 2000 Corporate Survey," from *Area Development Magazine,* December 2000.

10. Kendall Middlemas, "Forces Teamed Up to Lure Co. to Area," *Panama City News Herald,* April 20, 2001.

11. "Enterprise Zone in Gulf Has Expanded," *Star,* January 31, 2002, p. 1B.

12. Executive Order 99-275, state of Florida.

13. Enterprise Florida, "Announced Projects with Incentive Profile by County," current as of May 24, 2001.

14. "Announced Projects with Incentive Profile by County, Enterprise Florida, Inc.," EFI web site, current as of May 24, 2001; telephone interview with Clay Smallwood, October 25, 2001.

15. Interview with Clay Smallwood, February 8, 2001.

16. County Statistics, April 15, 2001, web site of Florida's Great Northwest, www.floridasgreatnorthwest.com.

17. Enterprise Florida, "Announced Projects with Incentive Profile by County," current as of May 24, 2001.

18. St. Joe Company News, press release, April 17, 2001, www.joe.com; "Port Gets $2 Million," *Star,* March 29, 2001, p. 1A.

19. Telephone interview with John Ray, legislative director, Enterprise Florida, May 2000.

20. Richard Williams, Executive Director, Opportunity Florida, to Kathryn Ziewitz, e-mail, January 28, 2002.

21. Remarks by Neal Wade to Apalachicola Chamber of Commerce, Apalachicola, Fla., June 7, 2000.

22. Interview with Jerry Ray, Jacksonville, Fla., May 9, 2000.

23. Telephone interview with Herbert H. Peyton, president of Gate Petroleum and St. Joe board director, May 2001.

24. Kendall Middlemas, "County Fares Well in Transportation Initiative," *Panama City News Herald,* January 14, 2000, p. 1A.

25. Florida Department of Transportation, *Mobility 2000: Building Roads for the 21st Century, Florida Intrastate Highway System 2000 through 2010,* January 2000.

26. Tim Croft, Freedom Capitol Bureau, title missing from web archives (story #260), *Panama City News Herald,* April 16, 1999, www.newsherald.com.

27. Telephone interview with Rep. Allan Bense (R-Panama City), April 1, 2002.

28. Steve Bornhoft, "We Are, All of Us, Stewards of the Land," *Panama City News Herald,* September 12, 1999, p. 1F.

29. Todd Twilley, "St. Joe Could Make Choice as Easy as A-B-C," *Panama City News Herald,* December 12, 2000, p. 1A.

30. Transportation Outreach Program web site, August 25, 2001, www11.myflorida.com/seaport/top.htm.

31. Florida Department of Transportation, *Year 2001 Transportation Outreach Program Project Recommendation by TOP Council,* January 8, 2001.

32. Nancy Cook Lauer, "Road Projects Take Off," *Tallahassee Democrat,* November 29, 2001, p. 1B.

33. Remarks by Neal Wade to Bay County League of Women Voters, May 23, 2001.

34. Cover letter accompanying Transportation Outreach Program application from Richard T. Roberts, executive director, Opportunity Florida, to Lorenzo Alexander, Seaport Office, Florida Department of Transportation, November 8, 2000.

35. Interview with Jerry Ray, May 9, 2000.

36. Remarks by John Pollack, PBS&J, public meeting, Port. St. Joe, Fla., December 13, 2001

37. Telephone interview with Sally Malone, Gulf County resident, November 3, 2001.

38. Draft Right-of-Way Exchange Agreement, DOT District Office of General Counsel, Chipley, Fla., September 18, 2000.

39. Telephone interview with Sally Malone, November 28, 2001.

40. Transportation Outreach Program 2002, Project Application Executive Summary Form for the Gulf to Bay Parkway, Opportunity Florida, November 2000.

41. "Hwy. 98 Realignment—Q&A on Issues," *Star,* November 29, 2001, p. 1A; telephone interview with Rich Brenner, retired insurance executive and Gulf County citizen, January 17, 2002.

42. Remarks of Sally Malone, public meeting, Port St. Joe, Fla., December 13, 2001.

43. Mark Kawar, "Gulf Backing U.S. 98 Shift," *Panama City News Herald,* January 10, 2002, p. 1A.

44. Clay Smallwood to the Gulf County Board of County Commissioners, letter and attachments, January 8, 2002.

45. Ibid.; Resolution, Board of County Commissioners, Gulf County, Fla., January 8, 2002.

46. Telephone interview with Billy Traylor, Gulf County commissioner, January 31, 2001.

47. Ibid.

48. Telephone interview with Richard Brenner, January 17, 2002.

49. Remarks of Richard Brenner at Board of County Commissioners meeting, January 8, 2002.

50. Telephone interview with Richard Brenner, January 17, 2002.

51. Wayne Childers, "Nostalgic for the Soviet Union? Move to Gulf County," *Franklin Chronicle* 10.17 (August 21–September 6, 2001): p. 3.

52. Remarks of John Pollard, PBS&J, public meeting on Hwy. 98 issue, Port St. Joe, Fla., December 13, 2001.

53. Bradley J. Hartman, Director, Office of Environmental Services, Florida Fish and Wildlife Conservation Commission, to Cherie Trainor, DCA, October 4, 1999.

54. Ibid.

55. Begos, "St. Joe Sets Sail," p. 1A.

56. Remarks by Neal Wade to League of Women Voters, Panama City, Fla., May 23, 2001.

57. Telephone interview with Tim Kitts, Bay Haven Charter School principal, September 21, 2001.

58. Interview with Talbot "Sandy" D'Alemberte, May 1, 2001.

59. Bechtel Infrastructure Corporation, *Feasibility Study,* p. 97.

60. PBS&J, First Annual Development of Regional Impact Report, prepared for Arvida, December 1, 2000, p. 31.

61. Interview with Tim Edmond, May 25, 2000.

62. Catherine McNaught, "Proposed Wastewater Plant Awaits Bottom Line," *Tallahassee Democrat,* October 12, 1999, p. 3A.

63. "Deed Received for Fresh Water Canal's Purchase," *Star,* September 6, 2001, p. 1A.

64. Notice of Proposed Agency Action, Individual Water Use Permit Application No. 1 05911, Northwest Florida Water Management District, December 29, 2000.

65. Karen Spencer, "Bay in Trouble, Water Expert Says," *Destin Log,* July 1, 1991.

66. Bay, Gulf, and Franklin Counties Community Health Task Force, Inc., *Community Health Needs Assessment*, prepared by the Big Bend Health Council, Panama City, Fla., 1998, pp. 330, 334.

67. Telephone interview with Mark Curenton, August 23, 2001.

68. Telephone interview with Ray Bye, president of research, FSU, July 2000.

69. Franklin County Property Appraiser's Office, Apalachicola, Fla.

70. Telephone interview with Frank Shaw Jr., August 2001.

71. Windy Twilley, "Summer Camps OK'd for Next Step," *Panama City News Herald*, Jan. 22, 2003.

72. Interview with Talbot "Sandy" D'Alemberte, May 1, 2001.

73. Bruce Ritchie, "Compromise Leaves Franklin County Untouched," *Tallahassee Democrat*, March 26, 2002, p. B1.

74. Telephone interview with Rep. Will Kendrick (D-Carrabelle), April 11, 2002.

75. Ibid.

76. Ibid.

77. Windy Twilley, "Summer Camps OK'd."

78. Remarks of Anne Rudloe, Franklin County Commission meeting, January 21, 2003.

Chapter 14. An Airport Taxis for Takeoff

Epigraph source: Quotation from Panama City–Bay County Airport Authority Transportation Outreach Program 2001 Proposal, November 2000, p. 3.

1. Interview with Randy Curtis, Panama City–Bay County airport manager, Panama City, Fla., April 12, 2001.

2. Ibid.

3. Remarks by Rep. Allan Bense, Panama City–Bay County Airport Authority meeting, Panama City, Fla., July 11, 2000.

4. Interview with Randy Curtis, April 12, 2001.

5. Telephone interview with Howard Menaker, manager, Public Affairs, Bechtel Infrastructure, September 2001.

6. Presentation by Bechtel Infrastructure, Panama City–Bay County Airport Authority meeting, Panama City, Fla., July 11, 2000.

7. Don Hodges, "One Citizen's Commentary on the Airport Relocation Feasibility Study," independent analysis on file with Bay County Public Library, November 16, 2000, p. 11.

8. Ibid., p. 2

9. St. Joe Company News, press release, April 17, 2001, www.joe.com.

10. Peter S. Rummell, CEO, St. Joe Company, to Donald Crisp, Chairman, Panama City–Bay County Airport Authority, November 17, 1999.

11. St. Joe Company, SEC Filing, 8-K, May 18, 2000, p. 40.

12. Bechtel Infrastructure Corporation, *Feasibility Study*, pp. 101–2.

13. Paul Swider, "Lobbyists: Pork Can Be Disguised," *Panama City News Herald*, October 25, 1997.

14. St. Joe Company, SEC Filing, 8-K, May 18, 2000, p. 52.

15. Standard and Poors, fact sheet, St. Joe Company, January 12, 2001.

16. Remarks by Danny Sparks, Bay County commissioner, Bay County Commission meeting, July 10, 2001.

17. Remarks by Bechtel Infrastructure Corporation spokesman, Panama City–Bay County Airport Authority meeting, Panama City, Fla., July 11, 2000.

18. "The St. Joe Company (NYSE:JOE) Reports Full Year Net EBITDA of $1.92 per Share, or $1.66 per Share Excluding Conservation Land Gains," St. Joe Earnings Report, February 6, 2002, p. 6.

19. Tim Croft, "New Airport: Numbers Have to Take Off First," *Panama City News Herald,* September 24, 2000.

20. Interview with Randy Curtis, April 12, 2001.

21. Panama City–Bay County International Airport, Transportation Outreach Program 2001 Proposal, p. 3.

22. Telephone interview with Wade Taylor, Lee County Economic Development Office, September 2001.

23. Telephone interview with Mike Ropa, Bay County commissioner, April 20, 2001.

24. Cox et al., *Closing the Gaps,* p. 185.

25. Cat Lazaroff, "Bush Orders Streamlined Transportation Project Reviews," Environmental News Service, 9-19-02, http:ens.news.com/ens/sep2002-09-19-06.asp.

26. Ibid.

27. Panama City–Bay County International Airport news release, April 17, 2001.

28. Remarks by John R. Middlemas, Bay County Planning Board meeting, Panama City, Fla., January 28, 2002.

Chapter 15. St. Joe and the Growth Machine

Epigraph source: Quoted in "Who Is St. Joe?" *Tallahassee,* January/February 2002, p. 39.

1. Frantz, "Florida's Largest Landholder."

2. Harvey Molotch, "The Political Economy of Growth Machines," *Journal of Urban Affairs* 15.1 (1993).

3. Telephone interview with Rep. Beverly Kilmer (R-Quincy), September 2001.

4. Interview with Peter Rummell, August 16, 2000.

5. Steve Bousquet, "Business Gets Bipartisan Support from Legislature," *Miami Herald,* July 9, 2000, sec. B.

6. Kam, "Florida Council of 100."

7. Jessica Cary, Enterprise Florida, Inc., to June Wiaz, e-mail, May 24, 2001.

8. Diane Rado, "Its Eyes, Hands on State Tax Dollars," *St. Petersburg Times Online,* August 20, 2000, www.sptimes.com; "Watchdog's Credibility at Risk," editorial, *St. Petersburg Times Online,* August 6, 2000, www.sptimes.com.

9. "Government Appointment: St. Joe Liaison," *Florida Trend,* February 2001, p. 38.

10. Bill Cotterell, "Controversial New Head at DMS," *Tallahassee Democrat,* September 6, 2000, p. 1B.

11. Michelle Pellemans and Margaret Talev, "Gift Case Tests Policy," *Tampa Tribune,* May 9, 1999, Florida/Metro, p. 1.

12. Tom Webb, "Sweet Deals Prove Costly for Bush," September 22, 1990, *Tampa Tribune,* p. 6A.

13. Pellemans and Talev, "Gift Case," p. 1.

14. Remarks by Charles Gauthier, State Department of Community Affairs, sector plan preliminary meeting, Chipley, Fla., April 27, 2001.

15. Interview with Tom Beck, division director, Department of Community Affairs, DCA office, Tallahassee, Fla., May 2000.

16. Kent Wetherell of Hopping, Green, Sams, and Smith (representing St. Joe Company), to Robert Cambric, Director, Apalachee Regional Planning Council, Blountstown, Fla., January 26, 1999.

17. Remarks by Secretary David Struhs, *Florida on the Line* radio program, WFSU, September 13, 2000.

18. Report of the Special Grand Jury on Air and Water Quality, First Judicial Circuit Court, Escambia County, June 10, 1999, p. 3.

19. Interview with Mel Leonard, June 9, 2000.

20. Interview with Linda Young, Tallahassee, Fla., November 10, 1999.

21. Interview with Bobby Cooley, Pensacola, Fla., March 3, 2000.

22. Ibid.

23. Escambia County Grand Jury report, office of assistant state attorney, Pensacola, Fla., June 1999, p. 83.

24. Florida Statutes 403.161, chapter 373.

25. James Burnett, Refuge Manager, St. Marks National Wildlife Refuge, to George Willson, Vice President for Conservation Lands, St. Joe Company, February 16, 2001.

26. Ibid.

27. Ibid.

28. Interview with Clay Smallwood, February 8, 2001.

29. Telephone interview with Randy Kautz, biologist, Florida Fish and Wildlife Conservation Commission, Oct. 21, 1999.

30. Col. Joe Miller, U.S. Army District Engineer, Jacksonville District Corps of Engineers, to Peter Rummell, CEO, St. Joe Company, January 25, 1999.

31. Remarks by Dave Tillis, St. Joe Company planning executive, pre-application conference for Pier Park Development of Regional Impact, Panama City Beach, Fla., March 15, 2000.

32. Telephone interview with Kevin Pope, director of Environmental Compliance, Leon County, August 1999.

33. Interview with Hildreth Cooper, Panama City, Fla., September 24, 1999.

34. Remarks by Billy Buzzett, December 7, 2001.

35. Interagency meeting on mitigating wetlands affected by Florida Department of Transportation.

36. Interview with Hildreth Cooper, September 24, 1999.

37. Craig Pittman, "Development vs. Environment Leads to Give and Take Meeting," *St. Petersburg Times,* April 21, 2002, p. 12A.

38. Telephone interview with Gary Knight, director, Florida Natural Areas Inventory program, December 21, 1999.

39. Remarks by Dave Tillis, March 15, 2000.

40. "Environmental Assessment for Issuance of an Incidental Take Permit under the Endangered Species Act," prepared by PBS&J for the St. Joe Company, finalized by U.S. Fish and Wildlife Service, Panama City Field Office, February 20, 2000, p. 12.

41. Cox et al., *Closing the Gaps,* p. 45.

42. Testimony of Thomas B. Evans Jr., before the U.S. House of Representatives, Com-

mittee on Resources, Subcommittee on Fisheries Conservation, Wildlife and Oceans, on H.R. 4070, May 11, 2000.

43. Telephone interview with Chris Schloesser, aide to Congressman Allen Boyd, May 11, 2000.

44. Coast Alliance of Washington D.C., "Facts on H.R. 4070," press release, May 11, 2000.

45. Remarks of Steve Seibert, secretary, Department of Community Affairs, Growth Management Regional Forum, Tallahassee, Fla., January 2000.

46. Carl Hiaasen, "Growth Management? What's That?" *Tallahassee Democrat,* November 6, 1999, p. 5A.

47. Steve Seibert to Jeb Bush, e-mail, November 1, 1999.

48. Associated Press, "Panel Tackles a Rewrite of Years-old Law," *Panama City News Herald,* July 17, 2000.

49. Charles Pattison, executive director, 1000 Friends, "Growth Report Is Seriously Flawed," *Tallahassee Democrat,* March 4, 2001, p. 3E.

50. "Gulf to Bay Highway in Portions of Gulf and Bay Counties: Year 2002 Transportation Outreach Program Application," August 2001, PBS&J, consultants to Opportunity Florida.

51. Rhodes, "Florida Growth Management," p. 13.

52. Hauserman, "Advisor's Job," p. 1B.

53. Remarks by Bob Cambric, State Department of Community Affairs, sector plan pre-scoping meeting, Chipley, Fla., April 27, 2001.

54. Telephone interview with Bob Cambric, Florida Department of Community Affairs, April 20, 2001.

55. Kristen Andersen, Planner, to Jonathan Mantay, Bay County Manager, and Terry Jernigan, Bay County Planning and Zoning Division Manager, memorandum, "Subject: Sector Plan Meeting," dated November 18, 1998.

56. Transportation Outreach Program 2001 Proposal, p. 15.

57. Bob Cambric, Florida Department of Community Affairs, to Planners in Bay County region, e-mail, April 19, 2001.

58. Interview with Cynthia Alexander, south Walton resident, Seagrove Beach, Fla., May 25, 2000.

59. "The Costliest Hurricanes in the United States, 1900–1996," National Hurricane Center, National Oceanic and Atmospheric Administration, www.nhc.noaa.gov/pastcost.html (September 24, 2001).

60. Kendall Middlemas, "County Planner Resigns," *Panama City News Herald,* December 15, 2000.

61. Telephone interview with Terry Jernigan, planning director, February 13, 2001.

62. Kendall Middlemas, "Sparks: Trip, Gifts Common Practice," *Panama City News Herald,* January 23, 1999.

63. Amended Presentment of Bay County Grand Jury, August 3, 2000.

64. Kendall Middlemas, "Letter Asks DEP to OK Exposed Pipe," *Panama City News Herald,* April 8, 2000.

65. Telephone interview with Daniel Meyer, general counsel, Public Employees for Environmental Responsibility, February 21, 2002.

66. Interview with John Hedrick, director of the Panhandle Citizens Coalition, Panama City, Fla., February 16, 2003.

67. Robert Rhodes, "Look to the Past to Manage Florida's Future Growth," editorial, *Tallahassee Democrat,* April 2, 2000, p. 3E.

68. "Silencing Opposition to Developers," editorial, *St. Petersburg Times Online,* February 13, 2002, www.sptimesonline.com.

69. Telephone interview with Rep. Allan Bense, April 1, 2002.

Chapter 16. The Two Bottom Lines: Profit and Quality of Life

Epigraph source: Fodor, *Better, Not Bigger,* p.141.

1. Telephone interview with Jerry Ray, July 2000.

2. Jane S. Shaw and Ronald. D. Utt, eds., *A Guide to Smart Growth: Shattering Myths, Providing Solutions* (Washington, D.C.: Heritage Foundation; Bozeman, Mont.: Political Economy Research Center, November 2000), p. 3.

3. Comments of Michael Busha, executive director, Treasure Coast Regional Planning Council at the Economic Development Workshop, sponsored by the Apalachee Regional Planning Council, DCA, and the Florida Sustainable Communities Network, Blountstown, Fla., April 26, 2000.

4. Meg Stevenson, "The Runaway Bride," *Defuniak Springs Herald Breeze,* March 1, 2001. p. 4-A.

5. Fodor, *Better, Not Bigger,* p. 13.

6. Ibid.

7. Springs Coast Ecosystem Management Area, Gulf Coast Conservancy, *Nature Pays Its Way,* brochure, printed with grant from Southwest Florida Water Management District, n.d.

8. Craig Evans, "Preserving the Rural Landscape Through Sustainable Economic Development," paper presented at Florida Sustainable Communities Network Statewide Roundtable, Tallahassee, Fla., May 15, 2000.

9. Telephone interview with James C. Nicholas, University of Florida professor of law and growth management expert, April 2000.

10. Fodor, *Better, Not Bigger,* p. 11

11. Interview with John Hedrick, February 16, 2003.

12. "The Fourth Branch," report of the Center for Public Integrity, April 2002, as reported by Bill Cotterell, *Tallahassee Democrat,* May 2, 2002, p. 9A.

13. Cox et al., *Closing the Gaps,* foreword.

14. Ibid.

15. Telephone interview with Tim Cannon, planner, Florida Department of Community Affairs, May 5, 2000.

16. "St. Joe Has Chance to Be Heroic at Coast," editorial, *Tallahassee Democrat,* March 19, 2002, p. 6A.

17. Telephone interview with John Ray, May 2000.

18. Margaret G. Thomas, Senior Resource Planner, Midwest Research Institute, Kansas City, "Redefining Economic Development," paper included in information packet distributed to attendees of "Civitas: Statewide Roundtable 2000," May 15–16, Tallahassee, Fla.

19. Remarks of Ernesto Sirolli, economist and small business development expert, Economic Development Workshop, sponsored by the Apalachee Regional Planning Council, DCA, and the Florida Sustainable Communities Network, Blountstown, Fla., April 26, 2000.

20. Bruce Katz and Jennifer Bradley, "Divided We Sprawl," *Atlantic Monthly,* December 1999, pp. 26–42.

21. Interview with Neal R. Peirce, Tallahassee, Fla., May 18, 2000.

22. Telephone interview with J. Don Ashley, April 30, 2002.

23. Don Ashley to June Wiaz, e-mail, May 2, 2002.

24. Telephone interview with Kim Ogren, program manager, Funders' Network for Smart Growth and Livable Communities, Collins Center, April 19, 2002.

25. Ibid.

26. Kim Ogren to Kathryn Ziewitz, e-mail, April 26, 2002.

Bibliography

Alfred I. duPont Testamentary Trust. *Estate of Alfred duPont and the Nemours Foundation.* Report. Jacksonville, Fla., Spring 1963.

Ball, Braden Lee. *Around West Florida in 80 Years.* Pensacola: University of West Florida Foundation, 1997.

Belin, J. C., and Braden Lee Ball. *The Edward Ball We Knew.* Pensacola: University of West Florida Foundation, 1998.

Bennett, Charles E. *Twelve on the River St. Johns.* Jacksonville: University of North Florida Press, 1989.

Brewton, Pete. *The Mafia, CIA and George Bush.* New York: S.P.I. Books, 1992.

Brooke, Steven. *Seaside.* Gretna, La.: Pelican Publishing, 1995.

Bruck, Connie. *The Predators' Ball.* New York: American Lawyer/Simon and Schuster, 1988.

Burnett, Gene M. *Florida's Past: People and Events that Shaped the State.* Vol. 1. Englewood, Fla.: Pineapple Press, 1986.

Carr, Archie. *A Naturalist in Florida: A Celebration of Eden.* New Haven, Conn.: Yale University Press, 1994.

Colburn, David R. "Florida Politics in the Twentieth Century." In *The New History of Florida,* edited by Michael Gannon. Tallahassee: University Presses of Florida, 1996.

Colby, Gerard. *Du Pont Dynasty: Behind the Nylon Curtain.* New York: Lyle Stuart, 1984.

Cowdrey, Albert E. *This Land, This South: An Environmental History.* New Perspectives on the South series, ed. Charles P. Roland. Lexington: University Press of Kentucky, 1983.

Cox, James, Randy Kautz, Maureen MacLaughlin, and Terry Gilbert. *Closing the Gaps in Florida's Wildlife Habitat Conservation System.* Tallahassee: Office of Environmental Service, Florida Game and Freshwater Fish Commission, 1994.

Danese, Tracy E. *Claude Pepper and Ed Ball: Politics, Purpose, and Power.* Gainesville: University Press of Florida, 2000.

Derr, Mark. *Some Kind of Paradise: A Chronicle of Man and the Land in Florida.* New York: William Morrow, 1989; Gainesville: University Press of Florida, 1998.

Doyle, Larry J., Dinesh C. Sharma, Albert C. Hine, Orrin H. Pilkey Jr., William J. Neal, Orrin H. Pilkey Sr., David Martin, and Daniel F. Belknap. *Living with the West Florida Shore.* Durham, N.C.: Duke University Press, 1984.

Fodor, Eben. *Better, Not Bigger.* Gabriola Island, B.C.: New Society Publishers, 1999.

Foglesong, Richard E. *Married to the Mouse: Walt Disney World and Orlando.* New Haven, Conn.: Yale University Press, 2001.

Frantz, Douglas, and Catherine Collins. *Celebration, U.S.A.: Living in Disney's Brave New Town.* New York: Henry Hold, 1999.

Golden Anniversary Celebration. Gulf County, Fla., June 4–16, 1975. Chattanooga, Tenn.: Great American Publishing Company, 1975.

Gore, Robert H. *The Gulf of Mexico.* Sarasota, Fla.: Pineapple Press, 1992.

Griffith, Leon Odell. *Ed Ball: Confusion to the Enemy.* Miami: Trend House, 1975.

Hawken, Paul. *The Ecology of Commerce: A Declaration of Sustainability.* New York: Harper Business, A Division of HarperCollins Publishers, 1993.

Hewlett, Richard Greening. *Jessie Ball duPont.* Gainesville: University Press of Florida, 1992.

Hiaasen, Carl. *Team Rodent: How Disney Devours the World.* New York: Ballantine, 1998.

Jahoda, Gloria. *The Other Florida.* New York: Charles Scribner's Sons, 1978.

James, Marquis. *Alfred I. duPont: The Family Rebel.* Indianapolis: Bobbs-Merrill, 1941.

Kunstler, James Howard. *The Geography of Nowhere.* New York: Simon and Schuster, 1993.

Landrum, Ney. "Study of the St. Joe Paper Company Land Using Activities in Leon County, Florida." Thesis submitted to Florida State University for M.A. degree, January 1956.

Mac, M. J., P. A. Opler, C. E. Puckett Haecker, and P. D. Doran. *Status and Trends of the National's Biological Resources,* Vol. 1. Reston, Va.: U.S. Department of the Interior, U.S. Geological Survey, 1998.

Mason, Raymond K., and Virginia Harrison. *Confusion to the Enemy: A Biography of Edward Ball.* New York: Dodd, Mead, 1976.

McGregory, Jerrilyn. *Wiregrass Country.* Jackson: University Press of Mississippi, 1997.

McPhee, John. *Encounters with the Archdruid.* New York: Noonday Press, 1971.

Miller, Gene. *Invitation to a Lynching: An Incredible Story of Murder and Justice by a Pulitzer Prize Winning Reporter.* Garden City, N.Y.: Doubleday, 1975.

Mosley, Leonard. *Blood Relations: The Rise and Fall of the du Ponts of Delaware.* New York: Atheneum, 1980.

Myers, Ronald L., and John J. Ewel, eds. Foreword by Marjorie H. Carr. *Ecosystems of Florida.* Orlando: University of Central Florida Press/Orlando, 1990.

The Nature Conservancy and Association for Biodiversity Information. *Precious Heritage: The Status of Biodiversity in the United States,* edited by Bruce A. Stein, Lynn S. Kutner, and Jonathan S. Adams. New York: Oxford University Press, 2000.

Nelson, Gil. *Exploring Wild Northwest Florida.* Sarasota, Fla.: Pineapple Press, 1995.

———. *The Trees of Florida.* Sarasota, Fla.: Pineapple Press, 1994.

Paisley, Clifton. *The Red Hills of Florida, 1528–1865.* Tuscaloosa: University of Alabama Press, 1989.

Peyton, Herbert H. *New Boy.* Jacksonville, Fla.: Gate Petroleum, 1997.

Pizzo, Stephen, Mary Fricker, and Paul Muolo. *Inside Job: The Looting of America's Savings and Loans.* New York: McGraw-Hill, 1989.

Ray, Janisse. *Ecology of a Cracker Childhood.* Minneapolis: Milkweed Editions, 1999.

Revels, Tracy. *Watery Eden: A History of Wakulla Springs.* Tallahassee, Fla.: Sentry Press, 2002.

Rogers, William Warren. *Outposts on the Gulf: Saint George Island and Apalachicola from Early Exploration to World War II.* Pensacola: University of West Florida Press, 1986.

Rowan, Robin Hill, and Clark Perry. *The Insider's Guide to Florida's Great Northwest.* Manteo, N.C.: Insiders' Guides and *Tallahassee Democrat,* 1995.

Scott, Peter Dale. *Deep Politics and the Death of JFK.* Berkeley and Los Angeles: University of California Press, 1993.

Sherrill, Robert. *Gothic Politics in the Deep South: Stars of the New Confederacy.* New York: Grossman Publishers, 1968.

Smith, Maureen. *The U.S. Paper Industry and Sustainable Production: An Argument for Restructuring.* Cambridge: MIT Press, 1997.

Wall, Joseph Frazier. *Alfred I. duPont: The Man and His Family.* New York: Oxford University Press, 1990.

Wilkinson, Alec. *Big Sugar: Seasons in the Cane Fields of Florida.* New York: Alfred A. Knopf, 1989.

Wilson, E. O. *Biophilia.* Cambridge: Harvard University Press, 1984.

Wolfe, S. H., J. A. Reidenauer, and D. B. Means. *An Ecological Characterization of the Florida Panhandle.* U.S. Fish and Wildlife Service Biological Report 88; Minerals Management Service OCS Study 88, 1988.

Womack, Marlene. *Along the Bay: A Pictorial History of Bay County.* Norfolk, Va.: Pictorial Heritage Publishing, Sponsored by Junior Service League of Panama City, 1994.

Zepezauer, Mark, and Arthur Naiman. *Take the Rich off Welfare.* Tucson, Ariz.: Odonian Press, 1996.

Index

Helms, Richard, 98
Henderson, Cynthia: background, 107, 273–74; and Gulfstream Land and Development, 274; as liaison to St. Joe Company, 236, 273; and SouthWood, 190; and Tew Cardenas, 274
Hendry, John, 162, 242, 243
Herty, Charles, 48, 61
Hess, Glenn, 182
Hewlett, Richard Greening, 38, 56
Hiaasen, Carl, 128–29, 288, 302
High, Robert King, 82
Highwaymen. *See* Gulf Coast Highway Association
Hilton, Charles, 293
Hilton Head Island, 158
Hinkle, Cliff, 249
Hobbs, G. M. "Mike," 111
Hodges, Don, 260–61
Hoffman, Al, 134
Holland, Spessard, 72, 82
Hopping, Green, Sams, and Smith, 272, 275
Hough, Marion, 207–9, 212, 215, 220, 296
Houston, Tex., 61, 110, 144
Howell, Billy, 75, 88–89, 225
Hunting, 33, 35, 157, 159–60
Hunt Oil, 65

Ickes, Harold, 47. *See also* Apalachicola National Forest
Infrastructure: and Bense, Allan, 238; civic, 314; costs, 171, 198, 238–57; in Florida Panhandle, 10, 12, 13, 149–50, 237–57; Hathaway Bridge, 238; health care, 249; interstate connector, 240; improvements, 231, 235; marinas and ports, 253–57; nature's, 307; pipelines, 293–96; roads, 237–41; sewerage, 252–53; strategic land donations for, 158, 303; voting on, 306; waste-water treatment, 253, 294; and water, 250–52. *See also* Panama City–Bay County Airport; Gulf Coast Parkway
Inman-Johnson, Dorothy, 105, 193
Interstate Commerce Commission, 58
International Paper, 65, 101
Intracoastal Waterway, 46, 52, 74, 141
Iran, 70
Ireland, 61–62, 72
Ivory-billed woodpecker, 33, 307

Jacksonville, Fla.: and Ball, Ed, 98; bridge toll, 71; Cross-Florida Canal, 93; and Dahl, James,

113; Florida National Bank, 73; Gran Central, 104; and Peyton, Herbert, 112, 154; and St. Joe headquarters, 122
James Madison Institute, 147, 150, 153–54, 272, 302
Jefferson-Smurfit. *See* Smurfit-Stone Corporation
Jernigan, Terry, 293
Johnson, Malcolm, 97
Jones, Duke, 118, 202

Kendrick, Will, 176, 256–57
Kennedy, John F., 73, 81–82, 93–94
Kent, Doug, 217, 220, 225
Kilmer, Bev, 175, 199, 234, 236, 240, 269
Kirk, Claude, 72, 76, 84
Knight, Gary, 285
Kraft paper, 48, 55, 74
Kunstler, James Howard, 162

Lake Wimico, 28, 141–42, 212
Ledsinger, Charles, 143
Lehman, Mel, 221–22
Lehman Brothers, 116, 154
Leonard, Mel, 278
Leon County, 63, 78, 177. *See also* Southwood Farm
Liberty County, 14, 32
Lightsey, Debbie, 196, 198
Lindner, Carl, 102, 114
Linton, Johnny, 224
Live oaks, 29–31. *See also* Forest products
Logging operations: clearcutting, 64, 67, 105, 141–42; "deadhead," 31; destructive practices, 67–68, 279–80; in 1800s, 31, 32; of hard-woods, 279, 282 (*see also* St. Joe Paper Company); in Liberty County, 32; railroads and, 30–32; stumping, 64. *See also* Gholson, Angus; Greenbelt tax; Silviculture
Longleaf pine: for building, 30; desirability of, 31; fire regime, 22; harvesting, 63–64; natural history, 22–23, 32–33, 66–67; and Port St. Joe, 42; and red-cockaded woodpeckers, 32, 105–6; at Southwood, 105–6
Lynch, John, 173

Maddox, Dave, 77
Maddox, Scott, 195
Maddox family, 59
Maloney, Joseph, 72, 82

Mantay, Jon, 290

Marcus, Nancy, 255

Mason, Raymond: and biography of Ed Ball, 60; and Charter Bankshares, 84, and Charter Company, 87, 98; and Epping Forest, 112; as possible successor to Ed Ball, 101–2. *See also* Charter Company

Matthews, Frank, 272, 298

McArdle, Larry, 212

McCarran, Pat, 58

McGovern, George, 89, 93

McGurk, Tom, 190, 194

McKay, Buddy, 226

Mead Company, 51–52, 55

Means, Bruce, 68

Meany, George, 82

Meyer, Daniel, 296

Mexico Beach, 80, 11, 286–87

Miami, Fla.: and Arvida developments, 132–33; and duPont, Jessie Ball, 39; Gran Central, 104, 134; and High, Robert King, 72; and Hoover, J. Edgar, 73; and Jahoda, Gloria, 71; and Revell, Walter, 153

Middlemas, John Robert, 266

Middlemas, Kendall, 294

Milken, Michael, 113, 116

Miller, Col. Joe, 283

Mills, William, 86

Mill View (development), 179, 220–22

Mineta, Norman, 266

Mixon, Wayne, 103

Mohr, Charles, 34

Molotch, Harvey, 269

Morrill, Thomas A., 97

Morse, Wayne, 81

Moses, Robert, 231

Motta, Jim, 132, 191

Moye, Tracy, 221–22

Moyers, Jim, 164, 166

Muir, John, 33

Muniz, Katie Baur, 269

Murley, Jim, 290

National Wildlife Federation, 296

Native Americans, 25, 27, 189

The Nature Conservancy: and biological hot spots, 20; and Everglades, 138; and St. Joe lands, 140–41, 152; and steephead ravines, 68; and Talisman, 137; and Topsail Hill, 15, 109

Naval stores, 29–30

Nedley, Robert, 53, 209, 210, 221, 227–28

Nemours Foundation: and Alfred I. duPont Trust, 101, 118; and Ball estate, 99; clinics, 219; founding, 50, 56–57; funding, 108, 114, 156; and Peyton, Herbert, 154; and Port St. Joe, 76, 155; and Wakulla Springs, 94, 97. *See also* duPont, Jessie Ball

New Urbanism, 125–26, 145, 162, 164, 184, 188, 302, 304

Nextel Partners, 233

Nicholas, James, 305

Nixon, Richard M., 89

Norman, Greg, 168

Northwest Florida Improvement Foundation, 155

Northwest Florida Water Management District, 140, 218, 250, 304

Ocean Reef, 125

Ochsner, Alton, 98–99

Ogren, Kim, 314

Ogren, Larry, 33

Oklawaha River, 93–94

Old Spanish Trail, 90, 145

1000 Friends of Florida, 176, 195, 296, 314

Panama Beach Development Company, 43, 55. *See also* Ball, Edward

Panama City, Fla.: annexations, 171; developments, 171–73; incorporation of, 40; marinas, 172; pulp mill, 48, 53; as tourist destination, 40; and U.S. Highway 98, 45. *See also* Panama City–Bay County Airport

Panama City–Bay County Regional Airport: Airport Authority, 258–66; Bechtel Infrastructure and, 259–63; costs of, 260, 264; Committee for Sensible Airport Development, 266; deficiencies of existing airport, 258–59; economic development associated with, 263–64; environmental impacts of, 265–66; and Federal Aviation Administration, 258–60, 262–64, 266; individuals associated with, 258–67; and St. Joe land donation, 259, 262; and seagrass, 259, 265; vote on, 267; and West Bay, 260, 265, 267; wetlands, 265–66

Panama City Beach, Fla., 233, 243, 247, 292, 312

Panama City News-Herald, 72, 203–4, 227

Panhandle. *See* Florida Panhandle

Ross, Jaimie, 178, 179, 180
Rudloe, Anne, 256–57
Rudloe, Jack, 97, 256–57
Rummell, Peter: and baby boomers, 160–61; and Bush, Jeb, 269; and changes in St. Joe Company, 121; and Codina, Armando, 135; development philosophy of, 158, 163, 268; and Disney Company, 108, 119, 122–23, 129 (*see also* Celebration, Fla.); family background, 123; and Florida State University, 248; and health care, 219; hiring of, 75, 95, 119; and mill closure, 205, 218; and Panama City airport, 237, 262, 263; and St. Joe Company political influence, 270; and schools, 246; and SouthWood, 185, 190; and U.S. Highway 98 relocation, 246; at Wakulla Springs, 97; at WaterColor groundbreaking, 11; work history, 123–25, 131–32. *See also* St. Joe Company

St. Andrew Bay, 29, 45, 159, 252
St. George Island, 40, 312
St. Joe/Arvida. *See* St. Joe Company
St. Joe Company: and Arvida purchase, 131–33 (*see also* Arvida Corporation); and company name, 120–21; conservation sales, 137, 139–42, 159, 308–9; Disney influence, 128–30; earnings, 122, 149; and economic development, 232; and ecotourism, 159; and Florida Audubon Society, 138; holdings, 3, 6; land donations, 192, 243, 249, 259, 269, 303; lobbyists, 272–73; management team, 18, 121, 129–33, 143–55; membership in associations, 272; paper mill cleanup, 208–11, 216, 217; political appointments, 135; profit goals, 9, 121; and Rummell, Peter, 120; stock, 263; subsidiaries, 6, 136–39 (*see also* Infrastructure); sugar tax opposition, 138 (*see also* Talisman Sugar); transition of company, 150, 157–58; visioning, 18
—commercial real estate: Advantis, 133; Arvida development, 311; Codina Group, 133–35
St. Joe Paper Company: and African Americans, 53 (*see also* Civil rights); articles of incorporation, 57, 104; and bleached pulp, 174; box plants, 61–62, 174; and clearcutting, 67–68, 105, 153; formation of, 51; housing program, 53; and Jacksonville, 77; land donations, 77; management, 102–3, 112; and Mill View development, 179, 220–

22; net income, 108, 112; pollution, 207–8; price fixing, 117; real estate, 103–11 (*see also* Southwood Properties, Topsail Hill); reorganization, 103–4, 199; sale of mill and box plants, 116–19; size, 101; stock holdings, 56 (*see also* Charter Company); stock offerings, 103, 112; water demands, 74; Woodlands division, 63–65, 168 (*see also* Greenbelt tax); wetlands draining, 69; World War II, 60–61. *See also* Ball, Ed; Belin, Jake; Taxes; Thornton, Winfred
—mill: buyers of, 116–19; capital from sale, 136; closing, 199, 234; construction of, 52, 54; dioxin from, 220–24; and discrimination, 89–90; duPonts and, 177; hazards, 88–89; modernization, 101; pollution, 92–93, 208–11, 213–14, 219; strike, 89–90; unions, 88–89
—subsidiaries (St. Joe Forest Products), 205–6, 211–12. *See also* Apalachicola Northern Railroad; Florida East Coast Industries; Florida National Banks
St. Joe Timberland, 66. *See also* Smallwood, Clay
St. Joseph Bay: connection to Apalachicola Northern Railroad, 41; dioxins, 213–14; fishing, 200; pulp waste, 213; shipping, 28, 41
St. Louis Lumber Company, 46–47
St. Marks Wildlife Refuge, 279
St. Teresa, Fla., 153–54
Sanders, Cheryl, 176
Sandestin (development), 4
Savings and loan institutions: and Bush, Jeb, 134; and Central Intelligence Agency, 110; and Drexel Burnham Lambert, 113–14; and Resolution Trust Corporation, 108–9, 144; and Topsail Hill, 108–9; and Twomey, Kevin, 143–44. *See also* Banks
Sawgrass (development), 125
Schloesser, Chris, 287
Schmitt, James, 115
Schultz, George, 260
Seibert, Steve, 148, 288
Shaw, Frank, 153–54, 190, 196, 248, 255
Sierra Club, 134, 176, 296
Sikes, Robert, 73, 76, 82
Silviculture: and Ball, Ed, 63; in Florida Panhandle, 69; practices, 63–67, 278–82; and St. Joe Paper, 63–65, 168; sustainable, 280; zoning, 79–80. *See also* Logging; Greenbelt tax
Sirolli, Ernesto, 311
Slash pines, 42, 63–64, 67, 160, 281

U.S. Highway 90: 27, 45
U.S. Highway 98: 45, 71, 176. *See also* Gulf Coast Highway
USS *Constitution,* 30

Vesco, Robert, 98
Virginia, 127–28, 133
Vogler II, Edward, 175, 289

Wachovia, 85–86
Wade, Neal: and Alabama jobs, 152–53; and Enterprise Florida, 271; and Franklin County, 174; as St. Joe vice president, 232–33, 236–37, 240, 246
Wakulla County, 71, 98, 141
Wakulla River, 28, 96–97
Wakulla Springs: acquisition by Ball, 22, 47; fence, 96–97; films made at, 21–22; lodge, 47, 61, 89, 95; productivity, 22; sold to state, 94, 97; uses of, 95–97, 138
Wall, Joseph Frazier, 46, 49
Wall Street: and Ball, Ed, 37; and Belin, Jake, 102; and Dillon Read and Company, 114–15; and New Urbanism, 184; and St. Joe Company, 122, 149
Wall Street Journal, 112
Walt Disney Company, 9, 108, 121, 174, 231. *See also* Disney Design and Development Company; Celebration, Fla.
Walton County: and affordable housing, 180, 181; beachfront, 43; and Choctawhatchee beach mouse, 16; Conservation and Development Trust, 15; development of, 1–2, 14; and Devil's Swamp, 140, 142; and duPont land purchases, 44; and Northwest Florida Improvement Foundation, 155; and St. Joe activities in, 14, 111, 140, 163–68; schools, 247; tax base, 312; tax disputes, 79; and Topsail Hill, 109–11; and water supply, 250; wetlands, 110, 140–41
Ward, George, 27
Warren, Fuller, 72, 77

Washington Post, 127
WaterColor: and affordable housing, 180; and Choctawhatchee beach mouse, 286; design of, 17, 163–67, 303; groundbreaking, 11, 17; inn, 263; as New Urbanist enclave, 11, 163; purchase of land for, 43; and storm water, 277; and Topsail Hill, 108, 164
WaterSound (development), 108, 167–68, 286
Webb, Mack, 80
Weidrich, Barbara, 166
West Bay Sector Plan, 267, 274, 289–92, 302. *See also* Panama City–Bay County Airport
WestCountry Financial. *See* Schmitt, James
Weston, Fla., 131, 303
Wetherell, T. Kent, 249, 274–75
Wetherell, Virginia, 274, 276
Wetlands: and Apollo Beach, 151; and bogs, 23; and Development of Regional Impacts, 183; and Gulf County, 245; in forests, 279; isolated, 282–83; mitigation, 284–85; and Panama City airport, 265–66; permits to fill, 236, 277; St. Joe Company and, 140, 172, 284–85; and schools, 247, 283; at SouthWood, 189–90; and Tate's Hell Swamp, 23, 28, 284; and U.S. Highway 98, 176, 242
Wewahitchka, Fla., 76
Willson, George, 33, 109, 141–42, 152, 255
Wilson Miller, 177–78, 274, 277
WindMark Beach, 162, 169, 241
Wittkopf, Frances, 173
Womack, Marlene, 65–66
Wood, G. Pierce, 52
Wood pulp, 48, 74. *See also* St. Joe Paper Company (mill)
WoodRun (subdivision), 172
World War II, 60–61. *See also* St. Joe Paper Company

Young, Linda, 213, 218, 278

Zimmerman, Nevin, 292

Kathryn Ziewitz is a freelance writer and educator living in Bay County, Florida. She has written articles for newspapers, magazines, and nonprofit organizations. From 1995 to 1997 she directed a grass-roots visioning project to lay the groundwork for revitalizing the waterfront community of St. Andrews in Panama City.

June Wiaz is a freelance environmental writer residing in Tallahassee. Before moving to Florida in 1996, she worked for the U.S. Environmental Protection Agency in Arlington, Virginia. Before EPA, she spent two years as a Peace Corps volunteer in Guatemala and worked as a policy analyst for the National Governors' Association and the American Association for the Advancement of Science.